King Lear AND THE GODS

King Lear

AND THE GODS

WILLIAM R. ELTON

THE UNIVERSITY PRESS OF KENTUCKY

This edition published in 1988 by
The University Press of Kentucky

Scholarly publisher for the Commonwealth,
serving Bellarmine College, Berea College, Centre
College of Kentucky, Eastern Kentucky University
The Filson Club, Georgetown College, Kentucky
Historical Society, Kentucky State University,
Morehead State University, Murray State University,
Northern Kentucky University, Transylvania University,
University of Kentucky, University of Louisville,
and Western Kentucky University.

Editorial and Sales Offices: Lexington, Kentucky 40506-0336

"King Lear" and the Gods was first published in 1966
by The Henry E. Huntington Library and Art Gallery;
second printing 1968.

Library of Congress Cataloging-in-Publication Data

Elton, William R., 1921-
King Lear and the gods / William R. Elton.
p. cm.
Reprint. Originally published: San Marino, Calif.: Huntington Library, 1966.
"King Lear studies, 1967-1987": p.
Includes index.
ISBN 0-8131-1640-6. ISBN 0-8131-0178-6 (pbk.)
1. Shakespeare, William, 1564-1616. King Lear. 2. Shakespeare, William, 1564-1616—Religion. 3. Religion in literature.
I. Title.
PR2819.E4 1988 87-26549
822.3C3—dc19

This book is printed on acid-free paper meeting
the requirements of the American National Standard
for Permanence of Paper for Printed Library Materials.
♾

CONTENTS

TO
WILLIAM RILEY PARKER
AND
HAROLD REINOEHL WALLEY
AND TO THE MEMORY OF
FRANK PERCY WILSON

ἦ μέγα μοι τὰ θεῶν μελεδήμαθ',
    ὅταν φρένας ἔλθῃ,
λύπας παραιρεῖ.
ξύνεσιν δέ τιν' ἐλπίδι κεύθων
λείπομαι ἔν τε τύχαις θνατῶν καὶ
    ἐν ἔργμασι λεύσσων.
ἄλλα γὰρ ἄλλοθεν ἀμείβεται,
μετὰ δ' ἵσταται ἀνδράσιν αἰὼν
πολυπλάνητος αἰεί.

—EURIPIDES, *Hippolytus*

εἰ θεοί τι δρῶσιν αἰσχρόν, οὐχ εἰσὶν
θεοί.

—EURIPIDES, *Fragmenta*

ACKNOWLEDGMENTS

TO THE LATE F. P. WILSON, who first encouraged its publication; to S. F. Johnson, who followed years of stimulating discussion with a painstaking reading of the manuscript; and, above all, to Harold R. Walley, who with rare patience and acumen guided its progress, I owe the appearance in print of this study. For various kinds of assistance I should thank, among many others: Don Cameron Allen, for the loan of materials; J. Leeds Barroll III; my colleagues, Robert F. Gleckner and Frederick J. Hoffman; my predecessors, particularly Robert B. Heilman; and the students in my Shakespeare seminar at the University of California, Riverside.

To the Trustees and Friends of the Huntington Library and to John E. Pomfret, its director, I am grateful for their assistance in the publication of this book. Through almost a decade as a reader I have compounded my indebtedness to the Huntington staff, including Miss Mary Isabel Fry of the Reference Department. That debt has grown to comprise members of the Publications Department, particularly Mrs. Nancy C. English, to whom I am obliged for her meticulous editing of a difficult manuscript. Although her devoted skill has greatly benefited the text, any errors of fact or interpretation which may remain are, needless to say, solely my responsibility.

Grants in support of this work have been generously provided by the American Council of Learned Societies, the Folger Shakespeare Library, the Huntington Library, and the University of California, Riverside. A summary of one chapter of the study, whose preliminary draft was completed in 1957, appeared in Helmut Bonheim, ed., *The King Lear Perplex* (San Francisco, 1960), pp. 174-176. Since the book's final version gained perspective while I was a Fulbright lecturer in India, I should like to acknowledge the assistance of Principal P. C. Joseph of the C. M. S. College, Kottayam, Kerala, and of Olive I. Reddick, the director of the Fulbright Program, India. I am, of course, indebted to the libraries which have facilitated my research. These include, in addition to the Huntington, the British Museum, the Columbia University Library, the Dr. Williams's Library, the Folger Shakespeare Library, the Harvard University

Library, the Library of Congress, the New York Public Library, the Union Theological Seminary Library, the University of California libraries at Berkeley, Los Angeles, and Riverside, and the Yale University Library. As the book was completed several years ago, I have not been able to take into account some relevant material which has appeared since that time.

W. R. E.

University of California, Riverside
September 1964

NOTE ON THE TEXT

In documentation I have preferred, wherever possible, to cite primary rather than secondary references; to quote rather than merely to paraphrase; and, particularly in view of my divergence from interpretative orthodoxy, to err on the side of abundance. I have normalized *i:j* and *u:v* forms and have expanded contractions. Unless otherwise stated, place of publication of books published in England is London. For convenience I have, unless noted, followed the Muir Arden text for quotations from *Lear*; the Globe text for other Shakespearean works; and the performance dates' limits for non-Shakespearean English Renaissance drama given in *Annals of English Drama 975-1700* by Alfred Harbage, revised by S. Schoenbaum (London, 1964). The following list includes editions employed and more frequently cited references.

BOOKS

Alemán, Mateo. *The Rogue: Or the Life of Guzman de Alfarache*, tr. James Mabbe (1623), introd. James Fitzmaurice-Kelly. 4 vols. London, 1924.

Bacon, Francis. *The Works of Francis Bacon*, ed. James Spedding et al. 14 vols. London, 1857-74.

Bible. [Geneva Version.] London, 1586.

Bradley, A. C. *Shakespearean Tragedy: Hamlet, Othello, King Lear, Macbeth.* New York, 1955.

Browne, Thomas. *The Works of Sir Thomas Browne*, ed. Geoffrey Keynes. 6 vols. London, 1928-31.

Busson, Henri. *Le rationalisme dans la littérature française de la Renaissance (1533-1601).* Paris, 1957.

Calvin, Jean. *The Institution of Christian Religion*, tr. Thomas Norton. London, 1587. (Referred to in text as *Institutes.*)

Cervantes Saavedra, Miguel de. *The Ingenious Gentleman, Don Quixote de la Mancha,* tr. Peter Motteux, introd. Henry Grattan Doyle. Modern Library. New York, 1950.

Chapman, George. *The Plays and Poems of George Chapman: The Tragedies*, ed. Thomas M. Parrott. London, 1910.

———. *The Plays and Poems of George Chapman: The Comedies,* ed. Thomas M. Parrott. London, 1914.

Curtius, Ernst Robert, *European Literature and the Latin Middle Ages*, tr. Willard R. Trask. New York, 1953.

Dante. *Tutte le opere di Dante Alighieri*, ed. Edward Moore. Oxford, 1894.

Donne, John. *The Poems of John Donne,* ed. Herbert J. C. Grierson. 2 vols. London, 1953.

Erasmus, Desiderius. *The Praise of Folly*, tr. John Wilson (1668). Ann Arbor, 1958.

Fitzherbert, Thomas. *The Second Part of a Treatise concerning Policy, and Religion.* [Douai?], 1610.

Hobbes, Thomas. *The English Works of Thomas Hobbes*, ed. Sir William Molesworth. 11 vols. London, 1839-45.

Hooker, Richard. *The Works of . . . Richard Hooker . . .*, ed. John Keble. 3 vols. Oxford, 1888.

Jonson, Ben. *Ben Jonson*, ed. C. H. Herford and Percy and Evelyn Simpson. 11 vols. Oxford, 1925-52.

The History of King Leir 1605, ed. W. W. Greg. Malone Society Reprints. [London], 1907. ("Corrigenda," *Collections*, Malone Society, IV [1956], p. 70.)

Marston, John. *The Plays of John Marston*, ed. H. Harvey Wood. 3 vols. Edinburgh, 1934-39.

Massinger, Philip. *The Dramatic Works of Massinger and Ford*, ed. Hartley Coleridge. London, 1863.

Montaigne, Michel Eyquem de. *Essays*, tr. John Florio. Everyman's Library. 3 vols. London, 1946.

Nashe, Thomas. *The Works of Thomas Nashe*, ed. Ronald B. McKerrow; rev. edn. with corrections and supplementary notes ed. F. P. Wilson. 5 vols. Oxford, 1958.

Shakespeare, William. *The Works of William Shakespeare*, ed. William George Clark and William Aldis Wright. Globe Edition. London, 1924.

———. *King Lear*, ed. Kenneth Muir. Arden Edition. London, 1952.

Sidney, Philip. *The Complete Works of Sir Philip Sidney*, ed. Albert Feuillerat. 4 vols. Cambridge, Eng., 1922-26.

Spenser, Edmund. *The Poetical Works of Edmund Spenser*, ed. J. C. Smith and E. De Sélincourt. London, 1924.

Tilley, Morris Palmer. *A Dictionary of the Proverbs in England in the Sixteenth and Seventeenth Centuries*. Ann Arbor, 1950.

Tourneur, Cyril. *The Works of Cyril Tourneur*, ed. Allardyce Nicoll. London, [1930].

Webster, John. *The Complete Works of John Webster*, ed. F. L. Lucas. 4 vols. London, 1927.

PERIODICALS

BHR	*Bibliothèque d'Humanisme et Renaissance*
JEGP	*Journal of English and Germanic Philology*
JWCI	*Journal of the Warburg and Courtauld Institutes*
MLN	*Modern Language Notes*
MLR	*Modern Language Review*
MP	*Modern Philology*
N&Q	*Notes and Queries*
SP	*Studies in Philology*
SQ	*Shakespeare Quarterly*

Part I

CHAPTER I

The Problem

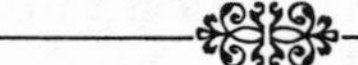

MOST RECENT INTERPRETATIONS of Shakespeare's *King Lear* have tended, in various ways, to identify it as a "Christian" play. The aim of this study, however, is not to determine whether it contains Christian references; rather, it is mainly to examine the validity of the currently widespread view that *Lear* is an optimistically Christian drama. This belief holds, first, that the protagonist, among other characters, is, consequent to his sufferings, "regenerated," "redeemed," or "saved," often by analogy with the morality-play tradition or with Dante's *Purgatorio* through which he is assumed to have passed on the way to his *Paradiso*. Second, corresponding to the meaningful suffering of the protagonist, supposedly there is in addition an intrinsic teleology, a cosmically derived plan, which somehow gives providential significance to the events of the tragedy.

Concerning the first point, instances are numerous, ranging from R. W. Chambers' attempt to improve on Bradley's "Redemption of King Lear": "If there were no more . . . than a tale of redemption through suffering, it would be as unbearable as the *Purgatorio* would be without the *Paradiso*. But *King Lear* is, like the *Paradiso*, a vast poem on the victory of true love"; "Lear, consoled, ends by teaching patience to Gloucester and to Cordelia."[1] Still further, some critics envision not only Christian optimism, but Christ Himself: like G. Wilson Knight, who sees in each Shakespearean tragic hero "a miniature Christ,"[2] J. Dover Wilson remarks, "It is impossible to contemplate the death of Lear without thinking of Calvary. . . ."[3] According to Geoffrey L. Bickersteth, Shakespeare "was unconsciously inspired by a story taken . . . from Christian mythology," with Cordelia in the

[1]R. W. Chambers, *King Lear* (Glasgow, 1940), pp. 49, 48; Bradley, p. 228.

[2]*Principles of Shakespearian Production with Especial Reference to the Tragedies* (1936), p. 231.

[3]*Six Tragedies of Shakespeare: An Introduction for the Plain Man* (1929), p. 46.

part of Christ.[4] As for Lear, there is no doubt that he has been improved, or regenerated: "... the 'spire of meaning' in this play," says John M. Lothian, "is the spiritual history or regeneration of King Lear. . . ."[5] To John F. Danby, the important point is the learning of patience: "*King Lear* in fact can be regarded as a study in patience unrewarded although achieved."[6] "Lear," insists S. L. Bethell, "after being bound upon his fiery wheel in this life, attaining humility and patience, is ... fit for heaven."[7]

In this "noblest spiritual utterance since *La Divina Commedia*," suggests Edgar I. Fripp, Lear achieves "lowliness, justice, tenderness," as Gloucester "attains," in his way, "patience and happy death."[8] Symptomatic of the *état présent* in *Lear* studies, Paul N. Siegel's recent book carries such views even further: "Lear's final conviction that Cordelia is alive might be regarded as the mysterious insight believed to be granted a man on the point of death." In his reconciliation with Cordelia

> It was as if from purgatory he had heard the celestial music and seen the angelic radiance that he was at last about to attain, a vision of what he would experience after death. . . . This miracle is the redemption of Lear for heaven, a redemption analogous to the redemption of mankind, for which the Son of God had come down to earth. The analogy between Cordelia and Christ, who redeemed human nature from the curse brought on it by Adam and Eve, is made unmistakable, although not crudely explicit. . . . Cordelia's ignominious death completes the analogy between her and Christ. . . . The "brand of heaven" . . . in releasing their [Cordelia's and Lear's] souls from the prison of their bodies, enabled them to become reunited in eternal bliss.[9]

[4] *The Golden World of 'King Lear*,' Annual Shakespeare Lecture of the British Academy, XXXII (1946), 26.

[5] *King Lear, a Tragic Reading of Life* (Toronto, 1949), p. 27.

[6] *Poets on Fortune's Hill: Studies in Sidney, Shakespeare, Beaumont & Fletcher* (1952), pp. 105, 108-127, containing essay reprinted from "'King Lear' and Christian Patience," *Cambridge Journal*, I (1948), 305-320; see also his *Shakespeare's Doctrine of Nature: A Study of King Lear* (1949); *King Lear* has the outline of a cross, he discloses in a later lecture, "The 'Major' Tragedies," at the Shakespeare Institute, Summer 1956, summary in *Shakespeare Newsletter*, VI (1956), 33.

[7] "Shakespeare's Imagery: The Diabolic Images in *Othello*," *Shakespeare Survey 5*, ed. Allardyce Nicoll (Cambridge, Eng., 1952), p. 78; see also his *Shakespeare & the Popular Dramatic Tradition* (1944), pp. 52-61 and passim.

[8] *Shakespeare: Man and Artist* (1938), II, 655-657.

[9] *Shakespearean Tragedy and the Elizabethan Compromise* (New York, 1957), pp. 185-186; see also his "Adversity and the Miracle of Love in *King Lear*," *SQ*, VI (1955), 325-336.

. . . I conceive, that every Tragedy, ought to be a very Solemn Lecture, inculcating a particular Providence, and shewing it plainly protecting the Good, and chastizing the Bad, or at least the Violent; and that, if it is otherwise, it is either an empty Amusement, or a scandalous and pernicious Libel upon the Government of the World.

—John Dennis, *The Advancement and Reformation of Modern Poetry* (1701), Epistle Dedicatory

While microcosmic suffering is, according to some critics, considered meaningful and, in the Dantean sense, ultimately "comic," the macrocosm, too, has a corollary orderliness. "In the play itself," affirms M. D. H. Parker, "there is nothing wanton. There is justice, mercy, sacrifice and redemption."[10] Natural law, in the traditional sense, presides over the tragedy: "Shakespeare," Hardin Craig asserts, "held very firmly to this belief in the ultimate punishment of the wicked, in other words, in eternal justice. He exemplifies it in all of his tragedies, and was certainly neither sceptical nor bewildered. . . . *King Lear* is based on the doctrine of eternal law. . . . Lear's faith in a divine providence, at least while he has his reason, is complete."[11] A study of "Heavenly Justice in the Tragedies of Shakespeare" by Carmen Rogers assures us that men act "Within the boundaries of a beneficent and divine order," whose "wheels of retribution move irrevocably, quickly, impartially, but compassionately."[12]

Once again, Siegel will have none of even Bradley's modified optimism concerning a Shakespearean tragic moral order. In Bradley's picture of a moral order which admits the continual engendering of evil and the destruction of good as well as evil, Siegel insists, four alterations must be made: "(1) Shakespearean tragedy conveys a sense of divine providence; (2) this divine providence visits a poetically appropriate retribution upon the guilty; (3) characters and action suggest analogies with the Bible story; (4) there are intimations of the heaven and hell of Christian religion." In short, Siegel's committed optimism revises Bradley "to make the order manifested

[10]*The Slave of Life: A Study of Shakespeare and the Idea of Justice* (1955), p. 135.

[11]"The Ethics of King Lear," *Philological Quarterly*, IV (1925), 105; cf. his "The Shackling of Accidents: A Study of Elizabethan Tragedy," *PQ*, XIX (1940), 1-19.

[12]In *Studies in Shakespeare*, ed. Arthur D. Matthews and Clark M. Emery (Coral Gables, Fla., 1953), pp. 117, 125.

in the course of the tragedies explicitly Christian, its laws the laws ordained by God. . . ."[13]

Although this has been the prevailing weight of much recent commentary, in contrast to that of previous periods, critics are not lacking who refuse to acknowledge the "Christian optimism" theory. In addition to those who pass over the matter in silence or who, like Bradley, are ambiguous on the issue, several writers have directly entered the lists against the prevailing interpretation. With regard to the first aspect, that of the meaningful suffering of the protagonist in relation to the outcome, E. K. Chambers counters R. W. Chambers' "final victory of good" with his own vision of the final victory of evil.[14] "We hardly," suggests Clifford Leech, "think of the dying Lear as going to his reward."[15] George Orwell doubts the tragedy's Christian morality.[16] L. L. Schücking enters a vigorous antithetical position, denying even Lear's purification, which Bradley would grant.[17] In surveying recent *Lear* criticism, R. W. Zandvoort comments on Bickersteth's identification above of Cordelia with Christ: "I would not be surprised if all this was thought rather bewildering. Some it may remind of medieval methods of biblical exegesis (Bickersteth himself uses the term 'anagogic' for the spiritual meaning he discovers in the play). . . . We will not cavil at this intepretation . . . by pointing out that Christ rescued his chosen ones from Hell *after* his crucifixion, whereas, if Cordelia entered a kingdom already divided against itself, she did so *before* being hanged." Further, observes Zandvoort, in a comment which underlines an anomalous situation, "What is important for our purpose, and symptomatic of at least one trend of contemporary criticism, is that an interpretation like this comes from a man who . . . is a serious scholar and not merely a religious enthusiast exploiting Shakespeare for his own purposes."[18]

13 Siegel, *Shakespearean Tragedy*, p. 82.

14 E. K. Chambers, *Shakespeare: A Survey* (1925), pp. 246-247; R. W. Chambers, *King Lear*, p. 25.

15 Review in *SQ*, V (1954), 89; cf. his *Shakespeare's Tragedies and Other Studies in Seventeenth Century Drama* (1950).

16 "Lear, Tolstoy and the Fool," *Shooting an Elephant and Other Essays* (1950), pp. 49-50.

17 Schücking, *Character Problems in Shakespeare's Plays* (1922), pp. 185-190.

18 "*King Lear:* The Scholars and the Critics," *Mededelingen Der Koninklijke Nederlandse Akademie van Wetenschappen, Afd. Letterkunde*. Nieuwe reeks, deel 19, No. 7 (Amsterdam, 1956), p. 241. Madeleine Doran raises pertinent questions regarding mod-

Elmer E. Stoll had earlier incredulously remarked of the consoling and Hegelian reconciliation proposed by such critics for the end, "if that be the sentiment of Shakespeare, his play should be by our bed's head, with the prayer-book"; such a conclusion, Stoll ironically called a "*Stimme von Oben*."[19] The optimistic renderings of Shakespeare's play have been diagnosed as follows: "a Christian dramatist is not likely on the face of it (and despite *King Lear*) to achieve" the hopelessness of Greek tragedy. "His audience are all too ready to substitute for the intangibles of calamity some simplified scale of rewards and punishments, to console themselves with an epilogic vision of Lear and Cordelia happily reunited in Heaven while Edmund, Goneril, and Regan are roasting in Hell, and this tendency is bound to detract from the tragic sense of death and disaster as absolute experiences . . . during which, rather than after which, Man realizes himself."[20] Or, as Dr. Johnson put it, regarding Nahum Tate's version, "In the present case the publick has decided";[21] and Johnson's "publick," it may be suggested, shares a tradition with the critical theory to be examined in the present study.

With regard to the second, or macrocosmic, aspect of the optimistic theory, opponents would deny the alleged universal order and benevolence. Such divergent critics as Bradley and Empson concur on this point: any theological interpretation of the world on Shakespeare's part is excluded from the great tragedies, says the first; "the attempts to fit Christian sentiments onto it [*Lear*] seem to me to falsify the play," agrees the second.[22] F. P. Wilson declares of that work: "No compensatory heaven is offered. Man has only himself and his own power and endurance to fall back on. These are very great, but when they fail only madness or death remains, and death is, if not nescience, escape into the unknown."[23] G. B. Harrison is one of the

---

ern Christian allegorizing of Shakespeare in "Some Renaissance Ovids," *Literature and Society*, ed. Bernice Slote (Lincoln, Neb., 1964), pp. 44-62, as does Roland M. Frye's *Shakespeare and Christian Doctrine* (Princeton, 1963).

19*Shakespeare Studies* (New York, 1927), pp. 183*n*, 182.

20John Peter, *Complaint and Satire in Early English Literature* (Oxford, 1956), pp. 211-212.

21In *A New Variorum Edition of Shakespeare: King Lear*, ed. Horace Howard Furness (Philadelphia, 1908), p. 419.

22Bradley, p. 222; William Empson, *The Structure of Complex Words* (1952), p. 8.

23*Elizabethan and Jacobean* (Oxford, 1945), p. 121; cf. p. 246.

few to commit what the optimistic critics might term a "vulgar error": "The lesson, motive and motto of *Lear* is contained in Gloucester's words" on the flies.[24] Like Arthur Sewell, D. G. James sees no clear sign of Christian doctrine in the play, which depicts a world of savagery and evil.[25] Finally, A. H. R. Fairchild contrasts *Lear* with the other tragedies, such as *Hamlet* and *Othello*, where Christian belief appears as an implied background; Hamlet's religious faith includes belief in God, the soul, and personal immortality, while "Othello, pagan though he is, believes in man's 'eternal Soul,' in prayer, in Heaven and its powers, apparently also in the Devil. Macbeth has a degree of religious awe: what he would 'highly,' that he would 'holily'; he believes in God, in prayer, and in some form of immortality." *King Lear*, says Fairchild, lacks such a background; yet "Paradoxically, what we may call religious beliefs are mentioned more frequently in *King Lear* than in the other tragedies; but they are the cries of natural man as he comes into conflict with forces aligned against him."[26]

In view of numerous such religious and antireligious interpretations as those exemplified above, this study proposes to examine the relevance to *King Lear* of the popular modern theory of Christian optimism. In order to determine its relevance, a detailed investigation of the characters' religious "belief speeches" in the light of Renaissance religious currents will be presented.

24*Shakespeare's Tragedies* (New York, 1952), p. 159.

25Sewell, *Character and Society in Shakespeare* (Oxford, 1951), esp. pp. 60-63; James, *The Dream of Learning* (Oxford, 1951), esp. pp. 120-121.

26*Shakespeare and the Tragic Theme*, Univ. of Missouri Studies, XXIX [XIX], No. 2 (Columbia, Mo., 1944), 49 ("*King Lear* is distinctly a pagan play").

CHAPTER II

Renaissance Concepts of Providence

There is 'twixt us and heaven a dark eclipse.
—Middleton, *The Old Law,* I.i.394

Ha, Ha, ô Democritus *thy Gods*
That governe the whole world! . . .
—Webster, *The White Devil,* I.i.2-3

IN THE LATTER HALF of the sixteenth century two attitudes toward divine providence, even among Christian believers, seem to have gained ground: first, that providence, if it existed, had little or no relation to the particular affairs of individual men; and, second, that it operated in ways bafflingly inscrutable and hidden to human reason. The first coincided with an Epicurean revival, which, along with Lucretius and the renewed ancient atomist tradition, Lucian, and such currents as Averroism, prevailed among those increasingly susceptible to skepticism. The second viewpoint, although also traditional, was emphasized, in addition to Montaignian and related influences, by the Reformers. Of these, Calvinists especially, dominating religious doctrine during a large part of the Elizabethan and Jacobean periods, implied in effect, if not necessarily in intention, an incomprehensible and unappealable God—a *Deus absconditus* (cf. Isaiah xlv.15) whose seemingly arbitrary judgments of election and reprobation were already determined, beyond the reach of human reason or experience.

New orientations between man and the heavenly powers were, in several directions, formed during the Renaissance, disintegrating the relative medieval sense of security, "die innere gläubige Sicherheit des mittelalterlichen in Gott gebetteten Menschen, die Goethesche 'ewige Ruh in Gott dem Herrn.'"[1] In his study of "The Rehabilita-

[1]Alfred Doren, "Fortuna im Mittelalter und in der Renaissance," London Univ., *Vorträge der Bibliothek Warburg, herausgegeben von Fritz Saxl, II. Vorträge, 1922-1923,* I. Teil (1924), p. 119; cf. Ramiro Ortiz, "*Fortuna labilis,*" *Storia di un motivo medievale* (Bucharest, 1927). Providence-questioning has, of course, recurred throughout religious history, e.g., in Job, Boethius, etc. This chapter sketches the special configuration which such questioning, owing to a new grouping of influences, seems to have assumed in the Renaissance.

tion of Epicurus and His Theory of Pleasure in the Early Renaissance," Don Cameron Allen has, moreover, demonstrated the return to the Epicurean pleasure doctrine, without considering the corollary Epicurean notion regarding providence.[2] The latter, perhaps held at the same time, was, as Surtz has indicated, the inexorable conclusion from Epicurus' premises: "The happy life of pleasure which is the final end of man is impossible without the elimination of the most serious hindrances to human joy," i.e., superstitious fears, and, to destroy those, "he does not annihilate the gods but makes them absolutely indifferent to human concerns."[3]

To Epicurus, paradoxically, those people "smitten with 'religious' dread" are truly impious, while those exhibit true piety who hold that the divine is immortal and happy, believing that the gods, "being endowed with prudence, cannot enter into the category of bunglers" and "know neither toil nor fatigue." Despite the fact, then, that Epicurus was apparently religious and believed in the gods, he supposedly viewed them as *rois fainéants* and held their perfect serenity to be inconsistent with their meddling in the human scene, "the turmoil of affairs, anxieties, and feelings of anger and benevolence"; and he concluded that "From their indestructibility . . . it follows that they are strangers to all suffering; nothing can cause them any joy or inflict on them any suffering from outside."[4]

In place of providence, the blind and fickle Fortuna, with her

[2]*SP*, XLI (1944), 1-15. See recent studies of *quattrocento* Epicurean revival, e.g., Eugenio Garin, "Ricerche sull' Epicureismo del Quattrocento," *La cultura filosofica del Rinascimento italiano* (Florence, 1961), pp. 72-92. See also the discussion in Walter Kaiser, *Praisers of Folly: Erasmus, Rabelais, Shakespeare* (Cambridge, Mass., 1963), passim.

[3]Edward L. Surtz, "Epicurus in Utopia," *ELH*, XVI (1949), 93.

[4]André Marie Jean Festugière, *Epicurus and His Gods* (Oxford, 1955), pp. 61, 60-61, 57, 58. See Cyril Bailey, *The Greek Atomists and Epicurus* (Oxford, 1928), p. 475. Epicurus (Bailey, p. 477) is said to have remarked with contempt: "If God listened to the prayers of men, all men would quickly have perished: for they are for ever praying for evil against one another"; Epicurus has no place for prayer to the gods, from whom man has nothing either to fear or hope.

Marcus Aurelius Antoninus expressed the cosmic alternatives of an age of crisis: "Either Providence, or Atoms"; "nothing but a medley and a dispersion" (*The Communings with Himself*, tr. C. R. Haines, Loeb Classical Lib. [1916], pp. 69, 253). And in a comment anticipatory of Lear's development he observes regarding the gods: "But if so be they take counsel about nothing at all—an impious belief—in good sooth let us have no more of sacrifices and prayers and oaths, nor do any other of these things every one of which is a recognition of the Gods as if they were at our side and dwelling amongst us . . ." (p. 155).

counterpoise, *virtù*, was reemphasized in, for example, the historical *scienza nuova* of Machiavelli; for him, as later for Napoleon, providence seemed on the side of the strongest battalion.[5] Drama, moreover, paralleled history, as one scholar has observed: "it seems hardly too much to call the tragedy of the sixteenth century the tragedy of Fortune." And, discussing the operations of fortune in the plays of Cintio, the same writer finds its employment to conform to the dramatic practice of Rucellai, Alamanni, Tasso, Ben Jonson, and Beaumont and Fletcher, as well as to the Renaissance view of life as "unstable, shifting, irrational, and unpredictable."[6] The latter view Machiavelli considered the reason for the widespread belief in fortune during his time. Even during the first half of the sixteenth century a passive reaction to the vagaries of providence appears in the Venetian humanist Pietro Alcyonio; offering no explanations for man's sufferings, his resignation, like Poggio Bracciolini's, was that of one to the way of the world.[7] Poggio's *The Misery of the Human Condition* stressed the antagonism of nature to human life. Another Italian humanist, Filippo Beroaldo, in his treatise *On Earthquake* saw no remedy against calamity, attributing man's unhappiness to the arbitrary and blind operations of fortune.[8] And about 1515 Giovanni Francesco Pico della Mirandola (1476-1533), nephew of the more noted Giovanni, felt called upon to explain *The True Causes of the Calamities of Our Times*, combatting the currently misleading fatalistic and astrological notions.[9] In addition, Niccolò Franco's *Dialogi Piacevoli* (Venice, 1542) considered in its sixth book "Se la Fortuna governa il mondo," observing "che il nome de la Fortuna e venuto quaggiuso in si fatta divotione, ch'ella sola si adora . . ." (sig. Miiii^{v}).

Accepting, on the other hand, the pseudonaturalistic astrological

[5]See Allen, "Renaissance Remedies for Fortune: Marlowe and the *Fortunati*," *SP*, XXXVIII (1941), 188-197; cf. Harry Levin, *The Overreacher: A Study of Christopher Marlowe* (Cambridge, Mass., 1952), pp. 25-26. In Dante, *Inferno*, Canto vii, Fortune is the handmaid of God; the Epicureans are in x.13-16. On providence as eliminated from history, see Francesco de Sanctis, *Storia della Letteratura Italiana* (Bari, 1925), I, 418.

[6]A. H. Gilbert, "Fortune in the Tragedies of Giraldi Cintio," *Renaissance Studies in Honor of Hardin Craig* (Stanford, 1941), pp. 43, 41, 32.

[7]Charles E. Trinkaus, *Adversity's Noblemen: The Italian Humanists on Happiness* (New York, 1940), pp. 123, 125-126, 134-137. Giovanni Poggio Bracciolini, *De miseria humanae conditionis*, in *Opera omnia* (Basel, [1538]), pp. 108-111.

[8]*Opusculum de terraemotu*, in *Varia . . . opuscula* (Basel, 1513), fol. 147.

[9]Trinkaus, *Adversity's Noblemen*, pp. 130-131.

determinism of events, the influential Pomponazzi (1462-1525), called the "last Scholastic and the first man of the Enlightenment," while viewing providence as God's eternal law, removed the Deity from direct and immediate relation with the world; the universe acts, he suggests, through "the heavens" determining particular occurrences.[10] Further, numerous Renaissance Italians, as a modern sociologist asserts, had relinquished the idea of divine power, while humanist historians tended to eliminate belief in miracles and to abandon the search for supernatural causation, content to leave such problems to theologians.[11] Finally, Roman Seneca, transmitting the idea of fortune and the truth of existence as uncertain, bequeathed also to Renaissance drama a Stoic sense of fatalism which ran counter to the conception of providence.

In Renaissance France, as in Italy, evidence for the disintegration of belief in providence appears plentiful, both in skeptical writings, necessarily less manifest because of the censorship, and in the pious attacks against proponents of skepticism. Indeed, toward the middle of the sixteenth century, as Henri Busson comments, "Il semble . . . que la foi à la providence diminue."[12]

For instance, Charles de Sainte-Marthe, *In psalmum nonagesimum* (1550), observes ". . . ces épicuriens impies se servir des raisons naturelles comme de machines de guerre pour jeter Dieu à bas de son trône, lui enlever sa Providence. . . ."[13] Popular in the Renaissance, Lu-

[10]John H. Randall, introd. on Pietro Pomponazzi, in *The Renaissance Philosophy of Man*, ed. Ernst Cassirer et al. (Chicago, 1948), pp. 268, 279; cf. Pomponazzi's view that, instead of providential rewards, the rewards of virtue and vice are in themselves alone (*De immortalitate animae*, Ch. xiv). See also Trinkaus, "The Problem of Free Will in the Renaissance and the Reformation," *Journal of the History of Ideas*, X (1949), 61-62. Cf. Giuseppe Saitta, *Il pensiero italiano nell' umanesimo e nel Rinascimento*, II (Bologna, 1950), 313-314, 320.

Coluccio Salutati had, after 1400, developed the view that human notions of the divine were bound to anthropomorphism; see Hans Baron, *The Crisis of the Early Italian Renaissance* (Princeton, 1955), II, 561. Telesio reduced the intervention of divine providence. While Giordano Bruno, Leo Spitzer's *Classical and Christian Ideas of World Harmony* (Baltimore, 1963), p. 130, reminds us, did not abandon Christian providence, he submerged it in the "*magnifica vicissitudine* of the law of metamorphosis."

[11]Alfred Wilhelm von Martin, *Sociology of the Renaissance* (1944), p. 19; cf. Eduard Fueter, *Geschichte der neueren Historiographie* (München, 1936).

[12]*Le rationalisme*, p. 521.

[13]Translated in Busson, *Le rationalisme*, p. 294. In his *Tischreden*, Luther had spoken of his terrible times in which the Epicureans, formerly thought to be extinct, were flourishing and threatened to engulf the entire world (Ewald M. Plass, *What Luther Says, an Anthology* [St. Louis, Mo., 1959], II, 785).

cian satirizes the absurdity of prayers; in *Zeus Rants* he ridicules those who give the name "order" to a blind tendency and "providence" to the natural order. Although influenced by Lucian, Erasmus, on the one hand, denounces his providential view as blasphemy,[14] while, on the other hand, Des Périers reveals the Lucianic attitude in his *Cymbalum mundi* (ca. 1529-1530) regarding the injustices of life.[15]

In England, Stephen Batman's *The Golden Booke of the Leaden Goddes* (1577) similarly mentions the Epicurean and Lucianic belief in the futility of prayers to Jupiter: "his want of Eares declare him to be indifferent unto all, not harkening more to one, then to an other" (fol. 1). In his preface (1563) to Volume II of *L'instruction chrétienne* (1564) Pierre Viret finds some who "jugent comme les epicuriens . . . de la providence de Dieu envers les hommes, comme s'il ne se mesloit point du gouvernement des choses humaines, ains qu'elles fussent gouvernées ou par fortune, ou par la prudence, ou par la folie des hommes, selon que les choses rencontrent."

These doubters of providence, "epicuriens et atheistes, desquels le nombre est beaucoup plus grand que plusieurs ne pensent," depress him because many are learned men:

> l'horreur me redouble encore d'avantage, quand je considere que plusieurs de ceux . . . qui sont mesme souventes fois estimez des plus savans, et des plus aigus et plus subtils esprits, sont non seulement infectez de cest execrable atheisme, mais aussi en font profession et en tiennent escole, et empoisonnent plusieurs personnes de tel poison. Parquoy nous sommes venus en un temps, auquel il y a danger que nous n'ayons plus de peine à combattre avec tels monstres qu'avec les superstitieux et idolatres, si Dieu n'y pourvoit, comme j'ay bonne esperance qu'il le fera.

Thus, Viret feels a real danger to exist from the Epicurean scoffers at providence: "Il nous devra pour le moins garder de tomber en l'erreur . . . des Epicuriens abbestis qui nient la providence de Dieu." The Stoics offer a similar peril in mingling God with nature: "et de tomber semblablement en l'erreur de ces pauvres philosophes nommez stoïciens, qui lient et assujettisent Dieu à nature et aux causes qu'ils appellent secondes. . . ." Those philosophers who say "qu'il n'y a aucune providence en luy, c'est à dire qu'ils estiment Dieu, comme

[14] Surtz, "Epicurus in Utopia," *ELH*, XVI, 93-94.

[15] C. A. Mayer, "The Lucianism of Des Périers," *BHR*, XII (1950), 203.

s'il estoit oiseux, et comme s'il n'avoit aucun soin de ses creatures pour les gouverner," believe God to be cruel.[16]

Similarly, Pierre du Val's *De la grandeur de Dieu* (1553, 1555) reproves

> Epicuriens et fols Empedoclistes
> Qui ne voulez aucun Dieu recevoir
> Ou lui ostez Providence et scavoir.[17]

Louis Leroy in the dedication to his translation of *Le Phedon de Platon traictant de l'immortalité de l'âme* (1553) attacks the atheism of those who ". . . nient la Providence divine . . . pour avoir grande occasion de servir à leurs concupiscences desordonnées et voluptés illicites."[18] The supposed Epicurean belief in *dieux fainéants* is condemned by Jean de Neufville in *De pulchritudine animi* (1556), remarking "la secte des épicuriens . . . de toutes les sectes la plus pernicieuse," a school which finds in Aristotle some support for its denial of providence.[19] In 1559 Gabriel Dupréau's *Nostrorum temporum calamitas* denounces the numerous disbelievers who doubted the existence of God and His providence;[20] while in 1569 his *De vitis, sectis, et dogmatibus omnium haereticorum* (Cologne, p. 70) declares that "Athei sunt, qui nullum esse Deum credunt . . . quique Dei providentiam e rebus humanis tollunt, omnia utique agi fato, animasque una cum corporibus interire arbitrantes." Ronsard, hymning the "goddess Eternity," in passages indicating the Epicurean notion of "careless gods," reminds Lovejoy as much of Lucretius as of Aristotle:

[16]Cited in Busson, *Le rationalisme*, pp. 518 and *n*, 490-491. Viret's *The Firste Parte of the Christian Instruction* appeared in 1565, and *A Christian Instruction* in 1573. Cf. Viret's *De la source & de la difference . . . de la vieille & nouvelle idolatrie* (Geneva, 1551), p. 32, which, like Batman, recalls the pagan custom "de paindre leur grand Dieu Jupiter, comme Plutharche le tesmoigne, sans oreilles. Aucuns disent qu'ilz la paignoyent aussi sans yeux." Their greatest theologians held that Jupiter "ne devoit point avoir de regard aux personnes" and therefore required neither eyes nor ears. See M. P. Nilsson, *A History of Greek Religion* (Oxford, 1949), p. 276, on the Athenians at the end of the third century, who held that the old gods either "are far away or have no ears. . ."

[17]In Busson, *Le rationalisme,* p. 581, citing from 1586 edition.

[18]Ibid., p. 285.

[19]Ibid., translation, p. 485.

[20]Busson, "Les noms des incrédules aux XVIe siècle," *BHR*, XVI (1954), 274; see also p. 277.

La premiere des Dieux, où bien loin de soucy
Et de l'humain travail qui nous tourmente icy.[21]

Comparable also is Ronsard's indignant demand for retribution from an apparently ineffectual divine providence:

Ne les puniras-tu souverain Createur?
Tiendras-tu leur parti? vieux-tu que l'on t'appele
Le Seigneur des larrons & le Dieu de querelle?[22]

Scornful of skeptics is the 1581 translator of Cicero's *De natura deorum*, a work which the former believes "n'avoir rien obmis de ce qui appartient aux discours et raisons qu'ameinent de nostre aage les mescreans, lucianistes, epicuriens, libertins qui comme serpens rampent et pullulent de jour en jour."[23] According to François de la Noue's work, translated as *The Politicke and Militarie Discourses* (1587 [1588]), France is overrun with Epicureans; and through some twenty pages he quotes in detail the arguments of the Epicures in the court, the armies, and the town.[24] In his *L'introduction . . . à l'apologie pour Hérodote* ([Geneva], 1566) Henri Estienne defends God against the charge of injustice. Besides the true atheists, he says, there is a whole group that, "non-obstant les remors de conscience, veulent contrefaire les atheistes." These "se faschent de ce qu'ils ne se peuvent oster de la fantasie qu'il n'y en ait un [Dieu], & qu'ils ont des remors de conscience alencontre du reniement de la providence de Dieu" (p. 118).[25]

In *Les trois véritez* (Bordeaux, 1595) Pierre Charron distinguishes, among three types of atheists, the Epicureans who seem to have some deity but hold it to be careless of this world and of us (p. 10). Jean Hotman's *Trois divers traittez sur la providence* (1596) asserts, against Pliny, that man is not less provided by nature than the ani-

[21] Arthur O. Lovejoy, *The Great Chain of Being: A Study of the History of an Idea* (Cambridge, Mass., 1936), p. 159; Ronsard, "Hymne de l'Éternité," *Oeuvres complètes*, ed. Paul Laumonier (Paris, 1914-19), IV, 160.

[22] "Remonstrance au peuple de France," *Oeuvres complètes*, V, 367.

[23] Guy Le Fèvre de la Boderie, in Busson, *Le rationalisme*, p. 588.

[24] "The 24. Discourse," pp. 312-334.

[25] "The term *Fortune*, so often employed by Montaigne, and in passages where he might have used that of Providence," recalls W. Carew Hazlitt (ed. *The Essays of Michel de Montaigne*, tr. Charles Cotton [New York, n.d.], p. 226*n*), "was censured by the doctors who examined his Essays, when he was at Rome in 1581." See *Oeuvres complètes de Michel de Montaigne*, ed. A. Armaingaud, VII (Paris, 1928), 281.

mals; he comments on Cicero's *De natura deorum* to show that providence has given man all he requires.[26] The extent of contemporary disbelief in watchful providence is suggested by Georges Pacard's *Théologie naturelle* (issued in 1579, 1606, and 1611): "Nous voyons . . . cette perverse opinion avoir saisi le cœur de la plupart des hommes que Dieu est voirement createur de toutes choses, mais qu'à present il ne se soucie aucunement de ce qui se fait ici-bas sur terre." Pacard distinguishes classes of infidels: the first holds with Averroës that if God governed this world "rien n'arriveroit par fortune et par cas"; the second agrees with Epicurus that "si Dieu avoit soin des choses basses et particulieres, cela diminueroit sa felicité"; others think that God would have the alternative of suppressing worldly evil or accepting responsibility for sin. Pacard opposes especially those who would replace God by "nature, fortune, or art" and suggests that the atheists confuse nature with God, that chance does not exist because the world is ordered, and as art proves man's intelligence, so the world demonstrates the wisdom of God.[27]

In his treatise on providence, *La constance et consolation ès calamitez publiques* (1595), Book II, the neo-Stoic Guillaume Du Vair gives evidence of those contemporaries who regarded providence as inactive or malicious. In the translation by Andrew Court (1622) Du Vair remarks that "most men turne their eyes" from providence

> and looke awrie upon it, striving to deceive themselves. . . . There hath bin truelie verie few, that durst bee so impious as flatly to denie it. . . . There are a number indeed, whose opinions I have heard . . . which acknowledging divine wisedome, and power in the first creation of the world, have taken the governement thereof from it . . . some attributing it unto that order, which they call Nature; some to a fatall necessitie, some others unto Chance, and Fortune. . . . (p. 64)

Having made these pronouncements regarding current skepticism of providence, Du Vair asserts that nature is not a power separate from God, as Vicomercato held, and that destiny is nothing but the foreknowledge of God (pp. 68-69).[28]

[26]In Busson, *Le rationalisme*, p. 515. For connections between human unprotectedness and questioning of providence, see Ch. viii below.

[27]Ibid., pp. 571, 570.

[28]In an extended examination of providence, J. C. Vanini, appearing to defend it while giving detailed arguments on both sides, supplies an indication of the ferment surrounding that doctrine: see *Amphitheatrum aeternae providentiae. . . . Adversus*

The year 1596, Busson observes (pp. 514-515), is peculiarly rich in apologies, a fact which suggests that the questioning apparently so plentiful since the middle of the century may have reached some sort of climax. About this time, too, in addition to works by Jean de Champagnac and Jean de Serres (John Serranus), appeared Hotman's *Trois divers traittez sur la providence*, cited above, which remarks that men still believe in God but doubt providence. Against the Peripatetics, "ceux qui confessent une divine providence seulement en ce qui se fait au ciel, et non pas en ce qui se fait sur la terre," Hotman establishes the reality of a particular providence. And, while he gives one chapter to the existence of God, he devotes most of the treatise to His providence, a proportion which may indicate something of the providence-questioning climate near the time of *King Lear*.

While in England unrestrained public expression of the Epicurean view of providence had to wait until later in the seventeenth century, promulgation of such ideas, as in Italy and France, occurred during the England of Shakespeare's time and earlier.[29] Since man, suggests Polydore Vergil's *Anglica historia* (Basel, 1546, 1555), is at the mercy of his luck, which "is extravagant . . . lavishly kind or cruelly perverse," he must accept his fate resignedly.[30] Coverdale alludes to "the number of them that say . . . God is in heaven and seeth us not, nor much passeth what we do."[31] And John Véron's *A Fruteful Treatise of Predestination and of the Divine Providence of God* [1561?] contains, the title continues, *an Apology of the Same, against Swynyshe Gruntinge of the Epicures and Atheystes of Oure Time*.

Affirming that God's providence extends to the smallest drop of

---

veteres philosophos, atheos, epicureos . . . (Lugduni, 1615). By opposing the skeptics with weak arguments, his accusers charged, he undermined orthodoxy. Vanini cites, *inter alia*, Diagoras' notion that, if providence ruled, there would be precise retribution of good and evil, which, in fact, does not occur. (Vanini was executed in 1619 for atheism.)

[29]Thomas F. Mayo, *Epicurus in England (1650-1725)* (Dallas, 1934), pp. xxiii-xxiv, cites English references of the early sixteenth century. See also Allen, "The Rehabilitation of Epicurus . . . ," *SP*, XLI, 1-3. C. T. Harrison, "The Ancient Atomists and English Literature of the Seventeenth Century," *Harvard Studies in Classical Philology*, XLV (1934), 3.

[30]Cited in Denys Hay, *Polydore Vergil: Renaissance Historian and Man of Letters* (Oxford, 1952), p. 140.

[31]*Remains of Myles Coverdale*, Parker Soc. (Cambridge, Eng., 1846), p. 231.

rain, Calvin, whose *Institutes* appears in influential Elizabethan translation,[32] especially aims at the Epicureans: "For to what end serveth it to confesse as Epicure doth, that there is a God which doth onely delight himselfe with idlenesse, having no care of the world?" (I.ii.2). "I speake not of the Epicurians," he explains, "(which pestilence the world hath alwayes beene filled with) which dreame of an idle and slouthfull God" (I.xvi.4). He reproaches, too, "the blasphemous sayings of the filthie dogg Lucretius" (I.v.5). While God's purposes are concealed from the depraved mind of man, fortune may not be said to rule: "how many a one is there," he complains, "that doeth not more thinke that men are rather whirled about & rowled by blinde unadvisednesse of fortune, than governed by providence of God?" (I.v.10). Not, he adds, "that we thinke that fortune ruleth the world & men, & unadvisedly tosseth al things up & down (for such beastlinesse ought to be farre from a Christian heart). . . ." Citing Augustine, Calvin declares, "Surely hee faineth not God to sit still idle in a watch toure . . ." (I.xvi.8). Resembling Pamela's argument against Cecropia in Sidney's *Arcadia*, Calvin's challenge to the Epicureans bids them explain how a "blind nature" can distinguish man from beast by endowing him with the excellences of the human soul. In opposition to Stoic fatalism, Calvin emphasizes the relevance of God's will (I.xvi.8).[33]

Ostensibly defending divine providence, Thomas Blundeville's translation of the precepts of Francesco Patrizi and Accontio Tridentino, *The True Order . . . of Wryting and Reading Hystories* (1574), admits that God "suffreth the wicked for the most part to live in prosperitie, and the good in adversitie . . ." (sig. [Fiii]). *Of the Ende of This Worlde* (1577) by Sheltoo à Geveren defines contemporary atheists as "men which neyther beleve there is any God, or divine providence at all." "And I feare me," he continues, "the most part of mankynd (. . . although they seeme never so spiritual . . . and woulde be counted Gospellers) by the like fictions . . . flatter themselves . . ." (sig. B1^{v}). Théodore de Bèze's *An Evident Display of Popish Practices, or Patched Pelagianisme* (1578) demands, "if . . . thou sayst" God "wincketh at" that which goes against a man, "howe muche doest thou differ from Epicurisme?" (p. 12). Abraham Flem-

[32]*The Institution of Christian Religion*, tr. Thomas Norton (1587).

[33]See Trinkaus, "Renaissance Problems in Calvin's Theology," *Studies in the Renaissance*, I (1954), 59-80.

ing's translation in 1579 of Bishop Synesius' *A Paradoxe* ... provides knowledge of Epicureanism: "Thus doubtfull of minde, and at defiance with destinie, as a favourer of Epicurus, I saide: What place is there left unto divine providence, seeing that all things fall out and happen to all men otherwise than they deserve..." (sig. [Avi^{v}]). Timothy Bright's *A Treatise . . . of English Medicines* (1580) remarks on "the Atheist of this age, who," rejecting providence, "so farre hath quenched those remnants of the light of the first creation, that all thinges seeme to him Fortune and Chaunce" (p. 9). Du Plessis Mornay's *De la verité de la religion chrestienne contre les athées, épicuriens* . . . (1582), translated into English (1587), assails those who deny providence, in their fear that God does not descend to particulars in this world subject to so many changes (Ch. xi).

From Elizabethan legal records testimony regarding Justice William Gardiner in 1582 discloses that he declared "that God hath nothing to do with the world since He created it, and that the world was not governed by Him"; another witness in 1588 attested the same person thought that God "had no government in the world."[34] Brian Melbancke in *Philotimus. The Warre betwixt Nature and Fortune* (1583) feels called upon to refute such heresy: "Far . . . be that from me, which Epicurus thinketh in Tullies bookes of the nature of the Gods, that nothinge is governed by the providence of God, bycause saith he, those that be immortall, take no pains, but being idle and vacant, trouble not themselves with any manner medling" (sig. [Yiii^{v}]).

Still another source of unrest regarding providence was Aristotle, as R. B., Esquire, insists in *The Difference betwene the Auncient Phisicke . . . and the Latter Phisicke* (1585). "Injurious" to providence is the Stagirite's teaching

> that God medleth not under the Moone . . . it maketh God to be the finall cause onely of motions. . . . And by this doctrine it must needes follow, that because the world is eternall without beginning & ending, and incorruptible, therefore it needeth not thy providence. . . . It also teacheth that thou O GOD . . . rulest under the Moone onely with a common influence and usuall course of second causes. . . .

"It is not enough," he notes, "to confesse that thou didst create all thinges, if it bee sayd also that thou hast forsaken those thinges as

[34] Leslie Hotson, *Shakespeare versus Shallow* (Boston, 1931), pp. 55, 57, 228-229.

soone as thou hast created them: as the Carpenter leaveth the house when he hath once made it. . . ." That such impious speculations were extant may be remarked in his expectation that his expression of pious views would be received with derision.[35]

Andreas Gerhard Hyperius' [Andreas Gerardus'] *A Speciall Treatise of Gods Providence* (1588?) assails supporters of chance, fortune, and destiny as deniers of providence. The argument of the Epicureans is that, if God is believed to care for human things, "his majestie in this point seemeth not a little to be hurt. . . . Which argument . . . flowed from out of the schoole of Epicurus . . ." (sig. B2^{v}). Directed, it would seem, at current unbelief, the author's strictures are intended to show "how fond and shamefull the cavillations of some men are, wherby they goe about to subvert and overthrowe particular providence" (sig. G1^{v}). John Hooper's *A Declaration of the X. Holie Commaundements* (ca. 1588) complains of "dailie used vices," the "most horrible abuse" of God's name being "among such as thinke there is no God to rewarde vertue, nor to punish vice, as the Epicures say, I woulde to God the same blasphemie had corrupted none that beare the name of christianitie" (fol. 33^{v}). And William Rankins, in *The English Ape* (1588), attacks the imitation of foreign ways and especially those that have "so stuffed England with their *Epicurisme*, and so replenished it with carelesse cogitations . . ." (p. 6).

In addition, Thomas Cooper's *An Admonition to the People of England* (1589), noting that "there are an infinite number of *Epicures*, and *Atheistes*" (p. 11), bears witness that "the schoole of *Epicure*, and the Atheists, is mightily increased in these dayes" (p. 118). That Epicureanism was common knowledge is suggested in Théodore de Bèze's *Job Expounded* (Cambridge, Eng., [1589?]): "Who knoweth not the wicked opinion of the *Epicures* attributing all things to the concourse or meeting of their small motes which they call *Atomi*?" (sig. [C7]). Like others, H. R. [Henry Roberts] assails those who exalt fortune above providence. In *A Defiance to Fortune* (1590), observing "But what vaine opinions they hold, that tearme thee a goddesse . . . for what can the servant doe without sufferance of the maister," he implies that, in his day, fortune was a live option against providence: "for what is fortune, but a fayned de-

[35]"The Authors obtestation . . . ," sigs. [6*v]-[7*], [8*v], [Aviii].

vise of mans spirite . . . so that . . . we must confesse, that all thinges are ruled and guided by the providence of God, and not by blinde fortune" (sig. M1^{v}). Many, concludes Roberts, "forgetting the honor of the true God, attribute al to fortune, which is nothing" (sig. M2).

More detailedly, *Propositions and Principles of Divinitie* (Edinburgh, 1591), of Théodore de Bèze and others, castigates varieties of contemporary questioning of providence:

> 1 Wherefore, we do condemne all ungodlie Epicures, who dreame of a certaine idle and daintie GOD, that neither regardeth his owne, nor yet other mens affaires: who also thinke, that all thinges are turned and rolled by the blind power of Fortune. . . .
>
> 2 . . . who make a subalternall or second providence, that is; do attribute unto the true God a generall kinde of providence, whereas they ascribe unto Saints or false Gods, a more speciall. . . .
>
> 3 . . . who faine a linking together of causes, & that there is a fatall destenie of things.
>
> 4 . . . that affirme heavenlie affaires, to be governed by God; and earthly things to be disposed, by the vertue, influence, and constellations of the Stars.
>
> 5 . . . who make Gods providence, to bee onely a bare knowledge of things . . . men and their affaires to bee guided by the power, but not by the appointment of God. (pp. 18-19)

Further indication that there was, at this time, questioning of providence occurs in Thomas Tymme's *A Plaine Discoverie of Ten English Lepers* (1592), which opposes "murmuring . . . against God. . . . For he can in no wise abide to be judged, and reprehended of ignorant men for the governement of his owne kingdome and common wealth. . . . Let no man medle with that which is beyond his skill." He notes that "Of this sort of murmurers, there are too many at this day among us, who in the time of scarcitie . . . do more like Pagans then Christians begin to murmur against God. . . . Other some there are which murmur against God, if they suffer any maner of affliction in this worlde . . ." (sigs. [L4]-M).

Again, reflecting foreign influences, the epistle to the reader in Thomas Bowes's translation of La Primaudaye's *The Second Part of the French Academie* (1594) fears that "this poison of Atheisme hath passed the narrow seas, & is landed in the hearts of no smal number . . ." (sig. b3^v). La Primaudaye notes, ". . . there are as many, yea moe at this day that doe openly shew themselves to be Atheists & Epicures, then there are of those that are taken for good Christians" (sig. A3^v).

In *Wits Miserie, and the Worlds Madnesse* (1596) Thomas Lodge, commenting on the Epicure's "many Imaginary worlds," evidences the frequent public expressions of such doubt:

this Devill . . . Blasphemy . . . is continually clamorous. . . . He haunts ordinaries, and places of exercise, schooles and houses of learning . . . if you talke of Divine justice, he saith there is no God: if he by sicknesse and plagues be forced to confesse him; he cals him tyrant, unjust, and without equitie. . . . (sigs. B, K)

Further evidence of Elizabethan disbelief in a just providence has been cited in connection with "The Problem of Justice in Marlowe's 'Hero and Leander.'"[36] Remarking that when Hero and Leander die in the Hellespont, the gods' divine justice is called into question, the discussion of Marlowe cites John Carpenter's *A Preparative to Contentation* (1597) clearly to show "That the concept of an unjust God was dangerously prevalent in England at the time of composition of these poems":

Herehence is also discried, that daungerous sin which hurteth mans soule with a desperate wound: *vz.* A deepe distrust of *the divine Providence*, by faith in the which, men have a chief comfort in this life, and without the which, they run into a labyrinth of errors. *Diagoras* the Atheist hath within his Schoole manie shrewd Schollers . . . and the *Protestant* is nothing scrupulous to pertake with the Peripatike, the Stoicke, the Epicure, the theefe, the murtherer, the perjurer, the bragging *Thraso*: yea, and . . . a thousand of them which go under this title [Protestant], shame not to halt between God and *Baal*, betweene *Moses* and *Corah*, betweene Christ and *Belial*. . . . But if they bee induced to graunt the beeing of GOD, yet imagine they, that God is either of no regarde or desire, or habilitie, to rewarde vertues with honours, or to defende the oppressed from theyr foes in this life, or to give victorie in battaile, or to punish horrible sinnes with horrible plagues. . . . (pp. 232, 234)[37]

Carpenter is aware that "in this world, *Diagoras* the Atheist . . . and the Cyclopicall Epicures, do take their pleasure to jeast at the provi-

[36]Paul W. Miller, in *N&Q*, N.S. IV (1957), 163-164.

[37]Carpenter's attack on Protestant recourse to Stoic and Epicurean ideas of providence is relevant to the discussion in Ch. ix below.

dence of God . . ." (p. 326). Machiavelli, he adds, jested at divine providence (p. 233). Doubters of providence emphasize "this heavy consideration . . . that the . . . wicked be preferred, and live in long prosperitie: that the unrighteous do unrighteously, & God (as *Job* saith) doth not charge them with follie, or plague them: that injustice and oppression is seene in the place of judgement . . ." (p. 278). Such discontent regarding providence is spread among "The common sort of men" who "do argue of the want of power and force in God," implying government by fortune. Even "manie of the godlie themselves . . . are by . . . such like spectacles, mooved to expostulate agaynst the Lorde . . . *should not the Judge of all the world do justice?*" There are "not a fewe" who are "desperate of GOD, and of the divine providence . . ." (pp. 279-280).

In 1597 George More's *A Demonstration of God in His Workes* indicates the many impious ones of Epicurus' "posteritie, worthily . . . to be termed Athiests" in "these latter wretched dayes" (p. 20). In 1597, too, Bacon remarks, if restraints were removed, "there is no heresy which strives with more zeal to spread and sow and multiply itself, than Atheism. Nor shall you see those who are fallen into this phrensy to breathe and importunately inculcate anything else almost, than speech tending to Atheism. . . ."[38] That scourge of God, Thomas Beard, in a chapter "Of Epicures and Atheists" in *The Theatre of Gods Judgements* (1597), scolds "Epicures and cursed Atheists, that deny the providence of God . . ." (p. 139). One of Beard's wicked targets is Marlowe, in whose writings lurks at least the suspicion of antiprovidential views. In such expressions as "the malice of the angry skies" and the equivocal treatment of Tamburlaine himself, and in Marlowe's dramatic attitude toward the Deity generally, may be implicit a dubiety in congruence with his life.[39] Indeed, Tamburlaine, like Faustus, views God as a repressive force, potentially an enemy. *Hero and Leander* mentions fate, by which "will in us is over-rul'd." Nowhere in Marlowe, it has been noted, is God seen as love and mercy; at best He is a legislator, with no visible effects of

[38] *Works,* VII, 251. Yet see Bacon's defense of Epicurus, in his sympathetic treatment of the school of Leucippus, Democritus, etc.: "But certainly he is traduced; for his words are noble and divine . . ." (*Works,* VI, 414).

[39] *Tamburlaine the Great* (1587-88), Pt. II, II.iv.11 (ed. U. M. Ellis-Fermor [1930]). See Jean Jacquot, "La pensée de Marlowe dans *Tamburlaine the Great*," *Études anglaises,* VI (1953), 339-340, 342-343.

justice on earth. The self is conceived as powerless before God.[40] Further, in such expressions as Spenser's

> if that carelesse heavens . . . despise
> The doome of just revenge, and take delight
> To see sad pageants of mens miseries,
> As bound by them to live in lives despight,[41]

may be instanced Douglas Bush's observation of Spenser's "painful struggle between his belief in a world evolving under divine providence and his vivid consciousness of a world of cruel strife and change."[42] William Vaughan's *The Golden-Grove* (1600) condemns "Atheists, and the hoggish sect of the Epicures . . ." (sig. [C8ᵛ]). Francis Meres's edition of Luis de Granada's *The Sinners Guyde* (1598) describes the Epicures as "the overthrowers and destroyers of all Philosophy, (for they denie the divine providence, and the immortalitie of soules) . . ." (p. 10).

Having paid his tribute to "epicuriens . . . et autres tels aveugles," Du Bartas, an influential figure in England, attacks, in Joshua Sylvester's translation of his *Semaines*, the Epicureans who say that the world was created by chance and those who deny a watchful providence:

> Fond *Epicure*, thou rather slept'st thy selfe,
> When thou did'st fancie such a sleepe-sicke Elfe.[43]

John Northbrooke's *Spiritus est vicarius Christi in terra* (1600) points to contemporary tendencies of those who "have in a very evill custome to say, this was Fortunes will, where they ought to say, this was Gods will," noting that "Fortune and chaunce, are the words of Heathen men, with the significations, whereof the minds of the godly ought not to be occupied" (foll. 24, 24ᵛ).

Sir William Cornwallis' *Discourses upon Seneca* (1601) assails the unprovidential worship of fortune and chance as a means of avoiding blame for our faults; those who do so imply that "by chance wee are governed, for so must they needes bee that allowe not their de-

40 *Marlowe's Poems*, ed. L. C. Martin (1931), Sestiad I, l. 168. See Paul H. Kocher, *Christopher Marlowe: A Study of His Thought, Learning, and Character* (Chapel Hill, N.C., 1946), p. 118.

41 *Faerie Queene*, II.i.36.

42 *Classical Influences in Renaissance Literature* (Cambridge, Mass., 1952), p. 56.

43 Guillaume de Salluste Du Bartas, *His Devine Weekes and Workes* (1605), p. 235.

signes premeditation without order: it is a shift to set up fortune, and the imputation of fortunes preposterous and disorderly working, it is our owne fault" (sig. E1^{v}). Epicureanism is expounded in the Englishman Nicolaus Hill's *Philosophia Epicurea, Democritiana, Theophrastica, proposita simpliciter* (Paris, 1601); in 1602, John Manningham calls Hill "a great profest philosopher," and Ben Jonson mentions his work in Epigram 133, written about 1610.[44] Du Plessis Mornay defends providence against fortune on the basis of divine workmanship, in *The True Knowledge of a Mans Owne Selfe,* translated by Anthony Munday in 1602 (sigs. L2-L4). Thomas Scott's *Foure Paradoxes* (1602) rebukes current "*Epicurian* folly" (sig. A4^{v}). In the same year, William Warner's *Albions England* attacks the "soule-blinded" Epicure and others who deny that the "All-powerfull, over all his Providence doth wate" (p. 314). John Davies of Hereford's *Mirum in Modum* (1602) demonstrates God's providence against atheists and evidences the climate:

> But with what words can I their blame bewray,
> That maugre all that ever can be saide,
> To prove this *God*; will all that *All* gainesay,
> And flat affirme, and speake as wellapaide,
> *There is no God. . . .*

Davies throughout is concerned to refute those who "impeach the *Providence* divine" (sigs. [H4], K2).

In 1603 Philemon Holland, some of whose work Shakespeare probably knew, in his translation of *The Philosophie, Commonlie Called, the Morals* of Plutarch complains of "these wretched daies, wherein Epicurisme beareth up the head as high as at any time ever before." He observes the Epicureans who,

> (drunken & intoxicate with false supposals, seeing in the conduct of this worlds affaires, some that be honest and vertuous, distressed, and oppressed by divers devices and practises; whereas others againe, who be naught and vicious, continue in repose, without any chastisement . . .) would needs take from God the dispose and government of humane affaires, holding and mainteining this point: That all things roll and run at a venture, and that there is no other cause of the good and evill accidents of this life, but either fortune or els the will of man. (p. 538)

[44] *Diary of John Manningham,* ed. John Bruce, Camden Soc. (Westminster, 1868), p. 60; reference dated Oct. 25, 1602; *Ben Jonson,* VIII, 87; XI, 32.

On the other hand, Plutarch, according to Holland, disposes of the emphasis on fortune, "shewing that it taketh away all distinction of good and evill." Plutarch, says Holland, "prooveth that prudence and wisedome, over-ruleth this blind fortune" (p. 229).

In 1604 Andrew Willet's *Thesaurus ecclesiæ* attacks "many carnall men, that cannot look into Gods providence," like the Epicures seeing all to be but fortune.[45] The author (Joseph Hall?) of *Two Guides to a Good Life* (1604) classifies four sorts of unbelievers: those who think there is no God and that the world is governed by the course of nature; those who, admitting God, feel He has no regard to men's lives; those who, believing in God and His providence, dismiss posthumous judgment or resurrection; and those who accept that which the former three reject and yet do ill ("The Genealogie of vertue," sigs. [E4^{v}]-[E5]). John Dove's *A Confutation of Atheisme* (1605), making the same kind of fourfold classification of unbelievers as the author of *Two Guides*, cites Epicurus among them (p. 2). In a translation dedicated to James, Pierre Le Loyer's *A Treatise of Specters* (1605) assails various points of the Epicurean religious position (foll. 24-32^{v}). In 1605, also, Thomas Tymme published his translation of Joseph Du Chesne, *The Practise of Chymicall . . . Physicke*, warning that "wee must not thinke that God hath so forsaken the frame of this world, that he sitteth idle," as do those who believe like the Epicures, acknowledging no other God but nature (sig. C2).

Since *Lear* was composed about 1605, previous citations and those to follow may indicate that the period surrounding its composition evinces concern regarding providence. In 1606, for example, Barnabe Rich (*Faultes*) argues: "They are much deceived, who would perswade the affaires of the world to bee turned about by chaunce, or uncertaintie. . . ." He opposes those who "would make God himselfe to be subject to the wheele of destinie . . ." (foll. 34, 33^{v}). In 1606, too, George Thomson's *Vindex veritatis* attacks the Stoic fatalistic view of providence (sigs. D3^{v}-D4). In the same year, Samuel Gardiner's *Doomes-Day Booke* complains, "The divinitie that the schoole of Epicures professeth . . . is. . . . There is nothing that remaineth after death" (p. 47). Again, Gulielmus Bucanus' *Institutions of Christian Religion* (1606) confutes "The errour of Epicures,

[45]Cambridge, Eng., p. 25.

& almost of all the Ethnicks, who supposed that fortune and chance ruled the world, and governed men . . . and that all effectes were produced by a casuall and accidentall application of the *agent* . . ." (p. 153). Nothing, he insists, comes by chance or fortune, although we, who are ignorant of true causes, may see things in that way. "*Chaunce* and *Fortune* are words of Heathens . . ." (p. 148).

In 1606, further, Thomas Fitzherbert's *The First Part of a Treatise concerning Policy, and Religion* (Douai), while it assails those who put nature in place of God (sig. [c5]), refers to atheists doubting providence (p. 233), while in *The Second Part* . . . ([Douai?], 1610) he affirms: ". . . I take Atheists, not only for those, who denie that there is a God, but also for such, as denie the particuler providence of God in the affaires of men" (pp. 69-70). Tourneur's atheist D'Amville, who in the timely *Atheist's Tragedie* (1607-1611) could have reflected some contemporary opinion, disdains God's presence in events:

> And I am of a confident beliefe,
> That ev'n the time, place, manner of our deathes,
> Doe Follow Fate with that necessitie;
> That makes us sure to dye. And in a thing
> Ordain'd so certainly unalterable,
> What can the use of providence prevaile? (I.ii.49-54)

In Webster's world, as in *The Duchess of Malfi* (1612-1614), capricious fortune is said to rule, and in *The White Devil* (1609-1612) the workings of providence are observed as lost:

> "While we looke up to heaven wee confound
> "Knowledge with knowledge. ô I am in a mist. (V.vi.259-260)

Chapman's Bussy D'Ambois operates in a world where "Fortune, not Reason, rules the state of things," where all men are "the spawn of Fortune," a world, in effect, where man falls "Before the frantic puffs of blind-born chance, / That pipes through empty men, and makes them dance."[46] Chapman's *Caesar and Pompey* (1599-1607), reflecting on the absence of justice in the world, attributes the heavens' disinclination to ameliorate such conditions to an inscrutable mystery.[47]

[46] *Bussy D'Ambois* (1600-04), I.i.1, 13; V.ii.44-45.

[47] V.ii.70-86. See Jean Jacquot, *George Chapman* (Paris, 1951), pp. 187-188. Plutarch observes that Pompey, after Pharsalia, uttered doubts concerning providence; Thomas North, tr. *The Lives of the Noble Grecians and Romanes . . . by . . . Plutarke* (1579), pp. 715-716.

The commentary on the Thirty-nine Articles by Thomas Rogers (1607) selects for condemnation "all Heretikes, and errors impugning . . . [God's] providence" in continuing and preserving the world, including "the Epicures, who thinke God is idle" and does not govern inferior things. It indicts also "The Stoike Philosophers, and the Manichies, who are the great patrones of Destinie, Fate, and Fortune."[48] Arthur Dent's *A Sermon of Gods Providence* (1611) cites "very many" who deny particular providence; although they condemn Epicurus' views of an idle God, they in effect embrace it (sig. [A5]).[49] In *The Gallants Burden* (1612) Thomas Adams notes "Epicures, that deny not a God, and a day of Judgement; but put it farre off . . ." (fol. 16v). Thomas Milles's edition of Pedro Mexía's *The Treasurie of Auncient and Moderne Times* (1613) speaks of "the instability of the world . . . which some have falsely attributed to Fortune . . . vanities holden by the *Gentiles* and *Ethnickes* . . ." (p. 655). Fortune is a "kinde of Idolatrie, or God of fooles," suggests Raleigh, who, with possible firsthand acquaintance, at the start of *The History of the World* (1614), reports: "Yet many of those that have seemed to excell in worldly wisdome, have gone about to disjoyne this coherence [between creation and providence]; the Epicure denying both Creation & Providence. . . ."[50] Like Raleigh, Donne had some personal knowledge, especially in his early years, of the naturalist traditions; in a sermon he reproves atheists who presume that "naturall accidents, casuall occurrencies, emergent contingencies" are matters which "would fall out though there were no God."[51] Lancelot Andrewes opposes those questioners of providence who effect a "curtaine" between God and man; those who cling to a providence of "generall things, not of particular"; and those who, admitting a "Providence both of generall and particular things," think "it is idle and not rewarding." Other men subscribe to both a general and a particular providence "which rewardeth good to the good, and evill to the evill. And this is the truth, which we hold."[52] Ultimately,

48*The Faith, Doctrine, and Religion . . . in 39 Articles* (Cambridge, Eng.), pp. 4-5.

49See also sigs. [A6]-[A7v], C3r-v.

50I.i.15, p. 19; Preface, sig. D2. See Ernest A. Strathmann, *Sir Walter Ralegh: A Study in Elizabethan Skepticism* (New York, 1951), p. 114; Raleigh, *The History of the World*, II.v.3, p. 299; II.xii.3, p. 413; II.xiii.5, p. 427; V.iii.12, p. 485.

51*The Sermons of John Donne*, ed. Evelyn M. Simpson and George R. Potter, VI (Berkeley, 1953), 217.

52Andrewes, *A Patterne of Catechisticall Doctrine* (1630), p. 55.

in the age of those who, like Hobbes, removed the Deity to a distant First Cause, Milton acknowledges that, concerning Adam's Fall, "many there be that complain of divin Providence. . . ."[53]

In addition to alterations in the traditional concepts of providence produced by Renaissance skeptical ferments, a second, and at least equally profound, revision was introduced by both devout Reformers and fideist Montaigne. The major change can be summarized: (1) Theologically, as a substitution for the medieval and Renaissance notion of *analogia entis* (or likeness between man and God) by the Reformers' voluntarist denial of any such likeness (at most, an *analogia fidei*). This change involved the breakdown of the traditional analogy between Creator and creature, in the reawakened consciousness of fallen man's rational incapacity. Beyond human reason, *totaliter aliter*, the transcendent, rather than immanent, Deity inscrutably hid himself. (2) In the secular realm, as a similar depreciation of human rationality and ability to know. Indeed, Montaigne's fideist demolition of the analogical, anthropomorphic Deity was, in effect, a Copernican revolution in the sphere of man's vanity, serving to distance him from God.[54]

[53]*Areopagitica* (1644), in *The Works of John Milton*, ed. Frank A. Patterson, IV (New York, 1931), 319; cf. IV, 312, on Epicurus and antiprovidential views. See Marjorie Hope Nicolson on "Milton and Hobbes," *SP*, XXIII (1926), 415.

Among numerous other references, see also S. I., *Bromleion* (1595), p. 160; Hieronymus Zanchius, *His Confession* . . . ([Cambridge, Eng.], 1599), sigs. [B7v]-[B8]; George Abbot, *An Exposition upon the Prophet Jonah* (1600), p. 195; Edward Hutchins, *Sampsons Jawbone* (1601), p. 140, petitioning God against "al Epicures and Atheists" who "disquiet . . . thy Church of England"; William Burton, [*Works*] (1602), sig. Kk1, regarding "the infinite swarmes of . . . Atheists . . . and of Epicures"; John Hull, *Saint Peters Prophesie of These Last Daies* (1611), sig. A3, "Epicures abound, Atheisme is ripe. . . . Gods providence rejected"; Helkiah Crooke, *Microcosmographia. A Description of the Body of Man* (1615), pp. 8-9; John de la Casa, *The Rich Cabinet*, tr. Thomas Gainsford (1616), fol. 47 (see also foll. 5v-6v); Robert Anton, *Vices Anotimie* (1617), sig. C2; C. B., in *Sir Thomas Overbury His Wife* (1616), sig. [¶5]; W. S., ibid., sig. [¶ 6v]; Sir Thomas Browne, *Works*, I, 26, 28; IV, 41; Robert Burton, *The Anatomy of Melancholy* (Oxford, 1621), pp. 765-766.

[54]Cf. Calvin, *Institutes*, II.ii.12. See Robert Hoopes, "Fideism and Skepticism during the Renaissance: Three Major Witnesses," *Huntington Library Quarterly*, XIV (1951), 319-347.

While Chapman in *Eugenia* supports the divine-human correspondence and the "Analogia mundi & corporis principium partium" (*The Poems of George Chapman*, ed. Phyllis B. Bartlett [New York, 1941], ll. 423-430, 721-745), Greville, because of "natural corruption," disputes such hopeful analogizing, e.g., in *A Treatise of Religion*, sts. 12-13, in *The Works in Verse and Prose . . . Fulke Greville, Lord Brooke*, ed. Alexander B. Grosart ([Blackburn], 1870), I, 243.

Relying on a tradition from Nicolaus de Cusa's *docta ignorantia*[55] through Ockham, Luther had already expressed the *Deus absconditus*. For Luther, indeed, at times God is not only hidden but angry, beyond reconciliation with fallen man.[56] He is even inimical, in the Job tradition, Luther's God being, it has been suggested, "not only *above* every human grasp, but in *antagonism* to it."[57]

In Montaigne's secular attack on divine analogy, demolishing Sebonde's hymn to man's privileged and glorious status under God, a new, impersonal, and unknowable providence is instated: "What greater vanitie can there be, than to goe about by our proportions and conjectures to guesse at God? And to governe both him and the world according to our capacitie and lawes?" Insisting on everything which, like an impenetrable screen, infinitely separates God from man—who is at best "neither above nor under the rest"—Montaigne delimits man's place in the cosmos (II, 216, 151). "... Éternel, intemporel, indéterminé, partout présent et agissant, mais dont on ne peut rien dire sinon qu'il Est," Montaigne's new distant, deperson-

[55]*Nicolai de Cusa opera omnia,* [Ser. 1], Vol. I: *De docta ignorantia*, ed. Ernst Hoffmann and Raymond Klibansky (Leipzig, 1932). See also *Schriften des Nikolaus von Cues,* ed. Hoffmann, Vol. III: *Vom verborgenen Gott. De Deo abscondito,* ed. Elisabeth Bohnenstaedt (Leipzig, 1940).

[56]*Werke,* I (Weimar, 1883), 139. While the *Deus absconditus* is essentially Lutheran, rather than Calvinist, the conception might also be derived from Calvinist premises. See Edward A. Dowey, *The Knowledge of God in Calvin's Theology* (New York, 1952); John Dillenberger, *God Hidden and Revealed: The Interpretation of Luther's Deus Absconditus and Its Significance for Religious Thought* (Philadelphia, 1953); Brian A. Gerrish, *Grace and Reason: A Study in the Theology of Luther* (Oxford, 1962).

Although receiving renewed emphasis at the Reformation, the *Deus absconditus* recurs in various forms throughout religious history: e.g., in Job; Ecclesiastes; Plato (e.g., *Parmenides, Phaedo, Symposium, Republic, Timaeus*); Philo (see Festugière, *La révélation d'Hermès Trismégiste,* II [Paris, 1949], 573-575; 585); Proclus (Festugière, IV [1954], 271-274; cf. IV, 307, on the *Agnostos theos*; see passim Vol. IV, which is subtitled "Le Dieu inconnu et la gnose"); Plotinus; Augustine; John Scotus Erigena; Anselm; Bonaventure; and Eckhart. "Negative theology," as in Dionysius the Pseudo-Areopagite and as developed by the cabalists, helped spread the *Deus absconditus* idea in the Renaissance. A significant English link in asserting the "unknown God" concept was John Colet, More's adviser and author of treatises on Dionysius.

[57]Rudolph Otto, *The Idea of the Holy* (1950), p. 185. Cf. Arthur Sewell, *Character and Society in Shakespeare* (Oxford, 1951), pp. 120-121: "Tragedy finds its origin not in a Christian idea of imperfection but in 'Renaissance anarchism.' . . . Shakespearian tragedy is the product of the change in men's minds—the Renaissance change—by which men came to feel themselves separate from God; by which, indeed, the idea of God receded from men's habitual certitudes and became no more and often less than an intellectual construction, a merely credible hypothesis, a Being remote and not certainly just or beneficent, perhaps the Enemy."

alized Deity rules over a world where all is "diversité, 'mutation et branle.' "[58]

Montaigne accepts the *Deus absconditus*: "Of all humane and ancient opinions concerning religion," he affirms, "I thinke that to have had more likelyhood and excuse, which knowledged and confessed God to be an incomprehensible power . . ." (II, 216). Considering the Christian God to be not unlike the Athenian, hidden and unknown, he observes: "We easily pronounce puissance, truth and justice; they be words importing some great matter, but that thing we neither see nor conceive. We say that God feareth, that God will be angry, and that God loveth. . . . They be all agitations . . . which according to our forme can have no place in God, nor we imagine them according to his." Hence, "*It onely belongs to God*," Montaigne deduces, "*to know himselfe, and interpret his owne workes*; and in our tongues he doth it improperly, to descend . . . to us, that . . . lie groveling on the ground" (II, 200).

Like Montaigne, Calvin has a low view of man's intellectual capacity and shares with him a skepticism regarding its use. If man's postlapsarian reason is dark and incapable, God is not to be understood but obeyed and his apparent injustices swallowed. Calvin insists that to be ignorant of many things "which it is neither graunted nor lawful to knowe" is to be learned (III.xxiii.8). Of "the same invisible God whose wisedome, power and justice is incomprehensible" (I.xiv.1), we are not, that is, to "take upon 's the mystery of things" (*Lear*, V.iii.16), as Montaigne and a host of Renaissance writers caution.

Both Montaigne and Calvin share, then, comparable views regarding not only the *debilitas rationis*, the limitation of human reason, but also the *Deus absconditus*, the hidden God. In addition, Calvin, like Montaigne, rejects anthropomorphism: "And the Anthropomorphites are also easily confuted which have imagined God to consist of a bodie . . . . such maner of speeches doe not so plainly expresse what God is, as they do apply the understanding of him to our slender capacitie" (I.xiii.1).

In both Montaigne and Calvin, God is distant from man, but in Calvin the Divinity comes at times to resemble a tyrant who arbi-

[58]Marcel Raymond, "Entre le fidéisme et le naturalisme (À propos de l'attitude religieuse de Montaigne)," *Festschrift für Ernst Tappolet* (Basel, 1935), p. 239.

trarily and unpredictably saves and damns, just as in Luther He seems at times the enemy. As Calvin memorably pronounces in his *horribile decretum*:

That therefore which the Scripture cleerely sheweth, we say that God by eternall and unchangeable counsell hath once appointed whome in time to come he would take to salvation, and on the other side whome he woulde condemne to destruction. This counsell as touching the elect, wee say to bee grounded uppon his free mercie without any respect of the worthinesse of man, but whome hee appointeth to damnation, to them by his just in deed and irreprehensible, but also incomprehensible judgement, the entry of life is foreclosed. (III.xxi.7)[59]

From the Calvinist premises it therefore emerges that, torn between its natural desire for justice and the mysterious ways of providence, mankind is helplessly and forever in the wrong before the divine tribunal.

In Calvin, law is rooted in divine omnipotence as unconditional and beyond human norms. Will stands for reason ("Stat pro ratione voluntas"), man's reason being enslaved to its depraved desires and darkened by the Fall. Supplanting the rational structure of moral law, the voluntarist tradition of Ockham and Calvin affirms that its rules exist, not through reason or knowledge, but simply because God has willed them. Hence, it is futile as well as wrong to demand the grounds of the divine decision. The culmination of this position appears in Pascal, who, following Isaiah and Jerome, declares, "Vere tu es Deus absconditus." Pascal defends God's ways against our own "miserable justice." Since the basis of God's justice, by definition, remains hidden, according to divine standards no human being suffers unjustly. In this way, God's justice and Pascal's title to "Athlete of the Faith" are both vindicated.[60]

In addition to such influences as Calvin and Montaigne, a third tendency, which may be labeled the Baconian, furthered the cloak-

[59]Cf. Calvin's remark that "it pleased God to *hide from us* al things to come, to this end that we should meete with them as things doutful, & not ceasse to set prepared remedies against them, til either they be overcome, or be past al help of care" (*Institutes*, I.xvii.4; italics mine).

[60]*Pascal's Pensées*, tr. H. F. Stewart (New York, 1950), Nos. 210*b*, 223, 247, 248, 514, 515. See also Lucien Goldmann, *Le Dieu caché: Étude sur la vision tragique dans les pensées de Pascal et dans le théâtre de Racine* (Paris, 1955 [1956]).

ing of God's providence.[61] Indeed, the *Deus absconditus* concept, by distancing God from man, encouraged the empiricist of the Renaissance, in effect, to substitute a visible second cause for the concealed First Cause, while maintaining at least the appearances of piety. Tending to shift "nature" from theology to empiricism, this third alienating factor seems to be reflected, for instance, in Lear's inquiries into the natural causation of things traditionally ascribed to heavenly causes.

[61]See Bacon, *Works*, III, 341-342.

CHAPTER III

Sidney's *Arcadia*: Four Attitudes to Providence

IN THE ENGLAND of Shakespeare's day the providential doctrines of Calvin, which I have summarized above, found a welcome home, the Genevan's influence exceeding, indeed, that of any other theologian. As Hooker observed, Calvin for a long period occupied the position which the "Master of Sentences" had held in the age of scholasticism, "so that the perfectest divines were judged they, which were skilfullest in Calvin's writings."[1] Although modern Anglicans, especially after the Oxford Movement, may tend to identify mainly the liberal or Anglo-Catholic branch as the true (Renaissance) Church of England, the fact remains that during Shakespeare's career the opposing side exerted a powerful enveloping force. Interestingly, the Arminians, seventeenth-century rebels against Calvinism, have been associated with the Anglo-Catholics of today.[2]

Unfortunately ignored is the fact that the strongest formulation of a basic Calvinist tenet (predestination) was made not by a Puritan but by an Anglican bishop, staunch defender of the Establishment and friend of John Donne, Joseph Hall.[3] That tenet, a modern anti-Puritan historian agrees, was crucially important for all brands of Protestantism.[4] In addition, the Thirty-nine Articles, known to every member of the Establishment, reflected Calvin's ideas.[5] In the universities, further, Calvinism was taught by such men as William Perkins and William Whitaker at Cambridge and John Reynolds at Oxford. G. R. Cragg concludes that the leaders of the Elizabethan

[1]*Of the Laws of Ecclesiastical Polity*, in *Works*, I, 139.

[2]Godfrey Davies, *The Early Stuarts 1603-1660* (Oxford, 1937), p. 69*n*.

[3]Charles H. George, "A Social Interpretation of English Puritanism," *Journal of Modern History*, XXV (1953), 330-331.

[4]A. L. Rowse, *The England of Elizabeth: The Structure of Society* (New York, 1951), p. 487.

[5]See Charles Hardwick, *A History of the Articles of Religion* (1888), p. 188.

church were Calvinists virtually to a man. Whitgift was no less a Calvinist than his Presbyterian opponent, Cartwright, his works being full of citations from Calvin in which the latter was utilized to contradict the main positions of the Puritans.[6]

So far as doctrine was concerned, the Calvinist struggle for England seemed victorious, John T. McNeill has concluded;[7] while the author of a monograph on the reception of Calvinist thought in England deduces that, though not everyone in sixteenth-century England was a Calvinist, almost everyone came in close contact with ideas which could have been accepted by Calvin.[8] For example, Calvinism, through Dean Nowell, permeated the official catechism, which Shakespeare probably studied.[9] Evidence, in fact, exists to show that, in 1604, at least, shortly before the appearance of *Lear*, Shakespeare was dwelling at the house of French Calvinists, whom he knew so intimately as to be involved in subsequent family litigation.[10] When, in addition, we recall that Shakespeare wrote *King Lear* under a sometime Scottish Calvinist monarch, we have indicated sufficient possibility of the influence of Calvinist-inspired views of the Deity and related conceptions of providence sketched above on the cosmic dimensions of Shakespeare's tragedy.

Between Calvin and Shakespeare's *Lear* still another link exists in Sidney's *Arcadia*, which includes possible Calvinist features. That Sidney's romance is a source of the Gloucester plot was pointed out as long ago as 1754 by Charlotte Lennox and has since been accepted in the scholarship; in addition, recent studies have indicated, without necessarily exhausting, the more general indebtedness of *King Lear* to the *Arcadia*.[11]

[6]Cragg, *From Puritanism to the Age of Reason* (Cambridge, Eng., 1950), p. 14.

[7]*The History and Character of Calvinism* (New York, 1954), p. 314. "It is unhistorical," adds William A. Curtis in *A History of Creeds and Confessions of Faith in Christendom and Beyond* (Edinburgh, 1911), p. 177, "to deny the Calvinism of the English Articles. . . ."

[8]Charles D. Cremeans, *The Reception of Calvinistic Thought in England*, Illinois Studies in the Social Sciences, XXXI, No. 1 (Urbana, Ill., 1949), 82.

[9]Thomas W. Baldwin, *William Shakspere's Petty School* (Urbana, Ill., 1943), p. 222.

[10]See E. K. Chambers, *William Shakespeare: A Study of Facts and Problems* (Oxford, 1930), I, 85; II, 94-95.

[11]Fitzroy Pyle, "'Twelfth Night,' 'King Lear' and 'Arcadia,'" *MLR*, XLIII (1948), 449-455; D. M. McKeithan, "*King Lear* and Sidney's *Arcadia*," *Studies in English*, Univ. of Texas Bull. No. 14 (1934), pp. 45-49; Hardin Craig, "Motivation in Shakespeare's Choice of Materials," *Shakespeare Survey 4* (1951), pp. 32-33; *The Complete Works*

When it is remembered that Sidney's education and adult friendships were to a large extent Calvinistic, it is not surprising that his major literary effort may reflect similar ideas. At Shrewsbury School, where Puritan officials were in charge, it may be assumed, says Sidney's chief modern biographer,[12] that the pronounced Puritan atmosphere left a strong impression; those officials included Ashton and Atkys, as well as Lawrence, who became master in 1568. We have a record of Sidney's purchase there of Calvin's Catechism; and there, as well as through his life, an intimate friend was the Calvinist Fulke Greville. At Oxford, where Puritans were then strong, Sidney's tutors were such Puritans as Laurence Humphrey and Nathaniel Baxter, later a vigorous Puritan controversialist. During his career Sidney moved among a circle of French Calvinist friends, including Languet and Du Plessis Mornay.[13] Sidney's name, as well as Arthur Golding's, is connected with the translation of Mornay's theological treatise *De la verité de la religion chrestienne*. The Puritan Golding also rendered large volumes of Calvin's sermons; and his Ovid's *Metamorphoses*, a version known to Shakespeare, introduces a demonstration that Ovid's cosmogony agrees exactly with that of Moses, a point of interest in relation to the *prisca theologia*, considered below.

In view of these facts, it comes at least within the range of possibility that a number of references to the heavens in the *Arcadia* may, in addition to their rhetorical conventionality, have a Calvinist tinge. In this acknowledged source Shakespeare—without necessarily reflecting its world view, which he might also have derived from the Renaissance climate, from Montaigne, and elsewhere—could have

---

of Shakespeare, ed. Craig (Chicago, 1951), pp. 980-981; Muir, pp. xxxviii-xlii; Muir and John F. Danby, "'Arcadia' and 'King Lear,'" *N&Q*, CXCV (Feb. 4, 1950), 49-51; William A. Armstrong, " 'King Lear' and Sidney's 'Arcadia,' " *Times Literary Supplement*, Oct. 14, 1949, p. 665. Steevens (New Variorum *Lear*, p. 252) connected Cordelia's and the *Arcadia*'s Philoclea's commingled smiles and tears.

12Malcolm W. Wallace, *The Life of Sir Philip Sidney* (Cambridge, Eng., 1915), pp. 43, 45, 98, 102, 103, 107, 183.

13On Sidney's French friends, see Lois Whitney, "Concerning Nature in *The Countesse of Pembrokes Arcadia*," *SP*, XXIV (1927), 209. See also A. G. D. Wiles, "Sir Philip Sidney: The English Huguenot," *Transactions of the Huguenot Society of South Carolina*, No. 45 (Charleston, 1940), pp. 24-37. On Sidney and his Protestant associates in their relations with King James's tutor, George Buchanan, see James E. Phillips, "George Buchanan and the Sidney Circle," *Huntington Library Quarterly*, XII (1948), 23-55.

confirmed some ideas about providence which may be echoed in his tragedy. Such ideas include the following attitudes toward providence, adumbrated, as subsequent instances will show, in the *Arcadia* and in *Lear* itself: the *Deus absconditus*; the gods as somehow not consonant with human happiness; human reason as corrupted and dark; man's position in relation to cosmic forces as one of helpless despair; and mankind a "worm." While such conceptions are, of course, not necessarily all in total accord with the intention of Calvin, they represent, at least in effect, feelings which the Calvinist premises could have produced.

The four major attitudes, which will be distinguished both in Sidney and in *Lear*, include: (1) the *prisca theologia*, or virtuous-heathen view, which may, in part, suggest the quasi-Christian aspect of such pre-Christian characters as Cordelia; (2) the atheistic view; (3) the superstitious view; and (4) the view which falls into none of the previous categories but is the result of human reaction to the effects of the hidden providence. These four viewpoints will be considered in turn, first, as they occur in the *Arcadia* and then, in the following chapters, as they reemerge in *King Lear*.

Regarding the Elizabethan attitudes present in the *Arcadia*, Sidney's actualizing propensities beyond his sources have been noted.[14] We may therefore admit the presence of traditional complaint patterns and of such conventions of the pastoral elegy as "The Riddle of this Painful Earth," the "feeling of bitter resentment against the cruel fate which blasts life in the bud," and the precedents of Bion, Theocritus, and Virgil's fifth eclogue,[15] as well as such later patterns

[14]See, e.g., Kenneth T. Rowe, *Romantic Love and Parental Authority in Sidney's Arcadia*, Univ. of Michigan Contributions in Modern Philology, No. 4 (Ann Arbor, 1947), p. 14. Also relating Sidney's work to contemporary sixteenth-century attitudes, numerous studies have traced the *Arcadia*'s Renaissance political reflections.

[15]George Norlin, "The Conventions of the Pastoral Elegy," *American Journal of Philology*, XXXII (1911), 306. Sidney's pastoral, it is evident, shares with *Lear* rhetorical formulas and conventional "set speeches" such as are discussed in Wolfgang Clemen's valuable *English Tragedy before Shakespeare: The Development of Dramatic Speech* (New York, 1961). Yet recognition of such "type speeches" (e.g., "The Prayer for Annihilation," "The Appeal to the Elements," "The 'Lugete-Topos'"), while generally enlightening, does not exclude awareness of their somewhat altered significance as they function contextually in the dramatic and historical particularity of the work of art. On Renaissance adaptations of the pastoral to contemporary concerns, see also S. K. Heninger, Jr., "The Renaissance Perversion of Pastoral," *Journal of the History of Ideas*, XXII (1961), 254-261, and Edward W. Tayler, *Nature and Art in Renaissance Literature* (New York, 1964).

as those of Tasso, Drummond, and Spenser,[16] without also excluding contemporary religious concerns. Whether Shakespeare's tragic cosmos was related to the *Trennung von Gott und Kreatur* implicit in Calvin and Montaigne and in the increasingly uncertain climate of the later Renaissance or to the Calvinist Sidney's intensification of the pastoral melancholy, the materials of cosmic despair available in Sidney's romance emerge in the deeper tones of Shakespeare's tragedy.

"Prisca Theologia"

> *The heathen remained in their own magic. But those who from the itch of corruption passed out into the light of Nature because they did not know God, yet have lived in purity, —these were children of the Free-will, and in them has the Spirit of Freedom revealed great wonders in their mystery, as is to be seen by the wisdom they have bequeathed to us.*
>
> —Jacob Boehme, *Mysterium pansophicum*

As recent studies have suggested, Pamela and certain other pagan characters in *Arcadia* exhibit virtues and pieties which, because of their purity, can be said to foreshadow Christian ones. Indeed, Sidney was one of a group of liberal Calvinists who, like the Catholics and unlike most Protestants, appeared to believe in the salvation of such heathens.[17]

In the controversy between De Andrade (Andradius), a Portuguese delegate to the Council of Trent, and Chemnitz, a Lutheran theologian, the latter attacked a conciliar canon (Sessio Sexta, Canon VII, published in 1569) which held: "If anyone should say that all the works which were done before justification, for whatever reason they were done, are sinful or deserve God's hatred; or that the more vehemently anyone strives to be in a fit state to receive grace, the more gravely he sins; let him be anathema,"[18] a Catholic position which led to a liberal view of the *prisca* and which ran counter to most Protestant opinion. Arguing from Augustine

[16]Spenser on Sidney's death, indicting the heavens which "foresaw, yet suffred this be so," "Astrophel," *Poetical Works,* p. 549, l. 10.

[17]D. P. Walker, "Ways of Dealing with Atheists: A Background to Pamela's Refutation of Cecropia," *BHR*, XVII (1955), 252-277. Cf. Louis Capéran, *Le problème du salut des infidèles* (Toulouse, 1934). See also Walker, "The *Prisca Theologia* in France," *JWCI*, XVII (1954), 204-259, and "Orpheus the Theologian and Renaissance Platonists," ibid., XVI (1953), 100-120.

[18]Quoted in Walker, "The *Prisca Theologia* in France," p. 257.

and St. Paul, Chemnitz further opposed the liberal views of Justin, Clement of Alexandria, and Epiphanius, who along with Eusebius, Lactantius, and Cyril were among the chief patristic inspirations for the *prisca theologia*. To claim that the Greeks were saved by philosophy, Chemnitz asserted, in the same way that the Jews were saved by the Law, is impious doctrine. In a refutation later typical of the anti-Calvinists, one which Samuel Harsnet himself used, Andradius declared that the damnation of virtuous pagans implied a cruel God.

Directly counter to the Tridentine canon, however, the thirteenth and eighteenth of the Thirty-nine Articles evince the impact of the Reformation on the Church of England with regard to the salvation of pagans:

13. Article. Of workes before Justification. Workes done before the grace of Christ, and the inspiration of his Spirit, are not pleasant to God, forasmuch as they spring not of Faith in Jesus Christ, neither doe they make men meete to receive grace . . . yea rather for that they are not done as God hath willed, and commanded them to be done, we doubt not but they have the nature of sinne.

In Article 18 we read:

Of obtaining eternall salvation onely by the name of Christ. They also are to be had accursed, that presume to say that every man shall be saved by the Lawe, or sect which he professeth, so that he be diligent to frame his life according to that Law, and the light of nature. For holy Scripture doth set out unto us onely the name of Jesus Christ, whereby men must be saved,[19]

once more a Reformation-influenced formulation.

Despite these obstacles to the *prisca theologia*, a few liberal Protestants, in addition to Catholics such as Parsons, were able to sustain their views; in such cases as Sidney, Mornay, Pacard, and Ramus, for example, the general inclination of Protestantism is opposed. These writers represent the positive position, held since Augustine, which has been conveniently summed up as follows:

the Gentiles as well as the Jews were being prepared for the Christian revelation. They had partial revelations, or reached God by natural reason, or learnt from the Mosaïc tradition. Some of them were possibly saved. The whole of religious truth is not plainly shown forth in the

[19]Thomas Rogers, *The Faith, Doctrine, and Religion . . . in 39 Articles* (Cambridge, Eng., 1607), pp. 56, 82-83.

Bible; valuable, indeed essential, help can be gained from non-canonical writers, both Christian and pagan.[20]

In effect, this meant that the more noble and respectable of the ancients could reach a rapprochement with the pious moderns, as forerunners and *prisci theologi.* Through typology and prefiguration, Adam, Moses, Abraham, Job, Zoroaster, Orpheus, Hermes Trismegistus, Pythagoras, Socrates, and Plato, for example, might, to an extent, share some measure of Christian truth; through their natural reason Gentiles as well as Jews were prepared for the Christian revelation, and Greek philosophy was propaedeutic to religious truth.

On the other hand, the illiberal attitude holds: "the Jewish revelation was the only pre-christian one. All the pagans were damned, and all their acts, thoughts and writings, were sinful and worthless, because they did not have faith in Christ. Everything in the Bible is true; nothing not in the Bible is true (with the possible exception of some things in Augustine)."[21] The effect of the ultimately victorious liberal view was obviously to sustain an interest in the classic past and to promote Platonism and neo-Platonism in Renaissance culture and religion; to encourage a cultural and religious tolerance which bridged the gap widened both by the Reformation and the Council of Trent; to integrate philosophy with religion; and to help foster an increasingly secular world. Viewed in the light of the liberal *prisca theologia* tradition, it may be suggested, Shakespeare's favorable treatment of certain pagans, including Cordelia and Edgar, leading exemplars of heathen virtue in *King Lear*, may indicate a position to be comprehended, at least in part, through Renaissance religious concerns.

Since Mornay's treatise, with whose translation Sidney was associated, takes the liberal Calvinist position, it may have provided, among other works, Sidney's reinforcement for the view. In addition to Mornay's *De la verité . . .*, which, as has been noted, is heavily Platonic and replete with the *prisca theologia* view, he would have found it in Ramus' *Commentarii de religione christiana*, in his friend Henri Estienne's collection of Orphica and other *prisca theologia* texts, and in the latter's edition of the Orphic hymns; probably he had read his cotranslator Golding's version of Ovid's *Metamorphoses*,

20Walker, "The *Prisca Theologia* in France," p. 252.

21Walker, "Ways of Dealing with Atheists," p. 262.

which ends with a harmony of the cosmogony of Moses and Ovid. The conclusion of D. P. Walker's study of Sidney and the *prisca theologia* observes that, in facilitating Mornay's translation into English and in depicting Pamela, Musidorus, and Pyrocles as pre-Christians who have attained religious truth, Sidney sided with the "liberal" camp and thus aided in the survival of Platonizing theology, which ultimately helped lead to the Cambridge Platonists.[22]

In addition, before *Lear* and the *Arcadia*, More's *Utopia* had, through the depiction of pagans, already established a mode of relatively safe and indirect commentary on Renaissance Christendom. All three works included favorable portrayals of virtuous heathens, who, despite their natural beliefs, approached the Christian ideal. Supporting such sympathetic conceptions, Erasmus, like Ficino in his work on Plotinus, held that God intended only a gradual revelation of the truth; thus, relying on reason alone, ancient philosophers might readily be converted to the reasonableness of the True Faith. For, by divine benevolence, the Book of Creation is set open before the philosophers of the Gentiles. Greater is God's written word, unknown to the heathens and revealed to Moses and the prophets, and greater still is the revelation through the Son; yet in the Book of Creation every creature is a letter inscribed by God's finger. The Utopians and similar heathens, believing in a Supreme Being who created and governed them, could read this Book of Creation well.

A "Grecian whom philosophie has brought to salvation," the *Arcadia*'s Pamela, in her prayer, shows a Christian frame of mind, lovingly submissive to the will of God: ". . . to whom nothing is either so great, that it may resist; or so small, that it is contemned . . . limite out some proportion of deliverance unto me, as to thee shall seem most convenient . . . let never their wickednes have such a hand, but that I may carie a pure minde in a pure bodie."[23]

She is a good pagan, who, through reading the book of nature, has reached the truth and preaches it, notably in her debate with the wicked atheist Cecropia. Confining herself to natural reason, her only means of communicating with the Machiavellian naturalist, Pamela distinguishes between two types of "nature": one, a religious person may worship, if by "nature" is meant "a nature of wisdom, goodness,

[22]Ibid., pp. 254-255, 276-277.

[23]*The Countesse of Pembrokes Arcadia,* in *Complete Works*, I, 382-383.

and providence, which knows what it doth"—i.e., *natura naturans*, or God; the other may not be worshiped, for it signifies the blind, automatic regularity of the created world. Her argument is from design, denying a universe of "chance," a term she uses, it has been suggested, with sophistical ambiguity;[24] and she concludes by threatening Cecropia with God's vengeance in a section entitled "The Auntes Atheisme refuted by the Neeces Divinitie":

> This worlde . . . cannot otherwise consist but by a minde of Wisedome, whiche governes it, which whether you wil allow to be the Creator thereof, as undoubtedly he is, or the soule and governour thereof, most certaine it is that whether he governe all, or make all, his power is above either his creatures, or his governement . . . he sees into the darkest of all naturall secretes, which is the harte of Man; and sees therein the deepest dissembled thoughts, nay sees the thoughts before they be thought . . . assure thy selfe . . . that the time will come, when thou shalt knowe that power by feeling it. . . . (I, 410)

In her prayer, her virtue, her hatred of atheism, and her loving submission to the divine will Pamela may seem to compensate for her ignorance of the Trinity and the coming of Christ; despite Milton's disparagement of Pamela's invocation as issuing "from the mouth of a Heathen Woman praying to a Heathen God,"[25] her attitude toward providence looks forward to the traditional Christian one of a watchful God who rewards good and punishes evil.

The Atheistic View

Let me not say Gods are not.
—Marston, *Sophonisba*, II.i

For this position Cecropia is the obvious candidate, as we have seen from Pamela's virtuous diatribe against her. Like Satan flattering Eve, Cecropia commences by praising her niece's beauty, "so if she coulde make her lesse feeling of those heavenly conceipts, that then she might easilie winde her to her croked bias." Taking up an ancient *topos*, she asserts that religion was introduced to keep men in check,[26] declaring the "zeale of Devotion" to be "the best bonde, which the

[24]Walker, "Ways of Dealing with Atheists," p. 271.

[25]Milton, attacking Charles I, who was supposed to have read the *Arcadia* in his last hours (*Eikonoklastes* [1649], p. 12). Walker ("Ways of Dealing with Atheists," pp. 264*n*, 276-277) would include also among the "saved," Musidorus and Pyrocles, judging by their discussion of the afterlife.

[26]With Cecropia on religion as politically devised restraint, cf. Marlowe, according to the well-known Baines note (see John Bakeless, *The Tragicall History of Christo-*

most politicke wittes have found, to holde mans witte in well doing . . . . these bugbeares of opinions brought by great Clearkes into the world . . . Feare, and indeede, foolish feare, and fearefull ignorance, was the first inventer of those conceates" (I, 406). Thunder, a significant instance, as I shall note in Shakespeare's play, is Cecropia's naturalistic illustration of this needless fear.

Among all creatures, further, only man foolishly avoids his own happiness by refusing to follow the course of his nature because of heavenly speculations: ". . . who while by the pregnancie of his imagination he strives to things supernaturall, meane-while he looseth his owne naturall felicitie." Serpentlike, she concludes: "Be wise, and that wisedome shalbe a God unto thee; be contented, and that is thy heaven." Prayer is unefficacious, and special providence is a mirage: "for els to thinke that those powers (if there be any such) above, are moved either by the eloquence of our prayers, or in a chafe by the folly of our actions; caries asmuch reason as if flies should thinke, that men take great care which of them hums sweetest, and which of them flies nimblest" (I, 406-407). Resembling Montaigne's "il nous faut abestir pour nous assagir" and Lear in some of his pessimistic later utterances, she holds the city of man to be, in appetite and other characteristics, not dissimilar to the world of beasts.

In reply, Pamela accuses her aunt of atheistic views, especially with regard to nature, in which term she distinguishes two meanings: (1) a beneficent, wise, and providential Designer (*natura naturans*); and (2) a fortuitous operation of chance (*natura naturata*).[27] God is

---

pher Marlowe [Cambridge, Mass., 1942], I, 111, and Paul H. Kocher, *Christopher Marlowe* [Chapel Hill, N.C., 1946], pp. 49-50); a Renaissance skeptical commonplace, it is heard also in antiquity, among the Sophists. Critias, in the fifth century B.C., points to fear of the gods as invented by men for restraint of the wicked. Democritus holds that wise men desired, by religion, to sublimate human fears deriving from divine manifestations in nature. La Primaudaye, *The Second Part of the French Academie* (1594), p. 579, assigns to the Epicures the notion that fear first made the gods. *Timor facit deos* is a view attributed to Renaissance atheists; e.g., Thomas Scott's *Foure Paradoxes* (1602), sig. [A5v], regarding such infidels: "*Religion* is a scarre-crow in thy eye. . . ." See also on the topic, fear made the gods, below, Ch. viii, n. 102. See below on the notion's recurrence in the Don Juan and thunder conventions.

[27]Pamela's distinction between "natures" is paralleled in Pacard and Mornay, both supporters of the *prisca theologia*. Chance, concealed under the cover of "nature," is rejected by Calvin as an explanation of events; he attacks contemporaries who "will not say, that they are by chaunce made different from brute beastes. But they pretende a cloke of nature, whom they account the maker of all things, and so do convey God away" (*Institutes*, I.v.4).

present and His providence real. Pamela's argument against chance, and from design, runs:

You saie, because we know not the causes of things, therefore feare was the mother of superstition: nay, because we know that each effect hath a cause, that hath engendred a true & lively devotion. For this goodly worke of which we are, and in which we live, hath not his being by Chaunce. . . . For if it be eternall (as you would seeme to conceive of it) Eternity, & Chaunce are things unsufferable together. (I, 407)

Attacking the skeptical or Aristotelian notion of the world's eternity, Pamela follows the commonplace pious belief in creation in time out of nothing, a view whose significance for *Lear* will be considered below: "And as absurd it is to thinke that if it had a beginning, his beginning was derived from Chaunce: for Chaunce could never make all thinges of nothing . . ." (I, 407). This world, she says, exhibits a design which could never have existed without a designer: ". . . Chaunce is variable, or els it is not to be called Chaunce: but we see this worke is steady and permanent. . . . perfect order, perfect beautie, perfect constancie, if these be the children of Chaunce, or Fortune the efficient of these, let Wisedome be counted the roote of wickednesse, and eternitie the fruite of her inconstancie" (I, 408).

Against Cecropia's definition of nature as chance, Pamela sets her own view of nature as design:

But you will say it is so by nature, as much as if you said it is so, because it is so: if you meane of many natures conspiring together, as in a popular governement to establish this fayre estate . . . that there must needes have bene a wisedome which made them concurre: for their natures beyng absolute contrarie, in nature rather woulde have sought each others ruine, then have served as well consorted partes to such an unexpressable harmonie. For that contrary things should meete to make up a perfection without a force and Wisedome above their powers, is absolutely impossible; unles you will flie to that hissed-out opinion of Chaunce again. (I, 408)

Should Cecropia agree that there is design in nature from eternity, perhaps adopting an Aristotelian position, she ought to avoid blasphemy in her definition of that nature: ". . . if you meane a Nature, as we speake of the fire, which goeth upward, it knowes not why: and of the nature of the Sea which in ebbing and flowing seemes to observe so just a daunce, and yet understands no musicke, it is but still the same absurditie subscribed with another title" (I, 408-409).

Partly because of Renaissance religious ferments and schisms, doubts regarding traditional views seem far from uncommon. As Busson and others observe regarding this "pullulement de doctrines," "La multiplicité des églises a fortement contribué à troubler les consciences au XVIe siècle."[28] The preface to Charles de Sainte-Marthe's *In psalmum nonagesimum* (1550) complains that ". . . l'unité chrétienne est aujourd'hui déchirée en tant de sectes . . . que l'athéisme élargit ses conquêtes";[29] La Noue's *The Politicke and Militarie Discourses* (1587 [1588]) notes three "dependances of Impietie" which have "infected all France": atheism, swearing and blasphemy, and a pernicious use of magic (p. 3).[30]

In England, Nashe, Bacon, and others blamed the numerous sects for the spread of atheism.[31] As Fulke Greville points out,

> I mean that many-headed separation,
> Which irreligious being, yet doth bear
> Religion's name, affects her reputation.[32]

In 1588 Franciscus Arcaeus' *A Most Excellent . . . Method of Curing Woundes*, translated by John Read, observes a number of infidel sects:

[28]Busson, *Le rationalisme*, p. 319*n*. See also Pierre Villey-Desmeserets, *Les sources & l'évolution des essais de Montaigne* (Paris, 1933), II, 151*n*-152*n*; Emile Bréhier, *Histoire de la philosophie*, I (Paris, 1926), 739.

[29]Busson, *Le rationalisme*, p. 293.

[30]Louis I. Bredvold, "Deism before Lord Herbert," *Papers of the Michigan Academy of Science, Arts and Letters*, IV, Pt. I (1925), 431-442, argues that evidence for a Renaissance skeptical climate is necessarily partial because of the censorship which prevented publication of significant elements of Renaissance thought (see n. 48 below). If he is correct, statistics regarding the proportion and kinds of religious writings deduced from the *Short-Title Catalogue* may, since the latter represents works which ordinarily passed the censor, be misleading. In his later plays Shakespeare resorted to Roman, Danish, Trojan, Greek, and ancient British and Scottish subject matter. Since the Act of Abuses passed by Parliament in 1606 to restrain use of the name of God in stage plays was related to a bill against "Swearing and Blasphemy" read in House of Commons on June 27, 1604, he could have had time, in writing *Lear*, to sense political winds. Through such multiple safeguards as paganism and antiquity, as well as the old age and madness of his protagonist, Shakespeare could have protected himself.

[31]Nashe, *Works*, I, 171-172; Bacon, *Works*, VI, 414.

[32]*The Works in Verse and Prose . . . Fulke Greville, Lord Brooke*, ed. Alexander B. Grosart ([Blackburn], 1870), I, 193.

some nulli fidians likewise be,
Some atheists temporisers, and
some machivells a griefe to see,
And some so stained are with vice,
that they more likely doe appeare,
Incarnet divells for to bee,
then such as live in Godlie feare. (sig. ¶¶¶.iii)

And Richard Barckley's *A Discourse of the Felicitie of Man* (1603) expresses a fear of the result of "the new Sectes and Schismes of these latter days . . . that by falling from one sect into another, many will become Atheistes . . ." (p. 427).

While the fragmentation of Renaissance religious belief proceeded apace, a Pyrrhonist crisis of thought in the late sixteenth and early seventeenth centuries developed which cast knowledge into doubt; this crisis was fostered by the publication of the works of Sextus Empiricus[33] (Latin versions in 1562 and 1569; a nonextant English translation of 1590 or 1591 referred to by Nashe in his preface to Sidney's *Astrophel and Stella*, 1591;[34] and an undated version apparently first published in 1651, said to be by Raleigh).[35] In addition to Aristotle, considered "le plus grand ennemi de la foi au XVIe siècle,"[36] Lucretian atomism permeated the ripening Renaissance. Allusions to a force resembling the nature of Lucretius are, for example, frequent in the later Jacobean drama; Bruno quotes freely from him in Italian works composed while Bruno was in England; Lucretius was widely available, and Montaigne's liberal citations from Lucretius made the latter still more accessible after 1603, when

[33]On Sextus see Richard H. Popkin, *The History of Scepticism from Erasmus to Descartes* (Assen, Neth., 1960), pp. 17-19. Although almost unknown in the Middle Ages, Sextus had a large impact on the late sixteenth and the seventeenth centuries. In 1562 Henri Estienne published a Latin edition of the *Hypotyposes*; in 1569 Sextus' works in Latin were published by Gentian Hervet. Popkin (p. 84) notes Sextus' utilization, around the turn of the century, by English and French opponents of astrology; e.g., 1601, John Chamber's *A Treatise against Judicial Astrologie*, pp. 22-24. In 1603 Christopher Heydon's *A Defence of Judiciall Astrologie* lists Sextus as an opponent; in 1605 Le Loyer's *A Treatise of Specters*, foll. 49-61, offered a reply to the Pyrrhonists.

On the Pyrrhonist crisis see Popkin, "The Sceptical Crisis and the Rise of Modern Philosophy: I," *Review of Metaphysics*, VII (1953), 132-151.

[34]Nashe, III, 332, 254-256; IV, 428-431; V, 120, 122.

[35]Ernest A. Strathmann, *Sir Walter Ralegh: A Study in Elizabethan Skepticism* (New York, 1951), p. 224; attribution is questioned in S. E. Sprott, "Ralegh's 'Sceptic.' . . ," *Philological Quarterly*, XLII (1963), 166-175.

[36]Busson, *Le rationalisme*, p. 28.

Florio's translation appeared.[37] Jonson indicates the debt to Montaigne when he writes in *Volpone* (1605-1606), about the time of *Lear*, that "All our *English* writers, / . . . Will deigne to steale out of" another well-known author "Almost as much, as from MONTAGNIE" (III.iv.87-90).[38]

In regard to Lucretius,[39] Sandys's tables of *editiones principes* and Munro's history of Lucretian scholarship show that both primary and secondary sources for the study of Lucretius, Democritus, and Epicurus were available well before the start of the seventeenth century.[40] Lucretius was published in 1473, Diogenes Laertius in 1533; well known in the early English Renaissance were Aristotle, Plutarch, Cicero, and Seneca, in addition to Hippocrates, Suidas, Stobaeus, and Athenaeus; still later, Burton's *The Anatomy of Melancholy* (1621) revealed an acquaintance with them all. Lucretius' master, Epicurus, is evident in the strictures of Augustine, Tertullian, and Lactantius, as well as in the Renaissance discussion of providence, illustrated above. More insidious, however, than the influence of Lucretius and subversive Averroism was that of Cicero, whose editors at times claimed that they were interested in his Latinity rather than in his ideas; the eclectic and respectable Cicero's Stoic empiricism, his praise of man, his doubts, and his universal deism helped make him a favorite of the sixteenth-century rationalist. Ques-

[37]See Villey-Desmeserets, "Montaigne et les poètes dramatiques anglais du temps de Shakespeare," *Revue d'histoire littéraire de la France*, XXIV (1917), 357-393.

[38]Although the relation has been debated, see George C. Taylor, *Shakspere's Debt to Montaigne* (Cambridge, Mass., 1925), p. 38: "In *Lear*, and in other plays after [Florio's translation in] 1603, the impression one gets of the forces of nature at play around us and outside us is vaster, more terrible, than before." The effect of Florio's translation of Montaigne is felt also in Marston; Anthony Caputi's *John Marston, Satirist* (Ithaca, N.Y., 1961), p. 58, observes that before 1603 his plays are weighted with Senecan borrowings, while after 1603 they are full of allusions to Florio's Montaigne.

[39]See C. T. Harrison, "The Ancient Atomists and English Literature of the Seventeenth Century," *Harvard Studies in Classical Philology*, XLV (1934), 1.

[40]H. A. J. Munro, *T. Lucreti Cari de rerum natura libri sex* (1920), I, 3-16. See also Cosmo A. Gordon, *A Bibliography of Lucretius* (1962). Cf. C.-A. Fusil, "La Renaissance de Lucrèce au XVIe siècle en France," *Revue du seizième siècle*, XV (1928), 134-150; G. R. Hocke, *Lukrez in Frankreich von der Renaissance bis zur Revolution* (Cologne, 1935); Simone Fraisse, *L'influence de Lucrèce en France au seizième siècle* (Paris, 1962); Eleonore Belowski, *Lukrez in der Französischen Literatur der Renaissance* (Berlin, 1934), in whose opinion the most influential idea of Lucretius in sixteenth-century poetry was the Venus Cult of Love as the generating power in nature (pp. 124-125).

tioning the existence of the gods, Cicero was often used to support the True Faith for having rejected the pagan deities.[41]

Still more than Cicero, however, Pliny, whom Shakespeare used, was reputedly atheistic, and his *Historia naturalis*, called the most popular natural history ever published, went through over thirty editions between 1469 and 1532.[42] More popular yet was Lucian, whose reputation in the sixteenth century was surpassed by that of few other ancient authors; about 270 printings of his works, or those attributed to him, appeared before 1550, the Greek text being printed more than sixty times between 1496 and 1550, while numerous Latin and vernacular translations were issued.[43] Bacon recognized Lucian as a "contemplative atheist,"[44] and Fitzherbert called him "an Atheistical pagan."[45] Notorious for his scoffing tone toward the gods, Lucian, a probable source of Shakespeare, bequeathed his name to Shakespeare's greatest English predecessor in the drama, Christopher Marlowe. Gabriel Harvey, after Marlowe's death, called him "a Lucian" or mocker of the gods.[46]

Despite recent revaluations of the extent and quality of Renaissance skepticism and the qualification of Busson by such recent critics as Febvre,[47] followed by Kristeller,[48] evidence exists to indicate

[41]Roland H. Bainton, "Changing Ideas and Ideals in the Sixteenth Century," *Journal of Modern History,* VIII (1936), 421-423; cf. Strathmann, *Sir Walter Ralegh*, p. 95.

[42]See Baldwin, "A Note upon William Shakespeare's Use of Pliny," in *Essays in Dramatic Literature: The Parrott Presentation Volume*, ed. Hardin Craig (Princeton, 1935), pp. 157-182; Busson, *Le rationalisme*, p. 39; E. W. Gudger, "Pliny's *Historia Naturalis*," *Isis*, VI (1924), 269-281.

[43]See C. R. Thompson, *The Translations of Lucian by Erasmus and St. Thomas More* (Ithaca, N.Y., 1940), p. 3; Baldwin, *William Shakspere's Small Latine & Lesse Greeke* (Urbana, Ill., 1944).

[44]*Works*, VI, 414.

[45]*Second Part of a Treatise*, p. 56.

[46]*The Works of Gabriel Harvey*, ed. Alexander B. Grosart, I (1884), 37.

[47]Lucien Febvre, *Le problème de l'incroyance au XVIe siècle: La religion de Rabelais* (Paris, 1942).

[48]Paul O. Kristeller's *The Classics and Renaissance Thought* (Cambridge, Mass., 1955), pp. 71-72, and "El mito del ateísmo renacentista y la tradición francesa del librepensamiento," *Notas y estudios de filosofía* (Tucumán, Argentina), IV, No. 13 (1953), 1-14, suggest that the extent of Renaissance atheism has been exaggerated.

Yet contrast Walker, "Ways of Dealing with Atheists," 255-256, holding that incontestable cases of Renaissance atheism exist. See also Revilo P. Oliver, review of Kristeller, *The Classics and Renaissance Thought*, in *Speculum*, XXXIV (1959), 289-291, and Edgar Wind, *Pagan Mysteries in the Renaissance* (New Haven, 1958), concerning a widespread Renaissance acroamatic tradition and the probability of frequently heterodox oral and esoteric views. Regarding such heterodoxy, Jeremy Corderoy's *A Warn-*

some contemporary disbelief, though not in the fashion formerly conceived by Pintard, Charbonnel, and Busson. In addition to the discussion earlier suggesting a providence-questioning climate, some more general instances may be cited. Roger Hutchinson in *The Image of God* (1560) attacks the "many late Libertines" (sig. Piiii^v); Calvin in the *Institutes* witnesses, "even at this day the earth beareth many monsterous spirites, which sticke not to abuse the whole seede of godhead that is sowen in mans nature, & to employ it to oppresse the name of God" (I.v.4); Jean de Neufville in *De pulchritudine animi* (1556), like Hervet, Postel, and others, writes "pour la multitude, grandissant de jour en jour, des épicuriens et des athées de ce siècle";[49] and Charles de Bourgueville in *L'athéomachie* describes the situation around 1560, listing among others "vrays atheistes . . . ne recoignoissans le Dieu Eternel" and those who deny immortality (Busson, p. 488).[50] Hugh Latimer's *The Seven Sermons* (1562), preached in 1549, cites the observation of "a great many in England" who discredit the immortality or the existence of the soul (fol. 65).

Marlowe, whose youthful indiscretion perhaps made him speak out where others were silent, has been thus summed up by Kocher: ". . . the cumulative force . . . is to show him as a propagandist and instigator of revolt against Christianity, anxious to proselytize others to his views. On this point the evidence seems to me quite decisive."[51]

---

ing for Worldlings (1608) offers a possibly revealing instance: the atheistic traveler, endeavoring to convert the Oxford student, asks him "come, where may we . . . talke freely, I would not bee heard. . . ." When the student assures him, "I wil locke my studie doore," the traveler declares, "Now we are in secret, I am bold to utter my mind . . ." (p. 9). Cf. Busson, "Les noms des incrédules au XVIe siècle," *BHR*, XVI (1954), 273, 277, recalling that the sixteenth century created the term "atheist" to meet a specific purpose; the article notes its use in Gentian Hervet as early as 1543 and in Gabriel Dupréau in 1559. For further documentation of Renaissance skepticism see also Don Cameron Allen, *Doubt's Boundless Sea: Skepticism and Faith in the Renaissance* (Baltimore, 1964).

49Cited in Busson, *Le rationalisme*, p. 484.

50In the 1564 edition of *L'athéomachie* (Busson, *Le rationalisme*, p. 487) the atheist is said to influence many others, as he

discourt d'une Ame impure
L'infinité de Nature
Et dict qu'il n'est autre Dieu. . . .
Du blaspheme de sa bouche
Maintz foibles espritz il touche. . . .

51*Christopher Marlowe*, pp. 31-32. Evidence recently made available by the cathedral and city archivist of Marlowe's native Canterbury suggests a family context of rebel-

Gabriel Harvey sketches the climate: "The Gospell taughte, not learned . . . every day, freshe span newe Opinions: Heresie in Divinitie. . . ."[52] Georges Pacard in *Théologie naturelle* (dedicated in 1574) observes, ". . . voyons la terre . . . couvert de deistes, epicuriens, atheistes et autres tels monstres."[53] Of bold deniers of God, who hold Christ's "truth is but a fable . . . this day, giveth feareful examples of too many," notes the English translator's dedicatory epistle to Pierre Viret's *An Epistle to the Faithfull* (1582, sig. [¶8ᵛ]).[54] *The Difference betwene the Auncient Phisicke . . . and the Latter Phisicke* (1585) by R. B., Esquire, laments those who follow natural causes, "whereby many of them become Atheists" (sig. [Aviᵛ]). Thomas Cooper in *An Admonition to the People of England* (1589) remarks that certain controversies have "wounded the hearts of an infinit nomber, causing them partly to revolt . . . to Atheisme . . ." (p. 121). In addition, Lyly's "Euphues and Atheos" suggests a debate of some contemporary relevance.[55]

In *Christs Teares over Jerusalem* (1593) Thomas Nashe—himself accused of "atheism" by Harvey—asserts, "These Atheists . . . are speciall men of witte. . . . It is the superaboundance of witte that makes Atheists"; and he admonishes

> University men that are called to preache at the Crosse and the Court, Arme your selves against nothing but Atheisme, meddle not so much with Sects & forraine opinions, but let Atheisme be the onely string you beate on; for there is no Sect now in *England* so scattered as Atheisme. . . . You are not halfe so wel acquainted as them that lyve continually about the Court and Citty, how many followers this damnable paradoxe hath: how many high wits it hath bewitcht. . . .

In addition, Nashe's *Pierce Penilesse* (1592) speaks of the pride of the learned, who "fetch the Articles of their Beleefe out of *Aristotle*,

---

lion (William Urry, "Marlowe and Canterbury," *Times Literary Supplement*, Feb. 13, 1964, p. 136). In addition to Marlowe, for example, his sister Ann was accused as "blasphemer of the name of God. . . ."

52 *Works*, ed. Grosart, I, 70-71.

53 Pacard, Dedication, in Busson, *Le rationalisme*, p. 568.

54 See also Viret, *The Second Part of the Demoniacke Worlde, or Worlde Possessed with Divels* (1583), sigs. [D5ᵛ]-[D6].

55 *The Complete Works of John Lyly*, ed. R. Warwick Bond (Oxford, 1902), I, 291-305. See also "A Dialogue betweene a Christian and an Atheist," which forms the substance of John Bate, *The Portraiture of Hypocrisie* (1589).

and thinke of heaven and hell as the Heathen Philosophers, take occasion to deride our Ecclesiasticall State, and all Ceremonies of Devine worship, as bug-beares and scar-crowes. . . . Hence Atheists triumph and rejoyce, and talke as prophanely of the Bible, as of Bevis of Hampton."[56]

The epistle to the reader of La Primaudaye's *The Second Part of the French Academie* (1594) remarks on the "violent course of Atheisme dayly spredde abroade . . ." (sig. b4^{v}) and declares that ". . . he that hath but halfe an eye may see, that there are a great many amongst us of those foolish men of whom *David* speaketh, *Who say in their hearts that there is no God*" (sig. b3^{v}). Marston's *Histrio-Mastix* (1589-1599) complains,

> Now is the time . . .
> Pitty and Piety are both exilde,
> *Religion* buried with our Fathers bones,
> In the cold earth; and nothing but her face,
> Left to adorne these grosse and impious times.[57]

Describing Du Plessis Mornay's *The True Knowledge of a Mans Owne Selfe*, the translator Munday's dedication (sigs. A3, [A5^{v}]) notes that Mornay aimed it at the reformation of a "mightie" atheist and "verie deepe disgrace of Religion by him daily committed. . . ." Munday recommends it as "a booke most needfull for these times . . . so mightie is the multitude of blasphemous Atheists. . . ." In 1601 Thomas Powell's *The Passionate Poet* gives a character of a contemporary atheist (sig. B3^{r-v}). Thomas Scott's *Foure Paradoxes* (1602) confutes the atheist who thinks God a fable and who assails religion with "contentious witt" (sigs. A4-[A5^{v}]).[58] In *A Perfume against the Noysome Pestilence* (1603), Roger Fenton lists among possible causes of the recent plague, ". . . whether the blasphemies of affected Atheists hath poysoned our ayre" (sigs. [A10^{v}]-[A11]).

In 1605 John Dove's *A Confutation of Atheisme* remarks ". . . *because now there are many* Atheistes, *it is to be wished that many would write against Atheisme*" (sig. A2), and he lashes out against

[56] *Works*, II, 124, 121-122; I, 172.

[57] *Plays*, III, 288. See also William Rankins, *Seaven Satyres* (1598), sig. B4.

[58] Similarly, Richard Rogers, *Seven Treatises* (1603), p. 595, addresses those "living among many Atheists. . . ."

"the swaggerers of our age, which are not ashamed to call them selves the damned crue: Of the salvation of such there is no hope" (p. 3). "These *English Italianat* and devils incarnat, doe holde," according to him, "these damnable opinions: That there was no creation of the world, that there shall be no day of judgement, no resurrection, no immortallitye of the soule, no hell . . ." (p. 4). In 1605, too, Joshua Sylvester's translation of Du Bartas' *His Devine Weekes and Workes* alludes to England and "*Thine un-controld bold open* Atheisme" (p. 62). John Day's *The Ile of Guls* (1606) contains the following dialogue:

> . . . Why you never light upon anie Atheistes, doe you?
> . . . Oh verie manie. . . . In the verie boosome of the Citie:
> and by your leave, heere and there one in the Court too. (sig. F)

Robert Pricket's *Times Anotomie* (1606) castigates those gallants "whose actions Atheismeticall, do seeme as if they scornde both heaven and hell . . . with their . . . godlesse blasphemy . . ." (sig. A2^{v}). Again, in 1606, *The Returne of the Knight of the Poste from Hell* mentions "publique Atheists who . . . only confirme themselves in Atheisme . . ." (sig. [D4^{v}]). Touching on the inward and outward skeptic, considered below, Arthur Newman's *The Bible-Bearer* (1607) observes: "There live now many Monsters in nature, Apostataes from God, Atheists in errour, Counterfeites of holynesse . . . worse than Atheists, for the Atheists professe themselves to bee (as they are) openly wicked, but the other by ill dissimulation, to be good" (sig. B1^{v}). Richard West's *The Court of Conscience* (1607) assails the

> unbeleeving villaine which doest thinke,
> That heaven & earth & all was made by nature,
> Not framd of God. . . . (sig. E3^{v})

Attacking also one who is "of no Religion, but a meere *Athiest*," Simion Grahame in *The Anatomie of Humors* (Edinburgh, 1609) later accuses, "Thou art a sighing *nulla-fidian*" (sigs. [C4], [G4]). Henry Peacham's *Minerva Britanna* (1612) shows the emblem of a hand striking at the heavens:

> The *Atheist* vile, that Giant-like attemptes,
> To bandie faction with Almightie JOVE. (p. 99)

In addition, Donne's "new Philosophy calls all in doubt" is but one expression of a documented period of naturalistic questioning.[59] Echoing Nashe, moreover, Ford's *'Tis Pity She's a Whore* (1629?-1633) takes note of

> wits that presum'd
> On wit too much, by striving how to prove
> There was no God . . .
> And fill'd the world with devilish atheism. (I.i.4-8)[60]

What these citations, and others which might be added,[61] may help to indicate is that, even if the charges of unbelief were exaggerated, ambiguous, and loose, as undoubtedly some were, they cannot entirely be dismissed as referring to nothing in the age. Evidencing wide interest and concern, they at least helped provide recognizable stereotypes for the stage. It is thus reasonable to assume that during the period of *Lear*'s original presentation Shakespeare's audience could probably have recognized and, in various ways, responded to a theatrical depiction of skepticism.

The use of the term "skepticism," following perhaps the best recent account of English Renaissance disbelief, implies "a tendency to challenge received opinions or the dicta of established authority and to submit them to the tests of reason and experience." Concerning himself with the challenge to dogmatism in religion, Strathmann adheres to a commonplace Renaissance convention of distinguishing between two types of religious skeptics, the "outward atheist," who gives vent freely to his doubts, and the more terrible "inward atheist," or Machiavellian hypocrite. Regarding the first of these, Strathmann provides a convenient summary:

[59]"An Anatomie of the World. . . . The First Anniversary," l. 205. See Bredvold, "The Naturalism of Donne in Relation to Some Renaissance Traditions," *JEGP*, XXII (1923), 471-502.

[60]*The Works of John Ford*, ed. William Gifford (1895), I, 113.

[61]I omit numerous other references: e.g., William Covell, *Polimanteia* (Cambridge, Eng., 1595), sig. Bb1v; John Deacon and John Walker, *Dialogicall Discourses* (1601), sig. [a4]; Dekker, *The Dead Terme* (1608), in *The Non-Dramatic Works of Thomas Dekker*, ed. Alexander B. Grosart, IV (1885), 54; Thomas Adams, *The Gallants Burden* (1612), fol. 16 (cf. foll. 16v-17); R. C., *The Times' Whistle* (ca. 1614-16), ed. J. M. Cowper, *E.E.T.S.*, No. 48 (1871), Satira 1, "Against the Atheists . . ."; John Stephens, *Satyrical Essayes Characters and Others* (1615), p. 214, on the atheist; *Machivells Dogge* (1617), sig. [D3v]. C. L. Barber, *Shakespeare's Festive Comedy* (Princeton, 1959), pp. 47-51, cites traditional folk skepticism in the Dymoke case (1601-10).

It is taken for granted that the atheist denies the existence of God, but the form of the denial is more likely to be refusal to credit the manifestations of His power than flat negation. He believes the world eternal, or he follows Lucretius and Epicurus in holding the creation to be an operation of chance. In applying to Omnipotent God the natural limitation "ex nihilo nihil fit" he draws a false conclusion. . . . With Epicurus the atheist believes providence faulty or nonexistent. If God made the world for man and controls its processes, why did He cover most of it with water, make half the land uninhabitable, and multiply such inconveniences as unseasonable storms, killing frosts, and creatures dangerous to man? Why do the righteous perish and the wicked prosper? . . . With few exceptions, he denies the immortality of the soul. He makes his point by blowing out a lighted candle: there, says he, is your soul at death. . . . man is no different from a beast, except that he is indebted to his nature (not God) "for the better composition of the two." . . . In general, the atheist attributes to nature what belongs to God.[62]

To summarize the criteria of the Renaissance skeptic: (1) he considers God's providence faulty; (2) he denies the immortality of the soul; (3) he holds man not different from a beast; (4) he denies creation *ex nihilo,* deriding the traditional tenet that God created the world out of nothing, and he ridicules it by applying it to a natural context, concluding *ex nihilo nihil fit*; and (5) he attributes to nature what belongs to God.

Recognizable in Renaissance terms, if not in our own, every major criterion of the outward skeptic becomes visible, among other elements, in Shakespeare's depiction of Lear, as will be more fully demonstrated below; indeed, in order to ensure that recognition, the dramatist sometimes repeats himself. It is desirable here to bring out aspects of his portrayal, overlooked by the modern reader, which could, in all probability, have been differently interpreted by the Renaissance spectator. As will be shown in a following chapter, the first three of the above criteria may be observed in Lear's final scene: (1) he questions—rather, he denounces—God's providence in allowing lower creatures to live, while Cordelia's existence is cut short by the horror of a senseless hanging; (2) pointedly and repeatedly, he questions the immortality of the soul; her death is final; she is dead as earth, not only to her father, it is implied, but eternally, without hope; and breath, not soul alone, is emphasized and equated with survival (as in the candle metaphor)—indeed, it can be shown that

[62]*Sir Walter Ralegh,* pp. 219, 86-87.

Lear's attitude toward Cordelia ("Thou'lt come no more," V.iii.307) is, in almost the same words, the precise attitude of the pagan mourner, as, for example, described below by Bishop Jewel in the sixteenth century; (3) man has no status differing from a beast's; dogs, horses, rats—the declining order is significant—have even the advantage of life. Lear's "Why?" it would seem, is the incessant "Why?" of the Renaissance skeptic. In addition, Lear's "Nothing will come of nothing," twice mentioned (I.i.90; I.iv.138-139), may be meaningful in the light of the Renaissance controversy over creation out of nothing. And finally, Lear's questions regarding the cause of thunder, and the cause *in nature* of hard hearts, may be connected with the last criterion, attribution to nature of what belongs to God.

While Cecropia, as has been noted, stands not alone but within an extant climate of Renaissance free thought, she represents, within that climate, one of two recognized types of skeptics, a distinction which, Strathmann remarks, is a commonplace in Renaissance discussions of atheism: (1) the "inward" atheist, Machiavellian and hypocritical; and (2) the "outward" atheist, who freely expresses his opinion.

The commonplace Renaissance distinction between the outward and the inward atheist, it seems not to have been emphasized, may owe part of its influence to a dualism established by Plato in the *Laws*:

> For whereas the one class will be quite frank in its language about the gods and about sacrifices and oaths, and by ridiculing other people will probably convert others to its views, unless it meets with punishment, the other class, while holding the same opinions as the former, yet being specially "gifted by nature" and being full of craft and guile, is the class out of which are manufactured many diviners and experts in all manner of jugglery; and from it, too, there spring sometimes tyrants and demagogues and generals, and those who plot by means of peculiar mystic rites of their own, and the devices of those who are called "sophists."[63]

In the Renaissance, to add to Strathmann's instances, Fitzherbert, among others, repeats the distinction between outward and inward atheists in the *Second Part of a Treatise*, with sidenote reference to "Plato II. de lege":

[63]Tr. R. G. Bury, Loeb Classical Lib. (1926), II, Bk. X, 381. Plato's *Laws* were available in Ficino's fifteenth-century translation.

And *Plato* in his booke of lawes, teaching that there are two kinds of Atheists, ordaineth severe punishments for them deviding the first kind into two sortes of men: the one of those, who though they held that there is no God at al, yet are so subtle, and craftie, that they dissemble their opinion, being nevertheles most wicked in life, and manners: whome he thinketh worthy not of one, but of many deathes: The other sort of *Atheists*, is of those, who though they thinke there is no divinitie, yea, and publikely speake and professe it, yet are of so good disposition by nature, that they live well, and vertuously: and for such he ordaineth five yeares imprisonment, and if they amend not therewith, that then they shalbe punished with death. The second kind of *Atheists*, are such, as though they beleeve, there is a God, yet denie his providence here on earth, and for such he assigneth perpetuall imprisonment, in such sort, that no free man, may ever have accesse unto hem, ordaining also, that when they die, their bodies shalbe caried out of the confines of the countrie, and left unburied. (pp. 73-74)[64]

The distinction between the inward and outward atheist appears also in Nashe, Bacon, Dove, and Burton and in William Vaughan's *The Golden-Grove* (1600, sig. C3^{v}).[65] While the outward atheist manifests himself clearly by his opinions, the inward atheist is known by his wicked conduct; as the epistle to the reader of La Primaudaye's *The Second Part of the French Academie*, discussing the inward atheist, observes, "the tree may be judged of by the fruites, & the outward effects of mens lives doe shew the inward affections of their hearts . . ." (sig. b3^{v}). *Saint Peters Prophesie of These Last Daies* (1611) by John Hull considers the "two-fold Atheist: the open . . . and the secret" (p. 232). Ultimately, in the seventeenth century the conventional antithesis of inward and outward atheist culminates in the central figures of Molière's great pair of consecutive comedies: the "faux dévot" hero of *Tartuffe* (1664) and the frankly skeptical hero of *Dom Juan* (1665).

In the inward category fall, together with Edmund and Cecropia, such Machiavellian villains as D'Amville of Tourneur's *The Atheist's Tragedie* and the Italianate politicians of Renaissance drama. "Thou

[64]Discussing atheism in his *Utopia*, another Catholic, More, borrows from the same *Laws* of Plato; cf. Leland Miles, "The Platonic Source of *Utopia*'s 'Minimum Religion,'" *Renaissance News*, IX (1956), 83-90. Instances of the Renaissance inward atheist are plentifully available in studies of Machiavelli's influence in England; see also the inward atheist or hypocrite described in Thomas Tymme's *A Plaine Discoverie of Ten English Lepers* (1592), sigs. E1v-[E4].

[65]See Strathmann, *Sir Walter Ralegh*, pp. 87*n*, 87-88.

hast . . . spoken," declares Viret's *The Second Part of the . . . Worlde Possessed with Divels* (1583), "of Libertine Atheistes, who dissemble their Atheisme, under the colour of havinge some Religion in them, so farre foorth as it tendeth either to their commodity or discommodity" (sig. [D8]). Cecropia, resembling the frequently mentioned Circe of antiatheistic apologetics, may openly support religion as socially useful but within herself believes, as Hooker would judge her, that "religion itself is a mere politic device," being one of the "wise malignants" who follow Machiavelli. In short, Cecropia shares with Shakespeare's Edmund, Goneril, and Regan, in Hooker's terms, a "resolved purpose of mind to reap in this world what sensual profit or pleasure soever the world yieldeth," mocking at religion with "a wanton superfluity of wit."[66] From this wickedly sensual category, Lear is, of course, excluded.

It is evident that, although she basely tries to convert Pamela to her views, Cecropia is, in general, sufficiently and unscrupulously covert and hypocritically Machiavellian to tend toward the category of inward atheist; and it is to this category that Edmund, not to speak of the dissembling sisters, specifically belongs. On the other hand, as the tragedy unfolds, Lear's views become more and more outspokenly skeptical with regard to the beneficence of the gods; I have indicated and shall demonstrate more fully in following chapters the congruence between his attitudes and those of the conventional Renaissance skeptical position that Strathmann has summarized. In paralleling Lear's emerging "outward" views with Edmund's "inward" views, Shakespeare has, by contrast, effectively purged Lear's skepticism of the conventional Renaissance connotations of moral depravity, all the more so as Lear's undissembled skeptical views are shown not to be a priori or innate but to develop through actual experience of the Powers of this world.

The Superstitious View

Of the *Arcadia*'s relevant characters, Basilius is interesting in connection with Shakespeare's play, for he is not only superstitious but

[66]*Ecclesiastical Polity*, in *Works*, II, 19-22. On Circe, see Merritt Y. Hughes, "Spenser's Acrasia and the Circe of the Renaissance," *Journal of the History of Ideas*, IV (1943), 381-399. According to Walker, "Ways of Dealing with Atheists," p. 266, Circe is mentioned very often in connection with atheism; and Pacard suggests that being enchanted by her is the same as being "ensorcelé par Satan." Walker, p. 257, agrees that Cecropia is an "inward atheist."

also a believer in free love. He supports an ethical naturalism which he uses to defend his passion for Zelmane, the course of free love being for him nature's course: "but that which most comforted him," says the narrator, "was his interpretation of the adulterie, which he thought he should commit with *Zelmane* . . ." (I, 328). Basilius' prognosticatory commitment clearly appears in the letter addressed to him by his sensible minister, Philanax. Learning of the oracle which has caused his credulous master fearfully to withdraw into rustic seclusion, Philanax declares:

wisdome and vertue be the only destinies appointed to man to follow, whence we ought to seeke al our knowledge, since they be such guydes as cannot faile . . . I would then have said, the heavenly powers to be reverenced, and not searched into; & their mercies rather by prayers to be sought, then their hidden councels by curiositie. These kind of soothsayers (since they have left us in our selves sufficient guides) to be nothing but fansie, wherein there must either be vanitie, or infalliblenes, & so, either not to be respected, or not to be prevented. . . . if this Oracle be to be accounted of, arme up your courage the more against it: for who wil stick to him that abandones himselfe? (I, 24-25)

In contrast to Basilius, Pamela attacks those who superstitiously blame fortune and chance, instead of relying on providence and the strength of their own virtue. In her fierce reply to Cecropia's substitution of chance for providence, we have already witnessed Pamela's pious disposition. "My deere and ever deere *Musidorus*," she reaffirms, "a greater wronge, doe you to your selfe, that will torment you thus with griefe, for the fault of fortune. Since a man is bound no further to himselfe, then to doe wisely; chaunce is only to trouble them, that stand upon chaunce" (II, 123). Similarly, the pious Philanax skeptically inquires, "Had the starres sent such an influence unto you . . . ?" (II, 181). Like the other sympathetic characters, Musidorus expresses opposition to astrological prophecies in the tale of his own life:

there were found numbers of Southsayers, who affirmed strange & incredible things should be performed by that childe; whether the heavens at that time listed to play with ignorant mankind, or that flatterie be so presumptuous, as even at times to borow the face of Divinitie. . . . the King of *Phrygia* (who over-superstitiously thought him selfe touched in the matter) sought by force to destroy the infant, to prevent his after-expectations. . . . Foolish man, either vainly fearing what was not to be feared, or not considering, that if it were a worke of the superiour powers, the heavens at length are never children. (I, 188)

So also, referring to Philanax's epistle to Basilius cited above, Kalander affirms: "the cause of all, hath beene the vanitie which possesseth many, who (making a perpetuall mansion of this poore baiting place of mans life) are desirous to know the certaintie of things to come; wherein there is nothing so certaine, as our continual uncertaintie" (I, 26).

"Deus Absconditus"

Mortality
Creeps on the dung of earth, and cannot reach
The riddles which are purpos'd by the gods.
—Ford, *The Broken Heart,* I.iii

This sense of the unsearchable and mysteriously hidden divine power, whose workings are beyond human reckoning, recurs in the *Arcadia.* Such concealed heavenly force, overshadowing mankind, is petitioned, for example, by the suffering and love-struck Philoclea: "My parents . . . have told me, that in these faire heavenly bodies, there are great hidden deities, which have their working in the ebbing & flowing of our estates" (I, 174). In similar fashion, Basilius hymns the sun-god, who is yet, paradoxically, concealed from mankind; although Apollo's "beames the greater world do light," they

ever shine, though hid from earth by earthly shade,
Whose lights do ever live, but in our darkenesse fade. (I, 328)

To Pyrocles, as he envisions his beloved Philoclea dead, the workings of the heavens are also hidden, even to the point where he doubts if there are any orderly powers at all: "O tyraunt heaven, traytor earth, blinde providence; no justice, how is this done? . . . hath this world a government? If it have," Pyrocles, anticipating Lear's "Pour on" (III.iv.18), exclaims, "let it poure out all his mischiefes upon me, and see whether it have power to make me more wretched then I am" (I, 483). Contemplating suicide, on account of the supposed death of Philoclea, Pyrocles kneels down and prays: "O great maker and great ruler of this worlde . . . to thee do I sacrifice this bloud of mine," recalling Gloucester's kneeling before his own "suicide"

(IV.vi.34-38). Pyrocles, alluding to the same power's "unsearchable minde," says that the ruler has "taken from me all meanes longer to abide . . ." (II, 105).

While agreeing with Pyrocles on the mystery of the divine will, his partner Musidorus bids him, on that very ground, however, to refrain from assailing it: "O blame not the heavens . . . as their course never alters, so is there nothing done by the unreacheable ruler of them, but hath an everlasting reason for it" (II, 164). Finally, at the trial of Pyrocles and Musidorus, the judge's own son and nephew, the narrator describes "Euarchus: whom the strange and secreate working of justice, had brought to be the judge over them . . ." (II, 177), as, in pleading with Euarchus, Pyrocles refers to the gods' "unsearchable wisedomes" (II, 203).

In addition to these instances of the hidden deities, further illustrations, also related to the "complaint" pattern, may be offered. While they may include commonplaces of the pastoral convention, they also suggest aspects of the fourth attitude toward the divine powers.

As the heavenly powers are mysterious, they are also, Arcadian personages imply, cruel and inimical. During the shipwreck of Pyrocles and Musidorus, the "heaven roaring out thunders the more amazed them, as having those powers for enimies" (I, 193). In his duel with Zelmane (i.e., Pyrocles) the fearless and vain Anaxius muses on "what spiteful God it should be . . . envying my glory . . ." (I, 518). "But when the conspired heavens had gotten this Subject of their wrath," says the heroic Musidorus, "upon so fit a place as the sea was, they streight began to breath out in boystrous windes some part of their malice against him" (I, 160). Elsewhere, the wicked Cecropia's son, Amphialus, is yet capable of feeling remorse for his slaying of Philoxenus and Parthenia, "wherein he found himselfe hated of the ever-ruling powers . . ." (I, 451).

When Pyrocles thinks his beloved Philoclea dead, he sees himself "the example of the heavens hate" (I, 484). Similarly, Philoclea, thinking her love gone, calls herself "the onely subject of the destinies displeasure" (I, 182). Among the shepherds, Agelastus sings an eclogue of "universall complaint in that universall mischiefe":

> Then since such pow'rs conspir'd unto our damage
> (Which may be know'n, but never help't with wailing). (II, 138)

To Zelmane, Dorus laments, "Alas . . . that it hath pleased the high powers to throwe us to such an estate, as the onely entercourse of our true friendshippe, must be a bartring of miseries" (I, 153), as Zelmane herself suggests "that the heavens have at all times a measure of their wrathefull harmes" (II, 9).

Indeed, injustice seems to be the heavens' rule. Mourning Philoclea, for example, Pyrocles demands, anticipating Lear, "what is the cause, that she, that heavenly creature, whose forme you have taken, should by the heavens be destined to so unripe an ende? Why should unjustice so prevaile?" (I, 487). A like lament inquires, "What can justice availe, to a man that tells not his owne case?" (II, 209); and an eclogue universally mourns, "Justice, justice is now (alas) oppressed" (I, 501).

Man's position in relation to the cosmic forces, as in the "man as tossed" topic considered below, is frequently seen in terms of helpless despair: "O strange mixture of humaine mindes!" grieves Gynecia, "onely so much good lefte, as to make us languish in our owne evills" (II, 11). "Woe to poore man," sings Basilius, "ech outward thing annoyes him . . . . So are we from our high creation slided" (I, 231). Similarly, a lament complains, "We Natures workes doo helpe, she us defaces . . . . her best child killeth" (I, 501). Echoing the convention of man as less provided than the lower beasts by stepmother nature, Musidorus, in the guise of Dorus, mourns: "O wretched mankind . . . . These beasts, like children to nature, inherite her blessings quietly; we, like bastards, are layd abroad, even as foundlinges to be trayned up by griefe and sorrow" (I, 154). The blind old Paphlagonian king laments to Leonatus, his son, who leads him, "feare not the danger of my blind steps, I cannot fall worse then I am. And doo not I pray thee, doo not obstinately continue to infect thee with my wretchednes. But flie, flie from this region, onely worthy of me" (I, 207; cf. Edgar, IV.i.24-26; and Gloucester, IV.i.15-17).

Human reason is frequently held to be corrupted and darkened in the *Arcadia*. "O accursed reason . . . thou dimme, nay blinde . . . in preventing" evils, moans the sorrowing Gynecia (II, 10). The Amazon lady sings of "poore Reasons overthrowe" (I, 76), as a Sestine laments "our darkned mindes" (II, 143). An eclogue, debating Passion versus Reason, deliberates their opposition. "Reason *hath eyes to see his owne ill case*" (I, 339), it declares, condemning "*feeble*

Reasons *spoiles*" (I, 340). Again, introducing the fourth book, the narrator contrasts our own with "the almightie wisedome," whose purpose it is "that humane reason may be the more humbled, and more willinglie geve place to divine providence" (II, 83).

Mankind is spoken of as a "worm." In her lovesickness, for example, Gynecia exclaims wretchedly, "O Sunne . . . art thou not ashamed to impart the clearnesse of thy presence to such a dust-creeping worme as I am?" (I, 145); and elsewhere she demands of her beloved Zelmane, "am I so vile a worme in your sight?" (II, 12). Musidorus, in the guise of Dorus, recites in an eclogue:

> Fortune, Nature, Love, long have contended about me,
> Which should most miseries, cast on a worme that I am. (II, 208)

"*Celestiall powers to wormes*," muses Amphialus, "Joves *children serve to claye*" (I, 397). And in his lament with Plangus, Basilius asks, "To harme us wormes should that high Justice leave / His nature?" (I, 228).[67]

In *Lear* the fourth and final position is, with dramatic logic, reserved for the protagonist. His changing attitudes toward the ambiguous heavens project the testing of providence which Shakespeare's tragedy would seem to consider. Against a background of characters who are relatively consistent and who may be associated with the three positions ascribed by Renaissance thought to pagans—atheistic, superstitious, or *prisca theologia*—Lear's experience of the heavens in relation to earth takes him from devotion to questioning of his deities. Framed, therefore, between total belief and total disbelief, Shakespeare's *King Lear* poses an ultimate question: given such an enigmatic universe as the *Arcadia* at least implicitly describes, what can man believe?

[67]Cf. Calvin's reference to man as a "worme of five feete long" (*Institutes*, I.v.4); ". . . the majestie of God," he holds, "is too high for mortall men, which creepe upon the grounde like wormes, to attaine unto it" (II.vi.4).

CHAPTER IV

From *Leir* to *Lear*

IN ORDER MORE FREELY to relate the problematic type of universe present in the *Arcadia* to the characters of the *Lear* plot, based partly, as scholars tend to agree, on the old chronicle play of *King Leir* (ca. 1588-1594),[1] Shakespeare would have had to banish the numerous direct Christian references of the dramatic source; the paganism of Shakespeare's tragedy, it may be suggested, is present in a proportion perhaps comparable to that in the *Arcadia.* In the nineteenth century, critics had already perceived the need for such de-Christianizing changes so that Shakespeare might, with less restriction, put the question boldly, "What are the gods?"[2]

The extreme Christianity of the so-called pre-Christian old source play has been emphasized as assuming the whole institution of Christian practices, offices, sacraments, liturgy, and creeds.[3] Rather than the gods, it supposes God alone, its worship being through the ecclesiastical system of the church. In addition to other differences between the two plays, it is important to note that the God of the source is not a *Deus absconditus* but a realizable and clearly just anthropomorphic deity; the change in Shakespeare's work is crucial to the sense of his tragedy. Indeed, the God of Leir is on occasion also the anthropomorphized Hebraic deity and bears his name. Significant is the distance the later drama has traveled, for Shakespeare's Lear at the end will inquire into "Things past all sence," rejecting Leir's quiescent acceptance of "Gods will" (ll. 1657-58). It may not be extreme, therefore, to infer that the old *Leir* looks back, in a sense, to the medieval, while the new *Lear* is relatively modern.

[1]See W. W. Greg, "The Date of *King Lear* and Shakespeare's Use of Earlier Versions of the Story," *The Library*, 4th Ser., XX (1940), 377-400. Muir, p. xxxii, suggests that Shakespeare carried the play in memory from having seen early performances; Hardin Craig, ed. *The Complete Works of Shakespeare* (Chicago, 1951), p. 980, agrees that the old play furnished events for *Lear.*

[2]E.g., Edward Dowden, *Shakspere: A Critical Study of His Mind and Art* (1875), p. 269.

[3]See H. B. Charlton, *Shakespearian Tragedy* (Cambridge, Eng., 1949), pp. 216-218.

For the old *Leir*'s God is just and vengeful against sinners. He instills conscience and remorse for evil and provides "heavens hate, earths scorne, and paynes of hell" (l. 1647), as well as the blessings of immortality. In *King Lear*, on the other hand, the gods are anything but the surest friends, while their justice is far from clear; there seem little obvious compensation and little or no preliminary savoring of the joys of immortality. In addition to its suffusion with Christian piety, the old *Leir* has another feature which is strikingly different from Shakespeare's play. It is that the characters, and especially Leir himself, do not generally change their views with regard to the heavens. Indeed, the old play's protagonist sustains an incessantly pious sententiousness.

A rapid sampling of belief references in the transparent old *Leir*, helping to show what Shakespeare probably had to work with, may illuminate religious attitudes of his tragedy. Regarding his dead queen, Leir begins by hoping her "soule . . . possest of heavenly joyes, / Doth ride in triumph 'mongst the Cherubins" (ll. 5-6). Following the *contemptus mundi* and *ars moriendi* traditions, he announces,

> And I would fayne resigne these earthly cares,
> And thinke upon the welfare of my soule. (ll. 27-28)

In contrast, Shakespeare's king abdicates not for pious, otherworldly reasons but, reversing the *ars moriendi* injunction, resigns for reasons of personal comfort (I.i.38-41); his first words after the abdication scene are, "Let me not stay a jot for dinner: go, get it ready" (I.iv.8-9).

In the old play the Nobles wish "That God had lent you an heyre indubitate" (l. 44), and Leir replies with an allusion to "heavenly powers" (l. 57) and to his daughters' marriages as promising a solution. In addition to the Nobles, Perillus is part of Leir's retinue. While, like Kent, foreshadowing his master's filial disappointment, Perillus differs from his counterpart in his pious insipidity. Like other characters, Perillus, too, alludes confidently to "heavenly powers" (l. 95). His master confesses,

> How deare my daughters are unto my soule,
> None knowes, but he, that knowes my thoghts & secret deeds.
> (ll. 204-205)

Rejected, however, by her father for her frankness, Cordella later has recourse only

> unto him which doth protect the just,
> In him will poore *Cordella* put her trust. (ll. 331-332)

Planning, with Cornwall, to share the kingdom, the King of Cambria conjectures, regarding Cordella's fate, whether "they meane to make a Nunne of her" (l. 461). Scornfully, Ragan informs Gonorill that Cordella "were right fit to make a Parsons wife" (l. 488). Invoking a Christ symbol, Leir declares, "I am as kind as is the Pellican" (l. 512), as he anticipates his daughters' marriage. Further, contemplating his retirement, Leir plans to "take me to my prayers and my beades," confident that his daughters "are the kindest Gyrles in Christendome" (ll. 557, 561).

Banished, Cordella accepts her fate as "the pleasure of my God: / And I do willingly imbrace the rod" (ll. 610-611). Seeing Mumford, who swears by St. Denis (l. 622), and his leader, the Gallian king, both disguised as pilgrims, Cordella addresses the latter as "Kind Palmer" (l. 644), while the Gallian king alludes to "holy Palmers" and "grieved soules" and bids "heaven . . . beare record of my words" (ll. 671-672, 674). Encouragingly, Mumford advises his king, who is enamored of Cordella, "Fayth, go to Church, to make the matter sure" (l. 733).

As at the beginning, Leir again stresses the *contemptus mundi* theme of old age:

> The neerer we do grow unto our graves,
> The lesse we do delight in worldly joyes. (ll. 820-821)

Piously, the king recalls the duty of his daughters who "by natures sacred law, / Do owe to me the tribute of their lives" (ll. 898-899). Amidst her troubles, Cordella retains her Christian faith and charity, still hopeful of her father's forgiveness and grace:

> I have bin over-negligent to day,
> In going to the Temple of my God,
> To render thanks for all his benefits,
> Which he miraculously hath bestowed on me, (ll. 1061-64)

and is grateful for a husband full of "care / To God" (ll. 1071-72). To regain Leir's love, Cordella vows,

> Bare foote I would on pilgrimage set forth . . .
> So he but to forgive me once would please,
> That his gray haires might go to heaven in peace.
> (ll. 1080-85)

Including her evil sisters and, presumably, the audience as well, Cordella begs,

> Yet God Forgive both him, and you and me,
> Even as I doe in perfit charity.
> I will to Church, and pray unto my Saviour,
> That ere I dye, I may obtayne his favour. (ll. 1090-93)

As she sees her father enter, bowed with grief, Ragan hypocritically kneels and welcomes him: "for Gods love, come" (l. 1135). Similarly, the Messenger insincerely prays, "The King of heaven preserve your Majesty" (l. 1164). For this villain, with "heart compact of Adamant" (l. 1212), terms his murderous profession "the gainefulst trade in Christendome!" (l. 1225). In contrast to the villainous characters, Cordella prays heaven's blessings upon her royal husband: "The King of heaven remunerate my Lord" (l. 1291). Again, discussing the murder of her father with Ragan, the Messenger is eager to exchange his wicked proficiency for money, exclaiming, "Oh, that I had ten hands by myracle" (l. 1328).

When his follower, Perillus, inquires what they should do should they be set upon, Leir responds with faith and an affirmation of the efficacy of prayer:

> Even pray to God, to blesse us from their hands:
> For fervent prayer much ill hap withstands,

to which Perillus agrees, "Ile sit and pray with you for company" (ll. 1448-50). Upon this pious scene the murderer enters, remarking that they "with pure zeale have prayed themselves asleepe. . . . / And are provided for another world" (ll. 1463-65). As the murderer approaches, Perillus exclaims, litany-fashion, "Deliver us, good Lord, from such as he" (l. 1506). Leir fears that this is the just revenge of Cordella, who is now Queen of France. Noting God's all-watchful providence, he is, however, happy at her fortune, "no thanks at all to me, / But unto God, who my injustice see" (ll. 1580-81). Resigning himself to the Messenger's blow, he rejects the latter's slanders:

> There lives not any under heavens bright eye,
> That can convict me of impiety....
> ... I am in true peace with all the world. (ll. 1600-03)

"You are the fitter," replies the villain, "for the King of heaven," denying his claim that he is "In charity with all the world" (ll. 1604-10). Demanding assurance that it is the evil daughters, not Cordella, who have employed the villain, Leir is told, "That to be true, in sight of heaven I sweare."

> *Leir*. Sweare not by heaven, for feare of punishment:
> The heavens are guiltlesse of such haynous acts....
> Sweare not by hell; for that stands gaping wide,
> To swallow thee, and if thou do this deed. (ll. 1625-33)

At this point, "Thunder and lightning" create panic in the would-be murderer's intention and awaken his conscience. Noteworthy is the crucial difference between Lear's defiant challenge to the thunder, culminating in a naturalistic question regarding its origin, and the Messenger's stupefied terror:

> Oh, but my conscience for this act doth tell,
> I get heavens hate, earths scorne, and paynes of hell.
> (ll. 1646-47)

"They blesse themselves," the directions read, both assassin and victim sharing the religious mood engendered by the thunder. The ever-pious Perillus takes this occasion to invoke the Hebraic deity:

> Oh just *Jehova*, whose almighty power
> Doth governe all things in this spacious world,
> How canst thou suffer such outragious acts (ll. 1649-51)

and in biblical language assails the "viperous generation and accurst" which seeks its father's blood (ll. 1653-54). More passively, Leir draws a most un-Lear-like moral:

> Ah, my true friend in all extremity,
> Let us submit us to the will of God:
> Things past all sence, let us not seeke to know;
> It is Gods will, and therefore must be so. (ll. 1655-58)

And he offers his life to the murderer, with his Christian forgiveness:

> My friend, I am prepared for the stroke:
> Strike when thou wilt, and I forgive thee here,
> Even from the very bottome of my heart. (ll. 1659-61)

Leir thus meekly quells the gigantic and Promethean conflict that Shakespeare's Lear provides. The old Leir, advocating a kind of religious passivity, would inevitably, perhaps, have appealed more to Tolstoy, while the Shakespearean Lear may be conceived as truly a restless Western force, in a sense, the epitome of the Spenglerian "Faustian" challenger. Like the Job of Théodore de Bèze's *Job Expounded* (1589?), the old Leir passively bears God's yoke, trusting in His wise, all-seeing providence.

Preparing to die, Leir goes through the *ars moriendi* routine, as Lear hardly does; he bids Perillus carry his blessing to Cordella and, following the Homilies' recipe for repentance, asks, like Lear, forgiveness of the one he has most injured, adding,

> Now, Lord, receyve me, for I come to thee,
> And dye, I hope, in perfit charity. (ll. 1670-71)

But the Messenger tells Leir that Perillus, too, must die; the king, affecting to misunderstand, replies,

> No doubt, he shal, when by the course of nature,
> He must surrender up his due to death:
> But that time shall not come, till God permit. (ll. 1677-79)

Like Gloucester, Perillus invokes the king's divine sanctity:

> Oh, but beware, how thou dost lay thy hand
> Upon the high anoynted of the Lord (ll. 1695-96)

and he paints a grim picture of punishments to come:

> Oh, then art thou for ever tyed in chaynes
> Of everlasting torments to indure,
> Even in the hotest hole of grisly hell,
> Such paynes, as never mortall toung can tell. (ll. 1735-38)

At this point, it conveniently thunders again; the Messenger quakes, and he drops his dagger. Leir exclaims, "O heavens be thanked, he wil spare my friend" (l. 1741), whereupon the murderer drops the other dagger meant for him and exits, bereft of his unlawful prey. As the Messenger again is frightened after the repeated thunder, Perillus observes, "Ah, now I see thou hast some sparke of grace" (l. 1749). Further, persuading Leir of Cordella's love for him, Perillus explains,

> No worldly gifts, but grace from God on hye,
> Doth nourish vertue and true charity. (ll. 1772-73)

If Perillus is correct, the king acknowledges, and

> If this third daughter play a kinder part,
> It comes of God, and not of my desert. (ll. 1789-90)

Unaware of events, Ragan is full of hypocritical foreboding (ll. 1899-1902). Like Albany, Cambria, however, replies:

> The heavens are just, and hate impiety,
> And will (no doubt) reveale such haynous crimes:
> Censure not any, till you know the right:
> Let him be Judge, that bringeth truth to light. (ll. 1909-12)

Miraculously brought to a table by Cordella, the old king is given restorative food. The unrecognized Cordella seizes this occasion for a syncretic exercise, mingling pagan and Old Testament narrative:

> And may that draught be unto him, as was
> That which old *Eson* dranke, which did renue
> His withered age, and made him young againe.
> And may that meat be unto him, as was
> That which *Elias* ate. . . . (ll. 2188-92)

Not to be outdone, Leir alludes to "the blessed Manna, / That raynd from heaven amongst the Israelites" (ll. 2202-03). Following her self-disclosure, Leir and Cordella strive to outdo each other in kneeling. While they thus alternately kneel, Leir blesses Cordella and hopes the blessing

which the God of *Abraham* gave
Unto the trybe of *Juda*, light on thee,
And multiply thy dayes, that thou mayst see
Thy childrens children prosper after thee.
Thy faults, which are just none that I do know,
God pardon on high, and I forgive below. (ll. 2326-31)

After the Gallian company enters, Mumford accepts command from his king and promises to fight to the death, swearing "by that sweet Saints bright eye" (l. 2411). The Gallian king invokes "God and our right for us," as later he shouts, "God and our right, Saint *Denis*, and Saint *George*" (ll. 2475, 2548). To Mumford on going to the wars, Cordella promises to "pray to God, to sheeld you from all harmes" (l. 2540), and Leir and Perillus echo her intention to pray. Yet when Cordella objects to Ragan being "so devoyd of grace" as to call her father a liar, Gonorill threatens her:

Peace (Puritan) dissembling hypocrite,
Which art so good, that thou wilt prove stark naught . . .
Ile make you wish your selfe in Purgatory. (ll. 2577-80)

Finally, having won a victory for Leir's party, the Gallian king announces, "Thanks be to God, your foes are overcome," to which the old king rejoins, "First to the heavens, next, thanks to you," and the victorious Gallian choruses, "Thank heavens, not me . . ." (ll. 2633-35, 2645).

In sum, the religious references in the old play are, for the most part, explicitly Christian, although hypocritically so in the case of the villainous daughters. Even the murderer heeds the voice of thunder and, dropping his sharpened dagger, slinks away. Divine and poetic justice rule all; the anonymous play never questions them or allows them to be questioned, and the work ceaselessly drums its pious message. Although both heroes demand pardon of those they have wronged, as set down in the Establishment Homilies, the old Leir follows the ordinances in the *ars moriendi* tradition, which Lear does not. In contrast to *Hamlet*, a Christianized version of the pre-Christian Amleth story, *Lear*, in Shakespeare's hands, becomes a paganized version of a Christian play.

We may deduce, therefore, that the old drama furnished a groundwork upon which Shakespeare constructed his variations: piety remained, to an extent, in the good characters, especially Cordelia and the interpolated Edgar; but the king himself and the added Gloucester are vastly different and more complex; further, they change and develop as the characters in the old *Leir* do not. The thunder is taken up and expanded into an all-encompassing storm, and Lear's attitudes toward it are a measure of his confused alterations; and, more significant, the thunder itself, perhaps for one of the first times in Christian literature, becomes ambiguous—not clearly on the side of God or the good. At one point, Lear goes so far as to seek a naturalistic explanation for God's "voice." From the old *Leir* the departures are, indeed, numerous; and those critics who still insist on viewing Shakespeare's play as a traditional drama of redemption might, comparing the two, measure the distance which Shakespeare has traveled into complexity, ambiguity, and dubiety in his new creation.

The foregoing chapters have attempted to sketch some of the evidence for the later Renaissance breakdown of a belief in providence, especially a personal providence, as a background for the comprehension of *King Lear*. In addition, they have indicated that the attitudes toward providence which the following chapters will examine in *Lear* are already present in one of its sources, Sidney's *Arcadia*. If Shakespeare were to make dramatic use of such points of view, he would have had to remove the patent and ubiquitous Christianity of another major source, the old *King Leir*; that he did so is established by an examination of the religious references in the earlier work.

Part II

CHAPTER V

Prisca Theologia: Cordelia and Edgar

Cordelia

We may consider initially the first of the four categories of pagan belief outlined above and one of its representatives, Cordelia. She speaks in just four scenes of the play and is the most taciturn of the main characters.[1] In Cordelia's resolution to "Love, and be silent" (I.i.62) we find the inception of a capability whose nature speaks louder than words; Cordelia absent is, perhaps, as powerful as Cordelia present. With only some hundred and fifteen lines, hers, in contrast to the "dread-bolted thunder" and its complementary hell-shrieking Bedlam, is a constant *argumentum ex silentio*.

"Grace" (I.i.273), the "bond" (I.i.93), "love" (I.i.62, 77; IV.iv. 28), "bless'd secrets" (IV.iv.15), "benediction" (IV.vii.58), "deep dread-bolted thunder" (IV.vii.33), "restoration" (IV.vii.26), "thy reverence" (IV.vii.29), "holy water" (IV.iii.31), "heavenly eyes"

[1]Cordelia has lines in I.i, IV.iv, IV.vii, V.iii, framing the play. Resembling, iconographically, "Truth shut in a cage," Cordelia will, like a "bird i' th' cage," be there later remanded. (Cf. Lear's other "poor fool," in whose case truth is also figured as whipped, I.iv.117-118, 190.) See, e.g., the allegory of Truth banished in Alemán's *Guzman de Alfarache*, II, 209, 211, 213. In addition, Cordelia's prediction to the evil sisters,

> Time shall unfold what plighted cunning hides;
> Who covers faults, at last with shame derides, (I.i.280-281)

parallels King James's proverbial "*Time* the Mother, will bring foorth *Veritie* her Daughter, in due season to perfection" (J. L. S., ed. *Flores Regii . . . Spoken by . . . James* [1627], No. 190). A favorite play of James, George Ruggle's *Ignoramus* (1615), in IV.xii, utilizes the proverb. Among numerous instances of the literary and iconographical formula *veritas filia temporis* and its variants, cf. *The Attic Nights of Aulus Gellius*, tr. John C. Rolfe, Loeb Classical Lib., II (1927), 394, 395; "Time trieth out both truth and also treason," *The Mirror for Magistrates*, ed. Lily B. Campbell (Cambridge, Eng., 1938), p. 370, l. 308; Timothy Bright, *A Treatise ... of English Medicines* (1580), p. 7; Thomas Tusser, *Five Hundreth Points of Good Husbandrie* (1604), p. 3; *Temporis filia veritas*, ed. F. P. Wilson, Luttrell Soc. Repr. No. 16 (Oxford, 1957); Shakespeare's *Rape of Lucrece*, l. 939; *The Christmas Prince* (1607-08), Malone Soc. Repr. (1922), p. 113, ll. 3399-3400; Nashe, III, 29. See also Tilley T580 ("Truth is time's daughter") and T591; Guillaume de La Perrière, *La morosophie* (Lyon, 1553), sigs. H4v-H5; Peter Pett, *Times Journey to Seeke His Daughter Truth* (1599); *The Arundel Harington Manuscript of Tudor Poetry*, ed. Ruth Hughey (Columbus, Ohio, 1960), II, 439; Fritz Saxl, "Veritas filia temporis," in *Philosophy and History: Essays Presented to Ernst Cassirer*, ed. Raymond Klibansky and H. J. Paton (Oxford, 1936), pp. 197-222; Donald J. Gordon, "'Veritas filia temporis'. . ." *JWCI*, III (1939-40), 228-240.

(IV.iii.31), "live and work / To match thy goodness" (IV.vii.1-2)—these are some relevant allusions, which, taken in their entirety, form a meaningful pattern of pious and reverent belief. Grace is asked both of, and later for, her father: "stood I within his grace" (I.i.273), she regretfully remarks of Lear; she feels herself cast out of grace beyond the merely familial; but it is a "grace" to which she ultimately returns, herself bearing it. To her, a believer in providence and divine justice, the gods are "kind Gods" (IV.vii.14); and it is to them that she prays for Lear's recovery, prayer for her appearing to have efficacy.

Cordelia's bond, ultimately merciful as it relates to an affirmation of absolute justice, in the opening scene contrasts with Edmund's announced relativism at the start of the second. Act I therefore seems to focus less on other aspects of Cordelia's character than on the significant issue of the destruction of the bond which she represents: in dialectic sequence Lear demolishes it; she affirms it; and Edmund provides a rationale for abrogating it by repudiating the law of nature and asserting the rule of natural impulse.

The bond as expression of natural law was a major Renaissance commonplace. As do Hooker and elsewhere Shakespeare himself, Richard Barckley, in *A Discourse of the Felicitie of Man* (1603), defines it:

> For whereas the great GOD of nature hath tyed together all his creations, with some meane things that agree and participate with the extremities, and hath composed the intelligible, ethereall, and elementarie world, by indissoluble meanes and bounds . . . between brute beastes, and those of a spirituall essence & understanding, which are Angels, he hath placed man, which combineth heaven and this elementary world together, whose one part is subject to death, and the other part immortall. . . . (p. 541)

In the family, says Leonard Wright's *A Display of Dutie* (1589, sig. A4), echoing a formula probably familiar to Shakespeare from Nowell's *Catechism*, "youth by law of Nature, are bound to honour, reverence, and obey their ancients."[2] Having announced her

[2]See Alexander Nowell, *Catechismus parvus* (1573), sig. [Avii]. Cf. the homily "An Exhortation concerning . . . Obedience . . .", *Certaine Sermons* (1587), sigs. J2v-J3, on the bond, and in relation to Shakespeare's degree speech in *Troilus and Cressida*. Cordelia's conception of duties is also the familiar Stoic one, as in Epictetus, *Discourses*: ". . . I ought not to be unfeeling . . . but should maintain my relations, both natural and acquired, as a religious man, as a son, a brother, a father, a citizen" (tr. W. A. Oldfather, Loeb Classical Lib. [1928], II, 23).

fidelity to the bond, "I love your Majesty / According to my bond; no more nor less," Cordelia continues with the orderly formula:

> You have begot me, bred me, lov'd me: I
> Return those duties back as are right fit,
> Obey you, love you, and most honour you. (I.i.92-93, 96-98)

Ironically, too late, Lear recalls to Regan the bond which he himself has broken:

> The offices of nature, bond of childhood,
> Effects of courtesy, dues of gratitude. (II.iv.180-181)

Again, Cordelia demonstrates her consistency with order, the principle of the bond, when she prays (IV.vii.14-16), "O you kind Gods, . . . / Th' untuned and jarring senses, O! wind up," where breach and discord are to be replaced by a cured wholeness and harmony, analogous to a restored cosmic harmony, related to the Platonic conception. Amidst her father's rash division of the country and the greedy scramblings of her sisters, on the one hand, and the imminent (I.ii.1-22) disorderly claim to private sensual privilege of Edmund, on the other, her reply, analogous to the divine order, is one of impulses restrained and duty obeyed, even at the cost of her dear father's love. Her response is one, moreover, which amidst the tragedy's reiterated breach-and-division imagery recalls, in contrast to Edmund's Sansloy, Spenser's Una and the never-entirely-absent motif of personal, political, and spiritual integrity. Like Shakespeare's royal patron, who had recently united Scotland and England, Cordelia is devoted to curing division. Strife between north and south, between such aptly named figures as Albany and Cornwall—compare the triple act-initiating references (I.i.1-2, II.i.11-14, III.i.19-21)—has its antithesis in Cordelia's healing and restoring forgiveness. She prays for a "cure" in "this great breach," in Lear's "abused nature," and her love would "repair those . . . harms" (IV.vii. 14-16, 26-29). Recalling the highest virtue as the highest love (the Augustinian *summum amor*), she summons up also the Boethian and Chaucerian bond of love. For it is love and its correlative, pity, which in *Lear* are the binding forces and which Cordelia preeminently reflects.

In contrast, the disorder consequent upon the breach of the bond of religion and of the law of nature is remarked by Fitzherbert in the *Second Part of a Treatise*: "Should not the world, by the breach of the common bond, fall to confusion, and man be overwhelmed with remediles miserie?" (p. 44). While Fitzherbert reflects a Catholic conception, Nashe notes contemporary threats to the unity of the English church; commenting on the bond, he complains, "*Bandes* are burst also, for our unitie is fallen into dissention" (I, 91).

Juxtaposing unity with disunity, the Renaissance *topos* comparing cosmic order and musical harmony appears in the headings of Pierre Viret's *Familiere . . . instruction en la doctrine chrestienne* ([Geneva?], 1559): "Comparaison de l'harmonie & de l'accord qui est en la diversité des tons, qui sont en la musique, avec l'accord & l'union que Dieu a mis entre les creatures. . . . Comparaison de l'art de musique, avec la providence de Dieu" (pp. 420-421, 424). In relating the harmony topic to Lear's sanity (IV.vii.16-17; cf. l. 25), Cordelia takes up, antithetically, the discordant musical image announced by Edmund: "my cue is villainous melancholy. . . . O! these eclipses do portend these divisions. *Fa sol, la, mi*" (I.ii.142-144), voicing the *diabolus in musica*, the devil's tritone.[3] Edmund's "divisions," moreover, may also contain a technical play on contrast and tension in music, while in another sense he foreshadows the discordant thunder and the "great breach" which Cordelia would heal. As John Thornborough's *A Discourse, Shewing the Great Happinesse . . . of England and Scotland, by Re-Uniting Them into One Great Britain* (1641, sig. [A12^v]), concludes, "Division is good in Musicke, ill in Kingdomes."

Such admonitions against the Serpent of Division as recur from *Gorboduc* (1562; reprinted in 1590 annexed to Lydgate's *Serpent of Division*) to the utterances of Shakespeare's royal patron would have been present in the playwright's mind. In addition, the divisive force of the passions, condemned in the Epistle of James, iv.1 ("From whence are warres and contentions among you? are they not hence, even of your lustes, that fight in your members?"), had political as well as personal overtones. While Hooker diagnoses pride, or "Immoderate swelling," as "a token of very imminent breach," setting "the whole world out of course," politically he ex-

[3]See Wilfrid Mellers, "La mélancholie au début du XVIIe siècle et le madrigal anglais," in *Musique et poésie au XVIe siècle*, Colloques internationaux du Centre National de la Recherche Scientifique (Paris, 1954), pp. 153-168.

presses an analogous fear of the Puritan intention to divide the realm into independent parishes, with the consequent disappearance of unity.[4] Resuming the traditional counsel against division of inheritance, King James himself warned his son to make the latter's "eldest sonne *Isaac*, leaving him all your kingdomes. . . . Otherwaies by deviding your kingdomes, ye shall leave the seede of division & discorde . . . as befell to this Ile, by the division . . . to the three sonnes of *Brutus*, *Locrine*, *Albanact*, and *Camber*."[5]

Cordelia unites in herself the Renaissance-sundered *pietas* and *sapientia*—"pietas," Petrarch had written, "est sapientia."[6] In contrast, violating the natural moral and Stoic virtues of prudence, justice, and temperance, Lear transgresses the prudence by which one governs oneself (*bonum proprium*), as well as the prudence by which one governs others (*bonum commune*). Indeed, human prudence and its cognate, divine providence, were regarded by Aquinas as analogies, and some Renaissance views held the one to be the counterpart of the other.[7] Unlike Lear, Cordelia, anticipating the higher virtues of faith, hope, and charity, seems to approach the contemplative virtues of wisdom (*sapientia*), knowledge (*scientia*), and understanding (*intellectus*).[8] In sum, she embodies Albany's association between "Wisdom and goodness" (IV.ii.38).

In opposition to the villains' rule by natural impulse and Gloucester's sense of astral domination, her attitude to such hyperbolic and conditional exclamations as Kent's "It is the stars, / The stars above us, govern our conditions" (IV.iii.33-34) would refer to the analogy of a higher wisdom. "Be govern'd by your knowledge, and proceed,"

[4]"A Learned Sermon of the Nature of Pride," *Works*, III, 602.

[5]*Basilicon Doron* (Edinburgh, 1603; *STC* 14349), p. 83. Proverbially, division is also condemned, as in Tilley A187: "He that gives All before he dies provides to suffer (is a fool)"; cf. Lear's "I gave you all" (II.iv.252) and Tilley D570, G308, on not parting with possessions before death.

[6]*De remediis utriusque fortunae* (Cremona, 1492), sig. b3. See Eugene F. Rice, Jr., *The Renaissance Idea of Wisdom* (Cambridge, Mass., 1958).

[7]St. Thomas Aquinas, *Truth*, tr. R. W. Mulligan, I (Chicago, 1952), Qu. V, Art. 5. Cf. W. L. Ysaac, "The Certitude of Providence in St. Thomas," *Modern Schoolman*, XXXVIII (1961), 305-323. See also Nannus Mirabellius, *Polyanthea* (Venice, 1592), s.v. "Providentia," "Prudentia," pp. 576-585.

[8]The four cardinal virtues, Prudence, Justice, Fortitude, and Temperance, decorated a triumph of James I in 1604 (Stephen Harrison, *The Arch's of Triumph* [1604], sig. H).

she requests the Doctor, "I' th' sway of your own will" (IV.vii.19-20), in one phrase summing up the precedence of reason and intellect over will which Lear had neglected. Like Albany, she might remark, "govern her" (V.iii.161), regarding the desperate Goneril of whom Edgar had exclaimed, "O indistinguish'd space of woman's will!" (IV.vi.273); and she would demur against such despairing pleas as Gloucester's to the gods' "great opposeless wills" (IV.vi.38). Hopefully and undespairingly, she demands, "What can man's wisdom . . . ?" (IV.iv.8). There is reverence, further, in her petition to Lear for blessing (IV.vii.57-58), exhibiting here as elsewhere a pious regard for those relations implicit in the bond, familial, political, and divine.[9]

Sharing Cordelia's view of the bond, Kent is its more aggressive defender against its enemies. "Such smiling rogues as these," he complains against Oswald, "Like rats, oft bite the holy cords a-twain / Which are too intrince t' unloose" (II.ii.74-76). Even against his beloved master, Kent, like Cordelia, affirms the bond. And, as Cordelia, in contrast to Lear, preserves a just distribution and propriety even in her private loyalties (I.i.100-104), so Kent's demands go no further than the modest and just distribution of mere acknowledgment (IV.vii.4-6). Moreover, although married, Cordelia seems chastely unmarried, and her virtue provides a contrast to Gloucester's adultery and the villains' lechery. Despite her piety, however, hers is not a cloistered virtue: Cordelia, for all her unworldliness, is in the world; Albany, for all his worldliness, at times seems out of it. For while he weds, and for some time continues unaware of, Goneril, Cordelia knows her sisters and knows the consequences of their flattery (I.i.269-271).[10]

[9]Although her wounded pride and edged irony in reply to her sisters are also evident, part of what may appear today as objectionable in Cordelia's initial response to Lear may be in the older tradition of righteousness, as expressed, e.g., in the *Inferno*, Canto viii (Dante to Filippo Argenti). In addition, Cordelia's "most small fault" (I.iv.275) may, as Lear later perceives it, anticipate his own consciousness of disproportion as "a man / More sinn'd against than sinning" (III.ii.59-60) and his view that "None does offend" (IV.vi.170).

[10]Cordelia's attitude accords also with James's, in warning against the flattery of monarchs; with her allusion to "that glib and oily art / To speak and purpose not" (I.i.224-225; cf. ll. 231-232) and her stress on deeds rather than hypocritical words (here and in I.i.77-78, 91-92; I.i.271-272, 280-281), compare James's counsel to his son against being "smoothed over with that flattering . . . sicknes," and against "the suspition of filthie proud hypocrisie and deceitfull dissimulation" (*Basilicon Doron*, pp. 16, 21).

To the Doctor's recommendation that Lear's sleep might be induced by "means . . . to provoke" it, by "many simples operative, whose power / Will close the eye of anguish" (IV.iv.11-15), Cordelia replies with a prayer:

> All bless'd secrets,
> All you unpublish'd virtues of the earth,
> Spring with my tears! be aidant and remediate
> In the good man's distress! (IV.iv.15-18)

Related to particular providence, which Gerardus' *A Speciall Treatise of Gods Providence* (1588?) endeavors to propound, is faith in "secret vertues." ". . . God," Gerardus explains, "hath instilled into every thing that he hath created certaine secret and peculiar vertues, which we cannot perceive in like maner to be in other things. So we see corn or grain properly to qualifie hunger, water to quench thirst . . ." (sig. Giii). "This universall Nature," acknowledges Du Chesne's *The Practise of Chymicall . . . Physicke* (1605), "is also taken for the divine vertue, which God hath put and implanted in all creatures: by the benefite whereof, certaine notes of the Divinitie, are to be discerned in them" (sig. B3^{v}). In addition, Timothy Bright's *A Treatise . . . of English Medicines* (1580) connects faith in providence (p. 9) with belief in native "virtues of the earth" (pp. 9-10, 23-24).[11]

Significantly, Cordelia's faith thus accords with Friar Laurence's confidence in the "virtues excellent" and "powerful grace" within "The earth that's nature's mother" (*Romeo and Juliet*, II.iii.9, 12-16). Similarly, Cordelia's undiminished faith may suggest that, as another and later priest (Gerard Manley Hopkins) affirmed, "nature is never spent," that "There lives the dearest freshness deep down things," and may imply as well a healing and providential nature, the *vis medicatrix naturae* of the ancients.[12] According respect to the

[11]See also Raleigh, *The History of the World* (1614), I.i.11, pp. 14-15. Tilley V88 ("Virtue is now in herbs and stones and words only").

[12]*Oeuvres complètes d'Hippocrates*, ed. É. Littré, V (Paris, 1846), 314-315. Galen refuted Epicureans who had attacked design by implying that the body resulted from chance. He argued that human physiology had been ordered in the best possible way (*On the Natural Faculties*, tr. Arthur J. Brock, Loeb Classical Lib. [1916], pp. xxix, 73). And Hippocrates, holding that nature is the physician of diseases, observed that providence is concerned with maintaining, as well as shaping, its creatures. See William A. Heidel, ". . . A Study of the Conception of Nature among the Pre-Socratics," *Proceedings of the American Academy of Arts and Sciences*, XLV (1910), 105-106.

secrets of nature, she does not, however, probe into forbidden knowledge of the mystery of things. Here, as in her reverential allusion to the "deep dread-bolted thunder" (IV.vii.33), for instance, she is far from the naturalistic explanations that less pious souls undertook. Eventually, Cordelia's optimistic confidence in the "unpublish'd virtues of the earth" is ironically to be echoed in Lear's bitter description of her corpse, "dead as earth."

Shakespeare allows Cordelia one allusion of an extremely conventional kind which may connect her with her ostensible paganism: "Myself could else out-frown false Fortune's frown" (V.iii.6), an observation any Renaissance Christian might have made, but one peculiarly fitting the Stoicism that Cordelia, both in speech and in silence, so eloquently exhibits.[13] As a pagan antedating Christ, existing under a natural rather than a revealed theology and under a dispensation of nature without grace, Cordelia appears limited to works. Like More's Utopians,[14] she, Edgar, and Kent perform good works ("live and work") without hope of grace or heaven but rather out of good conscience and mere recognition (IV.vii.1-4). In contrast to the despairing Gloucester, who suggests that "our mere defects" (IV.i.20) or deficiency of good works may prove more reliable and salutary or less hurtful to ourselves, Cordelia trusts in works or "means." In like fashion, Erasmus in his *Adagia* touches upon the secular pagan ideal: "Labor for the well-fare and profit of others, and in doing so, look for no other compensation than the satisfaction of having labored in the interest of the greatest possible number of one's fellow-men."[15] Such attitudes of paganism as are indicated in More and Erasmus are to be distinguished from a more orthodox Christian ideal as reflected, for instance, in the *Imitation of Christ*, where good works and good conscience are related to the desire and love of heaven and the right to supernatural reward because of divine ordination.[16]

[13]"Fortune and chaunce, are the words of Heathen men. . . ." John Northbrooke, *Spiritus est vicarius Christi in terra* (1600), fol. 24v; cf. Théodore de Bèze, *An Evident Display of Popish Practices, or Patched Pelagianisme* (1578), p. 90.

[14]*The Utopia of Sir Thomas More*, ed. J. H. Lupton (Oxford, 1895), pp. 193-194, 280-281.

[15]Paraphrased by Theodore C. Appelt, *Studies in the Contents and Sources of Erasmus' "Adagia"* (Chicago, 1942), p. 65.

[16]Edward L. Surtz, *The Praise of Wisdom: A Commentary on . . . St. Thomas More's Utopia* (Chicago, 1957), pp. 115-117; [Thomas a Kempis?], *The Imitation of Christ*, ed. Albert Hyma (New York, 1927), pp. 64-65, 146-150, 160-161.

Yet, ironically, good works, even on the earthly plane, seem, at best, of doubtful consequence, as Gloucester discovers. Edmund's repentant "some good I mean to do" and his plea for the hasty remission of his writ on Cordelia's life (V.iii.243-247) are followed some dozen lines later by the bearing in of his victim's corpse. Analogously, although Cordelia, near the close of the previous act, had demanded, "how shall I live and work," the reply appears in the event; despite their benevolent intentions, neither villain nor heroine "live and work." Again implying works, Cordelia exclaims in an analogical *entendre*: "O dear father! / It is thy business that I go about" (IV.iv.23-24); but it is a business of unhappy consequence to both. It is works, rather than mere words (I.i.62, 76-78), that Cordelia invokes against her hypocritical sisters. Similarly, Kent, who exemplifies works, finds his sorrowful reward in the death of his master, whôm he had faithfully served, and in his own "journey . . . shortly to go" (V.iii.321).[17]

It may be concluded that in the light of the evidence, implying a belief pattern of forgiveness; divine justice, kindness, and provi-

---

Such emphasis on works could have met with royal approval; for in 1604, at the Hampton Court conference, James expressed agreement with the Bishop of London's criticism of those "many" who "neglect holiness of life, presuming on persisting in Grace upon Predestination." "I approve it very well," the monarch observed, "as consonant with the place of Paul, 'Work out your salvation with fear and trembling'" (*A Complete Collection of State Trials*, ed. T. B. Howell et al., II [1816], 76). On the other hand, James's Calvinist training could have elicited sympathy with a later attitude of Gloucester toward works. Concerning the latter, see the present writer, "'Our Means Secure Us' (*King Lear*, IV.i.20)," *Neophilologus*, XLVII (1963), 225-227.

Yet, while the issue of works may be questionable, "*works*," as Thomas Adams' *Mystical Bedlam, or the World of Mad-men* (1615), p. 22, holds, "are infallible notes of the *hart*. I say not, that *works* determine a man to damnation or blisse: the decree of God orders that: but *works* distinguish of a good or bad man."

[17]See Tilley V81 ("Virtue is its own reward"). Cf. the Stoic doctrine of the "sufficiency of Virtue" or *sufficientia*; virtue, according to Chrysippus, does not allow addition (*accessio*). Like Cicero, Epictetus, and Marcus Aurelius, Seneca (e.g., in *Ad Lucilium epistolae morales*, tr. Richard M. Gummere, II [1920], 231) pronounces virtue its own reward.

That emphasis on works may also suggest an anti-Puritan bias is implied by Nashe (III, 389) in his lament concerning "good woorkes truste over the sea with Jacke a lent, the latter a popish symbol. Elsewhere, he assails those who take "the performance of good workes for Papistrie" (I, 22); and he asserts, "Those Preachers please best, which can fitte us with a cheape Religion, that preach Fayth, and all Fayth, and no Good-workes . . ." (II, 107). Robert Greene's *A Quip for an Upstart Courtier* (*The Life and Complete Works in Prose and Verse*, ed. Alexander B. Grosart [1881-86], XI, 280) also complains of those who "preach faith, faith, and say that doing of almes is papistry, but . . . have preached good workes quit out of our Parish."

dence; grace; good life and works, rather than faith alone; efficacy of prayer; the universal bond; deference toward divine manifestations, such as thunder; blessing; and governance by reason, Cordelia could in all probability have been identified as approximating the pagan *prisca theologia*, like Sidney's Pamela.[18] Contrary to Dante, who placed some virtuous heathens in the First Circle or Limbo of his *Inferno*, in Shakespeare's day the controversy over the *salut des infidèles* might, according to the indications in *King Lear*, have been decided in her favor.

Edgar

Flectere si nequeo superos, Acheronta movebo.
—*Aeneid*, VII.312

QUEST FOR IDENTITY

If Cordelia is silent and absent, Edgar seems loquacious and ubiquitous, a Proteus with more lines than anyone but the protagonist himself. The most enigmatic character in the play, perhaps, he occupies a role which is far out of proportion to his secondary-plot origin. Last to be introduced, excepting the Fool and Oswald, he is billed on the Quarto's title page with the titular hero. Initially delineated by Edmund as

a brother noble,
Whose nature is so far from doing harms
That he suspects none; on whose foolish honesty
My practices ride easy! (I.ii.186-189)

Edgar is, like the king, more trustful than Cordelia; his is a trust which arises more from nobility than credulousness. Readily persuaded by his worldly sophisticate brother and apparently little schooled in either human or cosmic evil, Edgar, in his eventual disillusionment, is analogous to Lear.

Paralleling Lear's persuasion by the evil sisters, and Gloucester's by Edmund, Edgar's is the last of three belief-and-reaction discharges

[18]With the Gentleman's allusion to Cordelia's shaking "The holy water from her heavenly eyes" (IV.iii.30-31), cf. Pierre Viret, *The Worlde Possessed with Devils*, published in English translation in 1583 (sig. Giii): "For the Panims beleeved as our Papistes now a daies doe, that sinnes were purged awaie by Holy water." Considering his probably divided audiences, Shakespeare's possible ambivalence may emerge when Lear's other "poor fool" mockingly refers to "holy-water" in its current sense of flattery (III.ii.10-11). Holy water as a Catholic "superstition" is alluded to often in one of the play's sources, Samuel Harsnet's *A Declaration of Egregious Popishe Impostures* (1603); cf. Richard Baddeley, *The Boy of Bilson* (1622), p. 24, "their Holy-Water . . . altogether superstitious. . ." Cf. *Titus Andronicus*, I.i.323; Tilley H532.

motivating the rapid unfolding of the plot. His Poor Tom initiates a series of disguises enforced by banishment and loss of patrimony and, as in Lear's case, loss of his status through usurpation. Concerning Tom o' Bedlam, he says, "That's something yet: Edgar I nothing am" (II.iii.21), a defect of identity already discovered by Lear (I.iv.234, 238). To Lear's question regarding his own identity, the Fool replies, "Lear's shadow" (I.iv.239). But the less-provided Edgar seems, in a sense, not even a shadow and is, for much of the drama, a series of personae. Indeed, Poor Tom speaks of having been made "to course his own shadow for a traitor" (III.iv.57).[19] By the second act, as *Mann ohne Schatten* and *hombre sin nombre*, Edgar is involved in a quest for his own identity and, under the newly recognized cosmic dispensation, for that of man himself.[20]

"Nothing" concludes his first soliloquy, just as the bare echo of a name introduces it: "I heard myself proclaim'd" (II.iii.1); and throughout, his identity, like Lear's, is in question. Edgar's "self" is a function of his vicissitudes. Outwardly, he regains his name with his defeat of Edmund and inwardly, at length, with his descent into feeling. His season in hell begins at the lowest human level, madman and beggar. This seems in response to Edmund's "descend: brother, I say!" (II.i.20). *Facilis descensus Averno.* A Virgil who is simultaneously captive in his own Inferno, Edgar conducts erring humanity through the conquest of its despair. Ironically, his outward for-

[19]See Helge Kökeritz, *Shakespeare's Pronunciation* (New Haven, 1953), pp. 100-101, on the "course-curse" pun in *King John* and *Love's Labour's Lost.*

[20]Cf. Kent's first inquiry: "What art thou that dost grumble there i' th' straw?" (III. iv.43). "What's he?" asks Lear. "Who's there? What is 't you seek?" echoes Kent. "What are you there? Your names?" choruses Gloucester (III.iv.129-131). When the Old Man demands of Tom, "Who's there?" (IV.i.24) and "Fellow, where goest?" (IV. i.29), Gloucester raises similar queries (IV.i.29, 40). Edgar as countryman compounds the confusion by quizzing Gloucester regarding the latter's supposed demonic tempter (IV.vi.67-68). When he offers sympathy, Gloucester again demands, ". . . what are you?" (IV.vi.221). At a parallel crisis, Edgar, as anonymous challenger, replies to the Herald who interrogates him, "Know, my name is lost . . ." (V.iii.121). Edmund's self-inflicted wound in his counterfeit duel may be ironically recalled at his fatal wounding in the real duel (V.iii.150). He dies partly through a lapse in his usual worldly providence, having failed before the battle to determine Edgar's identity, an imprudence he had himself recognized: "In wisdom I should ask thy name" (V.iii.141). Cf. John Ferne's *The Blazon of Gentrie* (1586), p. 322, indicating that the other combatant "bee equall in degree and estate to the approover: otherwise, he is not bounde to accept of him." As nameless stranger knight, having dealt his brother a death blow, Edgar is demanded by Edmund: "But what art thou / That hast this fortune on me?" To which, at this moment of his rightful return, Edgar can at last reply, "My name is Edgar, and thy father's son" (V.iii.164-165, 169).

tunes rise as he plunges deeper into human suffering. In that descent[21] he exemplifies the Shakespearean, as well as the Chaucerian, "Pite renneth sone in gentil herte." In his suffering ascent, Lear's godson, ultimately an inheritor of the kingdom, rises from madman and beggar, retrospectively servant,[22] to rustic countryman, messenger, and armed knight.

Edgar's confusion of personal identity parallels a Renaissance confusion and deception on the social and cosmic levels, for mistrust of knowledge and self (Montaigne's "Que sçais-je?" suggesting also "Que suis-je?") accompanied the Renaissance breakdown of social trust and hierarchical identity. Amidst such contemporary deteriorations of confidence, the *déclassé*, as well as the true-born, confidence man,[23] as picaro, crossbiter, or shifter, emerged; yet, contrary to expectations, "springes to catch woodcocks" often led, in the classic inversion, to "wily beguiled." Generally, the dictum of Nashe could have held true: "An extreme gull he is in this age, and no better, that beleeves a man for his swearing" (II, 179).

Professionally, Poor Tom himself, as beggar and pretended madman, occupied a recognized confidence role. Indeed, the Fool's perception of "handy-dandy" as the way of the world implied more than a mere child's game: for instance, Guzman de Alfarache, in Mabbe's 1623 translation of Alemán's work, recounts his "Conycatching trickes" in which "Roguish life, I learned to play at . . . Handy-Pandy. . . ."[24] Out of this world of mutual dupers and duped arose two conventional types of deceivers, the benevolent and the malevolent: those friends, for example, who dissimulate in order to restore Don Quixote to his senses, in contrast to Cervantes' Duke and Duchess, who gull others for their own amusement. In the more

[21]Cf. Tilley D204-205.

[22]Cf. Edgar's beast attributes, III.iv.94-95, and those proverbially ascribed to a good servant, Tilley S233; the latter does not, however, include John Hoskyns' characterization; see *The Life, Letters, and Writings of John Hoskyns 1566-1638*, ed. Louise B. Osborn (New Haven, 1937), p. 168, figure facing p. 168, and pp. 279-280.

[23]Cf. a motto of Herman Melville's *Confidence Man*, "No Trust." For the picaresque background of Edgar's Poor Tom role, see Erik von Kræmer, *Le type du faux mendiant dans les littératures romanes depuis le moyen âge jusqu'au XVIIe siècle*, Societas Scientiarum Fennica, Commentationes Humanarum Litterarum, Vol. XIII, No. 6 (Helsingfors, 1944).

[24]I, 251, 252. Lear's "handy-dandy, which is the justice, which is the thief?" (IV.vi. 155-156) is paralleled in Thomas Powell's *The Attourneys Academy* (1623), p. 217: ". . . to play at *handy dandy*, which is the Gardian, or which is the foole?"

intense climate of tragedy, Edgar functions as benevolent hoaxer to his father, while Edmund operates as malign paternal deceiver. Finally, it may be suggested, above the realm of personal and social illusion attended the divine tricksters, whose potential deceptiveness was mirrored in the theatrical illusion which is tragedy.

"MIME OF THE EPHEMERAL"

. . . a Protean actor variinge everie shape / with the occasion. . . .
—Massinger, *Believe as You List*, III.i

Concomitant with his other roles, Edgar, like Hamlet, assumes the role of actor. His entrance is theatrically announced by the malevolently histrionic and truly hypocritical Edmund: "and pat he comes, like the catastrophe of the old comedy" (I.ii.141-142). Like Hamlet, too, he assumes an antic disposition and prepares in public to don his Bedlam make-up (II.iii.9-12). On "this great stage of fools," Edgar's play-within-a-play employs theatrical asides, actors' terms, and quick change of symbolic garb. His "trade" plays "fool to sorrow" (IV.i. 38); his tears mar his "counterfeiting" (III.vi.60-61), and he cannot "daub it further" (IV.i.51).[25] Moreover, Edgar intensifies the emotional impact by showing it almost break through the limits of his actor's role as actor. If we consider that actors might be statutory vagabonds and rogues, often shelterless, Edgar's assumed outcast role and "roguish madness" (III.vii.103) foreshadow both Cordelia's coupling of Lear with "rogues forlorn" (IV.vii.39) and the king's reference to "poor rogues" (V.iii.13). Indeed, as the protagonists suggest the Renaissance idea of decay, Edgar, alluding to the world's "strange mutations" (IV.i.11), appears to act out the Renaissance notion of mutability.[26] While he partakes of the chameleon's dish as actor, he also stage-manages Gloucester's "suicide" (IV.vi) and remains to the end the *régisseur* of human compassion.

Counterpointing the lunatic king's alterations, Edgar's noble and unsuspecting nature becomes Poor Tom's depraved confusion. He parallels Gloucester, as well, suicidal temptation afflicting his nakedness, while the deadly sins, especially lechery, assail his imagination. In confessional forms demanded of the proud—a kind of subecho of

[25]Cf. Robert Bolton, *Some Generall Directions* . . . (1625), p. 59: "if thou dawb and dissemble."

[26]Cf. citations in Tilley C233 ("There is Change of all things").

Lear's pride—the demon-driven former servant exposes his vices.[27] Eventually, in his pessimism Edgar parallels Gloucester's darker utterances; and, as Edmund devises astrological and "auricular" explanations,[28] Edgar invents demons and miracles in connection with his father's belief.[29] Accommodating himself to Gloucester's credulity, Edmund in his false charge against Edgar describes him as

> Mumbling of wicked charms, conjuring the moon
> To stand auspicious mistress. (II.i.39-40)

Later, as Poor Tom, Edgar does mumble a charm (III.iv.123-127) as Gloucester enters, and in the latter's presence alludes to a fiend whose eyes were "two full moons" (IV.vi.70).

Through the mad Lear's perspective, Edgar's "nothing" (II.iii.21) has become the quintessential "thing itself" (III.iv.109), *res ipsa*, a visible theatrical response to the perpetual Renaissance enigma, the nature of man. As Petrarch had inquired, "Quis est . . . hominum . . . ?" *The Booke of Common Prayer* asked the Psalmist's question, "What is man that thou art mindfull of him."[30] To Hamlet's admiring "What a piece of work is a man!" (II.ii.316) Lear would reply, "Is man no more than this?" (III.iv.105).

As Edgar's role may appear, through two acts, dramatically disproportionate, it is appropriate to demand what relationship exists between his demonic concerns and the preoccupations of the protagonist. Why, in this mature achievement of his art, did the playwright risk such apparently unfunctional distraction?

[27] Like hell itself, Edgar's exorcism of *der Altböse Feind* may also be pre-Christian. In Hellenistic times, for instance, diagnosis of demonic possession forced intrusive spirits to confess their identity; and the connection between devils and vices is at least as old as Egyptian antiquity. On punishment of hell see, e.g., Virgil, *Aeneid*, Bk. VI, ll. 616-624 (tr. H. Rushton Fairclough, Loeb Classical Lib. [1916], Vol. I).

[28] Edmund's "auricular" arrangements for his father point forward to certain "ocular" ones.

[29] The duality of Gloucester's astrological and Edgar's demonological concerns has ancient philosophical prototypes. According to *De fato* (attributed to Plutarch, *Morals*, tr. Philemon Holland [1603], pp. 1048-54), three degrees of providence included, in addition to the reason or benevolent will of God expressing itself in universal laws, that of the stars watching over men, and that of the devils, which, on earth, observe human actions.

[30] 1590, sig. Aiiii^v^.

Exorcism

It is relevant to recall that Edgar's demonic references derive largely from Samuel Harsnet's *A Declaration of Egregious Popishe Impostures* (1603), denouncing instances of fraudulent possession and priestly exorcism. An inquiry into "Shakespeare's Interest in Harsnet's *Declaration*" suggests that it arose from Harsnet's indictment of the exorcising Robert Debdale, an early Shottery connection of the playwright.[31] While a possible reason for Shakespeare's awareness of the work, said to be the only book of polemical divinity he carefully and entirely read, it would not seem in itself sufficient to account for his manifest and public borrowing.

But if we investigate Harsnet's other possible links with the dramatist and with the latter's royal patron, some clearer motive for Shakespeare's indebtedness may emerge. First, as chaplain and secretary to Richard Bancroft, Bishop of London, Harsnet had been licenser of books for the press, and such a function could have brought his opinions to Shakespeare's attention. Such notice could, moreover, have been made still more likely by the fact that Bancroft himself was said to have written parts of Harsnet's *Declaration*. In 1604, on the death of Whitgift, James chose as Archbishop of Canterbury the same Bancroft who, aided by Harsnet, had with rigor and severity in the closing six years of Elizabeth's reign fought against sham demoniacs and exorcists. For example, public excitement had been aroused through an exorcising Puritan preacher, condemned as fraudulent in 1599 by a high commission including Bancroft and exposed by Harsnet in *A Discovery of the Fraudulent Practises of John Darrel* (1599).[32]

But it was against Roman Catholic exorcists that Harsnet's *Declaration* was mainly directed. Deriving from Bishop Bancroft's exposure of exorcistic trickery ascribed to Jesuits, the *Declaration* was caused to be written, or written, by him and published anonymously in 1603 by order of the Privy Council. Reissued in 1604 and 1605, it also shared in the anti-Catholic feeling surrounding the Gunpowder

[31]Robert Stevenson, in *PMLA*, LXVII (1952), 898-902; article repr. in *Shakespeare's Religious Frontier* (The Hague, 1958), pp. 62-66. On Harsnet cf. Muir, Appendix 7, pp. 253-256; "Samuel Harsnett and *King Lear*," *Review of English Studies*, N.S. II (1951), 11-21; "Shakespeare and Harsnett," *N&Q*, CXCVII (Dec. 20, 1952), pp. 555-556.

[32]Cf. John Darrell's *A Detection of That Sinnful . . . Discours, of Samuel Harshnet* (1600), pp. 7, 8.

Plot of November 5, 1605. Partly in consequence of such exposures, the Church of England, by official canon in the revised *Constitutions and Canons Ecclesiasticall* (1604), forbade any minister, without license, to cast out devils, "under paine of the imputation of Imposture, or Cousenage" (sig. [M4^{v}]).

Moreover, Harsnet had in a *cause célèbre* in 1599 licensed for the press his old friend John Hayward's *The First Part of the Life . . . of King Henrie the IIII*, eulogistically dedicated to the Earl of Essex, Southampton's friend. Presumed Shakespearean associations with the Essex group, as well as Harsnet's threatened share in Hayward's punishment, might also have linked the dramatist and Harsnet. Further, the latter, like Hayward, soon found favor under James, who became Shakespeare's royal patron; by 1605, Harsnet had been elected master of Pembroke Hall in succession to Lancelot Andrewes and was to rise higher.

Significantly for Shakespeare, Harsnet's exposure of demonic possession suited James, who employed him in investigations for which the king assumed credit. The monarch's interest in demoniacs appears, for instance, in his *Daemonologie* (Edinburgh, 1597): "whereby shal these possessed folks be discerned fra them that ar trubled with a natural Phrensie or Manie" (p. 70). During the first part of his reign, especially, his intense curiosity in the subject accompanied his increasing skepticism. About the time of *Lear*, for example, James had, in April 1605, proudly exposed the supernatural claims of Richard Haydock, the "Sleeping Preacher" of Oxford.[33] Sir Roger Wilbraham entered in his journal that "The king's majestie, sithence his happie comyng, by his owne skill hath discovered 2 notorious impostures." The second was "of a woman pretended to be bewitched, that cast up at her mouth pynnes, & pynnes were taken by divers in her fitts out of her brest."[34] On October 10, 1605, King James sent Robert Cecil his diagnosis of this woman, convinced that no demoniacal possession, though some fraud, existed in her case.[35] Both Ban-

[33]Cf. Edmund Lodge's *Illustrations of British History* (1838), III, 154-155, 157-160.

[34]*The Journal of Sir Roger Wilbraham . . . 1593-1616*, ed. Harold S. Scott, *Camden Miscellany*, X (1902), 69-70. See also an account of the woman in the *Diary of Walter Yonge, Esq.*, ed. George Roberts, Camden Soc. (1848), p. 12; C. L'Estrange Ewen, *Witchcraft in the Star Chamber* (1938), pp. 28-36. See G. L. Kittredge, "King James I and The Devil Is an Ass," *MP*, IX (1911), 207.

[35]See James's letter to Cecil of this date describing her confession. In addition, James diagnosed her swelling as having been "occasioned by the disease called the mother,

croft and Harsnet, moreover, appear to have played important parts in disclosing the pretense.[36]

When, in 1605-1606, *Volpone* was acted, Jonson could have gratified his king by inserting a scene of sham demoniacal possession: amid spasms, the advocate Voltore pretends to cast up pins. A decade later, Jonson repeated the compliment in *The Devil Is an Ass*, which contained a satirically topical demoniac scene that seems loosely related to the plot.[37] Commemorating royal acumen in that piece, Jonson, like Shakespeare in both *Lear* and *Macbeth* (1606), drew upon Harsnet to expose pretended possession. Besides *Volpone*, other plays about the time of *Lear* and *Macbeth* catered to James's interest in demonology. For example, Shakespeare's own King's Men also acted in Barnabe Barnes's *The Divils Charter: A Tragædie . . . of Pope Alexander the Sixt* before James on Candlemas Night, 1606/07, closing a season which had been opened by *Lear*, performed at court in Christmas, 1606. In addition, a comedy which James returned to

---

wherewith she was oftentimes vehemently afflicted. . . ." Historical Manuscripts Commission, *Calendar of the Manuscripts of . . . the Marquess of Salisbury . . . at Hatfield House, Hertfordshire*, Pt. XVII, ed. M. S. Giuseppi (1938), pp. 450-451. The woman's insensitivity to pain when she was stuck with pins (". . . Aciculis puncta, caruit omni sensu doloris," Robert Johnston, *Historia rerum Britannicarum* [Amsterdam, 1655], p. 401) has obvious affinities with Edgar's Tom o' Bedlam role.

In Lear's reference to "*Hysterica passio!*" as "this mother" which "swells up toward my heart" (II.iv.56-57), Shakespeare, as in Harsnet's case, may also recall a work by one of James's favorites: Edward Jorden's *A Brief Discourse of a Disease Called the Suffocation of the Mother* (1603). Physician to the queen and trusted by Robert Cecil, Jorden was also adviser to the king and in sympathy with his antiexorcistic and antiwitchcraft views. In his book, Jorden, complementing Harsnet's treatment of exorcism, offered a naturalistic explanation for the disease. Cf. Timothy Bright's *A Treatise . . . of English Medicines* (1615), p. 47, on the naturalistic cure of "All suffocations of the Matrix." Remedies for the illness, to which males too were prone, are suggested in *The Treasurie of Hidden Secrets* (1600), sig. [E3], "For the Mother that riseth upon a man . . . when the Mother riseth up to the heart. . . ." (In addition to its other significances, Lear's suppression of "the mother" may also suggest his antigenerative theme.)

Cf. Nashe, *The Unfortunate Traveller*, in *Works*, II, 318; *The Problemes of Aristotle* (1597), sig. H4; Jonson, *Poetaster* (1601), III.i.185; *Bartholomew Fair* (1614), I.v.168; Michael Drayton, *Poly-olbion* [1612], p. 102, "The Seaventh Song," ll. 19-28; *Celestina or the Tragi-Comedy of Calisto and Melibea*, tr. James Mabbe (1631), ed. H. Warner Allen (New York, [1923]), p. 118: "every minute I was ready to die with pain of the mother, which rising in my breast, swelled up to my throat, and was ready to stifle me. . . ."

[36]On Bancroft and Harsnet's role see Johnston, *Historia rerum Britannicarum*, p. 401.

[37]See Kittredge, in *MP*, IX, 195-209.

Cambridge to see again, George Ruggle's *Ignoramus* (performed in 1615), contains scenes mocking exorcism.

Shakespeare's apparent inclination to reach James's concerns,[38] fully evident in *Macbeth*, manifests itself in several ways in the almost contemporaneous *Lear*. As Theobald early pointed out regarding Edgar's assumed possession, "his whole Frenzy is Satire levell'd at a modern Fact, which made no little Noise at that Period of Time: and consequently, must have been a rapturous Entertainment to the Spectators, when it was first presented." Indeed, continues Theobald, "This Transaction was so rife in every Body's Mouth, upon the Accession of King *James* the 1st to the Crown; that our Poet thought proper to make his Court, by helping forward the Ridicule of it."[39]

Miracles

> *All the Spectators stood amaz'd, and some of the simpler Sort stuck not to cry out, A Miracle, a Miracle! No, no, cry'd Basil, no Miracle, no Miracle, but a Stratagem, a Stratagem.*
>
> —Cervantes, *Don Quixote*, Pt. II, Ch. xxi

James's demoniacal authority, Harsnet, may have provided suggestions not only for Edgar's Tom o' Bedlam but also for the other half of Edgar's interpolation, the "miracle" of Gloucester's salvation from suicide. "Thy life's a miracle" (IV.vi.55), he comforts his father. Both miracles and demonic possession were current topics of royal as well as popular interest. Concerning miracle-mongering, the monarch's distrust was expressed, for instance, in his saying: "False *Miracles* and lying newes, are the foode of Superstition, which by credulitie Deludes ignorant people."[40] Resembling in this the sympathetic King of France, a title which was, incidentally, included in

[38]Documented in Henry N. Paul, *The Royal Play of Macbeth* (New York, 1950).

[39]Lewis Theobald, ed. *The Works of Shakespeare* (1733), V, 163-164.

[40]J. L. S., ed. *Flores Regii . . . Spoken by . . . James* (1627), No. 188. Harsnet, *Declaration*, p. 1, refers to a Catholic "*penned booke of* Miracles . . . an English Treatise." "The Book of Miracles," ascribed to the Jesuit father Weston, allegedly contained an account of Catholic prodigies of exorcism.

Since exorcism, miracles, and superstition were joined with Catholicism in James's and the popular mind, anti-Catholic feeling, ca. 1605, is significant for our problem. In the same year as the Gunpowder Plot, James at Oxford advised students to fly Catholicism (*Calendar of State Papers . . . Venice . . . 1603-1607*, Sept. 14, 1605, p. 270), and in some early years of his reign, at least, James would have approved of plays satirizing Papists; see ibid., p. 361, June 14, 1606. From James's coin, an angel, the crosses were early in his reign removed, as was *et est mirabile* from Elizabeth's

James's style,[41] the English monarch's "reason" warred with "miracle" (cf. France at I.i.222-223, regarding a "faith that reason without miracle / Should never plant in me"). Such miracles included the curing of the "King's Evil," which James "knew a *Device*, to aggrandize the *Virtue* of Kings, when *Miracles* were in fashion; but he let the World believe it, though he smiled at it, in his own *Reason*."[42] A letter dated October 8, 1603, from London to Rome, explains that James "non vedeva come potessero guarire l'infermi senza miracolo, et qià li miracoli erano cessati et non se facevano più: et cosi haveva paura di commettere qualche superstitione. . . ."[43] Exhibiting the patent fraudulence of Edgar's "miracle," acted out before the audience, Shakespeare avoided direct verbal attack and yet seemed to demonstrate a method of such trickery. Earlier in his career a fraudulent miracle had already been depicted, in the second part of *Henry VI* (II.i.59-164), where Blind Simpcox's alleged restoration of sight at St. Alban's shrine is exposed.

Through Edgar's role, in turn, demonic possession and "miracles" are thus plainly shown to be frauds: the first, publicly assumed as part of a disguise during banishment; the second, a benevolent and admitted "trifling" (IV.vi.33) played, in the audience's full view, upon a suicidal and blind old man. For Harsnet in his *Declaration* had not only assailed pretended possession; he had also, like James, attacked as heathenish superstition the fraudulent belief in miracles.

Prognostications

Through a similar dramatic device, moreover, Shakespeare seems to have made contact with a third related concern of James, superstitious faith in astrological prognostications, especially those which

---

coin; in addition, James was loath to cross sufferers from the "King's Evil" with a coin, as Elizabeth had done (see Raymond Crawfurd, *The King's Evil* [Oxford, 1911], pp. 82-88). Confused overtones of the above, along with other meanings, may therefore be present in the mad Lear's exclamation ("No, they cannot touch me for coining; I am the king himself") at IV.vi.83-84.

[41]On his accession, James was proclaimed "King of the realms of England, France and Ireland." See S. T. Bindoff, "The Stuarts and Their Style," *English Historical Review*, LX (1945), 192.

[42]Arthur Wilson, *The History of Great Britain, Being the Life and Reign of King James the First* (1653), p. 289.

[43]Public Record Office, London, *Roman Transcripts*, Gen. Ser., Vol. LXXXVII, containing extracts from letters in the Archives of the Vatican, quoted in Crawfurd, *The King's Evil*, p. 83.

were personal and political.[44] First, hearing Edmund's soliloquy expose his amoral values and his plan to deprive Edgar (I.ii.1-22), then seeing the operation of the villain's plot to damage his brother in Gloucester's eyes (I.ii.28-106), the spectators, during Gloucester's next speech (I.ii.107-123), clearly observe how the gullible are taken in. For Gloucester, by way of commentary, offers a prognostication in which Edmund's patently false statements regarding Edgar are assumed to confirm the earl's own astrological fears. "This villain of mine," he exclaims, in excited confirmation, "comes under the prediction" (I.ii.114-115). In close juxtaposition, *Lear* and *Macbeth*, whose affinities with James's concerns seem beyond question, demonstrate the dangers of uncritical trust in such supernatural prognostications.

Indeed, in Shakespeare's play whatever "auricular assurance" (I.ii.94) of supernatural intervention arrives comes by way of the nameless and menacingly unclear "rumble" (III.ii.14) of the thunder from above and by way of the fraudulent "grumble" (III.iv.43) of Edgar's demons from below. As on the heath, Edgar thus serves ironically to confound spuriously infernal with dubiously supernal effects. In his demonic and miraculous portrayal the dramatic themes of human and cosmic alienation are emphasized. Hence, his role furnished more than an entertaining audience-pleaser or a flattering treatment of the royal patron's obsessions. By connecting the supposed machinations of hell and heaven and by revealing complementary below-stage echoes to the heaven-directed agitations of the protagonists, Edgar's apparently unfunctional interpolation in fact provides an effective contribution to the general thematic structure and unity.

FEELING AND STOICISM

> *the King is the* summum genus, *under whom are many subordinate degrees of men, till at last wee descend to the Begger the* Infima species *of mankinde, whose misery cannot be subdivided into any lesser fortune.*
>
> —Wye Saltonstall, *Picturæ loquentes* (1635)

[44]In regard to James's questioning of astrological prognostications, see below, Ch. vii. In his *Basilicon Doron*, p. 109, he affirms: ". . . all Prophecies, visions, and prophetick dreames are accomplished and ceased in Christ." Therefore, he urges, "take no heede to freets," a Scottish term signifying superstitions or omens, "either in dreames, or any other things: for that errour proceedeth of ignorance. . . ." Prognostications might involve the credulity of "simple creatures," or they might include

Gradually leaving "free things and happy shows behind" (III.vi.108), Edgar in his progression into the community of human suffering reaches a stage where it is still "portable" (III.vi.111). Comparing his sorrow with Lear's (III.vi.105-113), he underlines the analogy: "He childed as I father'd!" His sympathy suggests even a confusion in roles: "My tears begin to take his part so much" (III.vi.60); and, like his "better," he has suffered "false opinion" below, as well as "high noises" (III.vi.114-115) above. While the king conducts the protagonist's business, Edgar is left to voice its developing rationale, feeling. Ironically, only the mad beggar can give adequate expression to the disorder Lear experiences: "I will keep still," the king cries, clinging to Edgar, "with my philosopher" (III.iv.180).

By the third act the plea for feeling has come appropriately from the lowest of mankind, beggar and madman; these, like the tragedy's highest, experience most cruelly the want of pity. Since poverty could thus be seen as a symbol of human insensitivity, it is, significantly, their recognition of the poor and outcast that signals the high-ranking protagonists' progress in feeling. By the third act, too, Lear's *gradus* in compassion is ironically expressed toward the Fool, who in the first two acts had tutored him in practical "reason" (III.ii.72-73). For it is the tragedy's central act, after two introductory ones evoking practical considerations, that emphasizes feeling: Edgar's role as Poor Tom and his soliloquy (III.vi.105-113), for example, and Lear's buffeting by the storm and his madness, climaxed in the third act's closing scene by the passion of Gloucester's blinding.

Generally, madmen, beggars, and fools might have been considered immune to pain, being too low or insensitive for feeling. Paradoxically, therefore, the presence onstage of such characters as Poor Tom, thrusting pins into his bare flesh, would have provided a perverse and walking reminder of the problem of human feeling. For the audience, moreover, such demoniacal possession was attested by the absence of pain on pin-pricking. Edgar's "mortified bare arms" (II.iii.15) prepares for Gloucester's torment ("Bind fast his corky arms," III.vii.29), as does Edmund's self-wounding of his arm (II.i.34). And Tom's small piercings are merely dramatic analogues of

---

half-truths which were the devil's lures. Satan, James's *Daemonologie*, p. 22, observes, "will make his schollers to creepe in credite with Princes, by fore-telling them manie greate thinges; parte true, parte false: For if all were false, he would tyne credite at all handes; but alwaies doubtsome, as his Oracles were."

larger shocks. "In thy anointed flesh rash boarish fangs" (III.vii.57), cries Gloucester of Lear, to be followed by the earl's own ineffable passion, here ironically foreshadowed by him in reference to the king, "thy cruel nails / Pluck out his poor old eyes" (III.vii.55-56); Lear comments, on awaking, "I feel this pin prick" (IV.vii.56); and the state itself, at the end (V.iii.320), is described as "gor'd."

Like the Fool, simultaneously involved and disengaged, Edgar humanizes and translates for both characters and audience the almost unbearable suffering. As the Fool strives grotesquely toward the release of laughter, Edgar interposes the solace of tears (e.g., III.vi.60). To the spectators the innovation of Edgar's quick changes, like that of the Fool's rapid jesting, could have made him more theatrically acceptable. In addition, while the Fool's quasi-comic viewpoint permits a distancing on pain, Edgar's sympathetic perspective facilitates the pathos which, according to Walpole, makes a tragic view possible. Significantly, Sidney's *The Defence of Poesie* altered the Aristotelian terror and pity into admiration and commiseration; tragedy drew tears.[45] Indeed, it is Edgar himself who defines the direction of tragedy (IV.i.5): "The lamentable change is from the best."

Further, just as the Fool is fool to worldly imprudence, so Edgar is fool to its unhappy consequences. After the truth-speaking Cordelia is banished, the "practical" Fool appears (I.iv.100); and, after the latter vanishes (III.vi.88), Edgar, like Lear, remains, with overtones of theatrical self-reflexivity, as the fool of feeling: "Bad is the trade that must play the fool to sorrow" (IV.i.38). In a world where neither truth nor prudence suffices, neither honesty nor expediency, neither Cordelia nor the Fool (V.iii.305), feeling must suffice for knowledge. Given his incomprehensible universe, man cannot "see." That feeling is a kind of seeing, indeed, a prerequisite of it, the blinded Gloucester discovers: Man ". . . will not see / Because he does not feel" (IV.i.68-69). To Lear's "yet you see how this world goes," Gloucester can reply, "I see it feelingly" (IV.vi.149-150). Earlier, Lear similarly cues Edgar's first entrance as Mad Tom: "Expose thyself to feel what wretches feel" (III.iv.34).

In this world, too, while the villains are unfeeling and therefore morally blind, Gloucester becomes physically blind, and the eye of Lear's mind, his sanity, is put out. Further, Edgar, who would be

[45] *Complete Works,* III, 23-24.

thought a beast by the beasts, is pitied by Gloucester and Lear; the subjectivity of perception, its basis in feeling, is thus emphasized. Indeed, the limitations of ratiocination divorced from natural compassion become progressively visible to Lear and his followers. Such limitations, except perhaps for a brief final moment in Edmund's case, are invisible to the villains, precisely because they cannot feel.[46]

Apropos, in his revulsion against rationalism and Stoicism, Montaigne had already provided an influential Renaissance precedent more symptomatic than Seneca's. For, as unmoved mover, Seneca's good man will, in Lodge's words, "assist his neighbour that weepeth, without weeping himselfe," and will "doe all this with a peaceable minde."[47] But Seneca's denial of pity in part provoked seventeenth-century insistence on the benevolence of feeling, whose echoes may perhaps be overheard in Lear's denunciation of "hard hearts," Gloucester's expressions of feeling, and Edgar's self-characterization as "pregnant to good pity." In addition, the irony of Lear's reference to the frenzied and shivering beggar as "this philosopher" (III.iv.158), "noble philosopher" (III.iv.176), and "my philosopher" (III.iv.180), suggesting a visual commentary on Stoicism, recalls Montaigne's "I am no Philosopher: Evils oppresse me according as they waigh" (III, 189).[48] Despite the influence of Stoicism, then, opposition to its suppression of emotion was virtually a universally professed commonplace.

Feeling, moreover, shows the limitations of the Stoic refuge. Like Gloucester after his suicide attempt, Edgar attempts a stoical rec-

[46]In relation to Goneril's repudiation of pity (e.g., "Fools do those villains pity . . . ," IV.ii.54), uttered against her husband, Albany's observation that her death "Touches us not with pity" (V.iii.232) is poetically just.

[47]*The Workes of . . . Seneca,* tr. Thomas Lodge (1614), p. 608. Against Stoicism's limitations, the Epicureans were especially critical, e.g., Epicurus against Zeno (cf. the Stoic-Epicurean antithesis in Ch. ix below). To Lucian, a Stoic was a man who, facing a contradiction, was incapable of seeing it; cf. Marcel Caster, *Lucien et la pensée religieuse de son temps* (Paris, 1937), p. 160, and on providence, pp. 123-178.

[48]In Montaigne the rejection of Stoicism and its great chainwork of "Stoycall causes" is connected with his own idea of the "Dieu inconnaissable." (See his "Apology" and discussion above.) So, for Edgar, who parallels Lear's sufferings, the discovery of the limitations of Stoicism might thus be a point of contact with Lear's developing cosmic Epicureanism.

See W. Lee Ustick, "Changing Ideals of Aristocratic Character and Conduct in Seventeenth-Century England," *MP*, XXX (1932), 147-166 (p. 164: "One of the most notable traits of *l'honnête homme* of the late seventeenth century . . . is . . . his 'good Heart' "). See Henry W. Sams, "Anti-Stoicism in Seventeenth- and Early Eighteenth-

onciliation (IV.i.3-9).[49] But such Stoic comfort is at once shattered by the glimpse of his father, blinded, plunging Edgar more deeply into inconsolable feeling (IV.i.10-12). Stoicism appears presumption in such a universe. Still further, neither the Fool, schoolmaster in worldly providence (e.g., II.iv.67), nor Edgar in Stoic or syncretic providence (V.ii.9, 11), suits his words to his convictions. Recognizing the disparity between reason and feeling, the Fool, despite his practical counsel, suffers the storm with his master; and Edgar doles out Stoic consolation but cannot swallow his own *consolatio*. In his self-reflection (e.g., IV.i.10-12), and almost consistently throughout, Edgar in effect cancels out his own soothing advice to his father: "Bear free and patient thoughts" (IV.vi.80), much as, having counseled Gloucester, "Thou must be patient" (IV.vi.180), Lear, too, recks not his own rede.

In Edgar, the genealogy of the man of feeling recalls Renaissance countercurrents against Stoic rationalism and suppression of emotion. Like Gloucester and Lear, Edgar sees man "with too much weakness for the Stoic's pride" and offers with them a plea for *les misérables* in the indifferent new world recorded, for instance, in Bruegel. Against Stoic impassiveness, as well as current "hardening of heart" (III.vi.78-79), for example, the "good heart" also moves the perceptive, yet loyal, Kent and the aware, yet self-sacrificing, Cordelia. The staid Albany is "almost ready to dissolve" (V.iii.203). Indeed, Lear's tears, Gloucester exclaims, move even the tears of heaven: "Yet, poor old heart, he holp the heavens to rain" (III.vii.61).

Century England," *SP*, XLI (1944), 67. Marston, e.g., in *The Scourge of Villanie*, Satyre II, ll. 5-6 (*The Poems of John Marston*, ed. Arnold Davenport [Liverpool, 1961], p. 106), rejects the "Stoickes patience." Pandulpho, in his *Antonios Revenge* (1599-1601), IV.v (*Plays*, I, 121), remarks, "Man will breake out, despight Philosophie." See also, in Marston's *The Dutch Courtezan* (1603-04), I.ii (*Plays*, II, 80), Freevill on the folly of going against nature.

On the impracticality of the Stoic restraint, see also Sir Thomas Browne (*Works*, I, 67) and *Much Ado about Nothing* (V.i.35-38), denying that philosophers who generally banish emotion could yet patiently endure a private bodily pain; and Webster's *The Duchess of Malfi*, V.v.78-80, varying *Much Ado*'s toothache example: "there's Philosophy for you." Cf. *Taming of the Shrew*, I.i.29-31. In protest against the want of pity, see *Timon of Athens*, III.ii.93, IV.iii.492.

[49]Opening Act IV, Edgar's choral exposition at his nadir is preliminary to the momentary hopefulness of the same act's close. To know one is at the worst is some consolation. At a parallel point in *Macbeth* (IV.ii.23-24), Ross expresses a similar sentiment. Cf. Tilley T216 ("When Things are at the worst they will mend"); B59 ("When Bale is highest boot is next"); W892 ("When the World is at the worst it will mend"); D84; W918.

Further, as Lear verges on a cosmic Epicureanism, so Gloucester finds "Stoic" death by suicide and Stoic life by endurance both difficult; and, like Lear's, his end, as described by Edgar (V.iii.196-199), is hardly a Stoic one.

Having traversed heath storm and farmhouse ritual (III.vi), Edgar changes from mad beggar to rustic peasant. Suicide, a possible Stoic solution, Edgar denies his father. For the son life seems a "treasury," which some, through experience of life, would suicidally deplete (IV.vi.42-44). Yet, contrary to his advice to his father, Edgar sees later that painful clinging to life may itself be irrational, keeping us from cutting short our suffering:

> O! our lives' sweetness,
> That we the pain of death would hourly die
> Rather than die at once! (V.iii.184-186)[50]

And in further speeches Edgar evinces un-Stoic lapses as choral measurer of human pain. For instance, at the mad Lear's entrance Edgar exclaims: "O thou side-piercing sight!" (IV.vi.85); while at the king's encounter with Gloucester he admits, ". . . my heart breaks at it" (IV.vi.143). Finally, when Edgar's visible education in suffering has almost run its course, his "nothing" (II.iii.21) is more clearly defined. Feeling sustains identity. To Gloucester's "Now, good sir, what are you?" he can reply,

> A most poor man, made tame to Fortune's blows;
> Who, by the art of known and feeling sorrows,
> Am pregnant to good pity. (IV.vi.221-224)

Significantly, two of Edgar's cruxes may arise not only from immediate dramatic requirements but also, in adapting his language to his kinsmen, from his persistent role as "pregnant to good pity."

TWO CRUXES

"Ripeness Is All"

The first of Edgar's two cruxes involves "ripeness is all," and the context is Edgar's return, in haste, to save his father's life from the victorious forces of evil. Once again, this time passively, Gloucester

[50]See Tilley L254, which omits Erasmus' *Praise of Folly*, p. 50. The *topos* recurs in Osorio da Fonseca's *The Five Bookes*, tr. William Blandie (1576), fol. 86v. Cf. Browne, ". . . the long habit of living indisposeth us for dying . . ." (*Works*, IV, 44).

confesses suicidal yearnings. And once again Edgar must contrive, through some way comprehensible to the old man, to rescue him. In the initial suicide rescue (IV.vi), Edgar was reduced to the transparent acting out of a "miraculous" fraud, couched in terms calculated to convince his father. Now, again, Edgar must resort to any desperate remedy to move his father to further experience of life's chances:

> *Edg.* Away, old man! give me thy hand: away!
> King Lear hath lost, he and his daughter ta'en.
> Give me thy hand; come on.
> *Glou.* No further, sir; a man may rot even here.
> *Edg.* What! in ill thoughts again? Men must endure
> Their going hence, even as their coming hither:
> Ripeness is all. Come on.
> *Glou.* And that's true too. [*Exeunt.*] (V.ii.5-11)

In a resolute Christian interpretation it has been asserted that "By 'Ripeness is all,' then, Shakespeare means that the fruit will fall in its time, and man dies when God is ready."[51] So certain is this commentator that this is what "Shakespeare means" that he apparently rejects or minimizes a non-Christian interpretation. That he is partly right, but that he is too exclusive, in view of the complex and syncretic nature of the play, may be indicated by additional citations on both sides. "Men must endure their going hence" is the burden of the service for the "Buriall of the Dead" in *The Booke of Common Prayer*,[52] whose rhythms would have continued, especially in those recent times of plague, to ring in Jacobean minds; the text is from Job xiv.1-2, and the burden is acceptance: "Man that is borne of woman, is of short continuance. . . . He shooteth forth as a flower, & is cut downe. . . ." Dante (*Paradiso* xix.48) had spoken of Lucifer's unripe fall ("Per non aspettar lume, cadde acerbo"). The Homilies assert that "our life doeth lie in the hand of god, who will take it away when it pleseth him. . . ." Citing Wisdom vii.6, "all men . . . come into this worlde, and goe out of the same in lyke sort," the Homilies remind us of "our mortall and earthly generation."[53]

[51] James V. Cunningham, *Woe or Wonder: The Emotional Effect of Shakespearean Tragedy* (Denver, 1951), p. 14; see pp. 9-15.

[52] 1590, sig. Pviiv; the same citation appears in the Homilies, ". . . miserie of all mankind" (*Certaine Sermons* [1587], sig. B).

[53] *Certaine Sermons*, sigs. [Ll2v], B. Edgar's "ripeness" advice has affinities also with Leibnitz' counsel of *Fatum Christianum*: ". . . il y a Fatum Christianum, une Destinée

In *A Godlie and Learned Commentarie upon . . . Ecclesiastes* (1585) John Serranus argues "*That all things and enterprises hath their proper and set times*, and that, by the providence of GOD, both Nature her selfe, and also the fellowship of man are wisely governed. . . ."[54] The central text for the concept, Ecclesiastes, especially iii, dwells on the appointed time for all things. Similarly, Paracelsus advises: ". . . before the appointed time God gives no fruit; everything must come in due time. . . . And as in everything else, time must complete its cycle; whether a thing ripens sooner or later depends on God."[55] John Wilkins in *A Discourse concerning the Beauty of Providence* (1649) declares that the wisdom of providence "hath disposed to every thing its particular season. This is that which we call, the *fulnesse* of time, the *ripenesse* of season" (p. 8).

Yet the concept "men must endure their going hence, even as their coming hither" was a commonplace of the Renaissance. The pagan Plutarch had observed, ". . . it is no part of a man whose understanding is cleere . . . to be ignorant . . . that man is a mortall creature, or that he is borne upon this condition, once to die."[56] Thomas Adams' *Mystical Bedlam* (1615) restates the view: "If a man lookes into what *life* it selfe is, hee cannot but finde . . . that hee must die. *As soon as we are born, wee beginne to draw to our end.* Life it selfe is nothing, but a journey to death" (p. 80). Bacon ("Of Death")

---

certaine de toutes choses. . . ." *God. Guil. Leibnitii opera philosophica*, ed. Joannes E. Erdmann (Berlin, 1840), p. 764. See also S. F. Johnson, "*The Spanish Tragedy*, or Babylon Revisited," *Essays on Shakespeare and Elizabethan Drama in Honor of Hardin Craig*, ed. Richard Hosley (Columbia, Mo., 1962), pp. 27-28.

[54]Tr. John Stockwood, p. 163. See also Ecclesiastes viii.6. Cf. *The Colloquies of Erasmus*, tr. N. Bailey (1878), I, 184-185, in which one character observes, regarding the body, "So long we may stay in an Inn till the Host bids us be gone," and another recalls Plato, ". . . no staying any longer in it, than during the Pleasure of him that plac'd him there."

[55]*Selected Writings*, ed. Jolande Jacobi, tr. Norbert Guterman (New York, 1951), pp. 282-283.

[56]*Morals*, tr. Holland, p. 526. See the conventional collection in the "Epistles Consolatorie" of Angell Day's *The English Secretary* (1599), Pt. I, pp. 112-128; and Benjamin Boyce, "The Stoic *Consolatio* and Shakespeare," *PMLA*, LXIV (1949), 771-780. Ripeness is, indeed, a feature of Christian, as well as pagan, consolatory literature. See Erasmus' insistence on awaiting the "laufull day" set by "our soverayne capitayne" in *A Treatise Perswadynge a Man Patientlye to Suffre the Deth of His Frende* ([1532]), sig. Biii^{v}; and the uses of "ripeness" in Thomas Wilson's *Arte of Rhetorique* (1560), ed. G. H. Mair (Oxford, 1909), pp. 78, 83-84, and in Robert Southwell's *The Triumphs over Death* (1596), sigs. C2, [C4^{v}], D1^{v}.

reechoes the notion: "It is as natural to die as to be born."[57] Mutianus Rufus concurs: "Being born, we die, and the end hangs already from the beginning."[58] Seneca's *De remediis fortuitorum*, translated by Robert Whyttynton (1547), has "Reason" replying to "Sensualites'" "Thou shalt dye" with "Upon the condicion I entred that I shuld depart" (sig. Aiii). Montaigne had expressed the commonplace: "The same way you came from death to life, returne without passion or amazement, from life to death" (I, 87).

Indeed, the very image of "ripeness" is, in a sense, a naturalistic one, as suitable to pagans as to Christians. For instance, it is a recurrent and underlying metaphor in Epictetus: ". . . why do heads of grain grow? . . . is it not that they may also be harvested? Since they do not grow for themselves alone. . . . In like manner . . . in the case of men as well it is a curse never to die; it is like never growing ripe, never being harvested." God commands plants "when to ripen," and "they ripen; when again He bids them drop their fruit . . . they remain quiet and take their rest."[59] Moreover, a secular discussion of ripeness in relation to the moral virtue of "maturity" in action occurs in Sir Thomas Elyot's *The Governour* (1531), ripeness being the mean between behavioral extremes: ". . . ripe or redy, as frute whan it is ripe, it is at the very poynte to be gathered and eaten."[60] Elyot here closely resembles the pagan treatment of *maturitas* in the *Noctes Atticae* of Aulus Gellius (A.D. ca. 123-169), when the latter speaks of "grain and fruits . . . which are neither unripe and hard, nor falling and decayed, but full-grown and ripened in their proper time."[61] Ripeness is also, in fact, a notion which no atheist could gainsay. John Hull in *Saint Peters Prophesie of These Last Daies* (1611), for example, assails "these monster-bred Atheists," who, denying that God "sets up, and pulls downe . . . makes, and can destroy," hold that "every thing hath his time, the man like the beast, the beast like the hearbe . . ." (p. 9). Contextually, "ripeness" is in direct response to Gloucester's "rot," and a sequence of naturalistic images supports

[57] *Works*, VI, 380.

[58] Lewis W. Spitz, "The Conflict of Ideals in Mutianus Rufus," *JWCI*, XVI (1953), 136.

[59] Epictetus, *Discourses*, tr. W. A. Oldfather, Loeb Classical Lib. (1926), pp. 249, 101.

[60] *The Boke Named the Governour*, ed. H. H. S. Croft (1883), I, 244-245.

[61] *Attic Nights*, tr. Rolfe, II, 239, 241. Cf. Cicero, *De senectute*, Loeb Classical Lib. (1923), p. 83.

this sense: Lear's "He's dead and rotten" (V.iii.285), "She's dead as earth" (V.iii.261); Kent's "your first of difference and decay" (V.iii. 288); as well as Albany's "this great decay" (V.iii.297). Moreover, the commonplace had, in Shakespeare, already been mocked, in a series of *entendres*, by the libertine Jaques:

> And so, from hour to hour, we ripe and ripe,
> And then, from hour to hour, we rot and rot.[62]

Evidently, too, Edgar's remark has a demonstrable Stoic sense. The acceptance of passive resignation and endurance in a universe of suffering is both characteristically Stoic and an element of the Christian outlook, in both early times of Roman admixture and neo-Stoic Renaissance times of disintegration and crises. Indeed, the Stoic "men must endure," in part perhaps a reaction and a refuge in a universe ruled by a *Deus absconditus*, had been an answer of the ancients to an analogous crisis. Finally, Edgar's speech, containing one of the oldest of human commonplaces, is in the tradition of ancient consolatory oratory (e.g., all men must resign themselves to age and the coming of death) and was in the Renaissance proverbial (e.g., "He that is once born once must die," etc.).[63]

The affinity of Stoicism and Christianity was recognized by Fitzherbert, who lauds the Stoics' "doctrine of Gods particular providence . . . as is manifest in *Senica*," the latter requiring "a resignation of his wil, to the will of God, in the patient suffering, & willing acceptaunce, of all the calamities that it shall please God to lay uppon him in this life."[64] John Wilkins' *Discourse* (1649) cites the Stoics to support the alleged exclusively Christian idea; they have excellent passages, he asserts, and he concludes that, "if meer *reason* could advance *Heathen* men to such resolutions, much more then should a *Christians faith* in the Providence of God," advising a man to "turn *Stoick*" (pp. 109, 112).

[62] *As You Like It*, II.vii.26-27. Jaques's speech is, of course, a Renaissance *topos*. Cf. Day's *The English Secretary*, Pt. I, p. 116: "Knowe yee not, that all thinges doe by little and a little growe into ripenesse, and foorthwith by degrees fall into rottennesse?"

[63] Cf. André Marie Jean Festugière, *Personal Religion among the Greeks* (Berkeley, 1954), p. 52. On topical recurrence in ancient oratory see Stanley F. Bonner, *Roman Declamation in the Late Republic and Early Empire* (Liverpool, 1949). Such topics are preserved in Nannus Mirabellius, *Polyanthea*, and similar Renaissance florilegia. See Curtius, pp. 80-82; Tilley B140, D327, etc.; *2 Henry IV*, III.ii.42.

[64] *Second Part of a Treatise*, pp. 16-17, with sidenote reference to "Seneca. lib. 4 de benef. c.6."

In short, from one point of view, Christianity and Stoicism merge indistinguishably with regard to the harsh necessities of this temporary life and the need for endurance. For the Middle Ages, Boethius became a Christian symbol, later coming to be translated by Elizabeth. Polydore Vergil considers that in a world where fortune may be cruelly perverse man must accept his fate with resignation; but, as his modern editor notes,[65] he does not indicate whether he thought Stoicism or Christianity the superior guide to this virtue. We may compare the popular Renaissance neo-Stoic Guillaume Du Vair, who holds that bodily misfortunes, or those to our friends or possessions, are unimportant if we learn to keep our minds free from torment: "Griefe is not intollerable, but / unto them which thinke that it is so . . . what remedie but patience . . . ," as Edgar advises Gloucester (IV.vi.80), "Bear free and patient thoughts." Man, affirms Du Vair, citing a well-known *topos*, "commeth naked into the world, and shall goe naked out of / the world. . . ."[66] Closer, perhaps, to Edgar's "Men must endure / Their going hence, even as their coming hither" than many other parallels is the Stoic Epictetus' "I came into the world when it so pleased Him, and I leave it again at His pleasure. . . ."[67]

Further, according to the evidence, as *Lear* appears to be a play which seeks, on an ostensive level, the appurtenances of pagan local color, it is entirely in keeping that Gloucester should reach a position which is both quasi-pagan and quasi-Christian. The mingling of Stoic and Christian belief was encouraged, for example, in the dedication to Du Vair's *The Moral Philosophie of the Stoicks*, in which Thomas James (1598) advises: ". . . no kinde of philosophie is more profitable and neerer approching unto Christianitie . . . then the philosophie of the Stoicks."[68] "*Seneca* that christian Ethnicke (for so

[65]Denys Hay, *Polydore Vergil: Renaissance Historian and Man of Letters* (Oxford, 1952), pp. 139-140.

[66]*The Moral Philosophie of the Stoicks,* tr. Thomas James, ed. Rudolf Kirk (New Brunswick, N.J., 1951), p. 93.

[67]*Discourses,* tr. Oldfather, II, 237. Epictetus was known and translated in Shakespeare's day; an English translation appeared in 1567. See R. R. Bolgar, *The Classical Heritage and Its Beneficiaries* (Cambridge, Eng., 1958), pp. 512-513, listing versions published in French in 1544, 1567, 1591; German, 1534; and Italian, 1564. Marston in "To my equall Reader" prefixed to *The Fawne* (*Plays*, II, 143) speaks of "My bosome friend good Epictetus. . . ."

[68]Ed. Kirk, p. 45. On the difficulty of extricating Christianity from Stoicism, see, e.g., Harry A. Wolfson, "Philosophical Implications of the Pelagian Controversy,"

dooth *Erasmus* terme him, for his profound wisedome & deepe judgement)" is recalled in Nicholas Gyer's *The English Phlebotomy* (1592), sig. A4. In the epistle to his translation of *The Workes . . . of Seneca* (1620) Thomas Lodge bids the reader, "What a Stoicke hath written, Reade thou like a Christian" (sig. b). As early as 1567 James Sanford's introduction to his edition of *The Manuell of Epictetus* informs his Christian readers concerning the pagan philosophical work that "there can be no Booke to the wel framing of our life more profitable and necessary" (sig. [Aiii^{v}]). In 1606 Joseph Hall's *Heaven upon Earth*, explaining Stoic thought to Christian Englishmen, shows how a Christian might more readily than a heathen Stoic attain the peace of mind sought by Seneca.[69] Moreover, the works of Justus Lipsius, among others, consciously attempted a reconciliation between Stoicism and Christianity. "And that's true too" (V.ii.11) affirms the pagan Gloucester to his virtuous-heathen son, tentatively accepting a Stoicism which mediates between paganism and Christianity.

In addition, it may be recalled that in Sidney's *Arcadia*, employing a *consolatio* analogous to Edgar's, Philoclea, unrecognized, demands of Pyrocles, "if she be dead, was she not borne to die?" (I, 486). By contrast, the *Arcadia* also offers Cordelia-like intimations of unripeness. While Pamela alludes to Dorilaus' "unripe death" (I, 187), Pyrocles, thinking his beloved Philoclea dead, mourns, "what is the cause, that she, that heavenly creature . . . should by the heavens be destined to so unripe an ende? Why should unjustice so prevaile? Why was she seene to the world, so soone to be ravished from us?" (I, 487). Providence is impugned in Pyrocles' grief at her supposed unripe end: "Did she excell for this? have I prayed for this?" (I, 483). Like Lear over the corpse of Cordelia, Pyrocles, holding himself "to be the example of the heavens hate" (I, 484), exclaims: "Philoclea is dead, and yet Life is not ashamed to continue upon the earth" (I, 485). Again, "so often did an unspeakable horror strike his noble hart: to consider so unripe yeares, so fautles a beautie, the

---

Proceedings of the American Philosophical Society, CIII (1959), 562. "Il est incontestable que l'affirmation du Dieu Providence, du Destin, joue un très grand rôle dans la théologie stoïcienne," concludes Paul G. Chappuis, *La destinée de l'homme: De l'influence du Stoïcisme sur la pensée chrétienne primitive* (Geneva, 1926), p. 55.

[69] *Heaven upon Earth and Characters of Vertues and Vices*, ed. Rudolf Kirk (New Brunswick, N.J., 1948), pp. 19-51. Du Vair was a bishop of the Roman Catholic Church, while Joseph Hall was an Anglican bishop.

mansion of so pure goodnes, should have her youth so untimely cut off . . ." (II, 104).

Yet whatever religious or philosophical overtones "ripeness is all" may possess, it is apparent, first, that the phrase is motivated by dramatic exigencies. It is not uttered, in short, as conceptual *summa* but rather as conventional *suasoria* in impatient and practical urgency at a desperate moment. As elsewhere in relation to his father—for example, "Bear free and patient thoughts" (IV.vi.80)—Edgar is alleviatory, his tone palliative. Far from being decontextualized philosophic predication, the expression functions in relation to the dramatic sequence of events. Much critical speculation might benefit from Hobbes's reminder that context, if not all, may at least be a great deal: ". . . they that insist upon single texts, without considering the main design, can derive nothing from them clearly. . . ."[70]

Second, it is evident that such paternal exigencies had, in the "suicide" scene, previously produced in Edgar a similar linguistic accommodation. Finally, although the good characters tend to await "the mature time" (IV.vi.277) while the evil ones seize it,[71] it may

[70]*Leviathan*, in *English Works*, III, 602.

[71]From one point of view, Edgar's allusions to unfolding in time, like Cordelia's remark (I.i.280), may suggest a reference to the larger mysteries in which human actions move. In contrast, the time-serving villains, who seize the time and who, as Lady Macbeth advises, "Look like the time," hold with Edmund that "men / Are as the time is" (V.iii.31-32). See also II.iv.252 and IV.vi.265-266—the villains' "fruitfulness" is the "unripeness" of the virtuous. Appropriately, the wicked, who live for time, lament their own untimely dispatch: III.vii.97, IV.vi.252, V.iii.164. Indeed, Edmund himself fulfills Cordelia's first-act prediction (I.i.280), ending his confession with "the time will bring it out" (V.iii.163). In the stocks, Kent stoically accepts his "time" (II.ii.156). Yet, reading Cordelia's letter, he seems involved with the hope to redeem the dear time's waste (II.ii.168-170). The king's time is, however, unredeemable; not even Cordelia, the sequel shows, can ransom his time; note the Doctor's warning regarding Lear's "time . . . lost" (IV.vii.79-80). As earlier, Edgar had attended "the mature time" (IV.vi.277) to inform Albany of the plot against his life, so he promises him to reappear "When time shall serve" (V.i.48). Similarly, Kent had awaited "that full issue" (I.iv.3) for which he disguised himself in the fulfillment of his master's service. Now, at the fourth act's close, he observes: "'Tis time to look about" (IV.vii.92). In addition, Kent bids Cordelia preserve his incognito "Till time and I think meet" (IV.vii.11). Replying to Edmund's "your haste / Is now urged on you," Albany finally announces, "We will greet the time" (V.i.53-54). In turn, Cordelia's murder, preventable in time, is time-related; minutes too late, Edmund pleads, "Nay, send in time" (V.iii.247). Lear's "Never, never, never, never, never!" (V.iii.308) marks for him the end of possibilities in time, his temporalizing of the frequent "nothing" of the tragedy: man is "nothing" in time. While both the villains' time-space ambitions and the virtuous' vague anticipations of time redeemed seem equally unfulfilled, the play ends appropriately with a commentary on "The weight of this sad time" (V.iii.323).

be suggested that the crucial phrase seems somewhat apart from the attitude of Edgar as it is elsewhere developed in the play. In fact, Edgar appears shortly to undercut the crucial expression when, in an aside, he admits that endurance and ripeness are *not* all and that, indeed, suicide or death might be preferable to the drawn-out calamity of so long life (V.iii.184-186).

More striking, however, than any of these considerations regarding "ripeness is all" is the action of the play itself. If drama comprises the art of language and action, and the connections between them, it is worth noting that the action of the next scene comments on the language of this one. In at least one sense there (V.iii) "ripeness" is shown not to be all, when the young and most unripe Cordelia is carried onstage dead in her father's arms. Drama indicates not only by positive allusion; as in the thrice-mentioned reference to "miracles" in the dark graceless world of *King Lear* and in "Cordelia absent" it may also work by contrast and negative reminder. In view of the above, attempts to isolate "ripeness is all" as philosophical gem or as the epitome of Shakespeare's wisdom, apart from dramatic and contextual considerations, should be received with caution.

"*The Gods Are Just*"

Ye have heard that it hath bene said, An eye for an eye....
—Matthew v. 38

The second of Edgar's cruxes also involves a kinsman who has sought his life and who is now at point of death. As he had at two previous junctures accommodated himself to save his father's life, Edgar adopts his brother's verbal mode to ease the latter's death. For throughout, Edmund, like his colleagues, has followed the principle of personal, direct, and harshly "appropriate" retribution, or *lex talionis*. Literally precise and merciless eye-for-an-eye justice, it appears when Cornwall deprives Gloucester of sight on just such grounds. To the latter's defense of Lear:

> Because I would not see thy cruel nails
> Pluck out his poor old eyes . . .
> but I shall see
> The winged vengeance overtake such children,
> (III.vii.55-56, 64-65)

Cornwall replies, "See't shalt thou never" (III.vii.66). Pressing poetic justice still further, Regan urges that *both* eyes be extinguished:

"One side will mock another; th' other too" (III.vii.70). Such eye-for-an-eye implications had significantly been recognized by Edmund in his fear that Lear's great age

> had charms in it, whose title more,
> To pluck the common bosom on his side,
> And turn our impress'd lances in our eyes. (V.iii.49-51)

Cornwall's demand for immediate retribution, "I will have my revenge ere I depart his house" (III.v.1); Goneril's insistence that, since "'Tis his own blame," Lear "must needs taste his folly" (II.iv.292-293); as well as Regan's

> If it be true, all vengeance comes too short
> Which can pursue th' offender (II.i.88-89)

and

> O! Sir, to wilful men,
> The injuries that they themselves procure
> Must be their schoolmasters, (II.iv.304-306)

are examples of the sole "legal" principle to which Edmund's camp subscribes.[72]

When, therefore, the dying brother confesses and repents, Edgar eases his last moments by offering extenuating comfort in the only terms Edmund is able to comprehend, through the latter's own *lex talionis* formula:

> The Gods are just, and of our pleasant vices
> Make instruments to plague us;
> The dark and vicious place where thee he got
> Cost him his eyes. (V.iii.170-173)

Since Edmund's own "Hammurabian" view of justice seems here apotheosized, and the gods, through their "instruments," may be seen as gigantically cruel and precisely retributive avengers, the Bastard predictably concurs:

> Th' hast spoken right, 'tis true.
> The wheel is come full circle; I am here. (V.iii.173-174)

Edmund, who has, in contrast to the good characters, lived by retribution, dies by it. Indeed, his *lex talionis*, opposite to the *prisca* for-

[72]Contrast Aristotle, *Nicomachean Ethics*, tr. H. Rackham, Loeb Classical Lib. (1926), pp. 279-281: "Reciprocity however does not coincide either with Distributive or with Corrective Justice. . . . For in many cases Reciprocity is at variance with Justice."

giveness, is basically the primitive code in which guilt and causality were seen to be one. Heir of *Ananke*, the principle of retribution, causality is the necessity with which *Dike*, goddess of retribution, avenges evil; and in the same term, *Aitia*, the Greeks expressed both cause and guilt.[73]

In a universe where "Fair is foul, and foul is fair," Lear himself comes to abandon heavenly prayers and imprecations, divine and human "justicers," and the anticipated "tasting" of "wages" and "deservings." Since these imply a certain order in the universe, they seem irreconcilable with his growing sense of a mysterious cosmic irrationality. For the old king, indeed, such poetic justice eventually becomes a bitter mockery, as in

> Judicious punishment! 'twas this flesh begot
> Those pelican daughters. (III.iv.74-75)

In a world where distributive justice is not evident, retributive "justice" seems bitterly awry.

In contrast, just as Edmund's sense of lovelessness is quick to confuse lust and love—

> Yet Edmund was belov'd:
> The one the other poison'd for my sake,
> And after slew herself—(V.iii.239-241)

so the Bastard's dying moment is solaced by a kind of harsh and poetically "just" *Schadenfreude*: his father has "paid" with his eyes. Against the random "sport" of Gloucester's "flies" speech (IV.i.36-37) is posed the horrible pointedness of Edgar's "Gods are just" speech.[74] Both provide perspectives for viewing the action of the

[73]See Hans Kelsen, *Society and Nature: A Sociological Inquiry* (Chicago, 1943), pp. vii, 262-263; Anaximander, "All things pay retribution for their injustice one to another according to the ordinance of time," after Gilbert Murray, *Five Stages of Greek Religion* (Boston, [1951]), p. 33. Cf. the wheel of Justice (*Dike*) and Destiny (*Moira*) as the wheel of Time in Pindar's second Olympian ode (*The Odes of Pindar*, tr. John Sandys, Loeb Classical Lib. [1915], pp. 19, 21). On these lines as initiating the idea of the wheel of Fortune, see Gilbert Norwood, *Pindar* (Berkeley, 1945), pp. 253-255.

[74]In addition to its implicitly ironical and horrifying commentary on divine justice, Edgar's "just" may also ambiguously imply "ironically appropriate" or "precise," as in Lear's "Judicious punishment!" (III.iv.74), but Edmund seizes upon it for his own vindictive justification. In some aspects anticipating Edmund, the expedient and unscrupulous Laertes would, like Macbeth, "jump the life to come" (*Macbeth*, I.vii.7); he would send "Conscience and grace, to the profoundest pit" and "dare damnation"

play, and both are to be taken in the light of its developing dialectic. Ironically, both speeches revolve about the terrible gratuitousness of Gloucester's blinding, the first uttered by the sufferer shortly after the deed, the second by his loving son near the play's end. Since Edmund's harsh *lex talionis* is the precise opposite to Edgar's frequently expressed pity, an emotion the latter directs especially at his father, it seems unlikely to represent Edgar's outlook. To mistake these views, by ignoring dramatic context and exigencies, for those of Edgar or the tragedy itself, would thus seem to involve a misinterpretation.

Advocated by Puritans, who were both inimical to the stage and displeasing to James, such retribution would, furthermore, hardly have been applauded by many in Shakespeare's audience. Edgar's role, as already noted, reflected, in effect, a hostility to the exorcism that had been practiced by the Catholics and that had also, amidst public excitement, been performed by a Puritan preacher, who was notably attacked in Harsnet's *A Discovery of the Fraudulent Practises of John Darrel.* Among the Puritans endorsing severe retribution against adulterers was Thomas Cartwright, a leading exponent of Presbyterianism, who insisted on capital punishment. In reply, his antagonist, John Whitgift, Archbishop of Canterbury (1583-1604), argued that the New Testament had abrogated the Old Testament regarding judicial and ceremonial laws, such as death for adultery in Deuteronomy.[75] Concerning death for adultery, indeed, Shakespeare had already indicated an attitude shortly before our play, in *Measure for Measure*,[76] and appears to do so again in the person of Lear:

> I pardon that man's life. What was thy cause?
> Adultery?
> Thou shalt not die: die for adultery! No. (IV.vi.112-114)

(*Hamlet*, IV.v.132, 133). He, too, sees a "justice" in Claudius' death: "He is justly served; / It is a poison temper'd by himself" (V.ii.338-339), as well as a "justice" in his own: "I am justly kill'd with mine own treachery" (V.ii.318).

[75]See A. F. Scott Pearson, *Church & State: Political Aspects of Sixteenth Century Puritanism* (Cambridge, Eng., 1928), pp. 107-109; Thomas Cartwright, *The Second Replie . . . agaynst Maister Doctor Whitgiftes Second Answer touching the Churche Discipline* ([Heidelberg], 1575), pp. C-CIII; *The Works of John Whitgift, D.D.*, Parker Soc., I (Cambridge, Eng., 1851), 273.

[76]*Measure for Measure* is echoed a number of times in *Lear*; see Muir, pp. xxv-xxvi.

Blinding, moreover, as a punishment for adultery was also proposed, Becon insisting that English law was too lenient and that "Among the Locrensians the adulterers had both their eyes thrust out."[77] Yet the explicit horror of Gloucester's experience would, among other reasons, argue against dramatic endorsement of this attitude. Such a position seems echoed in Middleton's *The Family of Love* (ca. 1602-1607), where Mistress Glister exclaims, "Villanous lecher! . . . O for long nails to scratch out his eyes!" (IV.iii.115, 120-121),[78] and in S. S.'s *The Honest Lawyer* (ca. 1614-1615), where the Wife declares, "I cannot hold . . . my . . . nailes from scratching out a Leachers eyes" (1616, sig. [A4^v]).

In general, blindness and lechery, *concupiscentia oculorum*, were associated in the Renaissance view. The "eye is the broker of the heart to all sinne," notes Thomas Tymme's *A Plaine Discoverie of Ten English Lepers* (1592, sig. [H3]).[79] "Immoderate carnall copulation," observes *The Problemes of Aristotle* (1597), "doth destroy the sight . . ." (sig. E1^v). According to Bacon, carnal pleasure not only, as Cicero said, "blindfolds the eyes of the mind."[80] For ". . . much use of Venus," Bacon explains, recalling the speculation of the ancients, "doth dim the sight. . . ." "The cause," he continues, in a phrase reminiscent of Shakespeare's Sonnet 129, "is the expence of spirits."[81] Similarly, William Parkes's *The Curtaine-Drawer of the World* (1612) warns that lust is "the canker of health, the azure complectioner of the eyes" (p. 8). "Immoderate and unseasonable use [of Venus] . . . doth of all things . . . soonest induce blindnesse," declares Richard Banister's *A Treatise of . . . Diseases of the Eyes* (1622, sig. [L7^v]). In addition, the blinded Milton in his *Second*

[77]"An Homily against Whoredom and Uncleanness," *The Catechism of Thomas Becon, S.T.P.*, Parker Soc. (Cambridge, Eng., 1844), p. 649; see also *Certaine Sermons*, sig. L3^v.

[78]*The Works of Thomas Middleton*, ed. A. H. Bullen (1885).

[79]Among the advantages of blindness, remarks Anthony Munday's translation of the paradoxical *The Defence of Contraries* (1593), pp. 37-39, is the avoidance of concupiscent observation. Underlining the unawareness of Gloucester's earlier assurance, "I shall not need spectacles" (I.ii.35), *The Defence* ironically enumerates those advantages: the blind "have no need of spectacles."

[80]Cicero, *De senectute*, tr. William A. Falconer, Loeb Classical Lib. (1923), p. 51; cf. Thomas Lodge's *Wits Miserie, and the Worlds Madnesse* (1596), sig. [Giv]. On the connection between blindness and punishment in antiquity, see A. A. M. Esser, *Das Antlitz der Blindheit in der Antike* (Leiden, 1961).

[81]*Works*, II, 555-556.

Defence of the People of England (1654) seriously defended himself against charges of such retribution.[82]

But to assume that Shakespeare's spectators, including possible patrons of nearby stews, could sympathetically entertain the notion of ocular extrusion as "just" punishment for fornication may be doubtful. Since the audience was composed mostly of non-Puritans, presumably unfavorable to such extreme positions, it is more probable that Shakespeare would have chosen to indicate the horror, rather than the justice, of that punishment. Indeed, Edgar's pitying reference to Gloucester's "bleeding rings, / Their precious stones new lost" (V.iii.189-190), only some twenty lines later, like his earlier allusion, "Bless thy sweet eyes, they bleed" (IV.i.53), makes the possibility even more remote.[83] Nowhere else does Edgar partake of the world view which the evil characters express. Yet Edgar is, in addition, an actor; his language, as well as his costume, may, when occasion requires, be altered to suit the action.

Dramatic revelation proceeds also via the dialectic of action. "Remember," as Marston said of his own drama, "the life of these things consists in action."[84] Edgar's defeat of Edmund, followed by the latter's last-minute "conversion," may symbolize the conquest of good over evil. But the victory is essential for the larger irony of Lear's ambivalent defeat by cosmic forces, more clearly to follow. For if the good were not itself at least illusorily potent, whence would come the irony, the worth, of evil's power? Like the *Tragik des Zuspät*, the good is victorious in a momentary lull, essential to the succeeding horror of overwhelmingly irrational evil.

Such dialectic movements are exemplified in the restoration of Lear to Cordelia at the end of Act IV; the horror of Act V to follow; and, within Act V, a microcosm of the play in respect to this strategy—the repentance of Edmund, the expected salvation of Cordelia ("The Gods defend her!" "Great thing of us forgot!" etc.), and her wanton hanging. The dying Edmund is borne offstage at the very moment Lear enters with Cordelia dead in his arms; the first, one of her murderers, had almost saved the last. Verbally, the sequence is mediated by Albany's piously hopeful "The Gods defend her!"

[82]*The Works of John Milton*, ed. Frank A. Patterson, VIII (New York, 1933), 63.

[83]Cf. Dante's pitiful description (*Purgatorio* xxiii.31) of those whose eye-pits were like rings without gems ("Parean l' occhiaie anella senza gemme").

[84]Preface, *The Fawne* (1604-05), in *Plays*, II, 144.

(V.iii.255). This sharp ritual of exchange of murderer and victim and Albany's short prayer point up the irony of cosmic inequity, futility, and waste. Finally, at the moment when the justness of the heavens has been proclaimed, the defiantly heroic Lear is overwhelmed by those irrational cosmic forces over which even the greatest of men has no control.

Both of Edgar's cruxes, occurring in the two hurried last scenes, are effectively juxtaposed to the two sudden horrors of the play, Gloucester's blinding onstage and Cordelia's hanging offstage. Both are clearly exigently persuasive;[85] both are couched in terms acceptable to the character addressed; and both produce a reconciled acceptance ("And that's true too"; "Th' hast spoken right, 'tis true"). Considering dramatic shock, however, rather than putative philosophic or religious import, it emerges from the sequential irony that ripeness may *not* be all and that the gods may *not* be just. Since theatrical meanings involve also the actions they implicate, such negative significances may be as valid as the positive ones. In the overall dramatic dialectic, then, Edgar's choral verbalizations also help direct attention to the ironic and conflicting disparities of the action.

Finally, in Cordelia's "kind gods," Edgar voices no unequivocal confidence, his piety seeming largely filial. Although as Mad Tom he refers to "the sweet face of Heaven" (III.iv.89-90), echoing Lear's desperate prayer to the heavens' "sweet sway" (II.iv.192), the ejaculation is in keeping with the confessional tone of his lunatic speech and his mingled chime of catechism, homilies, and commandments. In addition, his sole favorable allusions to the heavens both occur in contexts such as earlier have been indicated: in his initial rescue of his father from suicidal despair, with the comforting assurance of "miraculous" intervention (IV.vi.73-74); and, in a similar context, in the second crux considered above.

Like Cordelia, he begs a paternal benediction (V.iii.195-196). As Cordelia forgives Lear, Edgar forgives his brother (V.iii.166). Further, like Cordelia and other characters, he makes the conventional Renaissance allusion to pagan fortune (IV.i.3, IV.vi.222). Yet, in contrast to that of Cordelia, his role is to remain on the scene of the world's "strange mutations"; here, lacking legitimate miracles,

[85]Cf. Edgar's instruction to his father, "Think that . . ." (IV.vi.73).

Edgar through his sympathy brings the comfort of illusion to the despairing and the suffering. For in the ironic universe of the tragedy life seems made bearable by illusion, as, ultimately, Lear's death appears attended by illusion.

Mirroring complementary aspects of the *prisca theologia* tradition, though involved with similar virtues, Cordelia emphasizes fidelity to truth and the bond, Edgar fidelity to feeling. To soothe his closest relatives *in extremis*, he seems willing to color his views; to gain her father's love, she is not. Where Cordelia could not do so, Edgar, in physical guise as Poor Tom, takes upon himself human iniquities. The pair recalls the complementary virtues of mercy and justice: Edgar's perspective is from below, as proxy for man; Cordelia's, also compassionate, seems more from above. In the absence of evidences of divine compassion here below, Edgar provides a humane sublunar substitute. Another of his related functions is to survive Cordelia and, with others, to represent human goodness in a denouement which ponders divine benevolence. Despite a deepening pessimism, he persists in charity, forgiveness, and love. Sharing the unresolved counterpoint at the play's end and matched against the relatively sustained cosmic optimism of Albany, Edgar is throughout the contrapuntal voice of human suffering.

CHAPTER VI

Pagan Atheism: Goneril and Regan, Edmund

As HAS BEEN INDICATED, Renaissance expectation was to view the pagan as "saved," superstitious, or atheistical. Through loose construction of both of these last terms, the superstitious person could in his deviation from the Christian mean also be considered atheistical, and so, by a similar construction, might the converse occur. But, in general, the distinctions established in an earlier chapter held good: the two were conventionally paired; the first erred by excessive and irrational fear of the deities, while the second erred by inadequate and too rational regard for the heavenly powers. As the whole problem of Renaissance "atheism" is vexed, suffering, it would seem, from an ambiguous use of terms, any attempt at definitive solution is here out of place. But whether or not atheists, in the modern sense, existed in Shakespeare's day, the facts are, first, that pagans could be, and often were, identified as such; and, second, that the religious Renaissance, far from being the relatively monolithic age that recent medievalizers seem to have projected, was fissured by incipient, if not fully formed, doubts.

Through the suggestion of Gloucester as related to the conventional Renaissance conception of the superstitious pagan and through the indication of Cordelia and Edgar as Renaissance "exempted" pagans, we are left with the alternatives that the Renaissance spectator could have with regard to an "ethnic": either (1) the latter was superstitious, (2) he was virtuous enough perhaps to become like the viewer himself, or finally (3) he was atheistic. This last alternative is clearly applicable, with the exception of Lear himself, to all the other major characters: to Goneril, to Regan, and to Edmund.

Whatever their particular religious inclination, however, pagans were, by definition, expected to be polytheistic and probably naturalistic—that is, to find divinity in nature itself through a kind of pantheism. These characteristics the personages in *King Lear* share;

but the particular bias the pagan *données* take in the individual cases is, of course, of primary interest. In Gloucester, as will be shown, polytheistic naturalism involves superstition; in Cordelia and Edgar the same groundwork also supports an exempted heathenism; but in the villainous trio the emphasis is on naturalism to a maximum degree and thus on a preoccupation with nature and with self, with a minimizing of supernatural interposition, unless that should immediately accrue to the benefit of the natural self.

Well known and frequently rehearsed in the scholarship is the tradition of the Machiavellian villain, with which the pagan naturalist in *Lear* becomes interwoven; this union is facilitated by the common ground of atheism which both types share, the Machiavellian, virtually by axiom, being a politic libertine and hypocritical disbeliever. Thus Shakespeare had at hand a conventional character type, already sketched, with some important differences, in Iago and elsewhere, by which he could make dramatically viable his pagan freethinkers and libertines.

Goneril and Regan

The horseleach hath two daughters which cry, Give, give.
—Proverbs xxx.15

Ethics, in the universe of Goneril, Regan, and Edmund, are Protagorean[1] and extemporized, in a Hobbesian *bellum omnium contra omnes*. As mankind, according to Hobbes, is determined by nature to acts of natural hatred and hostility, "What more savage, wild, and cruel, than man," observes Hooker, "if he see himself able either by fraud to overreach, or by power to overbear, the laws whereunto he should be subject?"[2] Although during the play *femina viro lupa*, at the end the sisters also tear animalistically at each other. "For whiles," points out Fitzherbert in the *Second Part of a Treatise*, "everie one seeketh his owne private good, without respect of the publike, all become for the most part treacherous, & perfidious, one towards an other: whereby there is neither anie true friendshipp amongst

[1] "The imagination of *Protagoras* is most false," notes John Serranus' *A Godlie and Learned Commentarie upon . . . Ecclesiastes*, tr. John Stockwood (1585), pp. 60-61, ". . . that man is the measure of all things . . . that things so farre have their being . . . after what sort men do . . . imagin of them, the which untruth . . . some frantike heads in our time have gone about to set abroach againe, under the name of Libertines, as if sinne were nothing else but a certaine imagination."

[2] Hobbes, *English Works,* III, 117; Hooker, *Ecclesiastical Polity,* in *Works,* II, 22.

them, nor care of covenant, or promise, nor respect of fidelity, nor regard of oath, nor consequently any common welth" (p. 71).

Analogously, a Renaissance audience could have interpreted Goneril's contempt for her "mild husband" (IV.ii.1) as disdain for the associations of that adjective. Stressing the body, rather than the soul, her scale of human value is measured in terms of force and physical *virtù*—when Albany calls her "a fiend," she retorts, "Marry, your manhood—mew!" (IV.ii.66, 68; cf. IV.ii.28). Her motive is rapidity in action, based upon will: "Our wishes on the way / May prove effects" (IV.ii.14-15).

Compared to direct action, ethical consideration is folly: "a moral fool" (IV.ii.58), she calls her husband. Thus pity is excluded from her cosmos:

> Fools do those villains pity who are punish'd
> Ere they have done their mischief, (IV.ii.54-55)

and the selfish end justifies the cruel means. "The ways to enrich," noted Bacon, "are many, and most of them foul."[3] "Honour" (IV.ii.53) is equated by her with action in defense of self-interest, twisted, as is "judgment" above, from its traditional uses; "honour" is clearer to her than it is to Hamlet, for she berates Albany in terms similar to those in which Hamlet accuses himself: "Milk-liver'd man! / That bear'st a cheek for blows, a head for wrongs" (IV.ii.50-51), a conception of honor she shares with Macbeth's own lady. Contempt for traditional values accompanies disdain for religious forms: "the text is foolish" (IV.ii.37), she sneers at Albany's warning. Returning evil for good—evil, be thou my good—Goneril and Regan parody Christian charity.

In fact, despite her paganism, the striking thing is that Goneril never mentions the gods at all, an indication that her Renaissance garb has completely covered her natural condition; totally self-preoccupied with her lusts and the expansion of her will, she is deaf to such counsels as Edgar's to Gloucester, "do but look up" (IV.vi.59), and Edgar's to Lear, "Look up, my Lord" (V.iii.312). Instead, Goneril bids Edmund, "Decline your head," her kiss "stretching" only his "spirits," in an amatory sense, "up into the air" (IV.ii.22-23).[4] In

[3] *Works*, VI, 461.

[4] Cf. Edmund, I.ii.22.

contrast to Cordelia's view of marriage, Goneril and Edmund here enact an adulterous and blasphemous parody, the ritual sealed appropriately by Edmund's "Yours in the ranks of death" (IV.ii.25). Like those of the wicked in *A Pake of Knaves* (after 1640) and unlike those of even such villains as Claudius, her eyes "Looke a Wayes douneward never on the skies" (p. 9).[5] The dimensions of the evil sisters' universe and their self-centeredness are described in Nathanael Carpenter's *Achitophel* (1629): "Having all their cares bounded in this world," such worldlings "runne alwayes in the same circle, and respect onely their owne center, disdaining . . . any interest in any superior Orbe. This, they esteeme their highest heaven; without the which . . . they can imagine neither *Locus* nor *Tempus*; neither place to containe their treasure, nor time to adde to their mortality . . ." (p. 55).

As Edgar complements Cordelia in goodness, moreover, Regan complements her sister in evil. Like Goneril, she reduces divine reason to practical consideration ("We shall further think of it," I.i.307)[6] and action ("our businesses, / Which craves the instant use," II.i.127-128); and, like her, she measures value by material gain.[7] *Déracinée*, like Goneril, Regan also spares mentioning the gods, except once, hypocritically,[8] before Lear, "O the blest Gods!" (II.iv.170)—a

[5]See F. P. Wilson, "Illustrations of Social Life II . . . ," *Shakespeare Survey 12* (Cambridge, Eng., 1959), p. 107. The injunction that man should look up at heaven rather than down at earth, as beasts do, occurring, e.g., in Petrarch, is a Renaissance *topos*.

[6]Cf. II.iv.236, 311, V.i.28; note "ignorance" in IV.v.9.

[7]Cf. Lear's comment regarding "What store" his evil daughter's "heart is made on" (III.vi.54) and Massinger's *The City Madam* (1632), IV.ii:

> Religion, conscience, charity, farewell!
> To me you are words only, and no more;
> All human happiness consists in store.
> (*Dramatic Works*, p. 332)

[8]"Yond simp'ring dame," charges Lear, ". . . minces virtue, and does shake the head / To hear of pleasure's name" (IV.vi.120-123). Since the same speech (112-114) rejects the death penalty for adultery, which Puritans had notoriously proposed, an implication of Puritan hypocrisy, as in *Measure for Measure*, may be present in these lines. Puritanism, as an inverted form of libertinism, recurs, for example, in such satire as Robert Anton's *The Philosophers Satyrs* (1616), sig. I3v:

> that *civill whore*,
> That in a *Puritans habit* dwells next *doore*,
> . . . with *Saintlike motion*,
> Minces the *pavement* with her *pure devotion*.

A suggestion of Puritan hypocrisy may also be implied in Goneril's sanctimonious indictment of knighthood, as represented in Lear's retinue (I.iv.249-257); efficient and utilitarian, the villains see little use in knighthood (e.g., II.iv.262-265).

silence which may be eloquent regarding her beliefs. She thus represents an antithesis to Gloucester's concern regarding the heavenly forces. Her ethics are pat. They involve vengeance of inordinate kind ("If it be true, all vengeance comes too short," II.i.88); a devilish parody of poetic justice (II.iv.304-306); an ironic perversion of the relation between goodness and pity ("it was he . . . / Who is too good to pity thee," III.vii.87-89); and the proper place of weakness vis-à-vis power ("I pray you, father, being weak, seem so," II.iv.203).

As a heathen villainess, sprung fully grown from the head of the Renaissance Machiavel, Goneril exhibits few differences from her sixteenth-century Italianate model; the implication is that, sharing the common ground of atheism, the pagan and the Machiavellian are expected to behave in a similar manner against God and their fellow men. Like all Machiavellian opportunists, the sisters, little worlds made cunningly, exist in a material time-space world, whose dimensions are present minutes rather than eternity. "And in good time you gave it" (II.iv.252), Regan sneers at her astounded father. Further, in contrast to Cordelia's "governance" and "knowledge," Goneril's ideals are practical judgment and action; remarking Lear's "poor judgment" (I.i.291) in worldly self-regard, she is quick to act in what she conceives as her own self-interest: "We must do something, and i' th' heat," she replies to Regan's "We shall further think of it" (I.i.307-308). Indeed, for her, "mind" (I.iii.16) is almost the same as will (cf. IV.ii.12-13, IV.vi.265), a far leap from the Aquinian or Hookerian *nous*, or reason; her world is a visible one, without cosmic hierarchy and principle, and must be constructed through frenzied acquisition, status claims, climbing, and opportunism; lacking Cordelia's bond, Goneril ironically creates disorder and is, in-

---

While Lear rejects "need" or utility alone as a relevant criterion, Goneril earlier denounces the "shame" of the knights' "disorder'd . . . debosh'd, and bold" manners: ". . . epicurism and lust / Makes it more like a tavern . . ." (I.iv.250-254). Cf. Malvolio, *Twelfth Night*, II.iii.96. Both Goneril and Regan invoke platitudes to justify inhospitality: cf. Regan's II.iv.242-244 and Tilley M729, "One Master in a house is enough"; and Goneril's I.iv.253-254 and Tilley W328, "Whoredom and grace can never bide in one place." The villains are intent on what Raleigh's *The History of the World* (1614), I.i.15, p. 21, describes as "*Machiavels two markes to shoote at . . . riches, and glorie.*" They are generally strangers to the feudal and nonutilitarian language of archery, hunting, and horsemanship, shared by Lear, Kent, and Edgar. Cf. James's commitment to the institution of knighthood, the king notoriously increasing the number of knights, as well as to the sport of hunting, on account of which he enlarged stables and kennels; indeed, he was held to devote more time to the chase than to serious affairs of state.

deed, in herself an aspect of disorder—chaos and evil being twins in the Elizabethan view.

Like Marlowe's Pride, the evil sisters "disdain to have any parents";[9] and they combine the features of the three daughters described in Nashe's *Christs Teares over Jerusalem* (1593), pride in gorgeous attire (cf. II.iv.271), delicacy, and disdain.[10] Moreover, in her pride Regan is like her sister, above the laws of God, man, and nature: "A peasant stand up thus!" (III.vii.79), she shouts, ironically regarding a point of protocol neglected by her betters. Similarly, it is ironical that Goneril should, at her moment of loss, summon up a legal reference. When Edmund falls at the hands of his brother, she shrieks,

> This is practice, Gloucester:
> By th' law of war thou wast not bound to answer
> An unknown opposite; (V.iii.151-153)

for immediately thereafter she exclaims, "the laws are mine, not thine: / Who can arraign me for't" (V.iii.158-159).

Parodying Genesis, Regan, in turn, creates chaos: giving herself to Edmund, she pronounces, "Witness the world, that I create thee here / My lord and master" (V.iii.78-79). "In my rights, / By me invested," she informs her sister and the latter's husband (V.iii.69-70). In like fashion, "They have made themselves," shouts Lady Macbeth, with unconscious irony, at her recalcitrant partner (I.vii.53). Similarly, Albany's reply to Goneril, "Thou changed and self-cover'd thing, for shame, / Be-monster not thy feature" (IV.ii.62-63), suggests self-generation and self-creation, monstering nature. In addition, since "cover," in a relevant sense, is used mainly of horses,[11] it suggests a link with the Ixion-centaur motif.

Where Edgar can be "pregnant to good pity," sympathy being a creative force, the evil sisters can only, like Iago, labor in sterile activity, bringing forth chaos (Iago's "Muse labours," for example,

[9] *The Tragical History of Doctor Faustus* (1588-92), ed. Frederick S. Boas (1932), II.ii.117.

[10] *Works,* II, 134-145.

[11] Cf. Lear's allusion to the "soiled horse," IV.vi.124; *Othello,* I.i.112-113. See Plutarch, *The Lives of the Noble Grecians and Romanes,* tr. Thomas North (1579), p. 54. Cf. the use of "coverd" in *double entendre,* Webster, *The White Devil,* I.ii.138; see Ch. vi of Thomas Blundeville's *The Foure Chiefest Offices Belonging to Horsemanship* (1609).

creating "this monstrous birth," II.i.128, I.iii.410). Paralleling Lady Macbeth in relation to her husband,[12] Goneril's injunction to Edmund, "Conceive" (IV.ii.24), and her use of "fruitfully" (IV.vi.266) involve an ironic reversal, as do her sneers at Albany's "cowish terror" (IV.ii.12). In Lear's "Centaurs" (IV.vi.126), as in his "Ha! Goneril, with a white beard!" (IV.vi.97), the reversal is further emphasized, the centaurs being male, notoriously addicted to rape.

In addition, for Regan as for Goneril the body and its uses are all that exist. Thus weakness of the body should be ruled by those who have strength (II.iv.148-149), where nature is equated with physical nature in the pagan sense; their contempt for the aged Lear is partly involved with their criterion of natural potency. Hence sexual concerns and jealousies arise, as in V.i.10-11, with regard to Edmund. Although Goneril exclaims over Edmund and Albany, "Oh! the difference of man and man" (IV.ii.26), the difference of woman and woman displays itself in the contrast between Cordelia's *sapientia* and the evil sisters' *sapientia carnis*. In Donne's terms ("Elegie III," l. 12), more "hot, wily, wild" than beasts, "Their blood," as Mendoza exclaims in Marston's *The Malcontent* (1600-1604), "is their onely God" (I.vi).[13]

Yet, while they can add, like Edmund and the accumulator Don Juan, they cannot, being a breed of barren metal, multiply. In acting alone, in uniting through lust, in being above the law, the sisters have in truth cast themselves outside order, which is the law of heaven, into chaos and loss. Theologically, then, Goneril and Regan as depraved pagans who never regard their gods are, like Cornwall and Oswald, atheists, reprobate by action and belief.

THE CHAOS OF QUANTITY

And thou shalt have more....
—Fool, *Lear*, I.iv.132

More! More! is the cry of a mistaken soul....
—Blake, "There Is No Natural Religion"

Goneril and Regan move within a universe of confused proportions in which the only unit of measurement is quantitative, and the main value word, "more."[14] Their motive is not service but the new

[12]Cf. the reversal in *Lear*, IV.v.3, "Your sister is the better soldier."

[13]*Plays*, I, 158.

[14]On the new quantitative outlook of the later Renaissance, see *Timon of Athens*; see also L. C. Knights, *Drama & Society in the Age of Jonson* (1937); John U. Nef,

appetitus divitiarum infinitus. For them "love" means both physical and material gratification. "I'll love thee much" (IV.v.21), Regan promises Oswald, if he lets her unseal the letter. Indeed, "love" early signified both "appraise, estimate or state the price or value of," as well as, from a different root, its more common meaning.[15] To Lear's love test, Goneril replies with a detailed and material catalog (I.i.55-61), and Regan estimates her love in the imagery of "metal" (I.i.69). While filial piety is for Cordelia an unshakable duty, for her sisters it is a means of extracting "more" from their father. Whereas, in reply, Cordelia asserts a fixed and due proportion, Lear's desire for "more" love violates the eternal bond of "proportion, season, form." As Antony, when asked "how much," was to observe, in another context, "There's beggary in the love that can be reckon'd" (*Antony and Cleopatra,* I.i.15). Though the king would "love" according to the affection tendered him, the good characters, such as Kent, demonstrate a love and service beyond price.

Indeed, as Goneril and Regan know the price of everything and the value of nothing, so Lear unvaluingly throws away a pearl richer than all his tribe. His initial question, "How much?" throws open the tragedy to the ironical consequences of posing quantitative human measurements against the cosmos. Further, the conjunction of ignoble quantitative attitudes seems acted out in the joint departure near the close of the first scene of the like-minded Lear and Burgundy and verbalized in the king's exit line, "Come, noble Burgundy" (I.i.266). Conflicting appraisals emerge when to Goneril's claim, "I have been worth the whistle," Albany rejoins with an estimate of her self-valuation: "You are not worth the dust . . ." (IV.ii.29, 30). Although, like the Stoics (for example, Epictetus[16]), Cordelia recognizes a distinction between outward and inward "worth" (IV.iv.10)—she is, says France, "herself a dowry" (I.i.241)—it is only the body and its show that exist for her sisters. While they, ac-

---

Cultural Foundations of Industrial Civilization (New York, 1960); and Edgar Zilsel, "The Sociological Roots of Science," *American Journal of Sociology,* XLVII (1942), 544-562. I am indebted to the discussion of "the values pattern" in Robert B. Heilman's *This Great Stage: Image and Structure in "King Lear"* (Baton Rouge, La., 1948).

[15]See Terry Hawkes, "'Love' in *King Lear,*" *Review of English Studies,* N.S. X (1959), 178-181.

[16]*Discourses,* tr. W. A. Oldfather, Loeb Classical Lib., I (1926), 35, 227; II (1928), 379.

ceding to his demand for "more" and professing "to love their father all," would violate their avowals, Cordelia would continue, in due proportion, her duties as daughter and wife (I.i.99-104). Previously, in the proposed, and severed, match between Burgundy and Cordelia, Shakespeare has effectively contrasted the antithetical values of quantity and the bond.

Later she is accompanied by the Doctor, who orders a louder music (IV.vii.25) which may "wind up" Lear's "untuned and jarring senses" (IV.vii.16) and restore him to his "better tune" (IV.iii. 40). Her healing "restoration" (IV.vii.26) extends even to the balance between the loss of his knights and the company of soldiers she issues to seek him: "A century send forth" (IV.iv.6). In contrast to her "numbers" and the ancient and hermetic Renaissance union between number and universal harmony, the villains' sterile quantitative chaos "untunes that string" and produces only harsh "divisions" (I.ii.144) and disharmony. In short, shattering the old personal bond of love as loyalty and service beyond compensation, the evil characters bring in the nexus of the new acquisitive society, lust and money.

Significantly, Goneril and Regan's conception of love as quantitative finds its seventeenth-century analogue in the quantitative lover, Don Juan; prefigured by Edmund, for him units of physical experience are endlessly computed and scored. Appropriately, the credo of Molière's Dom Juan, "that two and two make four . . . and that four and four make eight," evokes his valet's practical judgment, "Your religion is arithmetic, I see" (III.ii).[17]

In the seventeenth century's new atomistic and fragmented universe, "all in pieces, all coherence gone," the hard clarities of number began to be shored up against the frustrating mysteries of providence: if humankind could not "know," it could at least reckon. Circumscribing the limitless space of which the mathematician Pascal expressed terror, the seventeenth century commenced its quantification of mystery. Thus, despite his occasional bad dreams, mathematical man bounded himself, relatively, in a nutshell and counted himself a king of infinite space. But if Pascal could apply the game of chance to eternal bliss, and "infinity" come to replace eternity, what was to become of the valuation of man himself? In Lear's

[17] *The Dramatic Works of Molière,* tr. Charles H. Wall (1889), II, 95-96.

"nothing" and in the acquisitive scrambling of his villains Shakespeare, entering the world of quantity, provided an answer: "Nothing can come of nothing." ". . . what is man," demanded Pascal, "in Nature? A cypher compared with the Infinite. . . ."[18]

As in the case of Sophocles' Oedipus (the name suggesting "foot" or "measure"), number thus furnishes a grid against which the ironical evaluation of Shakespeare's characters might be perceived. Although Aeschylus' Prometheus considers number, which he invented for man, "prime sovereign of all sciences,"[19] man, in his pride, becomes not only the measurer but the measure. Yet, between Pythagorean number mysticism and Protagorean exaltation of man as the measure, Sophocles' chorus, adding up the sum of mortal generations of men, derives the total, zero. Like Sophocles, auditing the Protagorean equation of man as the center of the universe, Shakespeare reckons up and finds wanting man's traditional role as Creation's most exalted and cherished object.

In *Lear* those characters who are busily quantifying mystery finally divide up nothing and at the end become, like the hero of the first act, "an O without a figure." For it is an irony of calculation that precision is ultimately meaningless under the ambiguous "pudder" of the thunder and within a shifting world without a frame. Both the villains' ethic of calculation and the hero's hubristic *quid pro quo* are ironically thrown up against the screen of cosmic ambiguity. In Shakespeare, as in Sophocles, the self-confident pursuer and measurer becomes the thing enigmatically pursued and measured, but by mysterious divinities themselves beyond rational reckoning.

In this hard new world of number the Fool, many of whose jests involve figures, teaches Lear the simple arithmetic of division and subtraction (e.g., I.iv.124-133). But it is only at the close of two scenes of ciphering lessons (I.iv, v) that Lear's arithmetical proficiency is approved. When he can discern the obvious and see that "The reason why the seven stars are no mo than seven," which is "a pretty reason," is "Because they are not eight," Lear is declared to develop from a monarch imprudent to a fool practical.[20] "Yes, in-

[18]*Pascal's Pensées,* tr. H. F. Stewart (New York, 1950), p. 21.

[19]*Prometheus Bound,* in *Aeschylus: The Seven Plays,* tr. Lewis Campbell (1890), p. 314.

[20]The Fool's arithmetical exchange has some of the inane common sense of the fool in Middleton and Rowley's *The Changeling* (1622), III.iii.165-169 (*The Works of*

deed," the Fool, with ironic foreshadowing, applauds his graduation into the clear light of common sense, "thou would'st make a good Fool" (I.v.35-39). Between those two scenes, as well as in the next act, Goneril's "disquantitying" (I.iv.257) of her father's knights also offers him a vivid worldly lesson in lower mathematics. One hundred . . . fifty . . . five-and-twenty . . . ten . . . five . . . nothing. It is "as hard," complained Swift, "to get quit of *Number* as of *Hell*."[21] As Goneril continues inhumanly to subtract and divide, Lear, in his critique of practical "reason," cries, "O! reason not the need" (II.iv.266).[22]

Edmund

"Nomos" and "Physis"

The onely certain guide, infallible nature.
—Shadwell, *The Libertine*, I.i

Antithetical to Cordelia's maintenance of *lex aeterna* and the bond is Edmund, who, with the evil sisters, denies them. But while the sisters' wickedness is virtually an unpremeditated expression of their debased natures, Edmund's is more consciously rationalized and repentable. Thus Goneril and Regan correspond in their tacitly operative evil to Cordelia's tacitly operative good; and similarly Edmund as the *raisonneur* of naturalism parallels Edgar as a *raisonneur* of

---

Thomas Middleton, ed. A. H. Bullen [1885]). Cf. also Alexander Ross, *The New Planet No Planet* (1646), pp. 42-43, defending the inviolability of the "7. Starres" against revision by new speculations: "Let therefore the number of 7. remaine, it is a sacred number. . . ."

[21] *A Tale of a Tub*, ed. A. C. Guthkelch and D. Nichol Smith (Oxford, 1920), p. 55.

[22] Lear's "reason not the need" speech recalls the *topos* "natura paucis contenta." Cf. Tilley N45. A Stoic and Cynic commonplace, it suggests the "hard" primitivism of Kent as opposed to the libertine "Golden Age" and "soft" primitivism of Edmund. The *topos* recurs, e.g., in Cicero, *Tusculanae disputationes*, Bk. V, Ch. xxxiii; Seneca, Epistle XVI; Erasmus, *Adagia* ([Frankfurt am Main], 1629), p. 159; Montaigne, II, 165; Nashe, III, 243; Jonson, *The Staple of News* (1626), III.ii. See also C. T., *Laugh and Lie Downe* (included in Nicoll's edition of *The Works of Cyril Tourneur*): "I have beene verie well acquainted with kick-shoses, but now I have learned to satisfie Nature with a little" (1605, sigs. [Bivv]-C).

Analogous is another commonplace touched upon by Lear, "Nature's above art in that respect" (IV.vi.86). See Arthur O. Lovejoy, *Essays in the History of Ideas* (Baltimore, 1948), p. 330, and *A Documentary History of Primitivism and Related Ideas*, ed. Lovejoy et al. (Baltimore, 1935), pp. 207-208. See Marcus Aurelius Antoninus, *The Communings with Himself*, tr. C. R. Haines, Loeb Classical Lib. (1916), p. 301. It is a recurrent argument of Montaigne; see also Erasmus, *Praise of Folly*, and Tilley A330, among innumerable instances, as well as Edward W. Tayler, *Nature and Art in Renaissance Literature* (New York, 1964).

virtuous paganism. It may be significant, too, that the quartos refer to him not as Edmund but as "Bastard."

In his libertine naturalism Edmund witnesses the Jacobean disintegration of natural law and ethical absolutes; in the same year as *Lear*'s probable composition was published Samuel Daniel's "Ulisses and the Syren," in which the Syren, who perhaps significantly has the last word, observes,

That doth opinion onely cause,
That's out of custome bred,
Which makes us many other lawes
Then ever Nature did,[23]

corresponding to Edmund's

Wherefore should I
Stand in the plague of custom, and permit
The curiosity of nations to deprive me. (I.ii.2-4)

Physis takes priority over *nomos*.[24] This distinction between "natural right" and man-made law, between nature and convention, apparent in the Sophists, emerges in the Renaissance with the rediscovery of "nature" itself, challenging tradition on all human levels. Here the new relativistic skepticism is heard shattering the old absolutistic faith in the universality of God's law; in place of the latter an Epicurean libertinism is erected, whose model is Aretino and, even more, the Golden Age passage in Tasso's *Aminta*, a charter of freethinking sensualism.[25] "Thou, Nature, art my goddess," are Edmund's first soliloquizing words (I.ii.1); and commentators have apparently missed the point that its emphasis is exclusion ("to *thy*

[23]*The Complete Works . . . of Samuel Daniel*, ed. Alexander B. Grosart, I (1885), 271.

[24]While Edmund, representative of *physis*, repudiates *nomos*, Lear, chief supporter, by his position, of *nomos*, comes to repudiate both *nomos* and *physis*, both law and the generative principle.

Callicles (*Gorgias*, 483, *The Dialogues of Plato*, tr. Benjamin Jowett [Oxford, 1953], II, 577) distinguishes between conventional justice, made to protect the weak (cf. *Richard III*, V.iii.309-310), and "natural" justice, which the strong naturally employ against the weak. The latter view represents the *physis* of the nominalist-sophist villains, who, as in the blinding scene, oppose their "justice" against the *nomos* of the weak. Cf. also Thrasymachus (*Republic*, 338c, *Dialogues of Plato*, II, 176-177), holding that whoever acts in the interests of the stronger acts justly.

[25]Tasso's chorus ("O bella età de l'oro . . .") occurs at the end of the first act of *Aminta* (Torquato Tasso, *Opera*, ed. Bruno Maier [Milan, 1963], I, 123-127).

law / *My* services are bound," I.ii.1-2; italics mine), with the shock of recognition that what men have hitherto accepted by nature, natural law, is no longer "natural."

In the early seventeenth century, custom, previously associated with natural law, began to be seen as a hindrance to the operation of nature and to be classed with mere opinion; true nature was considered, as in some versions of modern psychology, to coincide with natural desires. Thus, within a century a major significance of that slippery word "nature" as natural *law*, or the absolute law of God, became metamorphosed to *natural* law, or the relative law of man. To this change Edmund, as a confessed naturalist, gives voice; and as a libertine naturalist, despite his pagan devotions to the fertility goddess Natura, he would tend to be considered an atheist. Moreover, we have seen that the Renaissance view of paganism led usually to three alternatives: *prisca theologia*, superstition, or atheism; it is clear that Edmund, falling into neither of the first two categories, may properly be classed in the third.

Continually the ambiguity of the term "law of nature" is complained of, and its validity itself is questioned. Even that staunch upholder of the law of nature, Hooker, comments on the term's ambiguity;[26] and a teacher of James I, George Buchanan, makes a similar point.[27] Indeed, in view of Renaissance confusion over the concept which Hooker elsewhere supports—"Obedience of creatures to the Law of Nature," echoes Webster's *The Devil's Law-Case* (1610-1619), "Is the stay of the whole world" (IV.ii.276-277)—and which was a doctrine of conservatism and stability against excessive individualism, the inroads made upon that concept become more understandable. In addition, other forces of dissolution were at work. The skeptics joined with the Epicureans against the law of nature. The latter posited pleasure as an end, while the former stressed the unknowableness of truth and thus set up utilitarianism or the customs of the country as relative guides.

[26] *Ecclesiastical Polity*, in *Works*, I, 222*n*.

[27] Buchanan, *The Powers of the Crown in Scotland . . . "De Jure Regni apud Scotos,"* tr. Charles F. Arrowood (Austin, Tex., 1949), pp. 46-47. Cf. Donne, *Biathanatos*, Facsimile Text Soc. (New York, 1930), pp. 36-38. Raleigh, *The History of the World*, Preface, sig. E2, remarks on the "ambiguity of this name," nature. Robert Boyle's *A Free Enquiry into the . . . Notion of Nature* (1685/6) catalogs ambiguities in the term. Cf. *The Tragical Reign of Selimus* (1586-93; pr. 1594), Malone Soc. Repr. (1908), ll. 113-114, on the questioning of natural law.

If, then, absolute law of nature is unacceptable, custom, habit, or, to use a favorite word, "opinion" must take its place. We comprehend Edmund's protest against the "plague of custom" (I.ii.3), all the more emphatic insofar as he sees it as merely relative custom which bars him, a bastard, as well as a younger son, from the advantages of his natural equals or inferiors. Apropos, Gloucester's first reference to his sons contrasts Edmund, the natural, with Edgar, "by order of law" (I.i.19). Basing his argument, like the other villains, on physical differences alone, Edmund sweeps aside custom which is accidental, as well as that which has traditional bases in natural law. Edmund is, like the *Arcadia*'s Cecropia, a defender of relative morals and man-made gods; they would both agree with Berecinthius in Massinger's *Believe as You List* (1631) that the gods and hell "are thinges wee make our selves."[28] Such, as Nashe says, "followe the Pironicks, whose position and opinion it is that there is no Hel or misery but opinion" (II, 116).[29] Similarly, Edmund's and Cecropia's naturalistic antinomianism is expressed also by the *Arcadia*'s Basilius: "Alas let not certaine imaginatife rules, whose trueth standes but upon opinion, keepe so wise a mind from gratefulnes and mercie . . ." (II, 43).[30]

[28]Ed. Charles J. Sisson, Malone Soc. Repr. (1927 [1928]), IV.iii, l. 2244.

[29]Cf. Peter Ure, "A Note on 'Opinion' in Daniel, Greville and Chapman," *MLR*, XLVI (1951), 331-338. See also Barnabe Rich, *Opinion Diefied. Discovering the Ingins . . . Set in This Age, Whereby to Catch Opinion* (1613).

[30]Cf. Cecropia at I, 406. "The basis for the distinction between moral and immoral, just and unjust, legal and illegal actions, is fanciful opinion—silly opinion at that," claims a participant in *The Dialogues of Guy de Brués* (1557), ed. Panos Paul Morphos, Johns Hopkins Studies in Romance Literatures and Languages, Extra Vol. XXX (Baltimore, 1953), p. 30; cf. Sextus Empiricus' tenth trope, "Outlines of Pyrrhonism," *Sextus Empiricus*, tr. R. G. Bury, Loeb Classical Lib. (1933), pp. 84-93; Donne, "Elegie XVII," ll. 48-51,

> The golden laws of nature are repeald . . .
> And we're made servants to opinion,

and "The Progresse of the Soule," ll. 518-520,

> Ther's nothing simply good, nor ill alone . . .
> The onely measure is, and judge, opinion.

While Hamlet asserts, "there is nothing either good or bad, but thinking makes it so" (II.ii.255-257), and Shakespeare's Troilus asks, "What is aught, but as 'tis valued?" (II.ii.52), Shadwell's Don John (*The Libertine* [1675; pr. 1676], Act II, p. 26) declares, "There's nothing good or ill, but as it seems to each man's natural appetite." Cf. Hermes in Lucian, *Zeus Rants* (tr. A. M. Harmon, Loeb Classical Lib. [1915], II, 169). Nashe observes, "our opinion (as *Sextus Empiricus* affirmeth) gives the name of good or ill to every thing" (III, 332); Nashe's observation is recalled in Thomas Rogers' statement that "There is no hell . . . but only . . . in mans opinion, as hold the Atheists . . ." (*The Faith, Doctrine, and Religion . . . in 39 Articles* [Cambridge, Eng., 1607], p. 74). Cf.

NATURE AS GODDESS

C'est Vénus tout entière à sa proie attachée.
—Racine, *Phèdre,* I.iii

Vere tument terrae et genitalia semina poscunt.
—Virgil, *Georgics,* II.324

Since nature is not to be bound by mere custom, which is seen to rule the world in place of nature, what is natural determines what is lawful. Hence, free reign is given to sensuality and libertinage with such absolute powers as a providential God, in practice, less invoked. While Montaigne, after much reflection, reaches the conclusion *sequere naturam,* that we should follow nature,[31] others, such as a speaker in Marguerite of Navarre's *L'heptaméron* (1559), also observe nature as guide—man, not nature, is perverse.[32] He is described by Malheureux in Marston's *The Dutch Courtezan* (II.i.) in similar terms:

> wretched man
> Whom nationall custome, Tyrannous respects
> Of slavish order, fetters, lames his power
> Calling that sinne in us, which in all things els
> Is natures highest virtue.[33]

Thus nature becomes goddess to Renaissance libertines, such as Edmund; no natural impulse, even incest, in Giovanni's claim (Ford's *'Tis Pity*), can be a priori barred.[34] François Garasse in *La doctrine curieuse des beaux esprits de ce temps* (Paris, 1623) sums up this tendency of libertinism and devotes the sixth book of that work to attacking the exclusive libertine worship of nature, which must be satisfied in all things. Like Giovanni, Eleazer, and D'Amville, Edmund invokes Nature and, in particular, perhaps Venus Genetrix, as the concluding line of his appeal (I.ii.22) may suggest.

Nashe, I, 216: "Custome is a Lawe, and Luste holdes it for a Lawe, to live without Lawe"; *Dialogues of Guy de Brués,* pp. 281-282: ". . . les loix ne valent rien, et . . . sont instituées par une seule opinion."

[31]Cf. *Letter-Book of Gabriel Harvey,* ed. E. J. L. Scott, Camden Soc. (1884), p. 87. Théophile de Viau, *Oeuvres complètes,* ed. Charles Alleaume (Paris, 1856), I, lxvi, argues, "J'approuve qu'un chacun suive en tout la nature."

[32]Ed. Michel François (Paris, 1960), p. 220. See Arthur A. Tilley, "Follow Nature," in his *Studies in the French Renaissance* (Cambridge, Eng., 1922), pp. 233-258.

[33]*Plays,* II, 83.

[34]Selimus, rebelling against his father, reasons like Edmund (*The Tragical Reign of Selimus,* ll. 352-360).

The goddess Nature whom Edmund worships was, in effect, increasingly reconciled with the orthodox Deity. Ronsard argues,

> Qui blasme la Nature il blasme Dieu supreme,
> Car la Nature & Dieu est presque chose mesme.[35]

Those who inclined to rest in nature, not the God of nature, often equated nature with the principle of fecundity. Significantly, Montaigne's "nostre grande et puissante mere nature"[36] was identified with the pagan goddess; and Richard Brathwaite's *Natures Embassie* (1621) cites "Nature the common mother (to use an Ethnicke induction) . . ." (p. 1).

Directly and by implication, evidence for Edmund's atheism has already been presented. His libertine sensuality conjoined with his materialistic naturalism is blasphemously expressed in the invitation of potency: "Now, gods, stand up for bastards!" (I.ii.22). This concludes a *topos* which Curtius has isolated, the invocation of Nature that in Edmund's soliloquy joins still another topic concerned with the goddess Nature; in Guillaume de Lorris' portion of *Le roman de la rose*, in Jean de Meun's continuation, in Alain de Lille's *De planctu naturæ*, and in Chaucer's Wife of Bath, the sensual Mother-of-us-all is celebrated. In Shakespeare's eleventh sonnet, further, nature as the plenitude principle is mentioned in a sense close to Edmund's. Although Curtius admits that the peregrinations of this *topos* since the Middle Ages are still to be examined, it is clear that in the Renaissance an exclusive worship of nature, at a time of increasing empirical interests and the breakdown of the medieval synthesis as well as the traditional law of nature, was one indication of libertine atheism. Like Bussy, "full-mann'd," Edmund would reject Macbeth's "supernatural soliciting" (I.iii.130); both his bastardy and his knavish prowess are the consequence of natural causation.[37]

[35]"Le Tombeau de Marguerite de France, Duchesse de Savoie," posthumous addition, *Oeuvres complètes,* ed. Paul Laumonier (Paris, 1914-19), VII, 513. Cf. Pliny, *Natural History,* Bk. II, Ch. vii.

[36]*Essais,* ed. Jean Plattard, II (Paris, 1960), 93.

[37]As libertinism is, in a sense, an extension of cosmic Epicureanism, Edmund may be seen as a reflection of the new cosmic order on the personal level. Cf. Don Cameron Allen, "The Rehabilitation of Epicurus and His Theory of Pleasure in the Early Renaissance," *SP*, XLI (1944), 1-15.

Pliny's *Natural History,* which anticipates other topics in *Lear,* also alludes to the invocation of Venus Genetrix (ed. Jacobus Dalecampius [1587], Bk. II, Ch. viii, p. 6, n.

PAGAN ATHEISM: GONERIL AND REGAN, EDMUND

ILLEGITIMACY

No sickly Fruit of faint Compliance He!
. . . stampt in Nature's Mint of Extacy! . . .
Conceiv'd in Rapture, and with Fire begot!
Strong as Necessity.
—Richard Savage, *The Bastard* (1728)

Despite Edmund's boast regarding the superiority of bastards,[38] Shakespeare's age tended to view them as unsettling figures. Bastards

---

h). Cf. Spenser's hymn to Venus (*Faerie Queene*, IV.x.44-47), a paraphrase of Lucretius, invocation to Aphrodite, at the start of Bk. I, *De rerum natura*, and illustrations given in *The Works of Edmund Spenser: A Variorum Edition*, ed. Edwin Greenlaw et al., IV (Baltimore, 1935), 233-237; Joachim du Bellay's translation into French of the Lucretian invocation in Louis Leroy's rendering of Plato's *Symposium* (Paris, 1558) and in Du Bellay's *Les oeuvres françoises* (Lyon, 1575), fol. 274r-v; and the celebration of Venus Genetrix in *Pervigilium veneris*. Edmund has been said to worship Aphrodite Pandemos. But see the tenth Orphic hymn, beginning "*O physi*," "O, Nature, Goddess, Mother of all, resourceful Mother"; Gustaf Fredén, *Orpheus and the Goddess of Nature*, Göteborgs Universitets Årsskrift, LXIV (Göteborg, 1958), pp. 15-16. Cf. Tribolo's nature-goddess statue in the Louvre, reproduced in Bertha H. Wiles, *The Fountains of Florentine Sculptors and Their Followers, from Donatello to Bernini* (Cambridge, Mass., 1938), fig. 167. Curtius, p. 107*n*, connects the Priapean deity with *physis*. From one point of view, Edmund's speech may be seen as a blasphemous parody of prayer; cf. the "Lover's Mass" as parody of the mass and an "observaunce of Venus goddes of love," discussed by Eleanor Prescott Hammond, "The Lover's Mass," *JEGP*, VII (1908), 95-104. Edmund's form of address is "thou"; his "services" are "due" to Nature in the double sense of votary and lover. Further, Goneril's remark to Edmund (IV.ii.23) appears to reinforce the sense of his invocation's concluding line; its *double entendre* appears also in Benjamin Rudyerd's *Le prince d' amour* (1660), p. 34. See also Hermann Kleinknecht, *Die Gebetsparodie in der Antike* (Stuttgart, 1937).

[38] A Renaissance *topos*, whose ubiquity may qualify Warner G. Rice's view ("The *Paradossi* of Ortensio Lando," *Essays and Studies in English and Comparative Literature* by Members of the English Dept. of the Univ. of Michigan, Univ. of Michigan Pubs., Language and Literature, VIII [Ann Arbor, 1932], 72) of the ultimate contribution of Lando (1543) to Edmund's speech. The natural superiority of bastards is discussed *inter alia* in Huarte de San Juan, *The Examination of Mens Wits* (1594), pp. 319-321; Erasmus, *Praise of Folly*, p. 13; Anthony Munday's tr. of Estienne's *Defence of Contraries* (tr. from Lando, 1593), sig. [O3v]; Webster's *Duchess of Malfi*, IV. i.42-44, and *The Devil's Law-Case*, IV.ii.275-280; *The Life and Death of the Lord Cromwell*, I.ii.63-83 (*The Shakespeare Apocrypha*, ed. C. F. Tucker Brooke [Oxford, 1908]); J. C. Vanini, in *De admirandis naturae* (Paris, 1616), pp. 321-322; Scipion Dupleix, *The Resolver; or Curiosities of Nature* (1635), pp. 34-35; *The Poems of Thomas Carew*, ed. Rhodes Dunlap (Oxford, 1949), pp. 98, 261, citing Euripides, Drayton, Donne, and Burton, who in turn cites Cardanus; Rochester, "A Satyr against Marriage," *Collected Works*, ed. John Hayward (1926), pp. 94-95; *The Night-Walker*, Oct. 1696, p. 9; Gaspar à Reies, *Elysius jucundarum quæstionum campus*, Qu. 76, cited (n.d.) in Pierre Bayle, *A General Dictionary*, V (1737), 308*n*. Note the contemptuous remark concerning the British in Fletcher's King's Men's play, *Bonduca* (1611-14), "Their Mothers got 'em sleeping . . ."; I.i (*The Works of Francis Beaumont and John Fletcher*, ed. A. R. Waller, VI [Cambridge, Eng., 1908], 80). See also Nashe, III, 365-366. Cf. Maurice Baudin, *Les bâtards au théâtre en France de la Renaissance à la fin du*

by chance are good, according to the Renaissance proverb, by nature bad.[39] Furthermore, Edmund's rebellion is not only against the stigma of bastardy but also, implicitly at least, against the very basis of nobility and monarchy, right by birth and inheritance: A *man*'s a man, for a' that. Specifically, as does Lear in dividing the kingdom, he also impugns the law of primogeniture—Shakespeare's "primogenitive and due of birth."[40] Gloucester, too, undermines primogeniture, as well as legitimacy, by considering Edgar "a son . . . by order of law, some year elder than" Edmund, ". . . no dearer in my account" (I.i.19-21). In denying these principles of order, and in stressing conception rather than birth, Edmund helps demolish the bond, which Lear, in actions as well as words, had already undermined.

Foil to the Duke of Albany, who upholds the state, Edmund is of the class determined by birth that, as Aristotle said, cannot make a civil society or state. They are not "stable in faith, nor honoured of men, nor beloved of God," according to William Clerke's *The Triall of Bastardie* (1594), sig. ***4^v^. Indeed, John Ferne's *The Blazon of Gentrie* (1586) declares that, with certain exceptions not applicable

XVIIIe siècle, Johns Hopkins Studies in Romance Literatures and Languages, Vol. XXI (Baltimore, 1932).

39Tilley B104. See also George Ruggle, *Ignoramus*, 2nd Prologue (1630, p. 12). John Ferne's *The Blazon of Gentrie* (1586), p. 279, cites the proverb: "It is against nature if any good thing do proceede from a Bastard, *Quia male geniti, male nati, male nutriti, & male edocti sunt*." The "adulterous" bastard (i.e., proceeding from adultery) "is excluded, not onely by the civill and ecclesiasticall lawes, but also by the lawe of God . . .", declares Henry Swinburne, *A Briefe Treatise of Testaments and Last Willes* (1590), fol. 199^v^.

40*Troilus and Cressida,* I.iii.106. Edmund's assault on the law is echoed by another younger brother in Webster's *A Cure for a Cuckold* (1624-ca. 1625), II.i.1-13. Cf. Edmund (I.ii.190): "Let me, if not by birth, have lands by wit," and Webster's young Rochfield (II.i.3-4). In *The Christmas Prince* see also *Periander* (1608), ll. 7738-39 (Malone Soc. Repr. [1922], p. 243). See Tilley B687, "The younger Brother has the more wit"; B688. Like Edmund, Webster's Rochfield, rejected by the law, turns outlaw and later repents; tonally, Rochfield's complaint against the inheritance law resembles Edmund's. Cf. John Earle's *Micro-Cosmographie* (1628), "A Younger Brother," on such disinherited ones' unlawful recourses; and Thomas Fuller, *The Holy and Prophane State* (Cambridge, Eng., 1642), Bk. I, Ch. xv. Thomas Wilson's *The State of England . . . 1600*, ed. F. J. Fisher, *Camden Miscellany*, XVI (1936), 24, observes of younger brothers that "their state is of all stations for gentlemen most miserable. . . ." Cf. Fletcher's *The Elder Brother* (1625?). Edmund's positions on primogeniture, nature, and custom recur in John Ap-Robert, *The Younger Brother His Apologie, Or A Fathers Free Power Disputed, For the Disposition of His Lands* . . . (Oxford, 1634), especially pp. 7-8, 24, 30-31. Among precedents involving omission of primogeniture, the author cites the example of "Leir" (p. 48), who aimed "to conferre the Kingdome wholly upon his younger Child *Cordeilla*. . ."

to Edmund, "a bastarde, shall not be admitted to the honour of combate . . ." (p. 315), while Sir Thomas Ridley's *A View of the Civile and Ecclesiastical Law* (1607) affirms, ". . . he that is a bastard can neither challenge Honour nor Armes from the Father or Mother," a restriction significant for *Lear*'s last act. Underlining the sensitivity involved, Ridley concludes, ". . . albeit it be no sin for a bastard to be a bastard, yet is it a defect in him to be such a one, and a thing easily subject to reproch" (p. 200). In contrast to the sympathetic Faulconbridge in *King John*, such are, for example, the aptly named Don John of *Much Ado* as well as Spurio of *The Revengers Tragædie* (1606-1607). In Spurio the pathos which Edmund conceals by his boasts wells up, summoned by the Duchess' sympathetic

> Oh what a griefe 'tis, that a man should live
> But once ith world, and then to live a Bastard,
> The curse a'the wombe, the theefe of Nature, . . .
> Halfe dambd in the conception, by the justice
> Of that unbribed everlasting law. (I.ii.179-184)

Here, and in such cases as Edmund's, illegitimacy becomes not only an occasion for the exploration of true versus false values, of legitimate versus illegitimate assumptions. It becomes also a motivation for filial rebellion and would-be parricide and, by analogy, rebellion against God. It is a motivation, too, for further experiments in the same line, Edmund becoming the respectable Albany's cuckolder. As Spurio reasons,

> For indeed a bastard by nature should make Cuckolds,
> Because he is the sonne of a Cuckold-maker. (I.ii.223-224)

Like Spurio's "I feele it swell me; my revenge is just!" Edmund's prayer-revenge soliloquy ends in a swelling crescendo (I.ii.20-22).[41]

Like a Vice Dissimulation or Faux Semblant, the Machiavellian

[41]Cf. Jonson's *Sejanus* (1603), Act V, l. 1: "Swell, swell, my joyes." In Euripides' *Hippolytus* is sketched a prototype of the bastard as sensitive and self-conscious figure, at odds with his father. Opposing an inverted form of *physis*, his puritanical pride, against the *nomos* or convention which stamps him illegitimate, he refers to himself as *nothos*, bastard (*Four Plays of Euripides*, tr. Augustus T. Murray [Stanford, 1931], p. 287). Indeed, his father expects Hippolytus, as Edmund in soliloquy does, to plead the natural antipathy of bastard and legitimate (p. 279). His opening speech, a prayer offering service to the goddess of chastity, also bears an inverted resemblance to Edmund's opening-soliloquy prayer offering service to the goddess of generation. See also Seneca's *Hippolytus*, tr. John Studley (1567), in *Seneca, His Tenne Tragedies*, ed. Thomas Newton (1581), Tudor Trans. (1927).

Edmund panders to Gloucester's fixed credulity. Continuing to gull Gloucester and slander Edgar, Edmund depicts the latter, for his father's benefit, in superstitious language as "Mumbling of wicked charms, conjuring the moon / To stand auspicious mistress" (II.i.39-40); "I told him," resumes Edmund,

> the revenging Gods
> 'Gainst parricides did all the thunder bend;
> Spoke with how manifold and strong a bond
> The child was bound to th' father, (II.i.45-48)

alluding to Gloucester's concern with nemesis, to the traditional notions of thunder as the divine voice, and to the all-uniting bond. Hypocritical, too, in the face of his ally, Cornwall, who has expounded an Edmundian position regarding personal responsibility, the Bastard piously exclaims: "O Heavens! that this treason were not, or not I the detector!" and "How malicious is my fortune, that I must repent to be just!" (III.v.12-13, 9-10).

In his practicality, amorality, and his ends-justify-the-means ethic, Edmund, no "bastard to the time,"[42] is at one with the evil sisters to whom he was "contracted" (V.iii.228), a term possessing not only a physical but an ethical, legal, and metaphysical significance as well. "Yours in the ranks of death," he loyally enjoins Goneril (IV.ii.25), a vow which implies that they are *of* the ranks of destruction and death. Rejecting mercy (V.i.65-68), he is the voice of rugged relativism. Though, like Goneril and Regan, Edmund wagers on the quick grab ("Briefness and Fortune, work!" [II.i.19]), "this fortune," at the play's end, turns against him: "But what art thou," he asks Edgar, "That hast this fortune on me?" (V.iii.164-165). To the very end, despite his repentance, he is inspired by the pragmatic test of fortunate or unfortunate outcome. Opportunism is all: "men / Are as the time is" (V.iii.31-32), anticipating Lady Macbeth's recipe for deceit: "To beguile the time, / Look like the time" (I.v.64-65).[43] To the Captain, a lesser Edmund, he declares shortly before Edmund himself has "done," "write happy when th' hast done" (V.iii.36).

Finally, in contrast to Lear, who is "every inch a king," Edmund

[42]*King John,* I.i.207.

[43]Cf. Alemán's *Guzman de Alfarache*, IV, 242: "Men must sell according to the season ['*El tiempo es el que lo vende*'], and make their market as the time serves."

is every other inch a gentleman.[44] His concern with honor and chivalry at the combat scene (cf. V.iii.141-145) points to his craving for respectability. His ironically self-preoccupied outcry, at sight of the sisters' bodies, "Yet Edmund was belov'd" (V.iii.239), significantly passive, indicates the similar basis of his needs. At the end his "single virtue" (V.iii.103), which he has "trusted," fails him; he had staked all against fortune on his solitary and self-sustaining *virtù*. As Edmund lives and dies by that "virtue"—"to be tender-minded," he warns the Captain, "Does not become a sword" (V.iii.32-33)—his repentance is also symbolically marked by his unsuccessful "token of reprieve" offered to the Captain: "take my sword" (V.iii.250).

THE FREE-WILL PROBLEM

> *C'est une plaisante chose à considérer, de ce qu'il y a des gens dans le monde qui, ayant renoncé à toutes les loix de Dieu . . . , s'en sont fait eux mesmes auxquelles ils obéissant exactement. . . .*
>
> —Pascal, *Pensées*, No. 412

In contrast to Christianity, which opens tragedy up to the illimitable mystery, Edmund finds his circle closed: the fortune upon which he wagered reveals itself to be a turning wheel. As in similar scenes in Marlowe's *Edward II* (1591-1593) and in *Macbeth*, for example, the larger villain is mirrored in the advice he bestows on the smaller; so young Mortimer in Marlowe's play, counseling Gurney in regicide, bids him act

> As thou intendest to rise by Mortimer,
> Who now makes Fortune's wheel turn as he please. (V.ii.52-53)[45]

Yet at the conclusion Edmund's wheel is seen to turn him. "The wheel is come full circle; I am here" (V.iii.174).

The wheels in *Lear* include the *Mirror-for-Magistrate*-like ones on which the wicked characters have ridden, of these only Edmund recognizing the futility of the ride as he drops off; the practical wheel

[44]Cf. Nashe, *Pierce Penilesse*, in *Works*, I, 176: "there is no friendship to be had with him that is resolute to doe or suffer any thing rather than to endure the destinie whereto he was borne: for he will not spare his owne Father or Brother, to make himselfe a Gentleman.

"*Fraunce, Italy*, and *Spaine*, are all full of these false hearted *Machivillions*. . . ."

[45]Ed. H. B. Charlton and R. D. Waller (1933).

which the prudent man will either dismount as it heads into peril or mount as it ascends, as the Fool advises (II.iv.71-74); the "wheel of fire, that mine own tears / Do scald like molten lead" (IV.vii.47-48), upon which Lear himself is bound; and, finally, the larger wheel, the unmentioned mysterious wheel of the universe and the "mysteries of things," which the Divine Power turns and whose meaning is not yet—if ever—revealed to mortals. In a final sense, whatever "meaning" *King Lear* has perhaps lies in the celebration of the mystery of that ultimate wheel.

Since Edmund conceives himself bound to a wheel, some question may be raised concerning the "freedom of will" often uniformly ascribed to Shakespeare's villains. Moreover, if the peculiarity of Edmund, among others of Shakespeare's villains, is understood, he may be seen in a different light from his compeers, with whom he is usually indiscriminately joined. While, for example, he shares certain attitudes of Iago, he does not share all of them. One of the obsessions of Edmund, for instance, is his bastardly birth (that "vicious mole of nature" in his "birth wherein" he is "not guilty") and its determining effect upon his life. Although he musters all his *virtù* against the misfortune of his coming into the world, partaking of the evil sisters' opportunistic morality, he is conscious of his social exclusion (I.ii.2-10) and lovelessness (V.iii.239). Sharing the deterministic overtones of the Bastard in *Much Ado*, Edmund might, in one sense, concur with Don John: "I cannot hide what I am" (I.iii.14).

In addition to those sensitivities deriving from an illegitimacy which his father insensitively emphasizes at the start of the play, Edmund comes to some self-knowledge of the evil determining his nature: "some good I mean to do / Despite of mine own nature" (V.iii.243-244). While, therefore, Edmund reveals the energetic Renaissance impulse of *virtù* or individualistic freedom against the powers of fortune, it is not the "freedom" which Iago espouses. When Edmund mocks Gloucester's trust in the stars, it is the irony that not the stars but the all-too-earthly and adulterous Gloucester himself caused his bastardy, which touches Edmund: "Fut! I should have been that I am had the maidenliest star in the firmament twinkled on my bastardizing" (I.ii.138-140). The Bastard, in effect, reveals the paradoxical determinism of the emancipated will.

In order to indicate a significant distinction of Edmund concerning free will, it may perhaps suffice to suggest that *King Lear* offers little evidence of the sort that *Othello* provides regarding its villainous *Geist der stets verneint*. One of Iago's most revealing speeches occurs in *Othello* at I.iii.322-330:

> Virtue! a fig! 'tis in ourselves that we are thus or thus. Our bodies are our gardens, to the which our wills are gardeners; so that if we will plant nettles, or sow lettuce, set hyssop and weed up thyme, supply it with one gender of herbs, or distract it with many, either to have it sterile with idleness, or manured with industry, why, the power and corrigible authority of this lies in our wills.

Man, according to Iago, has complete freedom, an idea not expressed by Edmund and one which St. Augustine labored, in his anti-Pelagian writings, to eradicate. While at the same time, of course, a prisoner of his own demonic will, Iago has succinctly and recognizably expressed the Pelagian heresy; that this is so may be seen in an apparently unstressed parallel from the writings of Pelagius:

> we have implanted in us by God a possibility for acting in both directions. It resembles, as I may say, a root which is most abundant in its produce of fruit. It yields and produces diversely according to man's will; and is capable, at the planter's own choice, of either shedding a beautiful bloom of virtues, or of bristling with the thorny thicket of vices. . . . But that we really do a good thing, or speak a good word, or think a good thought, proceeds from our own selves. . . . Nothing good, and nothing evil, on account of which we are deemed either laudable or blameworthy, is born with us, but is done by us: for we are born not fully developed, but with a capacity for either conduct; we are formed naturally without either virtue or vice; and previous to the action of our own proper will, the only thing in man is what God has formed in him.[46]

Like Iago, Pelagius attributes man's actions for good or ill to man's own independent will; and, like Iago, he proposes the potential in garden imagery, man being the gardener to his own body. In this crucial matter the fifth-century British monk and the Renaissance-conceived Eternal Demonic are seen to be at one; while, despite the usual tendency of critics to generalize about Shakespearean villains,

[46]Pelagius, as quoted by St. Augustine, *The Anti-Pelagian Works*, II, in *The Works of Aurelius Augustine*, ed. Marcus Dods, XII (Edinburgh, 1885), 19, 18, 58. See also Giovanni Pico della Mirandola, "Oration on the Dignity of Man," tr. Elizabeth L. Forbes (*The Renaissance Philosophy of Man*, ed. Ernst Cassirer et al. [Chicago, 1948], p. 225): "Whatever seeds each man cultivates will grow to maturity and bear in him their own fruit." Ultimately, of course, the garden imagery is biblical; cf. Matthew vii.18, which Augustine cites.

the Bastard that Shakespeare drew seems unpreoccupied by such pretensions.

THE DON JUAN CONVENTION

> *Felicity is a continual progress of the desire, from one object to another; the attaining of the former, being still but the way to the latter.*
>
> —Hobbes, *Leviathan*

As Edmund's hypocrisy foreshadows Molière's "faux dévot," Tartuffe, so, in refusing to accept any external restraint on his natural impulse, Edmund may be partly in the tradition of Molière's "grand seigneur méchant homme," the seducer-atheist, Dom Juan.[47] Edmund's lineage is like that assailed by Garasse in *La doctrine curieuse* . . . , cited above, whose sixth book concerns those libertine evil-doers who usurp the word "nature." In order to illuminate aspects of his character, it may be relevant to indicate certain affinities between Shakespeare's Edmund and some elements of the seventeenth-century Don Juan tradition.

Between *Lear* in 1605 and Shadwell's *The Libertine* in 1675, a figure of European drama was the rebellious and amoral libertine Don Juan, whose pattern of rebellion comprised usually such traits or tenets as the following: (1) pride, sensuality, and lust; (2) blasphemy and defiance of divine justice, divine power, and punishment; (3) relativism, disdain for natural law, and a contempt for human morality and law as mere "opinion"; (4) regard for nature as goddess, in place of God; (5) disbelief in providence, in favor of destiny, chance, or fortune; (6) naturalistic determinism along with insistence on his own *virtù*; (7) Epicureanism or Lucretianism and materialism; and (8) a defiant death, challenging the heavens. In addition, some type of would-be parricide may have been a feature. Since it is evident that, except for the eighth, such resemblances as those listed above, as well as a self-proclaimed handsomeness (I.ii.7-9) and a notable attractiveness to women, link Edmund to the Don Juan motif, a review of certain of its conventions may be appropriate.

Initiation of the Don Juan theme has been ascribed to Tirso de Molina's [Gabriel Téllez'] *El burlador de Sevilla y convidado de piedra*, which, though it was printed in 1630, may have been per-

[47] Tirso de Molina, who sketched Don Juan, also portrayed a female Tartuffe in his play *Marta la piadosa*.

formed as early as 1613.[48] Tirso drew upon old legends, whose elements were current in romances popular in Spain and other countries, and upon folk tales passed on by oral transmission.[49]

Among plays succeeding Tirso's in the convention is Dorimon's *Le festin de pierre ou le fils criminel* (first performed in 1658), subtitled in the second edition *L'athée foudroyé.* Its Don Juan figure is a *libertin de moeurs* as well as a *libertin de pensée*, who, it has been claimed, for the first time in the convention (in a long soliloquy at the start of I.iii) analyzes himself. Anticipated in this device, however, by Edmund's self-identifying soliloquy at the beginning of I.ii, Dorimon's Dom Jouan is followed in it by Molière, Rosimond, Shadwell, and others. Like Edmund, Dorimon's hero there reveals the motivation of his hatred and jealousy, his own despised state. In addition, like Shakespeare's villain, he claims nature as his goddess and insists on natural determinism and fate, rather than on providence, as the cause of his being:

> C'est au gré du destin que nous venons au jour.
> La nature est ma Mere et le sort m'a fait naistre,
> Et le Ciel est tout seul et mon Pere, et mon estre. (ll. 284-286)[50]

Like Edmund, too, he challenges law, including the claims of his gods, filial obligation, and the law of the land:

> Que le destin se bande ou pour, ou contre moy,
> Pere, Princes, ny Dieux ne me feront la loy. (ll. 291-292)

Close to Dorimon's is Villiers' play of the same name (first performed in 1659), in which the hero similarly announces,

> Que le sort soit prospere, ou qu'il soit ennuyeux,
> Je suis mon Roy, mon Maistre, et mon sort, et mes Dieux.
> (ll. 341-342)[51]

48See Leo Weinstein, *The Metamorphoses of Don Juan* (Stanford, 1959), p. 7. The characteristics listed above are only limitedly relevant to the Spanish priest Tirso's *Burlador*; apparently uniquely in the genre, it is believed to be involved in dogmatic polemics.

49See also *L'ateista fulminato*, scenario, published by F. de Simone Brouwer (1901), *Rendiconti della Reale Accademia dei Lincei*, in Enzo Petraccone, *La commedia dell' arte* (Naples, 1927). Before Tirso, Leucino in Juan de la Cueva's *El infamador* (produced in Seville, 1581) has been considered a type of Don Juan, as has Leonido in Lope Félix de Vega Carpio's *Fianza satisfecha* (1612-15). Two centuries after Tirso, by an intentional parallel, the victim of Kierkegaard's Don Juan (*Diary of a Seducer*), as, in another sense, of Shakespeare's, is named Cordelia.

50In *Le festin de pierre avant Molière*, ed. G. Gendarme de Bévotte (Paris, 1907).

51Ibid.

Defiantly he upholds as his sole legal criterion the pursuit of his natural impulses, insisting to the timid,

> Que le feu, le viol, le fer, le parricide,
> Et tout ce dont tu m'as si bien entretenu,
> Passe dans mon esprit comme non advenu;
> S'il en reste, ce n'est qu'une idée agreable,
> Quiconque vit ainsi ne peut estre blâmable,
> Il suit les sentimens de la Nature.... (ll. 1754-59)

While tolerant of parricide, he also resembles Shakespeare's Bastard in his sensual gratification. Indeed, he is the steadfast and unrepentant sensualist:

> mon cœur...
> Ne peut jamais souffrir ny remords, ny dédit;
> J'ay contenté mes sens, et pour ne te rien taire,
> Je le ferois encor s'il estoit à refaire. (ll. 1521-24)

In short, the heroes of Dorimon and Villiers are rebels against paternal authority. With courage never to submit or yield, the Don Juan figures refuse to bow to heavenly "tyranny." In this, they ironically resemble Shakespeare's hero, who dies after defying the heavens, rather than his villain, whose death is accompanied by repentance, an emotion they consider cowardly. Like Lear, too, they are not restrained from probing the mystery of things and extending their curiosity to the heavens themselves. In brief, like Edmund during the play and like Lear in the storm as well as at the conclusion, they prostrate themselves to no higher right or authority of rule.[52]

Further, in Molière's Dom Juan play (first performed in 1665), the hero-villain is a proud, self-sufficient atheist and hypocritical sensualist, whose only standard of behavior is the pleasure it brings: "... songeons seulement à ce qui nous peut donner du plaisir" (I.ii).[53] Recognizing, like his predecessors, no judgment as valid outside his own will, he proceeds unrepentantly from crime to crime. And, like them, he does not scruple to cast a glance into supernatural mysteries.

[52]Promethean analogies are discussed in the comparison of Aeschylus' *Prometheus Bound* and *Lear* in Ch. viii. Cf. also Micheline Sauvage, *Le cas Don Juan* (Paris, 1953): "... le mythe de don Juan se définit à l'intérieur du mythe de Prométhée" (p. 157). "Don Juan est le héros qui brave les Puissances (Dieu ... le Père), qui viole leur Ordre (le temps, la loi, la morale) ... qui ne partage pas les croyances collectives." His sword represents "le courage *humain* dressé contre une *transcendance* insupportable" (p. 122).

[53]*Oeuvres de Molière,* ed. Eugène Despois and Paul Mesnard, V (1880), 92.

Typically, again, the sole criterion of law as natural impulse is expressed by Dom Juan in the piece of Rosimond (Claude La Rose), *Le nouveau festin de pierre ou l'athée foudroyé* (1669):

> J'ose tout ce qui peut contenter mes désirs;
> Je n'examine point si j'ay droit de le faire:
> Tout est juste pour moy quand l'objet me peut plaire,
> Et ne prenant des lois que de ma passion. (I.ii)[54]

Moreover, of interest in relation to *Lear* is the fact that such plays, to reduce the risk of offense through irreligious expression, also employ the paganizing device. In Giacinto Andrea Cicognini (*Il convitato di pietra*, before 1650),[55] Dorimon, Villiers, and Rosimond the matter has generally been de-Christianized to remove possible provocation and to allow the dramatist greater freedom in thought and character. In Villiers, for instance, Jupiter (l. 891) replaces the Christian Deity, while the valet ridicules Neptune and the Tritons (ll. 1056-62), and repeatedly Dom Juan mocks the gods.

Supposedly the first English play in the convention,[56] Thomas Shadwell's *The Libertine* (performed in 1675) appears to have borrowed more heavily than has been noted from *Lear*. The Restoration dramatist, who knew and elsewhere adapted Shakespeare's work, said he put together this play in three weeks, "there being no Act in it, which cost me above five days writing . . . the Play-house having great occasion for a play."[57] Shadwell's Don John not only espouses

[54]In *Les contemporains de Molière*, ed. Victor Fournel (Paris, 1875), III, 328.

[55]On the question of Cicognini's authorship, raised by Benedetto Croce, see *The Year's Work in Modern Language Studies*, XXIV (1962), 284-285, citing a newly published letter of March 24, 1632, by Cicognini's father, Jacopo, regarding his son and the performance of a comedy called *Il convitato di pietra*.

[56]But see Fletcher's *The Wild Goose Chase* (1621[?]), where the libertine Mirabel keeps an extensive inventory of his conquests; Sir Aston Cokayne's *The Tragedy of Ovid* (1662), whose author probably knew the Italian *L'ateista fulminato*; Massinger's *The Unnatural Combat* (1621–ca. 1626), in which the libertine Malefort puts forth naturalistic arguments in defense of his sensual freedom and is killed by a lightning stroke; and C. S. sieur de la Croix's *L'inconstance punie*, published in 1630 but presumably available earlier, in which a rake braves the gods and is punished by lightning. Regarding other relevant plays, see John Harold Wilson, *The Influence of Beaumont and Fletcher on Restoration Drama* (Columbus, O., 1928).

[57]1676, Preface, sig. [A4v]. *The Libertine* is claimed by G. Gendarme de Bévotte (*La légende de Don Juan* [Paris, 1911], I, 191-192) to contain numerous original elements; yet the pursuit of the hero by two women at once is already in *Lear*, and Shadwell's Don John alludes to them in virtually the same terms as does Edmund.

and expands Edmund's naturalistic and sensually amoral views but seems, as in the thunder allusions below, to reflect Shakespeare's lines themselves; for example, Edmund muses,

> To both these sisters have I sworn my love; . . .
> . . . Neither can be enjoy'd
> If both remain alive . . . , (V.i.55, 58-59)

Albany later interjecting "'Tis she is sub-contracted to this lord" (V.iii.87). Reminiscently, Shadwell's Don John, at the opening of Act IV, observes, ". . . I have been contracted to both the Sisters, and this day resolve to marry 'em, and . . . enjoy them."

Before Hobbes[58] English libertine characterization in *Lear* and *The Atheist's Tragedie,* among others, had already delineated such views as Shadwell's villains express. Don John's follower, Shadwell's Don Lopez, flaunts their common deterministic notion: "All our actions are necessitated, none command their own wills. . . . What we are, we are by Nature." "If we be bad, 'tis Nature's fault that made us so," agrees Don John.[59] Further, Edmund's defiance of the rule of law and espousal of nature, as a continuing libertine commonplace of the seventeenth century, is apparent from Restoration drama, through which echo the doctrines of Rochester and other Renaissance rakes. Like Edmund, for example, Don John in Thomas Otway's *Don Carlos* (1676) resounds the Renaissance note:

> Why should dull Law rule Nature, who first made
> That Law, by which her self is now betray'd? . . .
> Law was an Innovation brought in since. (II.i.1-7)[60]

As late as 1675, in Shadwell, defiance of thunder to indicate the rebel against divine power was a readily identifiable theatrical convention. Anticipated in other Don Juan depictions, as well as in Lear himself, it appears also in *The Atheist's Tragedie* (1607-1611), whose villain, D'Amville, is related to Edmund and the rebellious Lear, as well as to the villain-hero of *Macbeth* (1606). Expressing the religious view of thunder, for example, Jean Bodin's *La demonomanie* (Paris, 1598) observes, "c'est Dieu qui gresle, tonne & foudroye"

[58]Thomas B. Stroup, "Shadwell's Use of Hobbes," *SP*, XXXV (1938), 405-432, omits the earlier development.

[59]*The Libertine,* Act III, pp. 39-40.

[60]*The Works of Thomas Otway,* ed. J. C. Ghosh (Oxford, 1932), Vol. I.

(sig. [Ccvii]), just as John Day's *The Travailes of the Three English Brothers* (1607) declares, ". . . the Gods speake in thunder."[61] Like Lear, however, in the storm scenes of Act III and at the end, Dorimon's Dom Jouan challenges that thunder:

> Ouy, ce fer armeroit ma main contre un Tonnere,
> [Luy montrant son espée.]
> Si le Ciel m'attaquoit, je luy ferois la guerre,
> Tout au moins je mourrois dans cette volonté. (ll. 1829-31)

Further, in Rosimond's Don Juan play (V.vii), the hero echoes Lear's defiance of the "sulph'rous and thought-executing fires" (III.ii.4):

> Quand la terre sous moy fondroit pour m'engloutir,
> Que chaque pas seroit un précipice, un gouffre,
> Qu'il pleuveroit sur moy de la flamme et du soulfre,
> Mon cœur ferme et constant ne pourroit s'ebranler,[62]

here resembling not only Villiers' protagonist ("Mais apprens que mon cœur ne se peut ébranler," l. 1510) but also the finally obdurate Macbeth:

> The mind I sway by and the heart I bear
> Shall never sag with doubt nor shake with fear. (V.iii.9-10)

Again, paralleling Lear's invitation to the "all-shaking thunder" to "strike" and the lightning to "singe my white head" (III.ii.6-7), Rosimond's hero cries,

> Et pour te faire voir qu'on ne peut m'y résoudre,
> Tonne quand il voudra, j'attens le coup de foudre. (V.vii)

Indeed, the titles themselves of the Don Juan plays indicate the role of the elements in relation to the central figure: *L'ateista fulminato*, the seventeenth-century Italian scenario of uncertain date; Dorimon's *Le festin de pierre ou le fils criminel*, whose subtitle was changed later to *L'athée foudroyé*; and Rosimond's *Le nouveau festin de pierre ou l'athée foudroyé*.

Lear's defiance of the traditional voice of the heavens ("Rumble thy bellyful!" [III.ii.14], etc.) is more explicitly revealed by Shad-

[61]Sig. [A4v]; cf. sig. B2.

[62]*Les contemporains de Molière*, ed. Fournel, III, 376.

well's Don John when caught in a dreadful storm: "let the Heav'ns do their worst," he challenges; "Let the Clowds roar on, and vomit all their Sulphur out. . . . you paltry foolish bugbear Thunder," he taunts, "am I the mark of your sensless rage?"[63] And Lear's powerful cosmic defiance (III.ii), like that of Rosimond above, may have left its mark upon Shadwell's memory: "rage! blow! . . . / You sulph'rous and thought-executing fires" (III.ii.1, 4), just as Kent's choral commentary,

> Such sheets of fire, such bursts of horrid thunder,
> Such groans of roaring wind and rain, I never
> Remember to have heard . . . , (III.ii.46-48)

reemerges at the same third-act point in Shadwell's play, where the Captain observes: "Such dreadful claps of Thunder I never yet remember'd" (p. 35). Hence, parallels as suggested here and above may indicate that the so-called first English Don Juan play, in addition to other origins, reached back some seventy years to Shakespeare's *Lear*. Well known as a Shakespeare adapter, Shadwell in *The Libertine* thus partly utilized *Lear*'s protagonist and villain for materials to depict his own libertine rebel.[64]

[63]*The Libertine*, Act III, pp. 35-36. Cf. atheistic thunder defiance in Jonson's *Sejanus*, Act II, ll. 159-162; Sejanus advises Drusus:

> Though heav'n drop sulphure, and hell belch out fire,
> Laugh at the idle terrors: Tell proud Jove,
> Betweene his power, and thine, there is no oddes.
> 'Twas onely feare, first, in the world made gods.

[64]In terms perhaps ultimately applicable to Shakespeare's hero as well, Coleridge admiringly remarked of Shadwell's Don John: "Who . . . can deny a portion of sublimity to the tremendous consistency with which he stands out the last fearful trial, like a second Prometheus?" (*Biographia Literaria*, ed. J. Shawcross [Oxford, 1907], II, 190). With intuitive awareness, Coleridge compares the intelligibility of the Don Juan figure and Milton's Satan (II, 186). For these two may be linked by the villain-hero convention; that convention may also connect Marlowe's heroic *révoltés* with Shakespeare's rebellious villain-hero pair, Edmund and Lear, and the consummate villain-hero, Macbeth, as well as with the Don Juan tradition of the seventeenth century. "The keynote of the seventeenth century," states Godfrey Davies' *The Early Stuarts 1603-1660* (Oxford, 1937), p. xix, "was revolt against authority," including, it might be added, a Promethean regicide.

In general, these "advanced" figures rebel against traditional notions of heavenly power and justice, providence and the other world, and involve themselves with libertinism or materialism of some kind. With still greater prescience, Coleridge associates this type of amoralist with a, by now, familiar history: ". . . nor . . . can it be denied . . . that the (so called) *system of nature* (i.e. materialism, with the utter rejection of moral responsibility, of a present providence, and of both present and future retribution) may influence the characters and actions of individuals, and even of com-

In addition, dedicated to the arch-libertine Rochester and produced in 1674, Nathaniel Lee's *The Tragedy of Nero* also maintains the convention of obdurate defiance of the thunder as a mark of the libertine-atheist. In his final speech, Nero, like the third- and last-act Lear, continues to brave the heavens. He avows, "If there be Gods, sure this must be their voice." Yet he challenges,

> If they have any Thunder, let it come;
> I'le stand the heavy shock, and brave my doom. (1675, p. 54)

Since of the two rebels against the heavens, Edmund, the villain, ultimately repents, and Lear, the hero, dies after assailing "heaven's vault" (V.iii.259), it may be significant that both these endings seem to involve seventeenth-century dramatic conventions. Except for the monk Tirso's Don Juan, who finally repents, the hero-villains of the other seventeenth-century Don Juan plays considered above die courageously challenging the divine powers; even Tirso's character, courageous also in the face of the supernatural, postpones, like Marlowe's Faustus, his repentance for a debauched life until it is too late. In *L'ateista fulminato* the prototypical character refuses to repent, while in Cicognini's *Il convitato de pietra*, Don Giovanni dies uncontrite. Similarly, the heroes of Dorimon and Villiers at their deaths refuse, considering repentance cowardly. Before he is, Faustus-like, swallowed up amid thunder and flames by earth, Molière's protagonist insists, "Non, non, il ne sera pas dit, quoi qu'il arrive, que je sois capable de me repentir" (V.v),[65] and he keeps his word.

Yet, in contrast to the ultimate defiance of the Don Juan figures, Edmund would seem in the issue of repentance to be paralleling other, and perhaps more indigenous, patterns. Among these may be suggested the convention in England of the repentant villain, represented, for example, by Faustus and by D'Amville in *The Atheist's Tragedie*, who, like Tirso's figure, acknowledge God too late; and a notion of some Elizabethans that the atheist, despite himself, could not completely stifle conscience: ". . . who is more feareful to die," asks Nashe, "or dies with more terror and afrightment, then an Athe-

munities, to a degree that almost does away the distinction between men and devils, and will make the page of the future historian resemble the narration of a madman's dreams" (*Biographia Literaria*, II, 186).

[65]*Oeuvres de Molière*, ed. Despois and Mesnard, V, 202.

ist" (II, 121). William Vaughan's *The Golden-Grove* (1600), after Calvin, affirms that the scorn of atheists is merely "laughter from the teeth outward" (sig. C2). In contrast to Macbeth's final obduracy, such last-minute conversions are conventional, for instance, in English Renaissance domestic tragedy.[66] Furthermore, Edmund's repentance, like D'Amville's disavowal of naturalism (V.ii.282-291) in *The Atheist's Tragedie*, has noteworthy affinities with the convention of the repentant rake in Restoration comedy and the repentant villain in Restoration tragedy.[67]

Although Edmund's last-minute *prise de conscience* anticipates the Restoration libertine conversions, also notable for their improbability, Shakespeare employs the conventional repentance device for his own ironical purposes. Edmund's contrition comes, in his own words, "pat . . . like the catastrophe of the old comedy" (I.ii.141-142), but it arrives too late to save his victim. The Bastard seems, indeed, one of Shakespeare's "fools of time, / Which die for goodness, who have lived for crime" (Sonnet 124). Moreover, his first-act "catastrophe of the old comedy" reference, if it calls to mind morality figures of punishment who visit judgment in this life on sinners,[68] may also suggest Edmund's own earlier atheistically sophisticated indifference to retribution. Finally, in Shakespeare's play the contrasting repentance of the villain serves paradoxically to emphasize the ultimately unreconciled defiance of the hero.

[66]See Henry Hitch Adams, *English Domestic or, Homiletic Tragedy 1575 to 1642* (New York, 1943), pp. 185-186. Cf. also the converted villain in Webster's *The Duchess of Malfi*; Shirley's theme of the roué's final conversion; and that of rebellious sons in the denouement of sentimental comedy. The repentance pattern is discussed in Arthur Sherbo's *English Sentimental Drama* (East Lansing, Mich., 1957), pp. 32-46.

[67]David S. Berkeley, "The Penitent Rake in Restoration Comedy," *MP*, XLIX (1952), 223-233, also notes the Restoration tragic convention of the penitent villain.

[68]E.g., Divyne Correctioun in Sir David Lindsay's *Ane Satyre of the Thrie Estaits*, Versions I (1540), II (1552), and III (1554); God's Visitation in *The Trial of Treasure* (1567); and Adversity in Skelton's *Magnificence* (1515-23).

CHAPTER VII

Pagan Superstition: Gloucester

SUMMARIZING RENAISSANCE ATTITUDES to pagan belief, I suggest that the age accepted the conventional dualism between superstition and atheism as extremes to the mean of true religion and that pagans, external to the Christian faith, regardless of time or place, were by definition held to share those extremes. Given the pagan premises of *King Lear*, therefore, it is reasonable to anticipate the usual superstitious attitudes ascribed to pagans in Renaissance treatises. What were the traits associated with the superstitious type, according to the Elizabethan view? Although astrological beliefs were widely held and were undoubtedly represented in Shakespeare's audience, a distinguishing factor was one of degree of anxious subservience to astral influences. Not to be equated with modern views, Renaissance conventions of the superstitious man included overemotional or vacillating and unstable dread before the all-determining heavens, an excess of helpless credulity or veneration before those powers, and an apparently unreasoning commitment to the special effects of celestial events upon individual lives and deeds.

In the convention from Theophrastus and Plutarch through Renaissance religious controversy and seventeenth-century "characters," the "superstitious" type became relatively well defined and readily recognizable. Indeed, in his writings King James repeatedly identified and condemned such superstitious excesses. Hence, it is not merely astrological leanings, shared by many Elizabethans, which define the superstitious man, but the excessive effect of similar beliefs on his general disposition and behavior. Despite the sympathy, therefore, which fellow believers might have accorded Gloucester's stellar fears, a priori, the Renaissance could have attributed such religious immoderateness to pagans.

First, the superstitious were fearful. Lacking faith in providence, they substituted a world filled with hidden menaces, dark threats, and frightening omens, a world in which the gods, if they existed, killed men for their sport. Just as he may, in part, suggest Theophrastus' Superstitious Man or *desidaimon*,[1] Gloucester may recall the evils of superstitious religion as described by Epicurus. The old earl's mysterious universe of fear-inspiring eclipses operating at the behest of blind forces, offering omens of worse to come, was far from the ideals of Epicurean ataraxy. Like Epicurus, Plutarch pictured the superstitious man as a victim of ominous dreams, apparitions, ghosts, horrible shapes, voices, visions of bottomless pits full of tortures and miseries. Thus, declares Plutarch, "unhappy and wretched superstition, by fearing overmuch and without reason, that which it imagineth to be nought, never taketh heed how it submitteth it selfe to all miseries."[2] Fear of demons, it may be noted, in connection with Edgar's feigned possession, was a feature of pagan religious anxiety, described by Hippocrates. Further, at the eclipse of the sun or moon, complains Seneca, "groundless superstition drives every one into panic."[3]

Similarly, Joseph Hall (*Characters of Vertues and Vices*, 1608) points out that "Superstition is Godlesse religion, devout impietie. The superstitious is fond in observation, servile in feare. . ." (p. 87). Regarding those who were disturbed by omens, William Blandie's translation of Osorio da Fonseca's *The Five Bookes* (1576) notes that in some instances ". . . all men that were wonderfully geven to that kind of religion, whom they tearmed fanaticall, were troubled with continuall feare, and care of the minde that bredde continuall doubt" (fol. 98v). In the *Diseases of the Time* (1622) Francis Rous observes, ". . . Superstition is a Bastard begotten by an . . . ignorant feare of the Deitie" (p. 51). "Skie-staring cocks-combs," as Jonson called them,[4] were the frequent butt of Elizabethan dramatists such as Jonson,

[1]*The Characters of Theophrastus*, tr. J. M. Edmonds, Loeb Classical Lib. (1929), pp. 78-83. See Peter J. Koets, *Deisidaimonia: A Contribution to the Knowledge of Religious Terminology in Greek* (Purmerend, Neth., 1929), for a classification of the term's usages.

[2]*Morals*, tr. Philemon Holland (1603), p. 262. On superstitious fear see Christopher Heydon, *A Defence of Judiciall Astrologie* (Cambridge, Eng., 1603), sig. [D2r-v]: ". . . as *Plutarch* noteth, the superstitious alwaies thinke the gods readie to doe hurt. By meanes whereof he accounteth them in worse case then malefactours or fugitives, who if they once recover the altar are there secured from Feare, where neverthelesse the superstitious are in greatest thraldome."

[3]*Physical Science in the Time of Nero, Being a Translation of the Quaestiones Naturales of Seneca*, tr. John Clarke (1910), p. 271.

[4]*Every Man Out of His Humour* (1599), III.vii.19. See Bertil Johansson, *Religion and Superstition in the Plays of Ben Jonson and Thomas Middleton* (Upsala, 1950).

Fletcher, and Middleton and earned the expressed opposition of such men of letters as Sidney and Harington.[5] Their perpetual unease is remarked, for example, by John Weemes: "The labourer after his labour findes his sleepe comfortable unto him, *Eccles.* 5.12. but the superstitious is as much troubled, when hee sleepeth, as when hee waketh . . . *dormit ratio sed vigilat semper metus,* his reason is asleepe, but his feare alwayes waketh."[6]

Second, the superstitious replaced providence with destiny, chance, or fate. But destiny, as Roger Hutchinson in *The Image of God* (1560) declared, made all things licit, for "If we think al thing to be governed by destini, we must nedes agre to the libertines, which make no difference betwene good and bad . . . calling notable vices, vocations commaunded of God" (sig. [Hvii^{r-v}]). Moreover, destiny detracted from God's sovereignty; those who believe in it, charges John Chamber in *A Treatise against Judicial Astrologie* (1601), "most blasphemously impeach the divine providence. For if all our actions depend of the stars, then may God have an everlasting playing day, and let the world wag" (p. 4). Obviously, then, destiny was incongruous with Christian faith. Citing the esteemed Sidney, probably the *Arcadia*'s Pamela-Cecropia episode, Henry Cuffe in *The Differences of the Ages of Mans Life* (1607) affirms ". . . Eternitie and Chance, being (as the learned *Sir Philip* observed) things unsufferable together; If Chanceable, then not Eternall" (p. 13); and William Covell's *Polimanteia* (Cambridge, Eng., 1595), which contains one of the first references to Shakespeare ("All praise worthy. . . . Sweet Shakspeare . . . ," sig. R2^{v}), having therefore been probably noticed by the dramatist, condemns those who put destiny and "cælestiall causes" in their prognostications superstitiously "before Gods promises" (sig. [G4^{v}]). In short, the future was in God's hands, and, as Chamber concludes, "none harken to Figure-flingers but Fooles, since God hath reserved the knowledge of future things to himselfe" (p. 77).

Third, believing in destiny rather than providence, the superstitious held their fate to be sealed at their nativity, the stars continuing to have power over men's lives. Any omen, therefore, of a planetary nature, especially an eclipse, was considered of great moment and

[5]See M. S. Goldman, "Sidney and Harington as Opponents of Superstition," *JEGP*, LIV (1955), 526-548.

[6]*A Treatise of the Foure Degenerate Sonnes* (1636), p. 19.

was sufficient to throw their lives into confusion. Although credence in judicial astrology was widespread, those many who, as Montaigne said, "estudient et glosent leurs Almanachs,"[7] were conceived in some quarters as superstitious violators of the commandment against worshiping false gods. Such writers, for example, as John Hooper, in *A Declaration of the X. Holie Commaundements* (ca. 1588), cite "the law of man" forbidding always "the superstition of fore-destenieng," condemning offenders to the sword and the loss of their heads (fol. 36ᵛ); while William Lambarde, linked with Shakespeare in several ways, in *Eirenarcha* (1592) classes among rogues those who pretend to skill in telling of destinies (p. 420).

Associated with paganism—Hooper's *Declaration* calls it "this Egyptiacall and Ethnickes foolishnes" (fol. 38)—illicit star knowledge in some circles evoked ridicule, especially among the clergy and the court; so fantastic, indeed, did predictions become that to "lie like an almanac" passed into proverb. Interestingly relevant to Gloucester's belief were the satirical mock prognostications, paralleling Gloucester's fearful reaction to eclipses, almost in his own words (I.ii.107-110): "Ecclipses both of Sun and Moone, with their dangerous and subsequent effects," sneers the epistle to the reader of *Vox Graculi, or Jacke Dawes Prognostication . . . for This Yeere 1623* (1622, sig. A2ᵛ), as does one Simon Smell-Knave's *Fearefull and Lamentable Effects of Two Dangerous Comets, Which Shall Appeare in the Yeere 1591* (1590?), of which in 1608 a plagiarism emerged, *The Penniles Parliament of Threed-bare Poets.* In his correspondence with Robert Cecil in 1605, the king himself composed a mock prognostication.[8] Weak Christians, he wrote in his *Daemonologie*

[7]*Essais,* ed. Jean Plattard, I (Paris, 1959), 55.

[8]King James jocularly predicted court news, including various romantic events among the nobility, as a result of the recent eclipse: "But now will I goe to hyer maitters & tell you . . . the effectis of this laite eclipse . . . for this yeare are verrie many & wondrouse . . . many other prodigiouse eventis are flowid from this eclipse. . . ." Letter (1605) in Hatfield MSS. 134/79/BM Microfilm M.485/30/, inscribed "7 October, His Majesty from Royston." Philopatris, *An Humble Petition Offered to the . . . Estates of This Present Parliament Assembled at Westminster Pallace* (1606), remarks, pp. 2-3, on "the eclipse of the Sunne seene here of late" in conjunction with dire earthly events, including the Gunpowder Plot, during "this yeare 1605." (See G. T. Buckley, "'These Late Eclipses' Again," *SQ,* XIII [1962], 253-256, for cautions regarding the usual dating of the 1605 eclipses of the sun and moon.)

Resembling James's view of political prognostications, an Elizabethan attitude is indicated in a letter in *Calendar of State Papers, Domestic . . . 1598-1601,* Feb. 18, 1601, p. 585, regarding the Essex affair: "A foolish prognostication of one Woodhouse con-

(Edinburgh, 1597), could be lured by the study of astrology, so that through curiosity they might exceed the lawful arts and invoke Satan, finding, however, their knowledge "nothing increased" (p. 11). In *Basilicon Doron* (Edinburgh, 1603) James further advises his son against necromancers, false prophets, and soothsayers (p. 57). Finally, in *Lear* the Fool himself provides an expression of the genre conventionally employed to satirize prognosticatory and astrological superstition (III.ii.80-96).

Since opponents of astrology tended to class it as a pagan superstition—compare "this Egyptiacall and Ethnickes foolishnes" above —astrology and paganism were closely linked. Thus, it is dramatically appropriate and, within the Renaissance conventional view, to be anticipated that Gloucester might be both pagan and superstitious in his Augustinian *caecitas*, ironically one of the "blinde prophets" whom Hooper, in the same context, condemns. In the same year as the probable composition of *Lear*, 1605, there appeared, dedicated to James I, a translation of Le Loyer's treatise, associating paganism with fear of eclipses and attempting to remove their terrifying aspect by a naturalistic explanation. Referring to the pagan Romans, Le Loyer asserts: "The thing that did most terrifie and astonish them . . . was an eclipse of the moone, which put them in a fansie and conceipt, that the gods were angry and displeased with them for that their enterprise." Interestingly, in view of Gloucester's later contact with demonology, Le Loyer, following Aquinas, suggests that the devil imprints in men's minds "a certaine terrour and feare of the puissance and power of the starres," so that "at this day there be many men that take all things unknowne unto them, to be Specters and Prodigies," being "afraide of them, without any just occasion,"[9] a perspective on Gloucester's position. Seneca, remarking "our terror of things that we suppose unprecedented, when they are not really unprecedented, but merely unusual," instances "superstitious fears inspired both privately and even for the safety of the State, if . . . the sun has been seen in eclipse . . . or . . . the moon. . . ."[10] Bacon's essay

siders this tumult the effect of an eclipse last year. . . . This eclipse, he says, shows the unfortunate state of sundry great persons, great destruction of many mean ones, and threatens death to ecclesiastical persons, lawyers, rulers, &c. . . . This book is called in, though it be but a toy."

[9] *A Treatise of Specters* (Stationers' Register, Jan. 11, 1605), foll. 137^{v}, 67^{r-v}.

[10] *Quaestiones naturales*, tr. Clarke, p. 228.

"Of Superstition" includes, among its causes, ". . . the taking an aim at divine matters by human, which cannot but breed mixture of imaginations: and, lastly, barbarous times, especially joined with calamities and disasters."[11]

Associating paganism and excessive astrological superstition, Renaissance explorers and travel writers provided evidence, moreover, regarding savage reactions to eclipses. Samuel Purchas, for example, in *Purchas His Pilgrimage* (1613) observes of the Moluccians, "If an Eclipse of the Sunne or Moone happen, they howle and make piteous lamentation, perswading themselves, that their King, or some great man amongst them will die. Experience thereof was the sixt of August 1599. when the Moone was eclipsed . . ." (p. 452); and Peter Martyr of Angleria in *De Novo Orbe, or the Historie of the West Indies* (1612) remarks that the natives "foretell the *Ecclipse* of the Moone. . . . At that tyme they . . . lyve sorrowfully . . . because they thinke some evill is foretolde thereby . . ." (sig. Rr4). Eclipses, noted Hobbes later, were to the unlettered a miracle still.[12]

In addition, among others of Gloucester's superstitious beliefs,[13] fairies were sometimes credited and often confused with devils. Renouncing "the faith of all Almanackes" and assailing prognosticators, the superstitious man at the end of S. S.'s *The Honest Lawyer* exclaims also against "Fairies . . . and divels" (1616, sig. K2v). Gloucester's gift to Edgar at the suicide scene reinvokes the old man's beliefs: "fairies and Gods / Prosper it with thee!" (IV.vi.29-30). Gloucester's reference here implies a paganism leaning toward superstition. Already, in the *Daemonologie* (1597), King James had condemned such beliefs as deluded paganism, mentioning

> spirites . . . called the *Phairie* . . . or our good neighboures . . . one of the sortes of illusiones that was rifest in the time of *Papistrie*: . . . vaine trattles founded upon that illusion . . . nor anie thing that ought to be beleeved

[11] *Works,* VI, 416.

[12] *English Works,* III, 429.

[13] E.g., in Gloucester's "I stumbled when I saw" (IV.i.19). Cf. a Renaissance, as well as an antique Roman, notion of stumbling as an unlucky omen. See, e.g., *3 Henry VI,* IV.vii.11-12. Identifying "The Superstitious," Joseph Hall in *Characters of Vertues and Vices* (1608) observes, "This man dares not stirre foorth . . . if hee stumbled at the threshold" (pp. 87-88). In a MS play of 1635, "Ominous," "A man fearefull of Superstitious Accidents," as well as of disaster-foretelling dreams, stumbles at his first entrance upon the threshold; see S. Schoenbaum, "*Wit's Triumvirate:* A Caroline Comedy Recovered," *Studies in English Literature,* IV (1964), 230.

by Christians . . . the devil illuded the senses of sundry simple creatures, in making them beleeve that they saw and harde such thinges as were nothing so indeed. . . . (pp. 73-74)[14]

In Gloucester, despite certain more sympathetic or ambiguous elements, we thus discern symptoms of an identifiable "superstitious" type who, as a rehearsal of some of his belief speeches will indicate, exhibits these traits. In his weak vacillation between terror and appeasement the earl is the antitype to his king's continuing defiance. Projecting his personal insecurities onto the screen of the cosmos—his fear, as Greville would say, fashioning gods unto man—he seems to create the gods in the counterpart of his own image. In contrast to Cordelia's steadfast faith and devotion, Gloucester's perfect fear casteth out love. His attitude to the governing powers is expressed symbolically in his passion, at the hands of Cornwall and Regan: "I am tied to th' stake, and I must stand the course" (III.vii.53). The implication of man as a baited bear torn, *pour le sport*, by human curs is present in the image, but the microcosmic image corresponds also to Gloucester's macrocosmic theology of pointlessly hostile divinities.

Moreover, a summary of Gloucester's expressions regarding himself and regarding the cosmos would show a certain congruence: in the first act he reveals himself to be credulous, rash, and vengeful, while he appeals blindly for harsh personal retribution to the heavens; he vacillates between sensual boasting regarding his adultery (I.i.9-24) and a misplaced sense of shame (II.i.93); he is melancholy,

[14]Cf. Samuel Harsnet's *A Declaration of Egregious Popishe Impostures* (1603), p. 134; Thomas Heywood's second part of *If You Know Not Me* (1605; pr. 1606), sig. F3r-v; William Warner, *A Continuance of Albions England* (1606), pp. 367-368; Samuel Rowlands, *More Knaves Yet?* (1612?), sig. F2; Hobbes, *English Works,* III, 9-10, 99-100.

As do others of his utterances, Poor Tom's "Bless thee from whirlwinds, star-blasting, and taking!" (III.iv.59-60) connects the protagonists, recalling both Gloucester's credulity and Lear's storm. "Whirlwinds" were fairy eddies, thought to lift and abduct people in the air; see Lewis Spence, *The Fairy Tradition in Britain* (1948), pp. 64-65, 175-176. The mock prognostication in Benjamin Rudyerd's *Le prince d'amour* (1660), p. 36, warns, in *double entendre,* "You shall have such great Whirlewinds, that many men shall be blown up, and not seen in the year after." Speaking of the fiend who "begins at curfew, and walks till the first cock," Edgar also recites a charm or spell (III.iv.118-119, 123-124) associated with fairies, which appears paralleled, in part, from Chaucer, in William Cartwright's *The Ordinary* (1634-35), III.i. Edgar's echoes of Gloucester's beliefs might in this case have reminded King James of "such kinde of Charmes as commonlie dafte wives uses" (*Daemonologie,* p. 11).

gloomy, and pessimistic, being struck by portents in eclipses, the ensuing decay of the world, the significance of predictions and almanacs, and the conviction that necessity rules via nativity and that the heavens, governing all, produce men's vices and virtues; in the third act he exhibits fear, suspicion, and desire for vengeance, while on a cosmic level he falls later into a kind of Stoic resignation and an acceptance of endurance and appeals to the presently kind gods for mercy; in the fourth act he shows humility and repentance, seeing man as the lowest animal, while ruling all are cruel gods, killing men for their sport; he expresses sympathy for the poor and views suicide as a release, while the gods are seen as punishing powers, alternately as possibly good, then as cruel and invincible, and as tyrants making men's lives unbearable;[15] later Gloucester is to repeat his conviction of the decay of the world, along with his acceptance of the truth, too, that "ripeness is all," while ironically the gods in his cruelly blinded eyes become "gentle."

After an interval following the first scene of the second act, the audience sees Gloucester again as fearful, gullible, and suspicious (III.iii.1-6, 8-22); but in III.vii.53, as has been noted, he evinces premonitory Stoic resignation to suffering contrived by evildoers, followed by sympathy for the victim, Lear, and desire for supernatural vengeance (III.vii.64-65), conceiving, as often, the gods in harmful terms, while his astral concerns recur in his reference to the "stelled fires" (III.vii.60; cf. 64-65). After his physical blinding and mental illumination regarding Edgar, he reverses his general position to exclaim, "Kind Gods, forgive me that, and prosper him!" (III. vii.91). But this crucial reversal occurs under the intense experience Gloucester has just suffered, and, as the sequence shows us, it is not a permanent change.

Yet, repentant grief dominates his mind, along with a newfound humility (IV.i.18-24). The gods, nevertheless, are still cruel, indeed, at their cruelest:

> As flies to wanton boys, are we to th' Gods;
> They kill us for their sport; (IV.i.36-37)

[15]Cf. Gloucester, IV.vi.62-64, and the Stoic position that courage expresses itself nobly in the face of tyranny by eluding its power in death. The Stoic doctrine of "reasonable departure" (*rationalis e vita excessus*) permitted suicide in similar circumstances. Cf. Hans F. A. von Arnim, ed. *Stoicorum veterum fragmenta* (Leipzig, 1903), III, 187-191.

while man is the lowest of animals: "I such a fellow saw, / Which made me think a man a worm" (IV.i.32-33). Gloucester's *Schicksal* vision is followed by expressions of humility and sympathy for the poor, as the heavens are reinvoked as punishment; there is a causal relationship suggested between man's degradation and heaven's plagues, paralleling the two speeches just cited; in short, the cosmic degradation implies the human one:

> Here, take this purse, thou whom the heav'ns plagues
> Have humbled to all strokes . . .
> Heavens, deal so still! (IV.i.64-66)

But, in apparent antithesis to the sportive infliction of the gods, there is supposedly, in addition, a reason for their torments—they operate by ordinances:

> Let the superfluous and lust-dieted man,
> That slaves your ordinance, that will not see
> Because he does not feel, feel your power quickly.
> (IV.i.67-69)

"The Charge of a Star"

In Gloucester's own words the overly susceptible type is thus readily recognized: the important exposition of I.ii points him out to the audience as, for example, credulous (ll.28-79) with regard to Edmund's manipulation of the forged letter; in I.ii.99-103 it shows him again to be uncritical, self-pitying, lacking objectivity in his appeal to "Heaven and earth!" and rash, impatient, and vengeful regarding Edgar's alleged misdeeds, the chaos and irresponsibility implicit in Lear's abdication being echoed in these lower quarters: "I would unstate myself to be in a due resolution." Having witnessed Gloucester's personal and family attitudes, the audience next observes the old earl as cosmic *Metaphysiker*:

> These late eclipses in the sun and moon portend no good to us . . . Nature finds itself scourg'd by the sequent effects. Love cools, friendship falls off, brothers divide: in cities, mutinies; in countries, discord; in palaces, treason. . . . This villain of mine comes under the prediction . . . all ruinous disorders follow us disquietly to our graves. (I.ii.107-120)

The speech reveals his position regarding eclipses in the sun and moon, and portents, as well as a fearful pessimism, involving the three analogical levels of family, state, and cosmos. Explicating his father's notions, Edmund comments on the old man's preconceptions:

> This is the excellent foppery[16] of the world, that, when we are sick in fortune, often the surfeits of our own behaviour, we make guilty of our disasters the sun, the moon, and stars; as if we were villains on necessity, fools by heavenly compulsion, knaves, thieves, and treachers by spherical predominance, drunkards, liars, and adulterers by an enforc'd obedience of planetary influence; and all that we are evil in, by a divine thrusting on. An admirable evasion of whoremaster man, to lay his goatish disposition to the charge of a star! My father compounded with my mother under the dragon's tail, and my nativity was under *Ursa major*; so that it follows I am rough and lecherous. . . . I should have been that I am had the maidenliest star in the firmament twinkled on my bastardizing. (I.ii.124-140)

Here are satirically reflected some bases of Gloucester's mode of thought, involving necessity and heavenly compulsion through nativity as causing man's virtues or vices.

The opposition between Edmund and Gloucester also reflects the Renaissance controversy over the validity of astrology, especially judicial astrology, a battle held to have begun in earnest in the early years of the seventeenth century.[17] Further, insofar as judicial astrology involves the particular details of individual lives, its crisis may be considered to parallel that concerning belief in special providence during the same period. Although Shakespeare could, with More, have noted regarding astrologers, "At hii regnant inter Christianos hodie,"[18] contemporary evidence makes it clear that Edmund's opposition to Gloucester's views, far from merely expressing villainy, was part of a continuing Renaissance debate. In the great argument between astrological supernaturalism and naturalistic self-dependence, Shakespeare here touches on a controversial issue which engaged not only his royal patron but also his probably divided audience.[19] Although the extent of Renaissance astrological credence has

16"Foppery" implied a foolish belief or superstition; see numerous references, e.g., John Gee, *The Foot Out of the Snare* (1624, *STC* 11701), p. 9.

17Walter B. Stone, "Shakespeare and the Sad Augurs," *JEGP*, LII (1953), 478.

18*The Utopia of Sir Thomas More*, ed. J. H. Lupton (Oxford, 1895), p. 186.

19While James would probably have shared a Renaissance ambivalence toward astrology, distinguishing natural and judicial forms, his *Daemonologie* reveals his dislike of such varieties of the latter as personal and political prognostications.

See Hugh G. Dick, introd., in Thomas Tomkis, *Albumazar: A Comedy*, Univ. of

been well documented, it seems not to have been sufficiently recognized that Edmund's opposing view was neither rare nor unique.

Even before Reginald Scot in *The Discoverie of Witchcraft* (1584) argued against superstitious believers, Thomas More's *A Dialogue concernynge Heresyes & Matters of Religion* (1528), in his *Workes* (1557), castigated those who blame destiny for their own misdeeds:

> if every misordred wretche myght alledge that his mischievous dede was his desteny. . . . they may be then wel aunswered with their owne wordes, as one of their sect was served . . . when he had robbed a man and was brought before the judges he could not deny the dede, but he sayde it was his desteny to do it, and therefore thei might not blame hym, thei aunswered him after his owne doctrine, that yf it were his desteny to steale, & that therfore they muste holde hym excused, than it was also their desteny to hange hym, and therfore he must as well hold them excused agayn. (p. 274)

William Fulke's *Antiprognosticon* in 1560 refuted dependence for human welfare upon the stars, stressing naturalistic causes:

> Sycknesse and healthe depende upon dyvers causes, but nothyng at al upon the course of the starres. for what way soever the starres runne their race, yf there be in the body abundance or defect, or from outward by corruption of the ayre infection it must nedes be sycke: and if none of these bee, though all the starres in heaven with all their oppositions and evil tokens shuld meete in the howse of sicknesse, yet the body shoulde bee whole, and in good healthe. (sig. [Dvii])

Like Edmund, the pious Roger Hutchinson in *The Image of God* denounces the tendency "to lay" human misdeeds "to the charge of a star": "if a thiefe come before you, he is not to be blamed, but his destiny: if an adultrer, an Idolatrer, an extortioner, you can laye nothynge to his charge, but to the starres which cause him to be naught, will he, nill he" (sig. [Hvii]). Earlier, Seneca reminds us

---

Calif. Pubs. in English, XIII (Berkeley, 1944), 31-33 and passim, regarding anti-astrological attitudes; concerning the importance accorded prognostications, however, see Stone, "Shakespeare and the Sad Augurs," pp. 457-479. A proverbial middle position is cited by Burton (*The Anatomy of Melancholy* [Oxford, 1621], p. 74): the stars "incline, but not compell." This *topos* is absorbed into an analogous view by Ovid in Sir Aston Cokayne's *The Tragedy of Ovid,* III.i (*The Dramatic Works of Sir Aston Cokain* [1874], p. 248). The proverbial "Astra inclinant, sed non urgent" in Erasmus' *Adagia* ([Frankfurt am Main], 1629), p. 533, recurs, e.g., in Alemán's *Guzman de Alfarache,* II, 262.

that we attribute to external fortune own our ill behavior.[20] A tutor of King James, George Buchanan, assails the disposition to ascribe to the innocent stars the blame for follies and crimes.[21] Further, Philip Stubbs's *The Second Part of the Anatomie of Abuses* (1583) advises, "it is the . . . wickednes of our owne harts, that draweth us to evill . . . and not the starres, or planets" (sig. [I5]). Some, complains John Carpenter's *A Preparative to Contentation* (1597), "stare on the Sunne, Moone, and Starres, and make fleshly reasons for those supernall things: howbeit, they have no reason for their own loose & filthy lives . . ." (p. 237). Sir William Cornwallis' *Discourses upon Seneca* (1601), rejecting the ascription to fortune, insists it is man's own fault: "so suffer wee our selves to ingrosse the commandements of lust and appetite, to embrace every thing that they see, and to devoure poyson, so it promiseth but sweetnes." Hence, he deduces, come "all that we call calamity, & think worthy of the bewayling" (sigs. E1^v-E2). ". . . When we lay our deserved afflictions upon fortune," we may merely be transferring our own guilt (sig. H5).

Like the villainous Edmund and Cassius, the virtuous Helena in *All's Well That Ends Well* eschews "heavenly compulsions" and points a similar moral (I.i.231-234).[22] For, as Webster's *The White Devil* observes,

> Thought, as a subtile Jugler, makes us deeme
> Things, supernaturall, which have cause
> Common as sickenesse. (IV.i.111-113)

In S. S.'s *The Honest Lawyer*, countering such fearful prognostications (e.g., "Most strange, and full of preposterous, prodigious, turbulent, dismall, fatall, amazing, terrifying . . . Wonders," sig. [B4]), Vaster exclaims,

20E.g., *Ad Luciliam epistolae morales*, tr. Richard M. Gummere, III (1925), 49.

21*Poëmata quæ extant* (Amsterdam, 1687), p. 469. See also Julius Firmicus Maternus' *Matheseos libri VIII*, ed. W. Kroll and F. Skutsch (Leipzig, 1897), I, 7, deploring the charge against astrologers of projecting men's vices onto the stars.

22Cf. Montaigne, III, 203, against blaming the stars. See also Pamela's remark against blaming fortune for one's own fault (*Arcadia*, I, 156). "Man is his own Star," says the poem "Upon an Honest Man's Fortune. By Mr. John Fletcher," appended to *The Honest Man's Fortune* (1613), in *The Works of Francis Beaumont and John Fletcher*, ed. A. R. Waller, X (Cambridge, Eng., 1912), 279; Constantia, in *The Chances* (1613-25), II.ii, refuses "To curse those stars, that men say govern us." Recalling Edmund's determinism, she recognizes, "Alas, I am the same still," and concludes, "Our own desires / Are our own fates, our own stars . . ." (ibid., IV [1906], 199).

> Hence, skie-consulting Gypsie: men commit
> Sinnes darke as night, and blame the starres for it. (sig. E3)

Robert Anton's *Vices Anotimie* (1617) notes, likewise, that "the superstitious world pinnes all their vitious lives and dispositions to opposite aspect of starres and celestiall bodyes . . . wee . . . Watch the Planets when they will bring us good or bad fortune, make theyr vertues the causes of our vices . . ." (sig. [B5ᵛ]). Similarly, Sir Thomas Browne argues, "Burden not the back of Aries, Leo, or Taurus, with thy faults, nor make Saturn, Mars, or Venus, guilty of thy Follies. Think not to fasten thy imperfections on the Stars. . . . Let celestial aspects admonish and advertise, not conclude and determine thy ways."[23]

Significantly, Gloucester's rejection of "the wisdom of Nature" which "can reason it thus and thus" (I.ii.108-109) seems to oppose naturalistic explanations of "these late eclipses in the sun and moon." For example, Le Loyer's *A Treatise of Specters*, cited above, observes, "And yet neverthelesse, the cause of the Moones eclipse is knowne to bee meerely naturall" (fol. 67). In 1605, also, an edition of Leonard and Thomas Digges's *A Prognostication* asserts "The naturall cause of the Sunne eclipsed," at the same time, however, being careful to remark regarding eclipses of the moon, "Some observe pestilent plagues, sudden battell, great dearth, to ensue these Eclipses . . ." (fol. 14). Richard Allestree's *1619. A New Almanacke and Prognostication* . . . (1618) speaks "Of the Eclipses of the Sunne and Moone, the naturall causes" (sig. B3).

Yet in the Renaissance reaction against naturalistic ascription of causes, many voices, insisting on supernatural dependence, joined. For example, although Louis Leroy's *Of the Interchangeable Course* . . . (1594) admits "theis things proceed (after the opinion of the *Naturalists*) from the fatall law of the world; and have their natural causes," he argues, "yet notwithstanding, the events of them do principally depend on the providence of God; who is above nature . . ." (fol. 126ᵛ).[24] While echoing Edmund's dismissal of planetary responsibility for human misdeeds, cited above, Browne, however,

[23] *Works*, I, 137.

[24] Cf. Guillaume Du Vair, *A Buckler against Adversitie: Or a Treatise of Constancie*, tr. Andrew Court (1622), pp. 65-69, who argues that it is providence that produces the regular order which is called "Nature"; nature did not "do all."

seems to share Gloucester's dissatisfaction with the "wisdom of Nature" (I.ii.108) which "reasons" out the cause of eclipses: "In the causes, nature and affections of the Eclipses of the Sun and Moon, there is most excellent speculation; but to . . . contemplate a reason why his Providence hath so disposed and ordered their motions in that vast circle as to conjoyn and obscure each other, is a sweeter piece of Reason, and a diviner point of Philosophy."[25] John Swan in 1635 continues to argue, partly in Gloucester's terms, for the supernatural significance of eclipses: "what are they," he exclaims in *Speculum mundi*, "but the Oracles of God? by which, changes, alterations, and sundrie calamities are threatned to the world."[26] As this instance and others may show, Gloucester's insistence on the portentousness of eclipses was a frequently professed view, countering the naturalistic position. Yet Edmund's rejection of the astrological version of special providence, according to which individual lives are shaped by planetary compulsions, was also professed. But such denials could have evoked Swan's indictment of one who rejects portents in eclipses: "And these, if any one contemne them, what doth he but despise the admonitions of God?" (p. 351).

Such controversial collocations as the views of Gloucester and Edmund have the advantage at once of revealing aspects of character, foreshadowing events, and engaging the attention of divergent factions within Shakespeare's audience. Elsewhere in Shakespearean drama, as in *Lear*, analogous interrogations and debates regarding individual will and cosmic destiny come early and frame the play. The Cassius-Brutus debate, for instance, occurs in I.ii.139-147 of *Julius Caesar*; Helena espouses the individual will in *All's Well* at I.i.231-234; and Iago upholds it in *Othello*, especially at I.iii.322-337. Edmund's reply, in effect, not only exposes his own traits but recapitulates and emphasizes Gloucester's supernatural attitude from a naturalistic viewpoint. The opening of the play thus furnishes multiple mirrors and perspectives for viewing the action. Its implicit debate, for example, introduces one of the tragedy's major questions, reemerging in Lear's puzzlement regarding the "cause in nature" (III.vi.78-79). Is the "wisdom of Nature," reasoning "it thus and thus" (I.ii.108-109), which Edmund represents and Gloucester finds

[25] *Works*, I, 20.

[26] Cambridge, Eng., p. 351.

inadequate, sufficient to explain the mysterious happenings of the universe? Such questions, moreover, could have aroused corollary interrogations regarding the cosmic governing force, providence, miracles, and the nature of the gods.

Despite Gloucester's fearful "over-belief," however, his dire prognostication is ironically fulfilled; as in *Macbeth*, omens are not entirely repudiated as false but are linked, in dramatically ironical terms, to the disasters of those who involve themselves with such forewarnings. On the other hand, the confident and mocking Edmund, who "should have been that I am had the maidenliest star in the firmament twinkled on my bastardizing," at the end attempts to violate his own individualistic determinism, "Despite of" his "own nature" (V.iii.244). Thus, near the start of the tragedy, the Renaissance dilemma is poised between two rival cosmic explanations: supernaturalism, in the astrological determinism of the aged earl; and its philosophical offspring, naturalism, in the materialist determinism of his illegitimate son. That, with dramatic craft, Shakespeare chooses to let us see Gloucester's position also through Edmund's skeptical yet complementary viewpoint (I.ii.124-140, 147-156) should not finally obscure the balanced irony with which the issues are presented.

Sub Specie Ludi

THE GODS' "DEAR SHELTER"

And that Bawde, / The skie, there . . .
—Tourneur, *The Atheist's Tragedie*, IV.iii.244-245

References to the heavenly bodies and the heavens themselves may, on Shakespeare's stage, have also alluded to a portion of its structure—"the coverings of the stage, which wee call the heavens," referred to in Heywood's *An Apology for Actors* (1612), sig. D2^{v}.[27] The Hope theater contract stipulates that the builder "shall also builde the Heavens all over the saide stage. . . ."[28] "If his Action prefigure passion," R. M.'s *Micrologia* (1629) describes the character of a Player, who "protests much by his painted Heavens . . . ready to pull *Jove* out of the Garret . . ." (sig. B3$^{r\text{-}v}$). This roof-canopy, or "roof" covering part of the stage, was called by the Fortune contract the

[27]Cf. John Melton, *Astrologaster, or, the Figure-caster* (1620), p. 31.

[28]E. K. Chambers, *The Elizabethan Stage* (Oxford, 1923), II, 466.

"shadowe or cover" and may, as Malone early suggested, have been painted a sky-blue color[29] and decorated on its underside with zodiacal signs and stars.[30]

If, as has been noted, Renaissance dramatic allusions abound to the stage structure and its zodiacal and starry decorations,[31] it may be possible to interpret, in their light, certain "heavenly" indications in *Lear*. That Shakespearean acting was accompanied by much gesture we gather, for instance, from *Hamlet* (III.ii.5-16) and *Titus Andronicus* (V.ii.17-18).[32] In *Titus*, shooting arrows tipped with messages for the gods, characters refer to hitting Virgo, Pallas, the moon, Jupiter, and Taurus as their targets, while probably pointing to the "heavens." Apropos, the marginal directions in the anonymous *Timon* (ca. 1581-1590?), which Shakespeare may have known, call

[29] *The Plays and Poems of William Shakespeare*, ed. Edmond Malone and James Boswell (1821), III, 108.

[30] See Thornton S. Graves, *The Court and the London Theatres during the Reign of Elizabeth* (Menasha, Wis., 1913), pp. 24-25, on the decorated heavens in the pageant-theater tradition and on the probability of such painted heavens in the drama.

[31] E.g., Sir Aston Cokayne's prefatory poem to Richard Brome's *Five New Playes* (1653), sig. A2v, contains a possible allusion to "*Taurus* in the Heaven." Cf. Chapman, *All Fools* (1599-1604; pr. 1605), Prologue, ll. 1-4; Nashe, III, 329. Like signs of the zodiac, the stars may have been mentioned in such allusions as Flamineo's (Webster, *The White Devil*, V.iv.120-121), when he questions the ghost by means of stage terms for heaven and hell. In addition, Heywood's Red Bull play, *The Rape of Lucrece* (1606-08), speaks of "starres / Stuck in yond' azure Rofe" (*The Dramatic Works of Thomas Heywood* [1874], V, 192), and the King's Men's pre-Globe *Edward III* (ca. 1590-95) alludes to "the great Starre-chamber ore our heads" (II.ii); the same company's *A Very Woman* (1634) by Massinger (II.iii) points to the "lights / That deck the heavenly canopy" (*Dramatic Works*, p. 373). Cf. Jonson's *Epicoene or the Silent Woman* (1609), III.i, which may, C. Walter Hodges suggests (*The Globe Restored: A Study of the Elizabethan Theatre* [New York, 1954], p. 70), allude to a painted heavens in the Bear Garden. "Heaven" is defined in Randle Cotgrave, *A Dictionarie of the French and English Tongues* (1611), s.v. "Volerie"; cf. "Dais." *Henslowe's Diary*, ed. R. A. Foakes and R. T. Rickert (Cambridge, Eng., 1961), p. 7, records payment for "mackinge the throne In the hevenes . . . 1595." See John C. Adams' *The Globe Playhouse: Its Design and Equipment* (Cambridge, Mass., 1942), p. 378*n*, for other possible Renaissance instances; a type of zodiacal design is described in George R. Kernodle's *From Art to Theatre: Form and Convention in the Renaissance* (Chicago, 1944), p. 142; see fig. p. 96. A Jacobean "heavens," with gods, sky, and stars, said to date from the first decade of the seventeenth century, is reproduced in Hodges, *The Globe Restored*, Pl. 56 (cf. pp. 70, 117), and in Hodges, "A Seventeenth-Century Heaven," *Theatre Notebook*, VI (1952), 59-60, Pls. 1, 2.

[32] Cf. also Shakespeare's *Rape of Lucrece*, ll. 1403-04; John Bulwer's *Chirologia* and *Chironomia* (1644). In the tradition of the Renaissance stage clown, the Fool (I.iv.153 and I.v.52-53), like Kent (II.ii.93-96), appears to utilize the platform-pit contiguity for bantering direct address. Cf. Kent, II.ii.161-163, for possibly theatrical, in addition to proverbial, allusion.

for "the sign of the 7 stars." Moreover, the English *Wagnerbook* (1594), Chapter xx, describing the Elizabethan stage, indicates a heaven with stars portraying "the whole Imperiall Army of the faire heavenly inhabitauntes." In addition, *The Birth of Hercules* (1597–ca. 1610) has the stage direction "Ad comœdiæ magnificentiam apprime conferet, ut cœlum Histrionium sit luna & stellis perspicue distinctum" (I.i). Also, Dekker's Fortune play, *The Whore of Babylon* (ca. 1606-1607; Q1, 1607), demands,

> Can yonder roofe, thats naild so fast with starres,
> Cover a head so impious, and not cracke? (sig. [A4v])[33]

Similarly, Lear's Fool, who elsewhere jests about stage properties (e.g., the "joint-stool," III.vi.52), may in his demand of Lear why "the seven stars are no mo than seven" (I.v.36) possibly be pointing to a theatrical property on this occasion perhaps visible both to hero and many spectators. Since the seven stars were a commonplace, the suggestion is not that they necessarily appeared on the Globe heavens but that "starry heavens" seem interestingly to recur in Renaissance staging.[34] Analogously, the Fool's preference for "a dry house" to "this rain-water out o' door" (III.ii.10-11) and Lear's resolution to "abjure all roofs" (II.iv.210) may have been accompanied by movements or gestures relating to the sheltering stage "heavens."

If such additional functional uses for stage structures are acceptable, it could follow that Shakespeare's actors and a portion, at least, of his spectators shared a common and continuously visible level of reference. Above Lear's "great stage of fools" (IV.vi.185) may have presided also Gloucester's sportively malign deities. Through the silent, yet ironically significant, presence of the gods and their heavens during the performance of human actions, Shakespeare could, in a manner imperceptible to later audiences, have utilized another level of theatrical meaning.

[33]Cf. the implication here of celestial solidity and Artemidorus of Parium's view, according to Seneca (*Quaestiones naturales*, tr. Clarke, p. 286), that "the upper regions of heaven are perfectly solid—a lofty thick vault, as hard as the roof of a house, formed by the accumulation of masses of atoms."

[34]Henslowe's inventory of the properties of the Admiral's Men for 1598 includes "the clothe of the Sone & Mone," suggesting that a painted cloth, as well as the painted heavens, might have served as visible astrological reference for Renaissance drama; see *Henslowe's Diary*, ed. Foakes and Rickert, p. 320.

MANKIND AS "SPORT"

Gloucester's

> As flies to wanton boys, are we to th' Gods;
> They kill us for their sport (IV.i.36-37)

is an instance of the *topos* of man, viewed from the perspective of the gods, *sub specie ludi*, as variously a trivial, ephemeral creature used for the amusement of higher powers (e.g., as fly, gilded butterfly, or caged bird); as a ball tossed in a tennis game; or as a mere player or entertainer on a stage ("this great stage of fools"), whose audience may be those higher powers. Increasingly, during the later Renaissance some, lacking reliance on a particular providence, felt themselves

> Servile to all the skyey influences,
> That dost this habitation . . .
> Hourly afflict. . . . (*Measure for Measure*, III.i.9-11)

In order to indicate that Gloucester's, like Lear's, is not an isolated expression in the period, further instances will be cited from the three above-mentioned related aspects of man-as-plaything *topos*.

Gloucester's insect-human analogy recurs also in Renaissance discussions of providence, as well as in Shakespeare's other pre-Christian British play, *Cymbeline*:

> No more, thou thunder-master, show
> Thy spite on mortal flies. (V.iv.30-31)

God's special providence, Mornay insists, is as admirable in a fly as in the universe.[35] Montaigne assails those who presume to know God's deeper concern for great things than for lesser, such as "the skip of a flea" (II, 235). The atheistic Cecropia in Sidney's *Arcadia* sets up the comparison between the indifference of gods to men and of men to flies. In reply, her pious niece Pamela reasons that, if God is "infinite, then must nothing, no not the estate of flies (which you with so unsaverie skorne did jest at) be unknowne unto him" (I, 406-407, 410).

Parallel elements to this *topos* have been suggested in the prefatory verse of Fernando de Rojas' *Comedia de Calisto y Melibea*, "*La Celestina*" (Toledo, 1500), which, like Gloucester, alludes to man's

[35] *A Woorke concerning the Trewnesse of the Christian Religion*, tr. Philip Sidney and Arthur Golding (1587), pp. 24-25.

insectlike, frail, and ephemeral helplessness: "alas . . . noblosas y flacas, nascido de ogaño."[36] Iconographically, the human-insect analogy,[37] as well as the world as puppet stage, may be realized in Bruegel's mid-sixteenth-century illustrations, which also suggest other *Lear* motifs, for example, the world as wheel and the world upside down. The human-insect analogy recurs frequently later, for instance, in Leopardi, Balzac, Dostoievsky, and Kafka, as it occurs earlier in Aeschylus, Aristophanes, and others.[38]

In addition to the "flies . . . sport" image, a similar one, that of a ball tossed by the gods, develops, after the Plautine model "enim vero di nos quasi pilas homines habent,"[39] into a Renaissance commonplace as uncertainty permeates the Elizabethan world picture. Calvin regrets "that the flesh stirreth" men "to murmure, as if God did to make himself pastime, tosse them like tennise balles" (*Institutes*, I.xvii.1). Sidney expresses the same apparent attitude of the gods toward man in the *Arcadia*: "in such a shadowe, or rather pit of darkenes, the wormish mankinde lives, that neither they knowe how to foresee, nor what to feare: and are but like tenisballs, tossed by the racket of the hyer powers," declares the narrator. "Then Fortune (as if she had made chases inow of the one side of that blooddy Tenis-court) went of the other side the line. . . ." "Balles to the starres, and thralles to Fortunes raigne," moans Plangus. "And why," asks Pamela, "shal we any longer flatter adversity? Why should we delight to make our selves any longer balls to injurious *Fortune*. . . ."[40] Mon-

[36]Facsimile, ed. Daniel Poyán Díaz (Coligny-Geneva, 1961), sig. [Aiiv].

[37]See Erasmus, *The Free Will*, in Erasmus and Luther, *Discourse on Free Will*, tr. and ed. Ernst F. Winter (New York, 1961), p. 89, comparing divine justice regarding flies, other insects, and men. Cf. Lear's "gilded butterflies" (V.iii.13), or courtiers, and Pope's "Ye tinsel Insects! whom a Court maintains" (*Epilogue to the Satires*, Dialogue II, l. 220, *The Poems of Alexander Pope*, ed. John Butt, IV [1939], 325).

[38]Cf. Ralph E. Matlaw, "Recurrent Imagery in Dostoevskij," *Harvard Slavic Studies*, III (1957), 201-225. Cf. Spenser's *Muiopotmos*. See the *topos* of man as fragile and ephemeral in Ecclesiastes, Job, and Pindar ("Creatures of a day, what is any one?" [*The Odes of Pindar*, tr. John Sandys, Loeb Classical Lib. (1915), p. 269, l. 95]), Plato, the Sophists (e.g., Prodicus, *The Hours*), and Plutarch, as well as in Aristophanes, *The Birds* (tr. Benjamin B. Rogers, Loeb Classical Lib. [1924], II, 199, ll. 686-687): men are said to be "feeble and wingless and brief, / Frail . . . gone in a day. . . ." Erasmus' *A Treatise Perswadynge a Man Patientlye to Suffre the Deth of His Frende* [1532], sig. Bii, cites Euripides and Pindar on the brevity of man's life. See the Aeschylean reference in Ch. viii below. See also Calvin, *Institutes*, III.ix.2.

[39]Plautus, Prologue, *Captives*, tr. Paul Nixon, Loeb Classical Lib., I (1928), 464, l. 22.

[40]II, 177; I, 390, 227, 508.

taigne, citing Plautus, observes, "The gods play at hand-ball with us, and tosse us up and downe on all hands. . . . The gods perdie doe reckon and racket us men as their tennis-balles" (III, 201).

Further, Richard Linche's *The Fountaine of Ancient Fiction* (1599), apparently from Cartari, develops the fortune-tennis image: "Like tennis-bals thou beat'st us to and fro . . ." (sig. Ziii^v). Greville's *Mustapha* (ca. 1594–ca.1596), altering the sport, exclaims, "But see! This Foot-ball to the Starres is come, / *Mustapha* I meane . . ." (IV. iv.21-22).[41] In similar terms, Orlando in *Charlemagne or the Distracted Emperor* (ca. 1600) complains: "I am the verye foote-ball of the starres / th' anottomye of fortune . . ." (II.i.636-637).[42] William Warner's *Albions England* (1602) speaks of those who are "tennis balles to every tongue of every Deitee" (p. 151).

The Shakespearean *Pericles* observes,

> A man whom both the waters and the wind,
> In that vast tennis-court, have made the ball
> For them to play upon. . . . (II.i.63-65)

Comparable is Edward Sharpham's *Cupids Whirligig* (1607), ". . . what Tennis-ball ha's fortune taken thee for, to tosse thee thus into my way?" "Others say . . . [the world is] like a Tennis-ball, and fortune keepes such a Racket with it, as it tosses it in to times hazzard, and that devoures all . . ." (sigs. C2, G3).[43] While Webster's *The White Devil* uses the image of "bandying at Tennis" (V.i.70), *The Duchess of Malfi* sounds the despairing keynote:

> We are meerely the Starres tennys-balls (strooke, and banded
> Which way please them). (V.iv.63-64)

An emblem in Henry Peacham's *Minerva Britanna* (1612) shows a hand bouncing a tennis ball out of heaven, with the headline "Sic nos Dij." Citing Plautus, Peacham considers the time

> when the Gods above, have struck us low,
> (For men as balls, within their handes are said). (p.113)

The comparison of men to tennis balls tossed by supernatural forces, it is interesting to note, occurs in two sources of *Lear* (the

[41]*Poems and Dramas of Fulke Greville*, ed. Geoffrey Bullough [1939], II, 115.

[42]Malone Soc. Repr. (1937 [1938]).

[43]See also sig. [G4] on life as a game of chess whose pieces are men "throwne at last" into one bag.

Arcadia, cited above, and Harsnet's *Declaration*, 1603), and in a possible third, Montaigne, also cited above; Harsnet refers to the "Witch of *Endor*, making them tennis-bals, for their devils to bandy on their stage" (p. 153). In addition, Massinger's fortune allusion (*The Bashful Lover*, 1636) notes, "We are her tennis-balls" (IV.i);[44] and Thomas Bretnor's *A New Almanacke . . . 1618* (1617) remarks,

> For man is like unto a Tennis ball,
> Now tost aloft, now dash'd against the wall. (fol. [13])[45]

WORLD AS STAGE

The metaphor of the world as a stage has been traced beyond Plautus to Plato: "May we not conceive each of us living to be a puppet of the Gods, either their plaything only, or created with a purpose?" and later, "man . . . is made to be the plaything of God, and this, truly considered, is the best of him."[46] For the sixteenth century the idea took on a new emphasis in Luther, who sees history as God's game; the divine game embraces even redemptive history.[47] Like others, Calvin uses a stage metaphor, speaking of "the theatre of the world."[48]

Further, for example, Vives' *Fabula de homine* asserts that man is

[44] *Dramatic Works*, p. 406.

[45] See also John Taylor, *The Praise . . . of Beggery . . .* (1621), sig. D2.

[46] *The Dialogues of Plato*, tr. Benjamin Jowett (Oxford, 1953), IV, 210 (*Laws*, 644d), 371 (*Laws*, 803c). Cf. also Lucian, *Menippus*, tr. A. M. Harmon, Loeb Classical Lib. (1925), IV, 99-101; see Rudolf Helm, *Lucian und Menipp* (Leipzig, 1906), pp. 45-53, for other instances; Clement of Alexandria, *The Exhortation to the Greeks*, tr. G. W. Butterworth, Loeb Classical Lib. (1919), pp. 135, 353. Horace (*Satires*, Bk. II, Satire VII, l. 82) views man as a puppet. Cicero, as well as Seneca and Boethius, compares life to a play. A leitmotiv of Apuleius is that man is a plaything in the hands of Fortune. Epictetus, as well as Lucian, recurs to the world-as-stage theme. Plotinus (*Ennéades*, tr. Émile Bréhier, III [Paris, 1956], 44-48) sees all of life as an act in roles distributed by the universal poet. The often-republished *Policraticus* of John of Salisbury helped sustain the notion of *theatrum mundi* for the Middle Ages as well as for the Renaissance. See Curtius, pp. 138-144; Jean Jacquot, "'Le théâtre du monde' de Shakespeare à Calderón," *Revue de littérature comparée*, XXXI (1957), 341-372; Antonio Vilanova, "El Tema del Gran Teatro del Mundo," *Boletín de la Real Academia de Buenas Letras de Barcelona*, XXIII (1950), 153-188. See also Jean Rousset, *La littérature de l'âge baroque en France: Circé et le Paon* (Paris, 1960). Instances of the topic, in both primary and secondary literature, are, of course, innumerable and beyond fuller recounting here.

[47] *Werke*, XLIV (Weimar, 1915), 285, 467, 470.

[48] *Institutes*, I.vi.2; I.xiv.20; II.vi.1; III.ix.2, among other instances.

a spectacle for the gods' enjoyment.[49] The gods, Francesco Patrizi comments, created man by a game.[50] Erasmus, in *The Praise of Folly,* among other works, emphasizes the world-as-stage idea and influences its use in later Erasmians, as well as in the *Quixote* of Cervantes.[51] Interestingly, Thomas Middleton's *The Blacke Booke* (1604) alludes to "this dustie *Theater* of the world" and refers to a place "Above the Stage-rayles of this earthen Globe" (sigs. B1, B1^{v}). In a letter of April 1605 Sir John Harington observes: "I conclude (as one pretily argued last day in the Schools,) that the world ys a stage and wee that lyve in yt are all stage players, some are good for many parts, some only for dumme shows, some deserve a *plaudite* some a *plorate*. . . . Once I played the foole. . . ."[52]

Anticipating the Shakespearean use of the idea, as in *Lear* and *2 Henry IV* (II.ii.154-156), "Well, thus we play the fools with the time, and the spirits of the wise sit in the clouds and mock us," the popular Renaissance poet Palingenius remarks: "So move they Goddes above to laugh wyth toyes and trifles vayne," and elsewhere:

> Here in this wretched mortall life, all men must foolishe be,
> And laughing stocks, and pageants fonde, unto the Gods in sky.

Perhaps, conjectures Palingenius, Jove purposely makes

> man thy laughing stocke. For nothing els to be
> The life of men on earth doth seeme, then staged Comedie.[53]

Suggesting the ratio of apes to man as man to gods, the same poet anticipates *Measure for Measure* (II.ii.107-123) and *Coriolanus* (V.iii. 182-185), where the hero exclaims: "The Gods look down, and this unnatural scene / They laugh at." Similarly, Shakespeare's Sonnet 15 emphasizes the idea of the world as stage subject to incomprehensible powers. The eighteenth-century antiquarian William Oldys

[49]Juan Luis Vives, *Opera* (Basel, 1555), I, 269-272; cf. II, 101; see "A Fable about Man," tr. Nancy Lenkeith, in *The Renaissance Philosophy of Man,* ed. Ernst Cassirer et al. (Chicago, 1948), pp. 387-393.

[50]*Della historia* (Venetia, 1560), fol. [49^{v}].

[51]Cf. Alemán's *Guzman de Alfarache,* II, 62, 114, 141.

[52]Letter in a Bodley manuscript (Rawlinson, B.162), quoted in Kathleen M. Lea, "Harington's *Folly,*" in *Elizabethan and Jacobean Studies Presented to Frank Percy Wilson* (Oxford, 1959), p. 42. See also Montaigne, III, 27 and passim; *Arcadia,* I, 333; II, 138; Spenser, "An Epitaph upon . . . Sidney . . . ," *Poetical Works,* p. 558, l. 36. Cf. "Tears of the Muses," ll. 157-168; Nashe, III, 284.

[53]*The Zodiake of Life,* tr. Barnabe Googe (1576), pp. 99, 203, [62].

reported the motto of Shakespeare's Globe Theatre, *Totus mundus agit histrionem*, which blazoned the idea of world as stage, where men must grunt and sweat under their heavy loads.[54] Among innumerable other references, the Induction to Marston's *Antonio and Mellida* (1599-1600) alludes to "this world's stage."[55] Donne repeats the *topos* of the world as stage, God having "made this World his Theatre, *ut exhibeatur ludus deorum*. . . ."[56] Regarding this stage-play world, Raleigh sustains the theatrical analogy when he declares, "Wee are all . . . become Comædians in religion," in our actions and in our lives renouncing the parts we profess to play.[57] George Ruggle's comedy *Ignoramus*, II.vi, contains the remark: "Totus mundus exercet histrionem" (1630, p. 63). And John Stephens' *Essayes and Characters, Ironicall, and Instructive* (1615) recites:

> The world appeares most like a Puppet-play,
> Wherein the motions, walke, performe and say,
> Nothing but what the master will advance;
> Though every tricke proclaimes dull ignorance. (p. 48)[58]

The world as stage in seventeenth-century drama was, of course, a major commonplace, handled memorably by Calderón de la Barca in *El gran teatro del mundo* (written ca. 1645-1650). In his *La vida es sueño* (written ca. 1631-1632) the imprisoned Prince Sigismondo reflects on the theater of the world and on life as a dream. Similarly, in the *Tempest*, where the stage manager Prospero remarks on the illusoriness of the world, the double theme is emphasized, and the Platonic distinction reaffirmed between appearance and reality. The world-as-stage *topos* impinges upon the world-as-dream convention, both, as in the church fathers and the *contemptus mundi* tradition, pointing to a Platonic sense of this world's unreality. It is, indeed, *King Lear* to which *La vida es sueño* bears significant resemblance, not only in the conventional descent of the hero from power to misery but also in Lear's confusion between appearance

[54]E. K. Chambers, *William Shakespeare: A Study of Facts and Problems* (Oxford, 1930), II, 278. Cf. Kent's "thou beacon to this under globe" (II.ii.163).

[55]*Plays*, I, 7.

[56]*The Sermons of John Donne*, ed. George R. Potter and Evelyn M. Simpson, I (Berkeley, 1953), 207. See Donne, "Holy Sonnets," VI, "This is my playes last scene . . .," and "Of the Progresse of the Soule. . . . The Second Anniversary," ll. 67-69; Webster, *The Duchess of Malfi*, IV.i.99-100.

[57]*The History of the World* (1614), Preface, sig. C2v.

[58]See Tilley W882.

and reality and the doubt of his own senses (e.g., I.iv.234-238). In his upside-down world of stage and dream the old king lacks criteria for the correctness of his sensory perceptions. Seeming to epitomize Lear's confusion, Mad Tom in the fantastic heath scene inquires, "Sleepest or wakest thou, jolly shepherd?" (III.vi.42).

Both as stage and as dream, the world shows Lear his own nakedness as actor in the unreal nightmare of the human condition, unprotected to his human and cosmic enemies. Near the play's midpoint the king recognizes the false assurance of his temporary garments in his borrowed role as actor on "this great stage of fools" and their misrepresentation of essentially unprotected man: "Off, off, you lendings! Come; unbutton here" (III.iv.111-112). As he has in the first scene doffed his crown, toward the end, uncovering from head to foot, he removes his boots: "Pull off my boots; harder, harder; so" (IV.vi.175). The king thus anticipates, as helpless Everyman, his concluding "Pray you, undo this button" (V.iii.309). "Unaccommodated man is no more but such a poor, bare, forked animal . . ." (III.iv.109-110). As Heywood's *An Apology for Actors* (1612) declares,

> then our play's begun,
> When we are borne, and to the world first enter,
> And all finde *Exits* when their parts are done. (sig. [a4v])

Like Lear, connecting the world-as-stage and clothing motifs, Raleigh observes of essential man: "Certainly there is no other account to be made of this ridiculous world, than to resolve, That the change of fortune on the great Theater, is but as the change of garments on the lesse. For when on the one and the other, every man weares but his owne skin; the Players are all alike."[59] When Don Quixote makes the same comparison, ". . . the Play done, and the Actors undress'd, they are all equal, and as they were before. . . . Death, which is the Catastrophe and End of the Action, strips the Actors of all their Marks of Distinction . . .," Sancho Panza acknowledges the ubiquity of the Renaissance commonplace: "A rare comparison . . . though not so new, but that I have heard it over and over."[60]

[59]*The History of the World,* Preface, sig. D2.

[60]*Don Quixote,* Pt. II, Ch. xii, p. 514. The clothing-stage motif is recurrent; e.g., in Marcus Aurelius Antoninus, *The Communings with Himself*, tr. C. R. Haines, Loeb Classical Lib. (1916), p. 323 and *n.*

CHAPTER VIII

Deus Absconditus: Lear

UP TO THIS POINT I have, in examining the major characters of *King Lear*, shown that they correspond closely to main Renaissance religious attitudes, especially those which Elizabethans would have attributed to heathens: *prisca theologia*, atheism, or superstition. To the first type, it has been indicated, belong Cordelia and Edgar; to the second belong Goneril, Regan, and Edmund; and to the third Gloucester corresponds. But what of the protagonist of the tragedy, Lear himself? An investigation of Lear's belief utterances excludes him from group one and, in a sense, from group three; moreover, he starts with no a priori negativist atheism, such as characterizes Goneril, Regan, and (except for his worship of the goddess Natura) Edmund. That Lear is not, according to the above categories, simply classifiable and that his various manifestations occupy the central interest of the play are, of course, to be expected in a work of such complexity that even at the present day it would be difficult to find scholars fully in agreement concerning its meaning.

Before discussing the lines themselves, we may inquire whether within the pagan scheme itself it is not possible further to distinguish a fourth religious stance. If pagans were superstitious, atheistical, or *prisci theologi*, none of these categories allows for the "representative" or prototypical pagan who does not happen to be a candidate for pre-Christian salvation—a polytheist-naturalist, in short, who starts with none of the anxieties of Gloucester, none of the rationalist contempt for the supernatural powers of Edmund, Goneril, and Regan, and none of the pre-Christian purity of Cordelia and Edgar. In other words, I have not till this point considered, in this ostensibly pagan play, a character who in his universal heroic strength can identifiably represent mankind as heathen, relatively unmarked by the eccentricities, admirable, absurd, or vicious, of the other personages. Without such a character to operate with, to poise against the forces to be explored, to offer values for the crucible of his tragic understanding, the play would collapse of its own inanition: powers of goodness ranged against powers of evil, and in the middle a weak old man blindly stumbling about, muttering of flies. In short, until now this analysis has lacked a hero, and in a real sense, ideologically, the play without Lear would be like *Hamlet* without the prince.

I conclude my previous statement—that an Elizabethan would have expected a pagan to be superstitious, atheistical, or "saved"—while true, to require qualification. For the "superstition" may be prima facie excessive and the product of fear, or it may be representatively and dignifiedly genuine from the heathen point of view and analogically correspond, on its own level, to that of a "believing" Renaissance Christian.[1] It is possible, then, that the *donnée* of the play includes, on a heroic level, a serious representation of pre-Christian pagan belief of elevated mind and strength. Whether this is true remains to be determined from an examination of the text of *King Lear*.

In considering the complex character of Lear, who as protagonist mirrors the thematic complexities of the play, we shall have to confront a technique different from that which depicted the relatively perspicuous portrayals of Gloucester, Cordelia, Edgar, Edmund, Goneril, and Regan; in Lear the threads of the work's central sense merge, unwind, come together and apart, on more than one level. If, therefore, among *King Lear*'s thematic preoccupations is belief, we might expect to find confluences and contradictions in belief, perhaps ambiguous, perhaps simultaneous; in short, I suggest that if *Lear* is, as many critics hold, Shakespeare's most complexly symphonic work its protagonist might, in all probability, be approached as a microcosm of that complexity.

The opening scene discovers to us a king apparently firm in his polytheistic-naturalistic faith, a ruler convinced of his dependence on the higher powers, who support him and from whom he derives his being and his end:

For, by the sacred radiance of the sun,
The mysteries of Hecate and the night,
By all the operation of the orbs
From whom we do exist and cease to be, (I.i.109-112)

[1]"If wee present a forreigne History," advises Thomas Heywood in *An Apology for Actors* (1612), "the subject is so intended, that in the lives of *Romans, Grecians,* or others, either the vertues of our Country-men are extolled, or their vices reproved . ." (sig. F3v).

he swears; and the extent and emphasis of the lines would seem, expositionally, to ensure our awareness of Lear's piety qua pagan, far from the self-sufficiency of the heathen atheists and the passive subservience of Gloucester. Thus it may be suggested that, just as Edgar and Cordelia function as norms of pre-Christian piety, Lear establishes himself at first as a norm of pagan fidelity. His confidence is a Plautine "Di me servant atque amant" (*Pseudolus*, l. 613). Hence, in a sense, the king is a "good" pagan, as who should say a "good" Catholic; he is, as we shall see, however, a more complex analogue of the Jacobean Christian believer, the spectator of Shakespeare's play.

"Thou Swear'st Thy Gods in Vain"

Of Jove, Appollo, of Mars, of swich rascaille!
—Chaucer, *Troilus and Criseyde*, Bk. V, l. 1853

Lear's preliminary heathen apologia, standard pagan fare, according to the Renaissance view, is reinforced by further interjections: "Now, by Apollo," he shouts at Kent, who significantly—and foreshadowingly—underlines Lear's religious exposition:

Now, by Apollo, King,
Thou swear'st thy Gods in vain. (I.i.160-161)

Again, the old king exclaims, "By Jupiter" (I.i.178), a divinity whose connection with Hecate, the goddess of the ghost world mentioned by Lear above, is interestingly suggested in Robert Estienne's *Thesaurus linguae latinae* (Basel, 1576), s.v. "Hecate": "Hecate . . . cui Jupiter elementa subjecit, & caelo hereboque potentem fecit. . . ." A fourth time Lear reinforces the conviction of his pagan reverence and piety when he swears "by the power that made me" (I.i.207).

Among the numerous possible avenues for Shakespeare's knowledge of pagan religion were, for example, Renaissance histories. Holinshed, containing Harrison's description of Britain, Chapter ix, "Of the ancient religion used in Albion," declares:

> Neither were these errors anie thing amended, by the comming in of Brute [Lear's ancestor], who no doubt added such devises unto the same, as he and his companie had learned before in Græcia . . . they honored the said Samothes himselfe under the name of Dis and Saturne: also Jupiter, Mars, Minerva, Mercurie, Apollo, Diana; and finallie Hercules.[2]

[2] *The First and Second Volumes of Chronicles* (1587), sig. [Civv].

Before Holinshed, Geoffrey of Monmouth describes Lear's father as having fallen on the temple of Apollo in Troynovant. Between Geoffrey and Holinshed, Wace repeats the account, placing the temple in "Londres." Other details of pagan worship could have been found in the *Arcadia*; in Boccaccio; in emblem books claiming to treat all the gods (Conti, Cartari, and Giraldi, the last reflecting the new sixteenth-century taste for archaeology), as well as in Ravisius Textor, Alciati, Symeoni, Sambucus, Whitney, and similar manuals; in Renaissance schoolbooks and literature generally, in Senecan drama and in Renaissance plays with pagan settings; in the syncretic Renaissance climate mingling classical, Celtic, and Germanic deities; and in Shakespeare's own favorite reading, including Plutarch, Virgil, and Ovid. From Ovid's less than reverent *Metamorphoses* Shakespeare could have absorbed notions of divine irrationality and caprice.[3]

SUN AND MOON

> *But they thought . . . the lightes of heaven to be governours of the world, and gods.*
>
> —Wisdom xiii.2

> *O toi, Soleil, ô toi qui rends le jour au monde,*
> *Que ne l'as-tu laissé dans une nuit profonde!*
>
> —Racine, *La Thébaïde*, I.i

The reign of the legendary Lear occupied an early era before Christ, Thomas Lanquet and Thomas Cooper's *An Epitome of Cronicles* (1559, fol. 37) and John Taylor's *A Memorial of All the English Monarchs . . . from Brute to King James* (1622, sig. B4) placing it in 844 B.C., while Lanquet and Cooper's "yere of the worlde" 3119 approximates Holinshed's "yeere of the world 3105."[4] Apropos, we may cite some Renaissance views of pre-Christian religious practice.

Some Utopians, says Thomas More, "worshyp for God the sunne, some the mone, some some other of the planetes."[5] Idolatry is reduced

[3]For sixteenth-century views on various national attitudes toward the gods, see Polydore Vergil's *De rerum inventoribus* (Strasbourg, 1606). Cf. *Leir*, Sc. v, ll. 416-419, connecting Dedalus and Troynovant. On Elizabethan notions of pre-Christian British origins, see Thomas D. Kendrick, *British Antiquity* (1950). In addition to Jean Seznec, *The Survival of the Pagan Gods* (New York, 1953), see also Ernest H. Wilkins, "Descriptions of Pagan Divinities from Petrarch to Chaucer," *Speculum*, XXXII (1957), 511-522.

[4]Holinshed, in the New Variorum *Lear*, p. 384. Taylor has illustrations of "Leire" and "Cordeilla." Richard Harvey's *Philadelphus* (1593), p. 30, gives the year 3122.

[5]*The Utopia of Sir Thomas More*, ed. J. H. Lupton (Oxford, 1895), p. 266.

in José de Acosta's account of his travels (1604) "to twoo heades, the one grounded uppon naturall things, the other upon things imagined and made by mans invention." The first is then divided into two: "for eyther the thing they worship is generall, as the Sunne, Moone, Fire, Earth and Elements, or else it is particular, as some certayne river. . . ."[6] William Warner's *Albions England* (1602) describes the reverence of pagans, "sacrificing as devoutly to a woodden Jupiter, as to a golden Jupiter . . . or," foreshadowing Edmund, "unreverent Priapus, as to the Sunne, the Starres, or amiable Venus" (sig. A3v).

Recalling by his language that Shakespeare had sketched, a year before *Lear*, a Moor of pagan origins,[7] Thomas Palmer's *An Essay of . . . Travailes* (1606) mentions "the Egyptians, the Assyrians, Philistines, and those uncircumcised people that worshipped strange GODS" and notes "the barbarous people of the East and West *Indies*, that worship the . . . Sunne, Moone, Starres . . ." (p. 74). The god secured unto men by nature is not God, argues John Dove's *A Confutation of Atheisme* (1605), since they worship the creature instead of the Creator and adore the sun and the moon (p. 1). Indicating a mode of transmission of such knowledge, Richard Brathwaite's *Natures Embassie* (1621) remarks that "we may reade in the ancient historians, of the Egyptians who adored . . . the Sunne, the Moone, the starres and inferiour lights" (p. 2).

Pre-Christian English deities are described and illustrated in Richard Verstegen's *A Restitution of Decayed Intelligence: In Antiquities. Concerning the . . . English Nation* (Antwerp, 1605). Reminiscent of Lear's "wheel of fire," Verstegen's "The Idol of the Sun" is illustrated and portrayed

> lyke half a naked man set upon a piller, his face . . . brightned with gleames of fyre, and holding with both his armes stretched out, a burning wheel before his brest: the wheel beeing to signify the cours which hee runneth round about the world; & the fyrie gleames & brightnes, the light and heat wherewith he warmeth & comforteth the things that live and grow. (p. 69)[8]

[6]*The Naturall and Morall Historie of the East and West Indies*, p. 332.

[7]See *Othello*, V.ii.351-355.

[8]Echoing Verstegen are Alexander Ross's *Pansebeia* (1658), p. 149, and Pierre Gautruche's *The Poetical Histories* (1671), p. 114. Gautruche notes that in Albion "Devotions were paid in the same manner" to the sun, "as to the *Mithra* of *Persia*, and to the Divinities of the East, that were reverenced for the Sun." On ancient worship of the sun and moon, see Robert Boyle, *A Free Enquiry into the . . . Notion of Nature* (1685/

The sun and moon in their eclipse are, for Gloucester, subjects of fearful speculation, auguring mysterious harm (I.ii.107-120). Lear, on the other hand, commences by worshiping the "sacred radiance of the sun" and "the operation of the orbs / From whom we exist and cease to be" as holy sources (I.i.109-112). This disjunction of the protagonists in tone and attitude in the opening act sets the stage for changes to ensue.[9]

"LUMEN NATURALE"

Natur und Geist—so spricht man nicht zu Christen.
Deshalb verbrennt man Atheisten.

—Goethe, *Faust*

That Lear, in addition to such deities as the sun and moon, refers to nature as his goddess (I.iv.284: "Hear, Nature, hear! dear Goddess, hear!") is, in the Renaissance view of pagan religion, to be expected. Brathwaite's *Natures Embassie* argues that the heathens "shew their Gods by deciphering an heavenly power . . . in . . . workes of Nature" (p. 2). Similarly, Lyly's *Euphues. The Anatomy of Wit* considers nature the only goddess of the heathens.[10] Warner's *Albions England* makes a similar point regarding "The greatest

6), pp. 84-93. Boyle recalls that Seneca, believing in the divinity of the sun, reprehended Epicurus for holding it to be a burning stone or an aggregate of fires. See Chapman's *The Masque of the Middle Temple and Lincoln's Inn* (1613), in *Plays and Poems: Comedies*, p. 443.

9Lear's curse, at I.iv.260, "Darkness and devils!" leads eventually into the obscurity of the villains, "threading dark-ey'd night" (II.i.119), and into the lust-ridden Edgar's demonic underworld, where "Nero is an angler in the Lake of Darkness" (III.vi. 6-7). Cf. IV.vi.126-131, concerning "darkness" beneath, and the Neronic tradition of the depraved emperor's curiosity concerning his birthplace; and cf. Edgar's reference to "The dark and vicious place where thee he got" (V.iii.172). The sun's radiance gives way to "sulph'rous and thought-executing fires" (III.ii.4). Finally, allusions to the sun no more recurring, except by the pathetic reminder of its absence in Gloucester's "Were all thy letters suns, I could not see" (IV.vi.141), mankind seems abandoned to darkness and the ceaseless mutability of the moon (V.iii.17-19). For Lear's night journey takes him from daylight's "sacred radiance" through the mysteries of darkness, to recognition of meaningless mutability, and finally to an at least implicit assault upon the divine mysteries and heaven itself. Counterpointing his dark pilgrimage is Kent, who, from the start, challengingly echoes Lear's "Now, by Apollo" with his own Apollo invocations (I.i.159-161) and who, in facetiously aureate terms—cf. Verstegen's description above—alludes to an "influence, like the wreath of radiant fire / On flick'ring Phoebus' front" (II.ii.108-109). And consequent to the "darker purpose," to which Lear, with dramatic irony, initially refers (I.i.36), is the *Höllenfahrt* of Edgar, with his riding imagery in the infernal scenes.

10*The Complete Works of John Lyly*, ed. R. Warwick Bond (1902), I, 192.

heathen Clarkes" (p. 320). "Before the lawe was given," explain the Homilies in *Certaine Sermons* (1587), "the law of nature onely" reigned "in the harts of men" (sig. L2^{v}).[11]

Furthermore, natural religion, being obeyed by men who had not had revealed to them the light of divine knowledge, was considered more vulnerable to doubt than revealed religion. ". . . I will treat of Atheisme," writes Fitzherbert concerning the pagans in the *Second Part of a Treatise*, to "prove that the same must needes growe of their religion . . ." (p. 60). For "the multitude, turpitude, and abjection of their gods, honoured with such detestable sacrifices, rites and ceremonies, that their beliefe . . . could not possiblie produce in time, any other effect in their common welth, then contempt of God, and of religion, that is to say, Atheysme . . ." (p. 48). Such latent skepticism within natural religion, he affirms, had already been instanced:

> But what doe I speake of contempt of the gods, growing of paganisme, seeing it is manifest, that it bred in verie manie meere Atheisme. Which was well observed by *Plutarck* in the *Egiptians*, whereby he also condemned at unawares the religion both of the *Greekes* and the *Romans*, which he professed himselfe. . . . it is no mervaile, if an infinit number of *Atheists*, did spring in time of *Paganisme*, out of these two fountaines, whereof *Plutarck* speaketh, to wit, ignorance of the true God, and the execrable superstition, of false, frivolous, and impious religion. (p. 69)

That Lear, as a devotee of a natural religion, might more easily than an adherent of a revealed faith decline into disbelief is evident from such Renaissance views as cited and is significant regarding his dramatic development. Indeed, a pagan, no matter how devout, might already be considered an atheist. Dove's *Confutation* observes that "Sometimes under the name of Atheists are comprehended Pagans, Infidels and Idolaters, all such as are ignorant of the true God, albeit in their kinde they be very devout, religious and godly" (p. 1). William Perkins in *A Treatise of Mans Imaginations* (Cambridge, Eng., 1607) speaks of Jews and Mohammedans as atheists (pp. 43-44). Robert Pricket's *Unto the Most High and Mightie . . . James . . . a Souldiers Resolution* (1603) refers to the time "since this Island first converted was from Pagan Athisme . . ." (sig. [A4^{v}]).

Hence, if Lear, with unerected wit and *lumen naturale*, might

[11]Following such writers as Mornay, Richard Barckley in *A Discourse of the Felicitie of Man* (1603), p. 598, notes that "Heathens sawe by instinct of nature, and by reason, that there is a God."

easily become an atheist to his natural religion, and, indeed, according to some Renaissance views, was already one, Shakespeare's depiction of his religious development could have occasioned little surprise and no reprehension. Moreover, since the dramatist had in hand a situation involving audience expectation, his expository task was reduced to the extent that Lear might have been expected to develop in the anticipated direction. It is to this dramatic problem that Dr. Johnson's complaint against Shakespeare's excessive expository allusion to the pagan deities seems to address itself. When Lear swears, "By Jupiter" (I.i.178), Johnson objects, "Sh[akespeare] makes his Lear too much a mythologist; he had 'Hecate' and 'Apollo' before."[12] In preparation for Lear's subsequent crisis of faith, however, it may be essential that the play emphasize his initial pagan devotion. Such underlining by repetition, indeed, is among the limited devices the hurried art of the theater can offer the playwright for the dramatic purpose of the reversal.

For if Lear were only a simple believer, as Gloucester seems a credulous man, the symphonic complexity which we sense, above all of Shakespeare's works, to be present in this play would be lacking. Certain countercurrents, anticipatory of Lear's later defiance, may, I suggest, be evident even in the beginning. In other words, having strongly established Lear's pagan piety at the start in order to have a norm against which to work and against which to measure Lear's departures at the end, Shakespeare would not have concluded his dramaturgical task; he would also have had to plant anticipations of that end, perceptible if muted, for such essential purposes as motivation and verisimilitude. What I am proposing is the obvious solution of a playwright's paradoxical task: how at the same time to establish character firmly and to allow for an eventual great, almost total, reversal of that character. For, if anything is clear in this tragedy, it is that the protagonist's faith in the gods whom he adores is severely shaken by the events of the tragedy. In addition to the outbursts of the storm in Act III, the closing speeches of Act V, Scene iii, give explicit evidence of Lear's loss of faith, just as, tacitly, the irony of sequence (discussed in Chapter xi) reveals it.

In order, therefore, to avoid a catastrophic last-minute introduc-

[12] In New Variorum *Lear*, p. 27. Cf. the similar complaint among modern critics: e.g., George S. Gordon, *Shakespearian Comedy* (1944), p. 121 (Lear swears "by too many Gods").

tion of a radically new orientation, i.e., Lear's later revulsion against the gods in a peripeteia of belief, Shakespeare, in the interests of verisimilitude, may have had to anticipate that change. It is conceivable, moreover, that elements of Lear's complexity which would have been fairly comprehensible to an Elizabethan audience, engaged in topical controversies, may have escaped the secular eye of modern criticism. In short, I suggest that even at the beginning certain allusions typical of pagan naturalism reveal a concurrence of counter-patterns accompanying Lear's firmly expressed heathen piety.

"Nothing Will Come of Nothing"

. . . ἴσα καὶ τὸ μηδὲν ζώσας ἐναριθμῶ.
—Sophocles, *Oedipus Tyrannos*

For we are borne at all adventure, and we shall be hereafter as though we had never beene.
—Wisdom ii.2

As has been observed, Lear in the opening scene staunchly reiterates his faith in his gods. Nevertheless, although neglected by critics unfamiliar with the dramatic importance of the Renaissance religious milieu, Lear's repeated exclamation in the first-act exposition, "Nothing will come of nothing," recalls a meaning that was centrally relevant to the religious crisis of Shakespeare's age. This twice-mentioned notion, expressed by Lear in two contrasting moods, angry and calm, occurs in the crucially expository first hundred lines of the play: "Nothing will come of nothing," he shouts (I.i.90) at Cordelia; while in a more reflective mood he replies to his Fool's "Can you make no use of nothing, Nuncle?" "Why, no, boy; nothing can be made out of nothing" (I.iv.136-139).

"Nothing," echoed throughout the play as an ironic refrain, is, in typically Shakespearean analogy, relevant to the individual, the family, the state, and the created universe; "nothing" and "something" are ironically substitutable in numerous ways, such as, for example, Goneril and Regan's acquisitions, something which results in nothing. Cordelia, who has nothing at the beginning ("that little-seeming substance," I.i.198), resembles Lear, who has nothing at the end. And the universe itself, upon whose substance and upon whose gods Lear relied, turns out, in a sense, to be nothing. In "nothing" and "something," then, we have a pair analogous to Shakespeare's "shadow" and "substance" and to the appearance-versus-reality motif which fills his dramas.

While "nothing will come of nothing" is a familiar proverbial expression, it is essential to inquire into its dramatic use, not only because "nothing" is a recurrent motif but also because both personal and cosmic implications seem to be present in the phrase. From the personal viewpoint it suggests that man, "this quintessence of dust," will, like chimney sweepers, return to his primary "nothing." After the emphatic "nothings" exchanged by Lear and Cordelia (I.i.87-90) and Lear's warning that "Nothing can come of nothing," the Fool applies the term to Lear himself (I.iv.200-202). With ironic ambiguity, the expression may point to the emptiness of Lear's *quid pro quo* ideal, as well as, more generally, to the futility of dependence on quantity. In like fashion, the futility of human pretension is mocked by Montaigne ("man is a thing of nothing," II, 199) and later by Pascal, who sees man as a nothing in comparison with the infinite.[13] From one point of view, then, Lear's expression may not so much question the orthodox position regarding Creation as imply that the creation out of nothing which man is will result in nothing, or that man, who is himself by origin a mere nothing, strives self-destructively to return to his original state. This *nostalgie du néant* is expressed, for example, by Antonio in Webster's *The Duchess of Malfi*, III.v.97-98:

> Heaven fashion'd us of nothing: and we strive,
> To bring our selves to nothing . . .

and in Donne's

> Wee seeme ambitious, Gods whole worke t'undoe;
> Of nothing hee made us, and we strive too,
> To bring our selves to nothing backe; . . .[14]

Similarly, the drift of the *Vernichtungsdrama*, as the storm scene (III.ii) indicates, is toward "nothing." Cursing the world, Lear wishes it to be annihilated (III.ii.7-8), just as he invokes sterility for his evil daughters. Having been deluded in the belief that man was "something," that the gods were "something," in the storm and afterward Lear discovers the "nothingness" of man and the protecting gods. His nihilistic crescendo assails the heavenly powers, deanthropomorphized during the violent storm into their elements. Such are the powers which sport with man, reducing his vaunted dignity below that of dogs, horses, and rats (V.iii.306) to a mere nothing.

13 *Pascal's Pensées*, tr. H. F. Stewart (New York, 1950), p. 21.

14 "An Anatomie of the World. . . . The First Anniversary," ll. 155-157.

Yet "nothing," a basic paradox of *King Lear*, has also a pointed religious irony in the play, which probes the reality of the heavens in regard to the realities of earth. A keystone of the accepted theology of Shakespeare's day was the paradox that God created the world out of nothing; and it was a keystone that was, at a time of increasing naturalism, materialism, and skepticism, in danger of crashing. So agitated were Elizabethan theologians concerning the retention of this paradox—which, in the Creation, has been considered a foundation of religion itself—that numerous polemicists, Catholics as well as Protestants, joined in its defense.

Belief in God the Creator of heaven and earth is evidently a theoretical basis and starting point of religious principles, a premise upon which others depend. Hence, the doctrine *ex nihilo*, formulated at the Fourth Lateran Council of 1215 (and reaffirmed by the Vatican Council of 1870),[15] was fundamental to providence and other basic articles of faith. Creation *ex nihilo*, indeed, implies providence.

Linking creation and providence, Raleigh, for example, appears to echo St. Augustine's view (*Confessions*, Bk. IV, Ch. xii): "non enim fecit atque abiit," the latter observes of God, "sed ex illo in illo sunt." Raleigh's *The History of the World* (1614; Preface, sig. D2) declares, ". . . these two glorious actions of the Almightie be so neare, and . . . linked together, that the one necessarily implyeth the other: Creation, inferring Providence: (for what Father forsaketh the child that he hath begotten?) and Providence presupposing Creation." Since created beings want in themselves the sufficient cause of their existence, they depend upon the acts of preservation of their Creator, who may direct them to the end for which he created them. Alluding to the divine word "par laquelle sont toutes chouses en leur nature et proprieté et condition, et sans la maintenance et gouvernement duquel toutes chouses seroyent en ung moment reduyctes a neant," Rabelais recalls, "comme de neant elles ont esté par luy produyctes en leur estre."[16] Hooker includes among "those principal spurs and motives unto all virtue" the resurrection of the dead, the providence of God, and "the creation of the world."[17]

That creation *ex nihilo* was affirmed against a solid front of philo-

[15]Heinrich Denzinger, *Enchiridion symbolorum* (Fribourg B., 1937), pp. 199, 491.

[16]*Oeuvres* (Paris, 1835), p. 350.

[17]*Ecclesiastical Polity*, in *Works*, II, 19.

sophical opinion is evidence of its tenacious hold, points out Arnold Williams in his study of Renaissance Bible commentaries, adding that, except for occasional deviations, this belief continues to the time of Milton.[18] Similarly, Paul H. Kocher concludes that Renaissance theologians of all faiths interpreted Scripture to signify that God created matter out of nothing.[19] Gabriel Harvey lists creation *ex nihilo* as one of the paradoxes so thoroughly canvased that everyone can write volumes on them.[20] Indeed, Don Cameron Allen indicates that the tenet did at this time excite feverish attention.[21] Hence, Lear's reply that "nothing can be made out of nothing" would, as another recent commentator deduces, "have struck original audiences as seriously, even ironically wrong. In its pagan doctrine it opposed a vital Christian tenet."[22]

Even intellectuals and relatively sophisticated independents claimed adherence to the doctrine in face of its clearly *credo-quia-absurdum* aspect. Yet if materialism, whose premise is naturalistically existent substance, accepted the paradox, its own existence would be threatened. Thus, the issue of the theological doctrine eventually became one which was crucial to scientific development. Further, if creation was not by the miracle *ex nihilo*, the miraculous incorruptibility of creation's heaven might also be questioned. In the crisis of Shakespeare's age both views came under scrutiny, especially after the discovery of the nova of 1572, while the shock of realization that the heavens might not be eternally changeless involved a corollary reinspection of the cherished Christian belief that the world was made for man. It is, at least partly, to a consideration of the last assumption that Shakespeare's tragedy, in the person of the protagonist, appears to relate itself.

18"Renaissance Commentaries on 'Genesis' and Some Elements of the Theology of *Paradise Lost*," *PMLA*, LVI (1941), 152-153.

19"The Old Cosmos: A Study in Elizabethan Science and Religion," *Huntington Library Quarterly*, XV (1952), 102. Kocher cites Andrew Willet, *Hexapla in Genesin* (1605); Du Bartas, *His Devine Weekes and Workes* (1605); Alexander Ross, *An Exposition on . . . Genesis* (1626).

20*Letter-Book of Gabriel Harvey*, ed. E. J. L. Scott, Camden Soc. (1884), pp. 10-11.

21"The Degeneration of Man and Renaissance Pessimism," *SP*, XXXV (1938), 210; see Allen's numerous contemporary citations, p. 210*n*.

22Paul A. Jorgensen, "Much Ado about *Nothing*," *SQ*, V (1954), 287. Cf. Correa M. Walsh, *The Doctrine of Creation* (1910); L. C. Martin, "Shakespeare, Lucretius, and the Commonplaces," *Review of English Studies*, XXI (1945), 174-182.

In orthodox fashion Petrarch condemns those contemporaries "Intending to defend the very famous or rather infamous little line of Persius: 'Nothing comes out of nothing, and nothing can return to nothing.'"[23] Righteously, too, Calvin, assailing the "common imagination in olde time among heathen men" regarding the origin of the world, insists on creation *ex nihilo* as proved by Genesis i, and denounces the opposing view as "this filthie errour."[24] Following Calvin, other Renaissance commentators on Genesis echo him and devote a section to demonstrating creation *ex nihilo* from the Bible and the church fathers. Among those who enlisted in defense of the paradox that something could be made out of nothing was Mutian: "We leave behind the entelechy of Aristotle and the ideas of Plato. God created all things from nothing."[25] Montaigne also rejects the vanity of human understanding which claims that "Because nothing is made of nothing: God was not able to frame the world without matter" (II, 229). The Catholic Robert Parsons notes the doctrine as an instance, beyond human capacity, of "high and hidden doctrine."[26] Identifying denial of creation *ex nihilo* with the pagan view, *The Difference betwene the Auncient Phisicke . . . and the Latter Phisicke* (1585) by R. B., Esquire, prays God to "teach, ayd, & assist thy servants against the heathnish and false Philosophie of Aristotle, which teacheth that . . . of nothyng, nothyng can be made . . ." (sig. 4*).

Furthermore, Sidney is at least twice connected with support of the orthodox tenet that God created the world out of nothing: the tenth chapter of his friend Mornay's *A Woorke concerning the Trewnesse of the Christian Religion* (1587), whose translation is ascribed to Sidney and Golding, is entitled "That GOD created the World of nothing; that is to say, without any matter or stuffe whereof to make it." And in the *Arcadia*, where Shakespeare would have seen it, Pamela refutes the atheistic Cecropia's dependence upon

[23]"On His Own Ignorance," tr. Hans Nachod, in *The Renaissance Philosophy of Man*, ed. Ernst Cassirer et al. (Chicago, 1948), p. 93.

[24]*A Commentarie of John Calvine, upon . . . Genesis*, tr. Thomas Tymme (1578), p. 26.

[25]Carl Krause, ed. *Der Briefwechsel des Mutianus Rufus*, Zeitschrift des Vereins für hessische Geschichte und Landeskunde, Neue Folge, Suppl. IX (Kassel, 1885), p. 445: "Relinquamus entelechiam Aristotelis, ideas Platonis. Deus ex nihilo cuncta creavit. . . ."

[26]Cited in Ernest A. Strathmann, *Sir Walter Ralegh: A Study in Elizabethan Skepticism* (New York, 1951), p. 108.

chance rather than providence: "for Chaunce could never make all thinges of nothing" (I, 407). In addition, La Primaudaye's *The Second Part of the French Academie* (1594) deals with objections, including Aristotelian, against creation *ex nihilo* (pp. 16-21). In 1590 Lodowick Lloyd's *The Consent of Time* asserts that "God made all things of nothing, against the rules of Philosophie, *Ex nihilo nihil fit* . . ." (sig. A1^{v}). Jean de Champagnac in his *Physique française* (1595) devotes a chapter to establishing that "la creation des choses venant de rien ne repugne à la lumière naturelle."[27] In contrast to the heathen Lear, Romeo, a Christian Italian, asserts an analogy to the paradox "of nothing first create" (I.i.183). A chorus in Greville's *Mustapha*, referring to creation, affirms that "From Nothing sprang this point."[28]

In 1598 Luis de Granada's *The Sinners Guyd*, issued by Francis Meres, bids us "consider . . . that God created this huge and admirable frame of the world, in a moment, and made it of nothing" (p. 17). Nashe's *Summers Last Will and Testament* (1592; pr. 1600) includes the remark: "This world is transitory; it was made of nothing, and it must to nothing."[29] Warner's *Albions England* alludes to "that unbounded *Power* that All of *No-thing* wrought" (p. 323). Symptomatically, the Janus-faced Bacon, though elsewhere not as convinced, manages, in at least one place, a fideist defense. He considers ". . . things . . . which we know by faith. First, that matter was created from nothing. . . . Creation out of nothing they [the old philosophies] cannot endure. . . . In these points . . . we must rest upon faith. . . ."[30]

In 1605 Dove's *Confutation* assails those who "holde these damnable opinions: That there was no creation of the world . . ." (p. 4). Holding that opposition to the orthodox view is "so weake, as is hardly worth the answering" and denying, with Mornay and Rob-

[27]In Busson, *Le rationalisme*, p. 507.

[28]*Poems and Dramas of Fulke Greville*, ed. Geoffrey Bullough [1939], II, 108.

[29]*Works*, III, 241.

[30]*Works*, V, 491. Further discussion and reference occur in Thomas Fowler, ed. *Bacon's Novum Organum* (Oxford, 1878), pp. 15, 490-491; Fowler's note (p. 491) observes of one of Bacon's formulations of the *ex nihilo* dogma: "It will be noticed that this statement saves the maxim from any theological objection." In his *Novum Organum*, Bacon affirms the Lucretian position "that 'nothing is produced from nothing' . . . the absolute quantum or sum total of matter remains unchanged, without increase or diminution" (*Works*, IV, 197; Lucretius, *De rerum natura*, ed. H. A. J. Munro [1920], I, 44-47, Bk. I, ll. 146-264); and he develops the view at length in *Works*, V, 426-429.

ert Parsons, that a rule of nature can hinder an omnipotent Deity, Raleigh makes acceptance of creation *ex nihilo* an act of faith.[31] Samuel Purchas in *Purchas His Pilgrimage* (1614) says of God's creation, "The action is creating, or making of nothing, to which is required a power supernaturall and infinite" (p. 6). A sidenote, citing Du Bartas, adds, "Nothing but Nothing had the Lord Almighty, Whereof, wherewith, whereby to build this city."

Orthodoxly, again, John Donne could several times proclaim his faith in the first nothing.[32] Sir William Cornwallis' *Essayes of Certaine Paradoxes* (1616), contributing "The Prayse of *Nothing*," opposes those

> Who in the deepes of Sciences do wade,
> Teaching that *Nought* of *Nothing* can be made....
> Sith to the making of this *All-Theater*:
> Nothing but *Nothing* had the *All-creator*. (sig. [F4^v])

In the same year Godfrey Goodman's *The Fall of Man* takes as dogma that "God created all things of nothing . . ." (p. 441), while Ralph Cudworth, still later, stoutly ridicules and refutes those atomists who denied creation out of nothing.[33] Sir Thomas Browne refers to the "nothing, out of which were made all things. . . ."[34] The atheist, explains Thomas Jackson's *A Treatise . . . of Unbeliefe* (1625), applies to omnipotent God the limitation *ex nihilo*; he draws a false conclusion "from a Maxime most true in a sense most impertinent" (p. 46). In *A Treatise of the Divine Essence and Attributes*, Part I (1628), moreover, Jackson identifies the opposite view as pagan as well as atheistic: "Of the Heathens, many did hold an uncreated *Chaos* præexistent to the *frame* of this Universe" (p. 16).[35]

Opposition to the orthodox position included adherents of Aris-

[31] *The History of the World*, Preface, sig. D3^v; see also II.xiii.7, p. 435.

[32] See, e.g., Donne, *Essays in Divinity*, ed. Evelyn M. Simpson (Oxford, 1952), pp. 19, 28-29.

[33] *The True Intellectual System of the Universe* (1678), pp. 16, 738-741 and passim.

[34] *Works*, I, 45.

[35] Upholding the orthodox position, see also Francesco Patrizi, cited in Benjamin Brickman, *An Introduction to Francesco Patrizi's Nova de Universis Philosophia* (New York, 1941), p. 39; Guillaume Postel, *De orbis concordia*, in Busson, *Le rationalisme*, pp. 278-279; William Perkins, *A Golden Chaine* (1592), sig. B4^v. "For that which to us Christians are as undoubted truths," declares David Person's *Varieties* (1635), sig. Ii2^v, to the philosophers "were dubitable grounds, grounded upon their physicall maxime. That *ex nihilo, nihil fiet*."

totle, of Lucretius, of the Paduan School, and of the Pyrrhonists.[36] Recognizing these enemies of faith, Donne confutes the Epicureans' disbelief in creation out of nothing, as well as "the quarelsome contending of *Sextus Empiricus* the *Pyrrhonian* . . . who . . . thinks he cuts off all Arguments against production of Nothing. . . ."[37]

In *The Dialogues of Guy de Brués* (1557) "Baïf" confutes "Ronsard," who holds experience teaches that, as a building may not be erected without stone, nothing can be created by nature without subsistent matter. "Baïf" attempts to show that, accepting the theory of philosophers and scientists regarding the impossibility of creation *ex nihilo*, we should fall into blasphemy and atheism.[38] Jean Bodin's *Methodus* (1583) asserts that the philosophers' postulate, nothing is born of nothing, was the cause of their other errors.[39] Pierre de Lostal's *Les discours philosophiques* (1579) argues, "C'est un axiome en la philosophie que de rien nulle chose ne peut estre faite, et mesmes l'experience nous sert de tesmoignage pour l'approbation d'iceluy."[40] Germbergius' *Carminum proverbialium* (1583) contains the axiom,[41] traceable to Persius' "de nihilo nihilum, in nihilum nil posse reverti"[42] and to Lucretius.[43] And Brian Melbancke's *Philotimus* (1583) refers to "Thy maister (that must be) Aristotle," whose "phisicks affirmes . . . ex nihilo nihil fit . . ." (sig. [Dii]).

Further, *The Prayse of Nothing* by E. D. (1585) cites "prophane antiquitie" and "their rule, that *Nihil ex Nihilo fit* . . ." (sig. [A4]).[44]

[36]Cf. Epicurus: ". . . nothing is created out of that which does not exist. . . ." Cyril Bailey, ed. *Epicurus: The Extant Remains* (Oxford, 1926), p. 21.

[37]*Essays in Divinity*, pp. 28-29. Before his ordination, however, Donne's position on creation *ex nihilo* was less certain; see Frank Manley, ed. *John Donne: The Anniversaries* (Baltimore, 1963), p. 183.

[38]Ed. Panos Paul Morphos, Johns Hopkins Studies in Romance Literatures and Languages, Extra Vol. XXX (Baltimore, 1953), pp. 34, 122.

[39]*Method for the Easy Comprehension of History*, tr. Beatrice Reynolds (New York, 1945), p. 308.

[40]In Busson, *Le rationalisme*, p. 393.

[41]Cited in Thomas W. Baldwin, *William Shakspere's Small Latine & Lesse Greeke* (Urbana, Ill., 1944), II, 543.

[42]*Juvenal and Persius*, Satire III, tr. G. G. Ramsay, Loeb Classical Lib. (1918), pp. 352-353, l. 84.

[43]See Lucretius, *De rerum natura*, ed. Munro, I, 44, Bk. I, ll. 155-158.

[44]*The Prayse of Nothing* is attributed to Edward Daunce, rather than Edward Dyer, by Ralph M. Sargent, "The Authorship of *The Prayse of Nothing*," *The Library*, 4th Ser., XII (1931), 322-331.

In Marlowe's *The Jew of Malta* (ca. 1589-1590) the Machiavellian and materialist atheist, Barabas, like Lear, outside the Christian faith, appears to confute the orthodox view: "Christians . . . / Of naught is nothing made" (I.ii.104-105).[45] In his *De principiis rerum naturalium,* kept by him in manuscript and posthumously published (1596), Francesco Vicomercato opposes creation *ex nihilo* and affirms *ex nihilo nihil*: ". . . physici omnes in id consensere, ex nihilo nil gigni." He professes not to know where theologians found their distinction between generation, which implies a preexisting subject, and creation out of nothing (fol. 49). Typical of the new scientists and one of the most eminent of the age, the mathematician Thomas Harriot, Raleigh's protégé, is described by Aubrey as follows: Harriot "did not like (or valued not) the old storie of the Creation of the World. He could not beleeve the old position; he would say *ex nihilo nihil fit*."[46] Finally, Hobbes offers the materialistic rebuttal: ". . . because nothing, however it be multiplied, will for ever be nothing."[47]

See also *Boece*, Bk. V, Prosa 1, ll. 46-55, stating the motto but removing the restriction from God (*The Complete Works of Geoffrey Chaucer*, ed. F. N. Robinson [1933]).

45Ed. H. S. Bennett (1931).

46Aubrey (*Aubrey's Brief Lives*, ed. Oliver L. Dick [1949], p. 123) provides the ironical sequel regarding Harriot: "But a *nihilum* killed him at last: for in the top of his Nose came a little red speck (exceeding small) which grew bigger and bigger, and at last killed him." See also Anthony à Wood, *Athenae Oxonienses*, II (1815), 300-301.

47*English Works*, I, 212. See also *The Works of Gabriel Harvey*, ed. Alexander B. Grosart, I (1884), 70, complaining of his time: "Something made of Nothing, in spite of Nature." In *The First Part of the Return from Parnassus* (1599-1601), ll. 900-901, it is mockingly observed: "thats a rare wit that can make somthinke of nothinge" (*The Three Parnassus Plays*, ed. J. B. Leishman [1949]). See Marston's poems from *Love's Martyr* (1601) in *The Poems of John Marston*, ed. Arnold Davenport (Liverpool, 1961), p. 177, ll. 5-6. William Camden's *Remaines* (1605), in the section on impresas, quotes "Ex nihilo nihil" (p. 167). Chapman's *Bussy D'Ambois* has "Nothing is made of nought, of all things made" (V.iv.86); his *All Fools* facetiously applies the maxim to cuckolds: "Created they were not, for *Ex nihilo nihil fit*" (V.ii.281-282). The "common-sense" view appears in George Wilkins' *The Miseries of Inforst Mariage* (1605-06; pr. 1607), whose title page states, "As it is now playd by his Majesties Servants"; paralleling the Fool's exchange with Lear (I.iv.135-144), cf. the Clown, sig. A2v. See in Nathan Field's *A Woman Is a Weather-cocke* (1609-10), II.i, the Page's remark (1612, sig. E2). Tyssot de Patot, cited in D. R. McKee, *Simon Tyssot de Patot and the Seventeenth-Century Background of Critical Deism*, Johns Hopkins Studies in Romance Literatures and Languages, XL (Baltimore, 1941), 25 and *n*. Translation of Persius, *The Works of John Dryden*, ed. Sir Walter Scott, XIII (Edinburgh, 1887), 238, ll. 158-160. See the discussion of *ex nihilo nihil fit* in Henry Knight Miller, "The Paradoxical Encomium with Special Reference to Its Vogue in England, 1600-1800," *MP*, LIII (1956), 163-165.

Now from one point of view Lear's clearly recognizable affirmation of the skeptical Renaissance tag was entirely in keeping with the characterization and milieu of a pagan man living before the Christian illumination; for pagans, as indicated above, were supposed, philosophically, to believe with Aristotle that nothing could come of nothing, Bacon observing that "Creation out of nothing" the pagan philosophies could "not endure."[48] Shakespeare has here seized upon a perfect dramatic ambivalence, for, from the viewpoint of the pagan realism the playwright proposes, Lear could be a pious man; from the viewpoint of a Renaissance spectator his speech was one of the clearest indications of skepticism. Thus, Lear as pagan was expected to hold such a view; but, in the analogical transformation by which Lear was both heathen and Renaissance contemporary, an ambivalence was set up by which he was both "pious" and "skeptical" at the same time. In other words, in rejecting creation *ex nihilo*, Lear was a pious pagan but a skeptical Christian; and the manifold hermeneutic of the Renaissance allowed for such a multiple interpretation. Dramatically, then, Lear's speech functioned both as contribution to local color and atmospheric verisimilitude, from a pagan standpoint, and as anticipation, from a Christian standpoint, of Lear's eventual rejection of the gods. Any apparent confusion in this account should, I trust, be attributed to the confusion in the multiple vision of the Elizabethan age, to its illogical syncretism, and to its mingling of disparate and divided worlds.

Once again, Lear asserts his polytheistic belief, addressing nature as "dear Goddess," just as in that other pre-Christian British play of *Cymbeline*, Belarius, a British nobleman, sympathetically invokes her: "O thou goddess, Thou divine Nature" (IV.ii.168-169). Thus Lear's invocation of nature as goddess is closer to that of Belarius than to that of Edmund, who claims exclusive veneration (I.ii.1-2). For Edmund is a votary negating other obligations, and his prayer is addressed also to his own natural sensuality, while Lear's devotions are part of a more widespread and more responsible bond. Yet, a similar divinity is named, the fructifying goddess whom antiquity and the Middle Ages, as well as the Renaissance, knew: "Hear, Nature, hear!" the old king appeals, "dear Goddess, hear!" (I.iv.284).

[48]The concept of creation *ex nihilo*, according to Louis H. Gray, *Encyclopædia of Religion and Ethics*, ed. James Hastings (Edinburgh, 1954), IV, 126, was apparently unknown in Western and Near Eastern antiquity.

Directly, or by implication, Lear continues to invoke this goddess for his curses; nature betrayed requires Nature to wreak vengeance. As a "good" pagan, Lear feels entitled to call upon the services of his heathen dispensation; and, in cursing his ungrateful elder daughters, Lear is well repaid by the gods whom he worships. "Blasts and fogs upon thee!" (I.iv.308), he wishes Goneril, much like another and less worthy heathen, the freckled son of Sycorax.[49]

As in the first act, Lear in Act II still plays the pious pagan: "By Jupiter, I swear, no," which, as before, Kent answers with, "By Juno, I swear, ay" (II.iv.21-22).[50] The king refers, in II.iv.108, to Nature, "When Nature, being oppress'd, commands the mind / To suffer with the body," but it is a sense of human nature, of natural condition, perhaps as a derivative of the all-embracing Nature that Lear implies. Continually he appeals for divine vengeance, again with satisfying results, this time against Goneril (II.iv.163-165). Other elements of nature are also called upon (II.iv.166-169). Here, as elsewhere, Lear is motivated by a polytheistic animism, in which all nature is alive and shares in the divine.

Yet, as his sufferings intensify, the old man's tones become more pleading, and for the first time the great word "if" enters his prayers:

> O Heavens,
> If you do love old men, if your sweet sway
> Allow obedience, if you yourselves are old,
> Make it your cause; send down and take my part! (II.iv.191-194)

[49]*Tempest,* II.ii.1-2. Such references to nature are conventions of drama set in pre-Christian eras; cf. *Gorboduc,* I.ii.11; 1.ii.174; I.ii.220; II.i.81; II.i.140-141; IV.ii.15-16; IV.ii.125; IV.ii.155, 162-164; IV.ii.244-247; IV.ii.259-260; V.ii.16 (*Chief Pre-Shakespearean Dramas,* ed. Joseph Quincy Adams [Boston, 1924]). Yet in the pre-Christian British plays of *Gorboduc* and *Cymbeline,* in contrast with *Lear,* a relatively responsive heaven seems to operate; see J. M. Nosworthy, ed. *Cymbeline,* Arden Shakespeare (1955), p. xxxiv. The uniqueness and deliberateness of Shakespeare's methods in *Lear* are thus emphasized by contrast with *Cymbeline,* as well as by the demonstrable care he took to depart from the providential old *Leir.*

[50]The traditional dissension of Jupiter and Juno (cf. Montaigne, III, 77) anticipates, in Kent's remark, the disintegration of Lear's pagan pantheon; the king has, according to Kent (I.i.161), sworn his gods in vain. Cicero, *De natura deorum,* in . . . *On the Nature of the Gods* . . . (tr. H. M. Poteat [Chicago, 1950]), p. 251, indicates his derivation of Juno from *iuvare,* to help; the clash of Jupiter and Juno may foreshadow some impediment in the workings of a helpful pagan providence. Cf. Stephen Batman's *The Golden Booke of the Leaden Goddes* (1577), fol. 2. The etymology of Jupiter appears also in *Narcissus: A Twelfe Night Merriment . . . 1602,* ed. Margaret L. Lee (1893), p. 33; *Pedantius* (1581), ed. G. C. Moore Smith, in *Materialien zur Kunde des älteren englischen Dramas,* VIII (Louvain, 1905), l. 111 and p. 162. See additional references in D. P. Walker, "The *Prisca Theologia* in France," *JWCI,*

A new and relative humility obtrudes with a new and still unspoken doubt; unrequited suffering, unavenged bestiality, bespeak a less creditable divinity. Lear's reliance upon "the power that made me" (I.i.207) begins to sway, and he takes on some of the tone of Gloucester under duress (III.vii.91, IV.vi.219-220), a tone anticipated at the end of Act I, when Lear shouts, "O! let me not be mad, not mad, sweet heaven!" (v.46), an early foreshadowing of a later development. Throughout the second act his personal doubt increases with his bewilderment and his insecurity. As the ground reels under his feet, he clutches at the heavens more wildly, more pathetically; and his curses, for a time, diminish in virulence, as his subjective state struggles for purchase.

> I do not bid the thunder-bearer shoot,
> Nor tell tales of thee to high-judging Jove,

with enormous and yet deceptive control, he advises Goneril (II.iv. 229-230).

No longer sure of himself, the gods, or anything else, keenly aware for the first time of human bestiality, a bestiality ironically that he himself from his own flesh has bred, the old man resolves to try the shelter of the heavens and to taste the community of animals in animal form, "To be a comrade with the wolf and owl" (II.iv.212). Already Lear had made the human-beast equation, which is to be a major motif of the tragedy; see, for example, "thy wolvish visage" (I.iv.317), "Most serpent-like" (II.iv.162), etc. But the identification, consummated in the dog-horse-rat allusion at the end, is fully explicit at II.iv.269, when he conditionally declares, "Man's life is cheap as beast's."

Beast in Man

> *Who knoweth whether the spirite of man ascende upwarde, and the spirite of the beast descende downwarde to the earth?*
> —Ecclesiastes iii.21

> *Ne vois-tu pas du Ciel ces petits animaux . . .*
> *Ces petits animaux qu'on appelle les hommes!*
> —Ronsard, "Remonstrance au peuple de France"

At this point, it is possible to suggest that another counterpattern has crossed the exposition of Lear's pagan piety; and, in addition, a

XVII (1954), 224*n*. The Jupiter-*juvare* etymology is discussed, with some credence, in Giorgio del Vecchio, *Justice: An Historical and Philosophical Essay* (New York, 1953), pp. 3-4.

progression toward his ultimate religious disillusionment has been sketched. For the beast-in-man pattern, so often noted by old- and new-style image-*Forscher*, though less often related to its intellectual context, is a significant aspect of the king's piety-skepticism configuration.

Lear's view that man, despite his pretensions, is no higher than a beast is a standard skeptical concept which, heard in the sixteenth century, receives stronger affirmation in the seventeenth and eighteenth centuries; Lovejoy, Boas, and others have traced the unhappy descent of man's pride.[51] Like Swift's Yahoos, Goneril and Regan help to destroy that medieval and Renaissance pride in the unique and exemplary possession of a rational soul, that "dignity of man" which the "wars of truth" help to demolish. Leonardo described man as *prima bestia infra le animali*. As in Bruegel, mankind in *Lear* might be termed "der Mensch am Rande des menschlichen." Goethe's Mephistopheles sneers at man,

> Er nennt's Vernunft und braucht's allein,
> Nur tierischer als jedes Tier zu sein,[52]

mankind becoming later in Nietzsche, "das Tier 'Mensch'"; Swift, told that someone was a fellow Protestant, recalled that the rat is a

[51]See *A Documentary History of Primitivism and Related Ideas*, ed. Arthur O. Lovejoy et al. (Baltimore, 1935); cf. Lovejoy's studies on primitivism and on the great chain of being and his "'Pride' in Eighteenth-Century Thought," *MLN*, XXXVI (1921), 31-37; George Boas, *The Happy Beast in French Thought of the Seventeenth Century* (Baltimore, 1933); Hester Hastings, *Man and Beast in French Thought of the Eighteenth Century*, Johns Hopkins Studies in Romance Literatures and Languages, Vol. XXVII (Baltimore, 1936).

Cf. the beast-in-man topic in the second-century attack on the Christian conception of human centrality, notably by Celsus, whom Origen accused of speaking like an Epicurean (Origen, *Contra Celsum*, tr. Henry Chadwick [Cambridge, Eng., 1953]). Like Celsus, Antiphon scornfully assails "man, who claims to be, of all animals, the one most like God" (cited in Mario Untersteiner, *The Sophists*, tr. Kathleen Freeman [New York, 1954], p. 253). Pomponazzi (in *Renaissance Philosophy of Man*, ed. Cassirer et al., p. 377), suggesting that some men are "far crueler than any beast," cites Aristotle's *Ethica* vii: "An evil man is ten thousand times worse than a beast." Like Pliny, Epictetus (*Discourses*, tr. W. A. Oldfather, Loeb Classical Lib., I [1926], Bk. I, Ch. xvi) indicates the unprovided state of man compared with that of beasts. Cf. also the seventeenth-century libertine attack on human pride, e.g., in Rochester and in Madame Antoinette Deshoulières (in *Les derniers libertins*, ed. Frédéric Lachèvre [Paris, 1924], pp. 74, 76, 77):

> L'homme ose se dire le maistre
> Des animaux, qui sont peut-estre
> Plus libres qu'il ne l'est, plus doux, plus généreux. . . .

"Sans loix," beasts are yet just and are "moins barbares que nous."

[52]Prologue, ll. 285-286 (*Goethes Faust*, ed. Georg Witkowski [Leiden, 1936], I, 164).

fellow creature; and Lear in his last lines, over the body of Cordelia, demands, "Why should a dog, a horse, a rat, have life, / And thou no breath at all?" (V.iii.306-307), the culmination of the beast imagery of the play.

Indeed, Lear's descending animal order in this speech is significant, for that is the order in the drama; to appreciate *King Lear,* less a twentieth-century naturalistic view than a more exalted medieval and early Renaissance view of man's hierarchical place and potential is requisite. For, disordering the great chain of being, the play's lines seem to reverse the great self-flattering tradition from Aquinas to Hooker: man *is* no more than this.

Significant also is the Montaignian shift from Lear's self-proclaimed wrathful "Dragon" (I.i.122) to Gloucester's "made me think a man a worm" (IV.i.33), utilizing "dragon's" archaic equivalent at its furthest remove.[53] Man's wormlike descent, expressed in Job (xxv.6), in Calvin, and in Sidney's *Arcadia,* is confirmed by the imagery in *Lear,* a development recapitulated in Lear's final abrupt shift from the highest in the animal order to the lowest. Although *Lear,* of all the tragedies, has the most animal allusions and comparisons, its last such reference is to the rat.[54]

Numerous apologetic tracts demonstrate the skeptical affiliations of Lear's position regarding the relative place of man and beasts. In *A Warning for Worldlings* (1608) Jeremy Corderoy's student disputes with the atheist traveler who will not excel man above beasts (pp. 163-168). The first part of Charles de Bourgueville's *L'athéomachie* (1564) contains a refutation of numerous objections to

[53]The dragon is the symbol of the king (e.g., Henry Peacham, *Minerva Britanna* [1612], p. 30); of pride (e.g., Spenser, *Faerie Queene,* I.iv.10.5). On the dragon ensign and traditions of British kingship, see J. S. P. Tatlock, "The Dragons of Wessex and Wales," *Speculum,* VIII (1933), 223-235; Sydney Anglo, "The *British History* in Early Tudor Propaganda," *Bulletin of the John Rylands Library,* XLIV (1961), 17-48. In his royal arms, however, James replaced Elizabeth's dragon, borne by her father, Henry VIII, with his own Scottish unicorn. Between Lear's "Dragon" king and Gloucester's wormlike man stands (linked to the earl's son who was conceived "under the dragon's tail," I.ii.135-136) the king's "serpent-like" daughter (II.iv.162; cf. I.iv.297, V.iii.85).

[54]Although dogs and horses were often considered beasts superior in intelligence, Lear's sudden shift to rats is dramatic in its encompassing even the lowest and most vicious beast. On the superiority of the former two, see La Primaudaye's *The Third Volume of the French Academie,* tr. R. Dolman (1601), p. 373; Epictetus, *Discourses,* tr. Oldfather, II (1928), 421; Adriano Banchieri's mock-heroic *The Noblenesse of the Asse* (1595), sigs. B2-B3v. According to Audrey Yoder, *Animal Analogy in Shakespeare's Character Portrayal* (New York, 1947), p. 65, *Lear* among the tragedies has the largest number (171) of beast references.

the existence of God and immortality, as well as of the peripatetic principle *nihil ex nihilo*, by which the creation is denied, and of the "ressemblance des animaux avec l'homme."[55] By this point in the play Lear has become involved with the last two of these skeptical positions, as, finally, he will touch upon another of these, the question of immortality. In his influential *Second Part of the French Academie* (1594) La Primaudaye describes the complaint of atheists who say "that God or Nature had brought men into the worlde, onely to make them more miserable and more wretched then all other creatures: so that they can finde no better happinesse and felicitie for themselves, then during their life to become like to beastes . . ." (p. 591).[56]

For the sixteenth century the *locus classicus* of the beast-in-man notion, as of "theriophily" and similar ideas generally, was Montaigne, who was, in turn, anticipated by Plutarch's Gryllus, Lando, Erasmus, and others. Echoing, without wholly agreeing with, the notorious seventh book of Pliny's *Natural History*, Montaigne provides close anticipations, with which may be compared both Lear's "Man's life is cheap as beast's" and "Is man no more than this? Consider him well. Thou ow'st the worm no silk, the beast no hide, the sheep no wool, the cat no perfume. Ha! here's three on's are sophisticated; thou art the thing itself; unaccommodated man is no more but such a poor, bare, forked animal as thou art" (III.iv.105-111). The Plinian complaint, says Montaigne, holds that man

> is the onely forsaken and out-cast creature, naked on the bare earth, fast bound and swathed, having nothing to cover and arme himselfe withall but the spoile of others; whereas Nature hath clad and mantled all other creatures, some with shels, some with huskes, with rindes, with haire, with wooll, with stings, with bristles, with hides, with mosse, with feathers, with skales, with fleeces, and with silke . . . And hath fenced and armed them with clawes, with nailes, with talons, with hoofes, with teeth, with stings, and with hornes, both to assaile others and to defend themselves. . . . (II, 147)

While man only, "(Oh silly wretched man) can neither goe, nor speake, nor shift, nor feed himselfe, unlesse it be to whine and weepe onely . . ." (II, 147). The essayist continues:

[55] In Busson, *Le rationalisme*, p. 488.

[56] Cf. Robert Anton, *The Philosophers Satyrs* (1616), sig. [C4].

Truely, when I consider man all naked . . . and view his defects, his naturall subjection, and manifold imperfections; I finde we have had much more reason to hide and cover our nakedness, than any creature else. We may be excused for borrowing those which nature had therein favored more than us, with their beauties to adorne us, and under their spoiles of wooll, of haire, of feathers, and of silke to shroud us. (II, 181)

Montaigne argues, therefore, ". . . that our wisedome should learne of beasts, the most profitable documents, belonging to the chiefest and most necessary parts of our life. . . . Wherewith men have done, as perfumers do with oyle, they have adulterated her [nature], with so many argumentations, and sofisticated her . . ." (III, 305).

Furthermore, Montaigne rejects man's alleged superiority. Citing Pliny's "Solum certum, nihil esse certi, et homine nihil miserius aut superbius. . . . This onely is sure, that there is nothing sure; and nothing more miserable, and yet more arrogant then man," Montaigne, like characters in *Lear*, observes, "This many-headed, divers-armed, and furiously-raging monster, is man; wretched weake and miserable man: whom if you consider well, what is he, but a crawling, and ever-moving Ants-neast?" (II, 333, 169). "Mans impudency, touching beasts," incites him to demand, "Were it not a sottish arrogancie, that wee should thinke our selves to be the perfectest thing of this Universe?" (II, 143, 237). Montaigne concludes:

We are neither above nor under the rest: what ever is under the coape of heaven (saith the wise man) runneth one law, and followeth one fortune. . . . Some difference there is, there are orders and degrees; but all is under the visage of one-same nature. . . . Miserable man with all his wit cannot in effect goe beyond it: he is embraced, and engaged, and as other creatures of his ranke are, he is subjected in like bondes, and without any prerogative or essentiall pre-excellencie, what ever Privilege he assume unto himselfe, he is of very meane condition. (II, 151)[57]

[57]Cf. Busson, *Le rationalisme*, pp. 40-41. In Ambroise Paré's *De la nature des bestes brutes* (1570), appearing one year before Montaigne's *Apologie*, Montaigne found Pliny's contrast of naked man with animals protected and clothed by nature (Pierre Villey-Desmeserets, *Les sources & l'évolution des essais de Montaigne* [Paris, 1933], II, 177*n*). Montaigne's skeptical denial of man's exaltation above the beast involves also a denial of Pliny's view concerning man's unique helplessness (II, 148); cf. II, 149-150. *The Problemes of Aristotle* (1597), sig. I2v, argues against the view that man is "in woorser case" than the animals. See, recalling Pliny, Joseph Hall, *The Discovery of a New World*, ed. Huntington Brown (Cambridge, Mass., 1937), pp. 78-79. Like Montaigne, Helkiah Crooke exhibits an anti-Plinian position concerning man's supposed helpless state in his *Microcosmographia. A Description of the Body of Man* (1615), as does Browne in his *Religio medici* (1635), *Works*, I, 25. The Plinian theme

In addition, Marston's malcontent Lampatho, in *What You Will* (1601), II.i, describes man as more wretched than a beast.[58] Further, echoing Pliny and the passage in Montaigne, *The Pilgrimage of Man, Wandering in a Wildernes of Woe* (1606) considers man as "of all other creatures . . . most miserable in his birth." While "Beastes & Birdes are brought into the world, either covered with haire, feathers, or wooll," man only is "excepted." For he at birth "seemeth . . . but the similitude of a poore Worme, that commeth creeping out of the earth. . . ." "Yet," the *Pilgrimage* concludes, "for all this, he nameth himselfe the Prince of all other creatures." Regarding man, requiring "nourishment and cloathing, to comfort the infirmitie of his nature," the *Pilgrimage* asks, "who would thinke that such a miserable creature (by succession of time) would become so proud and lofty?" (sigs. A2-A4).

Similarly, Greville's *Mustapha* declares that "Our Beasts are no more delicate than we" (Chorus Secundus).[59] And Pierre Du Moulin's *Heraclitus: or Meditations upon the Vanity & Misery of Humane Life* (1609) notes that man, who is "borne immoveable," alone ". . . hath need of habiliments: for hee which is the most noble in the world, is ashamed to shew his nakednesse, & therefore hideth himselfe under the spoiles of other Creatures. Hee is subject to more maladies, then all the Beasts together." Like Lear, man is not uniquely "ague-proof" (IV.vi.107); on the contrary, says Du Moulin, of "divers sorts of Agues . . . Man only is capable to discerne these differences, and to feele their effects."[60]

---

is heard in Roger Coke's *Justice Vindicated* (1660), pp. 5-6. Anticipating such motifs and language in *Lear* (e.g., II.iv.266-272) is Thomas Tymme's *A Plaine Discoverie of Ten English Lepers* (1592), sigs. [F3v]-[F4]. The *topos* connecting the assault on human pride with man's theft of garments from lower creatures to protect his defenseless native state recurs in Robert Parsons' *The First Booke of the Christian Exercise* ([Rouen], 1582), p. 312. On naked man himself, cf. Thomas Fenne, *Fennes Fruites* (1590), sigs. B1v-B2; cf. *The Workes of . . . Seneca*, tr. Thomas Lodge (1614), p. 335. (In Fenne, sigs. [O4v]-P, occurs an apparently unnoted version of the Lear story.) See also John Taylor, *Superbiae Flagellum, or, The Whip of Pride* (1621), sigs. C3v-C4.

[58] *Plays*, II, 257.

[59] *Poems and Dramas*, ed. Bullough, II, 95.

[60] Tr. R. S. (Oxford), pp. 7-8. Cf. Kent's remark to Lear (V.iii.288), "from your first of difference and decay." Connecting human nakedness and the Promethean motif (discussed below) is the myth in Plato's *Protagoras*, 320d-322a (*The Dialogues of Plato*, tr. Benjamin Jowett [Oxford, 1953], I, 145-147): Epimetheus had improvidently distributed all natural defenses to the animals, leaving nothing for man; whereupon his brother, Prometheus, to save man, stole fire on his behalf.

The convention of birds, among other animals, as particularly happy in contrast to man, appears, for instance, in Marston's *The Dutch Courtezan.* Enviously comparing the state of "free-borne birdes" with that of man, Malheureux there (II.i) parallels Edmund's rebellion against "the plague of custom" and "the curiosity of nations," i.e., national law, as opposed to natural law.[61] The topical envy of "the silliest, fairest birds," who are set against humankind in its restraints, recurs in *Periander* (ll. 7604-21) in a libertine plea for natural freedom from human law.[62] Webster's *The Duchess of Malfi* echoes the convention:

> DUCHESS. The Birds, that live i'th field
> On the wilde benefit of Nature, live
> Happier then we . . . . (III.v.25-27)

In contrast, Lear's wistful implication of the happy state even of "birds i' th' cage" (V.iii.9) is ironically followed by Edmund's brutal "Take them away" (V.iii.19), much as the Duchess' "birds" speech above is succeeded by the villainous Bosola's entrance: "You are *happily* oreta'ne."[63]

That "theriophily," or the exaltation of the state of beasts in relation to that of man, tended to be a device of disillusioned skepticism as well as libertinism is evident not only from Jacobean but also from later literature. Besides the "Satyr against Mankind" of the arch-libertine Rochester, for instance, Nicholas Rowe's *The Fair Penitent* (1703) voices it in the person of the immoral Lothario:

> I wou'd not turn aside from my least Pleasure,
> Tho' all thy Force were arm'd to bar my Way;
> But like the Birds, great Nature's happy Commoners . . .
> Rifle the Sweets, and taste the choicest Fruits,
> Yet scorn to ask the Lordly Owners leave. (II.ii)[64]

[61]*Plays,* II, 83.

[62]In *The Christmas Prince,* Malone Soc. Repr. (1922), p. 239. See discussion of Edmund above.

[63]III.v.29 (italics mine); in addition, Lear's cage reference lends partial recollection to another passage in Webster's play: "didst thou ever see a Larke in a cage? . . . this world is like her little turfe of grasse, and the Heaven ore our heades, like her looking glasse, onely gives us a miserable knowledge of the small compasse of our prison" (IV.ii.128-131). Cf. *Macbeth,* IV.ii.31-32; and Matthew vi.26.

[64]On the "happy beast," see also Erasmus, *Praise of Folly,* p. 55; Nashe, II, 113. Faustus' damnation in Marlowe is accompanied by the envious cry, "all beasts are happy," V.ii.180 (*The Tragical History of Doctor Faustus,* ed. Frederick S. Boas

Finally, if any further evidence were required of the skeptical character of Lear's beast-in-man view with its assault on special providence, Tourneur's *The Atheist's Tragedie*, which probably owes much to Shakespeare's tragedy, with its avowedly atheistical D'Amville and Borachio, may furnish it:

> [*D'Amville.*] Observ'st thou not the very selfe same course
> Of revolution both in Man and Beast?
>
> *Bor.* The same. For birth, growth, state, decay
> and death, (I.i.8-10)

where the exposition of the attitude immediately identifies the speakers. Even more pointedly, in reply to the claim that beasts are more privileged and happier than men, a character in Nathan Field's *Amends for Ladies* (ca. 1610-1611) observes, "You argue like an Atheist" (1639, sig. F2[r-v]).

What the Thunder Said

> *C'est le pur sang du Dieu qui lance le tonnerre....*
> —Racine, *Iphigénie*, V.iv

In considering Lear's relationship to the gods, which, first, we have seen to be confident and unquestioning reliance and, next, to be a kind of bewilderment, we arrive at a major turning point, where the apparent avenger—the invoker of revenge—seems to become the "Avengers'" victim. In short, Lear's active state enters the realm of *passive* affliction: "I am a man / More sinn'd against than sinning" (III.ii.59-60). In effect, Lear recognizes, at the moment of his imprecations against others, himself as a victim. It is a moment of anagnorisis, to be followed by later ones; and it occurs on the heath, amidst thunder and lightning, at the end of his prayer to the gods:

[1932]). Like Faustus, Donne's poetic expression compares the happier state of conscienceless beasts, "lecherous goats" and "serpents envious" ("Holy Sonnets," IX: "If Poysonous mineralls . . ."). William Baldwin's popular *A Treatise of Morall Philosophie* (1591), reprinted at least seventeen times between 1547 and 1640, cites Menander (fol. 45), "All beasts are happier & far wiser then man." Cf. Aristophanes, *The Birds* (tr. Benjamin B. Rogers, Loeb Classical Lib. [1924], II, 237, ll. 1088-95), contrasting the happy state of birds with the toils and rigors of mankind. See also Burton, *The Anatomy of Melancholy* (Oxford, 1621), p. 658, quoting Lydgate, and Lydgate's "The Flour of Curtesye," in Walter W. Skeat, ed. *The Complete Works of Geoffrey Chaucer*, Supplement (Oxford, 1897), p. 268.

Let the great Gods,
That keep this dreadful pudder o'er our heads,
Find out their enemies now . . .
close pent-up guilts,
Rive your concealing continents, and cry
These dreadful summoners grace. I am a man
More sinn'd against than sinning. (III.ii.49-60)

The "good" pagan, confident in his deities, becomes, after Lear's significant "if" speech to the gods,

O Heavens,
If you do love old men, if your sweet sway
Allow obedience . . . , (II.iv.191-193)

more placating and more fearful, at the same time referring both to "great Gods" and "dreadful pudder." While the thunder of the heavens beats at his ears, and the thunder inside his brain beats at his mind, threatening his sanity, Lear revises his view of the gods. They *seem* to side with destruction, and in an appropriate antifertility ritual he prays all the four personified elements to let loose their force, "this extremity of the skies" (III.iv.104-105), with the thunder, traditionally the divine voice, especially invoked against human baseness (as in III.ii.6-9); the appeal, in its imagery, microcosmically parallels Lear with universal Nature, both having improvidentially and injudiciously brought to birth unnatural creatures.

During the storm the bareheaded old king's reborn attitude toward the heavens accompanies his revised attitude toward mankind, just as Gloucester's sense of divine arbitrariness in the "flies" speech accompanies his degraded notion of man as a worm. "Rumble thy bellyful," Lear shouts at the elements, which his pagan perspective endows with animism, an aspect of divinity, almost a Spinozistic *Deus sive Natura.*

Spit, fire! spout, rain!
Nor rain, wind, thunder, fire, are my daughters:
I tax you not, you elements, with unkindness;
I never gave you kingdom, call'd you children,
You owe me no subscription: then let fall
Your horrible pleasure . . . , (III.ii.14-19)

a phrase which may imply "horrifying will" and suggests also a paradox which is inherent in Lear's new-found ambivalence toward the ruling powers. Those who at the outset were the powers that made him, that gave him life, and by whom he swore, those he was so sure were his—echoing or anticipating the traditional motto of English sovereigns, the countersign chosen by Richard I in 1198, *Dieu et mon droict*—now are in command of the "dreadful pudder" threatening "horrible pleasure" to their victim:

> here I stand, your slave,
> A poor, infirm, weak, and despis'd old man.
> But yet I call you servile ministers,
> That will with two pernicious daughters join
> Your high-engender'd battles 'gainst a head
> So old and white as this. O, ho! 'tis foul.
> (III.ii.19-24)

The elements, personified, are servile intermediaries of the gods and, joined with the daughters, perform an unworthily cruel function against an even more abject slave. Lear's speech is *in extremis*, pitiful and self-pitying, far from the confidence of Act I. Peripeteia and anagnorisis coincide; suffering becomes "knowledge," *pathema, mathema*.

In his obsession with justice, human and divine, Lear, we have seen, interprets the "dreadful pudder" (significantly a *confused* noise) also as an instrument of justice against the enemies of the gods (III.ii.49-53). But justice cuts all ways; it is a knife-edge also directed at himself and at his keen recollection of his own injustice. Thus Lear's self-knowledge, previously lacking, becomes reconstructed under the auspices of a new view of the heavens, powers which in his mind and, he implies, in the view of others must seem ambiguous. Like Milton, therefore, at a time of similar dubious battle, Lear attempts to "justify" the gods. Significantly, at this point the gods seem in some need of justification; and it is evident how far we have traveled from Lear's initial confident credo. "Poor naked wretches," his great prayer to humanity runs,

> whereso'er you are,
> That bide the pelting of this pitiless storm,
> How shall your houseless heads and unfed sides,
> Your loop'd and window'd raggedness, defend you
> From seasons such as these? O! I have ta'en
> Too little care of this. Take physic, Pomp;
> Expose thyself to feel what wretches feel,
> That thou mayst shake the superflux to them,
> And show the Heavens more just. (III.iv.28-36)

In this speech the intensifier "more" may suggest the heavens' want of even such secondary testimony; divine justice, along with Lear himself, undergoes a test in Act III; and charity from above, Lear moderately proposes, would then be manifested in human charity.

The storm, symbol of cosmic cruelty as well as, perhaps, cosmic vengeance, produces in man himself, unprotected by the skins of other creatures and lacking the gods' special providence, a death wish coupled with a grave symbol: "Thou wert better," Lear advises "Poor Tom," "in a grave than to answer with thy uncover'd body this extremity of the skies" (III.iv.103-105). What has happened is, analogically, the naked revelation of the heavens at a time when bare, unprotected man reveals himself for what he is, the most vulnerable of creatures. As noted elsewhere, the heavens and man correspond, both in the Renaissance analogical scheme and in the drama itself (explicitly, for instance, at III.i.10). Hence, at this middle of Lear's tragic journey his attitude toward the gods, as toward man, is, despite his sad need to "show the Heavens more just," one of confusion and disappointment.

It is to be expected, therefore, that Lear's piety-skepticism configuration, which I have indicated earlier, should at this point weigh more heavily toward the latter pole. And, indeed, in sequence Lear gives voice to a further series of notions which the Renaissance spectator would probably have associated with questioning rather than acceptance. It should be emphasized, however, that, while no attempt is here made to label Lear a mere skeptic, as a pagan such an attitude in him would not have seemed implausible or offensive, although the starting premise of his characterization is that, as a pagan, he is fundamentally pious. The complexity of the drama and the varying viewpoints involved allow for a free and ironical interplay of seemingly contradictory positions.

At this midpoint of the drama, when Lear could be expected to begin his questioning of the gods, the old man, his wits unsettled by ingratitude within and the storm without, delays his acceptance of Gloucester's fire and food to address the ragged, supposedly mad, and demon-possessed Edgar. "First," he begs, "let me talk with this philosopher. / What is the cause of thunder?" (III.iv.158-159).

The role of the thunder in this play is a consequential one. It might be argued that the Fool, in his pointed worldly prudence, is the counterpoise to the thunder in its cosmic ambiguity. Moreover, their ironical juxtaposition underlines the incongruity between human calculation and incalculable mystery. From both directions they offer wisdom or warning to Lear; in both directions Lear has given offense and requires forgiveness. And it might be concluded that the king is caught, literally and figuratively, externally and internally, between the Fool and the thunder, imprudence and anger, untruth and consequences. Yet, in contrast to the morality-play tradition, and to the convention general in Renaissance drama as well as in other of Shakespeare's plays, of the thunder as the unequivocal voice of heaven, this common device is, in Lear, ambiguously presented. For it is not clear whose side the thunder is on, for whom it acts, and to what ends; what is clear is that it numinously accompanies human suffering.

Thus, when Lear asks of Edgar, whom he takes to be a "philosopher,"[65] most likely a natural philosopher, "What is the cause of thunder?" he is both reinforcing the impression we receive, at this juncture, of his failing faith in the gods and running counter to a convention almost universally identified with piety. Previously, in his repeated observation "Nothing will come of nothing," he at the same time expressed himself as a pagan would regarding a fundamental Christian tenet and foreshadowed the decline in his own reverence. Now, however, in his deeply revealing madness he expresses an attitude which more surely associates itself with doubt, for it is one which suggests the abandonment of a strong religious and literary tradition, shared by both pagan and Christian alike (although the ancients also took a skeptical view), and one which simultaneously in its probing of causation in the natural realm seeks for a cause beyond the divine. In contrast to Bacon's "Of Atheism," ". . . troubles and adversities do more bow men's minds to religion,"[66] Lear, in his suffering, seems to bow the other way.

In his second allusion to thunder Lear sees it as a destructive force afflicting all mankind, including himself; he summons it not as a mere agent of divine justice but nihilistically, as an agent of dissolution,

[65]Cf. *As You Like It*, III.ii.21-33. See also Simon Harward, *A Discourse of the Severall Kinds and Causes of Lightnings* (1607), sig. C3, on "the generall naturall cause which the Philosophers doe give of Thunders and Lightenings. . . ." Cf. Lyly, "Euphues and Atheos," *Complete Works*, ed. Bond, I, 293; Lyly's anecdote recurs in similar language in John Carpenter, *A Preparative to Contentation* (1597), p. 277.

[66]*Works*, VI, 414.

of the "nothing" into which he presently wishes the creation to dissolve. Thus dramatic irony was at work, also, in his repeated "Nothing will come of nothing."

Lear's early reference to the thunder is relatively assured; thunder is the clear instrument of the gods' vengeance, and the gods are the clear agents of justice. His first allusion implies a court, a judge, and an executioner who could be summoned in a just cause. "I do not bid the thunder-bearer shoot," with exploding patience he assures Goneril, "Nor tell tales of thee to high-judging Jove" (II.iv.229-230). He *could*, in other words, if he would, have her punished by Jupiter's justice which sits high and watchful in the heavens.

Here, the king takes the traditional view, expressed, for example, in Calvin's belief in God's power "sometime to shake the heaven with noise of thunders . . ."[67] and in Cicero's *De natura deorum* as the third of Cleanthes' reasons for belief in deity, "the terror we experience in the presence of thunderbolts. . . ."[68] In homiletic references, such as Bishop Pilkington's to storms as the instruments of God's wrath;[69] in Corderoy's "A . . . use of these fearfull thunders . . . is to confute such as you";[70] in Donne's "he may heare God . . . in the voice of Thunder";[71] in poems, where the "celestial thunderbolt" of *Purgatorio* (xii.28-29) recurs, as in Donne's "Litany" (XXIV), alluding to God's "threats in thunder"; and even in Renaissance historiography, such as Polydore Vergil's *Anglica historia*, where storms have the moral purpose of warning men of their evil ways, thunder was a clearly meaningful and divinely inspired phenomenon.

The pre-Christian English thunder-god is described in John Clapham's *The Historie of Great Britannie* (1606). The Saxons, he says, "painted *Thor* with a Scepter in his hand, after the same manner that the Poets used to describe the image of *Jupiter*: and him they reverenced as the commander and disposer of Thunder . . ." (p. 194).

[67]*Institutes,* I.v.5. Calvin describes thunder as God's voice: *Sermons . . . upon the Booke of Job* (1584), p. 676. See the Calvinist Canephius' [pseud. Mornay's] *Athéomachie* ([Geneva], 1582), poem prefacing the book.

[68]. . . *On the Nature of the Gods* . . . , tr. H. M. Poteat (Chicago, 1950), p. 231.

[69]*The Works of James Pilkington,* Parker Soc. (Cambridge, Eng., 1842), p. 177.

[70]*A Warning for Worldlings,* p. 72.

[71]*The Sermons of John Donne,* ed. Evelyn M. Simpson and George R. Potter, X (Berkeley, 1962), 110.

Similarly, Camden's *Britain* (1610) observes that "Jupiter, whom the Greekes, of *Thunder* call Βροντῶος, and the Latines *Tonans*, that is, *Thunderer* was worshipped of the Gaules under the name of *Taranis*, there be writers, not a few that have reported. But *Taran* with the Britans betokeneth *Thunder*. In which signification the Germanes seeme to have named Jupiter, *Thonder* . . ." (p. 17). Appropriately, a land grant of King Edward the Elder (A.D. 901) begins: "In the name of the High Thunderer, Creator of the world."[72]

Mentioning "thunderbolts for *Joves* avengefull threate" (*Faerie Queene*, IV.v.37.4), Spenser elsewhere asserts that beneath God's feet are to be found

> Thunder, and lightning, and tempestuous fyre,
> The instruments of his avenging yre.[73]

Lyly continues the pious convention in "Euphues and Atheos," where the godless one is warned, "thou shalt see him appeare in thundringes and lyghtninges."[74] Marlowe employs thunder as a sign of divine anger: in *Faustus* the power of generating thunder and lightning is, as in Job, a divine attribute, and Faustus' ability to "rend the clouds" and produce the effect will unseat Jove and gain him "a deity" (I.i.60-64).[75] Mustapha in *The Tragical Reign of Selimus* refers to

[72]*English Historical Documents c. 500-1042*, ed. Dorothy Whitelock, I (New York, 1955), 499; see also p. 490. Belief in thunder and lightning as instruments of retribution is widely held among primitive peoples (cf. discussion of *lex talionis* above). See Hans Kelsen, *Society and Nature: A Sociological Inquiry* (Chicago, 1943), p. 116. See also Raffaele Pettazzoni, *The All-Knowing God: Researches into Early Religion and Culture* (1956).

Euripides' Medea pronounces a self-curse, invoking a divine bolt from heaven to pass through her brain (*Four Plays of Euripides*, tr. Augustus T. Murray [Stanford, 1931], p. 120). Adopting the device, Senecan tragedy in prayer invokes heavenly power against an enemy or against the speaker himself, an invocation often involving the destruction of the world. See *Seneca, His Tenne Tragedies*, ed. Thomas Newton (1581), Tudor Trans. (1927); Seneca's plays frequently call down Jove's thunder against wickedness (e.g., I, 92; II, 79, 155, 223, 224).

On lightning as sulphurous, note Seneca, *Quaestiones naturales*, tr. John Clarke (1910), p. 97: ". . . wherever lightning has struck there is sure always to be a smell of sulphur . . . a substance . . . naturally poisonous. . . ." Connecting the elements with the Centaur daughters, Lear's later allusion is to "the sulphurous pit" (IV.vi.130) beneath the girdle.

[73]"An Hymne of Heavenly Beautie," *Poetical Works*, p. 598, ll. 180-182.

[74]*Complete Works*, ed. Bond, I, 295; cf. D. P. Walker, "Ways of Dealing with Atheists: A Background to Pamela's Refutation of Cecropia," *BHR*, XVII (1955), 273.

[75]See also *Tamburlaine the Great*, Pt. I, II.iii.19; Pt. II, I.ii.24; II.ii.7, 13; II.iii.1-2; V.i.182-184 (ed. U. M. Ellis-Fermor [1930]). See Paul H. Kocher, *Christopher Mar-*

"th' almighties thunderbolt."[76] Analogous are *Love's Labour's Lost*, "Thy eye Jove's lightning bears, thy voice his dreadful thunder" (IV.ii.119), and *2 Henry VI*, "O that I were a god, to shoot forth thunder" (IV.i.104), as well as *Pericles* (V.i.200-201) and *Cymbeline* (V.iv), where Zeus descends in thunder and lightning and throws a thunderbolt. Greville in *Mustapha* (II.i.6-7) and Massinger in *The Unnatural Combat* (V.ii) employ the divine-thunder device; indeed, as has been indicated, Elizabethan playwrights conventionally invoked belief in thunder as the voice of the Divine Judge.

Further, Anthony Copley's *A Fig for Fortune* (1596) alludes to the "Revenge" of Jove's "Thunder-boltes" (sig. [C4v]), as does, in the same year, Christopher Middleton's *History of Heaven*, Jove's thunder striking his victim dead (sig. C2). La Primaudaye's *The Third Volume of the French Academie* (1601) remarks on "many excellent points of doctrine concerning the providence of God . . . taught us . . . by meanes of . . . thunders . . ." (p. 238). *The Whipper of the Satyre* (1601) advises:

> But let the Heavens frowne, the Welkin thunder,
> Perhaps weele feare a little, and minde our God.
> (sig. [A7v])

Chapman's note to "Eugenia," "The dreadfull Thunder, the Almightie word" (l. 744), reads: ". . . The word, intended by the

lowe: A Study of His Thought, Learning, and Character (Chapel Hill, N.C., 1946), p. 102: "This, surely, is the unity, and the only unity, underlying all the diversity of the religious attitudes in both *Tamburlaine* plays—that God is a god of thunder." In Job xxxviii.34-35, lightning and rain are described as beyond human capacity to produce. But by magic, as the Evil Angel counsels, Faustus might become "on earth as Jove is in the sky, / Lord and commander of these elements" (I.i.77-78). Cf. the *Aeneid*, tr. Thomas Phaer (1584), sig. Kii, regarding Salmoneus in the Underworld (for his impiety struck by a thunderbolt):

> For he the flames of god, and thondring soundes
> would counterfeat. . . .
> And honors due to God usurping tooke of every rout.

The question of wresting control of the thunder is thus adumbrated not only in the *Aeneid* and *Faustus* but, by implication, also in the Promethean challenge. Further, since possession of power over the thunder was a mark of the sky-god (see James G. Frazer, *The Golden Bough* [1957], I, 197, 210-211; II, 927-928), such naturalistic explanation as Lear demands might be construed, in effect, as verging on human usurpation of a traditionally divine mystery. Cf. Webster's *The Duchess of Malfi*, III.v.116, and parallels cited by Robert W. Dent (*John Webster's Borrowing* [Berkeley, 1960]): Jacques Hurault, *Politicke . . . Discourses*, tr. Arthur Golding (1595), p. 56; Plutarch, *Morals*, tr. Philemon Holland (1603), p. 295, ". . . God indeed hateth and punisheth those who will seeme to imitate thunder. . . ."

[76] Malone Soc. Repr. (1908), l. 129.

Thunder; which divine Scripture call[s] *Gods voice*."[77] Like Mornay (citing Seneca) in *A Woorke concerning the Trewnesse of the Christian Religion* (1587, p. 11), Henry Smith in *Gods Arrow against Atheists* (1604, p. 2) employs the standard illustration, after Suetonius, of Caligula's fear of divine thunder, as does Brathwaite's *Natures Embassie* (p. 36).[78] Finally, Thomas Wilson's *A Christian Dictionary* (1622), citing Psalm xviii.13 and Exodus xix.16, defines thunder as "a witnesse of Gods power, and serveth to strike terror and feare into men, that the godly may be humbled, and the better subdued unto God; and the wicked confounded and left without excuse" (sig. [Vv7v]).[79]

In the fourth act a further reference to thunder appears, and there we should expect Lear to be even less firmly attached to his early standpoint. Still deranged, Lear not only does not fear, but is even more explicitly dubious about, the thunder: "When the rain came to wet me once and the wind to make me chatter, when the thunder would not peace at my bidding, there I found 'em, there I smelt 'em out" (IV.vi.102-105). The lunatic king has significantly lost all sense of his capacity to "bid the thunder-bearer shoot" in the latter's role as "high-judging Jove." His insane chatter reveals the deep impression made upon his mind by the fact that the thunder was not only beyond his control but, more significantly, beyond any control, beyond any meaning perceptible to him. Lear's insights into the characters of his daughters and the nature of the cosmic powers, he indicates, arrive at the same time, during the storm on the heath.

Seeking to identify a skeptic to his audience, an Elizabethan dram-

[77] *The Poems of George Chapman*, ed. Phyllis B. Bartlett (New York, 1941), p. 289. Cf. Chapman's *Bussy D'Ambois,* I.i.36-37, III.ii.4-5.

[78] The *exemplum* of Caligula and the thunder seems to have been a common one; e.g., Calvin, *Institutes,* I.iii.2, and Alexander Ross, *The New Planet No Planet* (1646), p. 42.

[79] See also Fitzherbert, *Second Part of a Treatise*, pp. 61-63; William Vaughan's *The Spirit of Detraction . . . to Be Perused by the Libertines of This Age* (1611), p. 253. "At the hearing of this horrid *Thunder*," reports *Looke Up and See Wonders* (1628), pp. 15-16, "all men . . . were so terrified, that they fell on their knees, and not onely thought, but sayd, that verily *the day of Judgement was come*." Similarly, the *Diary of Walter Yonge, Esq.*, Camden Soc. (1848), p. 15, speaks of a "mighty and terrible thunder" during a dramatic presentation of Judgment Day in 1607, which "threw down the house . . . and killed the greatest part" of the audience. Cf. Lear's speech on the criminals who should tremble amidst the thunder (III.ii.51-57) and Tilley T118 ("When it thunders the Thief becomes honest"); and in contrast see J81 ("Far from Jove . . . far from thunder . . .").

atist might be able to do so by having him reject the divine admonition in thunder, for as Nashe in *Christs Teares over Jerusalem* expressed it, "Who heareth the thunder, that thinkes not of God?"[80] In contrast, the atheist, notes John Stephens' *Satyrical Essayes Characters and Others* (1615), "turnes *Divinity* into *colorable inventions of Philosophy*" (p. 214).[81] In his question inquiring into causes, the king leans more toward the tradition of the ancient skeptics than of the probable source play, *King Leir,* discussed earlier, which, in its Christian piety, shows a murderer frightened into repentance by a sudden clap of heaven-sent thunder. Since Shakespeare probably adapted his tragedy partly from this old drama, the altered conception of the religious role of thunder is significant. Either he replaced the pious view because he felt that the skeptical notion of thunder was more pagan, or, as seems likelier, he wished to use Lear's attitude toward thunder as a measuring device for his increasing doubt; but it is possible that both reasons, complexly related, were implicit in the change. It is important to recognize, therefore, that the thunder, in more than one way, is bound up with Lear's religious transformations. For *King Lear* probes still more daringly than Marlowe's drama: "When I behold the heavens," cries Faustus, "then I repent" (II.ii.1).

Indeed, questioning of the divine provenance and providential power of thunder has been shown earlier to mark not only Renaissance skepticism but also the seventeenth-century Don Juan convention. Not only does Lear inquire into its naturalistic causation and cast doubt on its providential benevolence; like the Don Juan figure considered above, he unrepentantly both challenges and defies the thunder to do its worst.

That differences existed between orthodox and naturalist adherents over the origin of thunder is indicated, for example, by Bishop

[80] *Works,* II, 121; cf. II, 23.

[81] Cf. the Don Juan convention discussed above and Shadwell's *Psyche* (1675), in *The Complete Works of Thomas Shadwell,* ed. Montague Summers (1927), II, 300:

> *Ch. Pr.* You have provok'd Heav'ns wrath again.
> Heav'n does again to you in Thunder speak!
> *Nican.* 'Twas nothing but a petty cloud did break;
> What, can your Priesthoods grave Philosophy
> So much amaz'd at common Thunder be?

See also Thomas Randolph's *The Muses Looking-Glasse* (Oxford, 1638), p. 24. The divine-thunder convention is burlesqued in Alessandro Tassoni's mock-heroic *La secchia rapita* (Paris, 1622), as well as in Buckingham's *The Rehearsal* (1671).

John Jewel. "They leese themselves," he remarks of the professors of human knowledge, when "They seek the depth and bottom of natural causes; the change of the elements; the impressions in the air; the causes of . . . thunder and lightning. . . ." That knowledge, Jewel declares, "is uncertain" and "not fit for every man to understand. . . ."[82] Although such questions had, as Ovid suggests, interested mankind from the time of Protagoras ("whither Jove or else the wynds in breaking clowdes doo thunder"),[83] those interrogations had a special point during the later period. For instance, Alexander Ross's *The New Planet No Planet* (1646) asserts: "Then whatsoever Naturalists affirme peremptorily of the thunder, I will with *Job* and *David*, acknowledge God to be the onely cause," having announced that "all the thundering disputations of Philosophers, and the small sparkes of light or knowledge which they have of naturall causes, are but toyes. . . . Therefore, in spight of all Naturalists, let us acknowledge . . . that it is the Lord that maketh the thunder . . ." (p. 42).[84]

If any further proof were needed that attitudes toward thunder on the Renaissance stage were clues to the religious positions of the characters, we may recall *Julius Caesar* (e.g., I.iii.46-56), where attitudes to the thunder help define the actors; the same tragedy, like *Lear*, also utilizes Stoic and Epicurean views, considered below, for developing character delineation. We may glance again at Tourneur's

[82]*The Works of John Jewel. . . . The Fourth Portion*, Parker Soc. (Cambridge, Eng., 1850), p. 1183. Joseph Hall (*Works*, ed. Philip Wynter [Oxford, 1863], VII, 599) defends piety, while recognizing a threat: "Perhaps the presumption of man will be finding out the natural causes of this fearful uproar in the clouds; but the working by means derogates nothing from the God of nature. Neither yet are all thunders natural. . . ."

[83]*Metamorphoses*, tr. Arthur Golding (1567), Bk. XV, fol. 187v.

[84]Regarding naturalistic accounts, see William Fulke's *A Goodly Gallery* (1571), foll. 24, 30; Pliny, *The Historie of the World*, tr. Philemon Holland (1601), Bk. II, Ch. xliii, pp. 20-21; La Primaudaye, *The Third Volume of the French Academie* (1601), p. 200; Bartholomaeus Anglicus, *De proprietatibus rerum*, tr. John Trevisa (Westminster, 1495), foll. 160v, 163v; Lucretius, *De rerum natura*, ed. Munro, I, 257, Bk. VI, ll. 160-172; Seneca, *Quaestiones naturales*, tr. Clarke, pp. 98-99. See also S. K. Heninger, Jr., *A Handbook of Renaissance Meteorology* (Durham, N.C., 1960).

See the naturalistic account of Du Bartas, *His Devine Weekes and Workes*, tr. Joshua Sylvester (1605), pp. 54-55, deriving from Aristotle and Lucretius; Henri Guy, "La science et la morale de Du Bartas d'après 'La première semaine,'" *Annales du Midi*, XIV (1902), 465, suggests also Pliny and Seneca. Despite his naturalistic explanation, Du Bartas, as significant transitional figure, maintains his pious allegiance, e.g., "la seule main du Dieu darde-tonnerre" (*The Works of . . . Du Bartas*, ed. Urban T. Holmes, Jr., et al., II [Chapel Hill, N.C., 1938], 265, l. 1153).

The Atheist's Tragedie, where the avowed atheist D'Amville knows that thunder is merely a physical phenomenon:

> What!
> Doest start at thunder? Credit my beliefe,
> T'is a meere effect of nature. (II.iv.163-165)

In contrast, the faithful Castabella presents the orthodox view: "O patient Heav'n! Why doest thou not expresse / Thy wrath in thunderbolts . . ." (IV.iii.177-178); and even D'Amville himself, when fearfully facing death, discards his skeptical attitude.[85] In addition, *The Revengers Tragædie* sounds thunder three times in answer to petitions to God or as sign of His approval. And finally, if Lear tends, at one point, to parallel the atheist D'Amville's position, they both resemble that of eminent Renaissance naturalists, whom the popular mind would associate with skepticism. For such probings regarding the cause of thunder were, in the Renaissance, earmarks of the revived tradition of classical skepticism, which included Leucippus, Democritus, Aristotle, Epicurus, Lucretius, and Pliny, all of whom tended to explain thunder in naturalistic terms. With regard to this phenomenon, Pierre Boaistuau in his *Theatrum mundi* (1581, pp. 92-93), Vicomercato in *Sur les quatre livres des météorologiques* (1556), and Dolet, a leader of the Paduan school, for whom "La suprême science, c'est de connaître les causes, puisque tout a une cause naturelle," also carried on, in the sixteenth century, the ancient skeptical tradition.[86]

It may be significant that parallel to Lear's reproach of the gods for their indifference to human suffering and misdeeds are passages

[85]D'Amville's etiology of thunder is verbally anticipated by an oft-reprinted scientific almanac, popular through the latter half of the sixteenth century and reissued in 1605, Leonard and Thomas Digges's *A Prognostication*. John Churton Collins, ed. *The Plays and Poems of Cyril Tourneur* (1878), I, 160, mistakenly declares of D'Amville's description, "This is taken from Lucretius; cf. *De Rer. Nat.*, vi. 270 seqq." Digges's explanation of thunder seems also to be echoed in Thomas Hill's *A Contemplation of Mysteries* (1571), p. 53. Simon Harward's *A Discourse of the Severall Kinds and Causes of Lightnings* (1607), sig. C3^{r-v}, offers the conventional naturalistic explanation, ultimately in the tradition of Aristotle (*Meteorologica*, tr. H. D. P. Lee, Loeb Classical Lib. [1952], pp. 223-231, 237-241); cf. also Aristophanes, *The Clouds* (tr. Rogers, I, 301-305), resembling accounts of Digges, Hill, and Tourneur.

[86]In Busson, *Le rationalisme*, pp. 209-210; 116-117. That among the ancients naturalistic views of thunder might be considered dangerous is attested by Bacon (*Works*, IV, 88): "For we see among the Greeks that those who first proposed to men's then uninitiated ears the natural causes for thunder and for storms, were thereupon found guilty of impiety."

from Lucian, who was usually regarded in Shakespeare's time as a skeptic or atheist. Included by Erasmus in his *Adagia*, Lucian influenced also his *Colloquies* and *Praise of Folly*. Lucian's *Dialogues* were translated into Latin by Erasmus and More in 1506 and by Nicolas Bérauld in 1515. In Shakespeare's day Gabriel Harvey notes that Lucian was "never so much" studied.[87] Several times reprinted in sixteenth-century England[88] and available in numerous continental editions, the *Dialogues* in whole or in part, by their irreverent irony toward the anthropomorphized gods, helped undermine credulity. If, as his modern translators say, Lucian in antiquity turned people from paganism to Christianity,[89] he may have served a contrary subversive purpose in the Renaissance. Indeed, Erasmus, who also translated the *Timon*, was accused of sharing Lucian's skepticism, and the outraged Luther declared that the former was worse than the latter.[90]

Lucian's criticism of providence is epitomized in his two dialogues, *Zeus Catechized* and *Zeus Rants*. Included in his arguments are the injustice of events, the misfortune of good people, and the triumph of evil.[91] Just as Aristophanes' *Clouds* had previously employed the example of the lightning falling by chance,[92] the so-called divine thunder, Lucian asserts, falls without reason, or even does not fall at all. Thus, this world's affairs, far from being controlled by an attentive and benevolent deity, run at hazard. For the Renaissance, Lucianic influence in the sixteenth century may be instanced from Des Périers' *Cymbalum mundi* (ca. 1529-1530). In its debate between an Epicurean and a Stoic, its dialogue implies that life's injustice proves there are no gods and that, even if they exist, they cannot intervene in human affairs. When the Stoic inquires, "Do you close your ears even to Jupiter's thunder, atheist?" the Epicurean responds, "I clearly cannot shut out the thunder; whether it is Jupiter's thunder, you know better than I perhaps: you may have inter-

[87] *Works*, ed. Grosart, I, 69.

[88] 1521, 1528, 1530?, n.d. (ed. Elyot), 1593 (ed. Giles Fletcher).

[89] *The Works of Lucian*, tr. H. W. and F. G. Fowler (Oxford, 1905).

[90] See C. R. Thompson, *The Translations of Lucian by Erasmus and St. Thomas More* (Ithaca, N.Y., 1940), p. 45; Luther, *Tischreden*, in *Werke*, III (Weimar, 1914), 136-137.

[91] Tr. A. M. Harmon, Loeb Classical Lib. (1915), II, 81-87, 119-123, 163-165.

[92] Tr. Rogers, I, 303.

viewed the gods."[93] For the Renaissance providential concerns sketched earlier appear to have had their ancient prototypes in the central second-century conflict between Epicureans and Stoics over divine providence.[94] And, in the view of the miracle-scorning Lucian, Epicurus above all grasped the nature of things and understood the truth.[95]

In Lucian's dialogue, *Timon, or the Misanthrope*, which may have been used by Shakespeare, Zeus is mocked for his senility and the lack of his former vigor.[96] Moreover, Zeus is assailed for failing in his function as "Lord of the Lightning" and "Loud-thunderer": "Where now is your pealing levin, your rolling thunder and your blazing, flashing, horrid bolt? . . . You neither hear perjurers nor see wrong-doers."[97] In their duty of finding out and punishing malefactors and perjurers, Lucian's Timon discovers the gods remiss, and it is to this function that the mad Lear hopefully alludes:

> Let the great Gods,
> That keep this dreadful pudder o'er our heads,
> Find out their enemies now. Tremble, thou wretch,
> That hast within thee undivulged crimes,
> Unwhipp'd of Justice; hide thee, thou bloody hand,
> Thou perjur'd, and thou simular of virtue.
> (III.ii.49-54)

Thunder as especially directed at perjurers,[98] like the controversy over its divine origin, goes back at least to Aristophanes. In his *Clouds*, for instance, when Jupiter is asserted to hurl his thunder at the perjured, the naturalistic and skeptical "Socrates" objects that, instead, he smites the tall oaks (cf. *Lear*, III.ii.5). ". . . What prompted

[93]C. A. Mayer, "The Lucianism of Des Périers," *BHR*, XII (1950), 197-199.

[94]See Marcel Caster, *Lucien et la pensée religieuse de son temps* (Paris, 1937), p. 132. Miracles and thunder were evidently expressions of providential intervention. On the Stoic-Epicurean antithesis, see Ch. ix below.

[95]Lucian, *Alexander the False Prophet*, tr. Harmon, Loeb Classical Lib., IV (1925), 209; see also p. 253.

[96]Cf. Lear (although in a different tone) to the heavens: "if you yourselves are old" (II.iv.193).

[97]Tr. Harmon, Loeb Classical Lib., II (1915), 327-329.

[98]See Alexander Ross, *The New Planet No Planet* (1646), p. 42; *The Bastard* (pr. 1652) of Cosmo Manuche (?), p. 18.

those strokes? *They* never forswore. . . ."[99] In Shakespeare's age, also, divine thunder as utilized to excite fear and self-exposure in criminals recurs, for example, in Palingenius, *The Zodiake of Life*, tr. Barnabe Googe (1576, p. 3): "And when the lightnings thunder rores, then gilty trembleth he. . . ."[100]

Complainingly, Timon carries tales to Zeus of his mistreatment by those to whom Timon has been most generous, "making them rich when they were wretchedly poor before and helping all who were in want." "Now," he adds, "that I have become poor thereby I am no longer recognized or even looked at by the men who formerly cringed and kowtowed and hung upon my nod."[101] Like Lucian's personage, Lear suffers ingratitude from those he has most benefited and receives no help from the "Loud-thunderer" whose aid he invokes. Concerning Goneril's ingratitude, however, Lear claims, in a type of *preteritio*, to avoid such Lucianic "tale-bearing" to the gods:

> I do not bid the thunder-bearer shoot,
> Nor tell tales of thee to high-judging Jove.
> (II.iv.229-230)

Finally, Shakespeare could have recalled the criterion of attitudes to thunder as a clue to religious belief from the *Arcadia*. In the crucial exchange between the atheistic Cecropia and the pious Pamela, the former skeptically observes: "Feare, and indeede, foolish feare, and fearefull ignorance, was the first inventer of those conceates. For, when they heard it thunder, not knowing the naturall cause, they thought there was some angrie body above, that spake so lowde: and ever the lesse they did perceive, the more they did conceive" (I, 406).[102]

99*The Clouds*, ll. 395-402 (tr. Rogers, I, 303). Citing Seneca's *Quaestiones naturales*, ii.2, c. 42 and 43, however, Fitzherbert's *Second Part of a Treatise* demands, "what is so foolish as to beleeve, that Jupiter, some tyme with his thunderbolt striketh . . . pillers, yea, and his owne images, and leaveth wicked men untouched . . ." (pp. 62-63). On the oak, sacred to Jove, and thunder see, e.g., Thomas Powell, *The Passionate Poet* (1601), sig. [E4v].

100See La Primaudaye, *The Second Part of the French Academie* (1594), p. 578. See also Tilley T118 and C609 ("A quiet Conscience sleeps in thunder"); with the latter cf. *Macbeth*, IV.i.85-86.

101Lucian, tr. Harmon, II, 331.

102Cf. Seneca: the ancients used Jove's thunder as a device to provoke "fear . . . essential to restrain the passions of the ignorant . . . so it was to terrify those wretches, against whose passions innocence is no protection unless backed up by fear, that they

It may be concluded that in his attitudes to thunder Lear was again: either (1) representing a pagan point of view, typified by the ancient skeptical tradition regarding the natural causation of that heavenly phenomenon, or (2) expressing an increasing doubt as to the reliability of the gods. In the first case, as heathen, Lear would have given no offense to his Elizabethan audience, while in the second case his developing distrust of "ethnic" deities could be construed as a fortunate change toward a theologically more enlightened position. Probably, as in the tenet *ex nihilo* and in other analogous instances, Shakespeare seized on an ambiguous idea which could be exploited in both directions for the complex ends of his multiply significant tragedy.

Lear and Prometheus

ἴδεσθέ μ' οἷα πρὸς θεῶν πάσχω θεός.

—Aeschylus, *Prometheus Bound*, l. 92

And he . . . counteth me as one of his enemies.

—Job xix.11

A royal demigod, Lear in the first scene is the thunderer against mankind. Rashly, he strikes his thunder at Cordelia and Kent, and without consultation. "Let kinges learne this," cautions Fitzherbert's *Second Part of a Treatise*, "that Jupiters owne judgement suffiseth not, when he is to strike any thing with his thunderbolt" (p. 63).[103] Furiously banishing Kent, the king, vicar on earth[104] of *Jupiter Altitonans* and *executor divinae Providentiae*, roars, "Away! By Jupiter, / This shall not be revok'd" (I.i.178-179). Being not among those "that have power to hurt and will do none" and neglecting

---

placed over us in the heavens the image of an avenger, and him well armed" (*Quaestiones naturales*, tr. Clarke, p. 90). See also Petronius, "Primus in orbe deos fecit timor, ardua caelo / fulmina cum caderent . . ." (*Petronius*, tr. Michael Heseltine, Loeb Classical Lib. [1913], p. 342). The *Arcadia* presents not only the skeptical view of thunder but repeated references to the orthodox view: e.g., ". . . let the heavens heare, and if I lie, let them answer me with a deadly thunderbolt" (I, 369); ". . . the heaven roaring out thunders the more amazed them, as having those powers for enimies" (I, 193). Cf. Ch. iii, n. 26.

[103]Cf. Seneca, *Quaestiones naturales*, tr. Clarke, pp. 88-91.

[104]On king as vicar of God, among innumerable references, see *Certaine Sermons* (1587), sig. [Ll7]; James, *Basilicon Doron* (Edinburgh, 1603), p. 2; James ("The King's Speech to the Parliament, 1610") in Joseph R. Tanner, *Constitutional Documents . . . James I* (Cambridge, Eng., 1930), p. 15; Thomas Bilson, *A Sermon Preached at Westminster . . .* (1603), sig. [A6].

"the king-becoming graces,"[105] the fretful Lear allows no room "betwixt" his "sentence and" his "power" (I.i.170). As in the Renaissance proverb, "Where Wrath is joined with power there are thunderbolts" (Tilley W934). By the third act, however, his initial contention proven wrong, he is shown "Contending with the fretful elements" (III.i.4). After his unreasoning thunder hurled against Cordelia and Kent, heaven ironically throws its own irrational "pudder" back at him; and he, too, like his victims, becomes "More sinn'd against than sinning" (III.ii.60). The third crescendo is heard during the last stage of the dialectic, following Cordelia's murder; having in Act III defied their elemental "servile ministers" (III.ii.21),[106] Lear finally challenges the heavens themselves (V.iii.257-259). The thunder is angrily flung back at the gods, and Lear can echo the Promethean conclusion, "O Earth, thou beholdest my wrong!" (l. 1093).

The Promethean analogy is more explicit in Lear's cry, "O Regan! she hath tied / Sharp-tooth'd unkindness, like a vulture, here" (II.iv.135-136). Mentioned in a source work (Samuel Harsnet's *A Declaration of Egregious Popishe Impostures*: "*Prometheus* with his Vulture," p. 73), Lear's reference evokes not only such Prometheus-alluding antecedents as Ovid's *Metamorphoses* (Bk. I, fol. 2), Virgil's sixth *Eclogue*, *Love's Labour's Lost* (IV.iii.304), and *Othello* (V.ii.12), as well as recurrent Renaissance iconography, but also, inevitably, Aeschylus' fifth-century tragedy, *Prometheus Bound*.[107] To

[105]Sonnet 94; *Macbeth*, IV.iii.91.

[106]Lear's phrase appears in Lewis Campbell's translation of Aeschylus' *Prometheus Bound*, from which lines are here cited (*Aeschylus: The Seven Plays* [1890]); Hermes, sent by Zeus, is so addressed by Prometheus, p. 333.

[107]Cf. *Titus Andronicus*, II.i.17. See also Olga Raggio, "The Myth of Prometheus," *JWCI*, XXI (1958), 44-62 (p. 57, n. 71, erroneously alludes to the Aldine edition of Aeschylus, Venice, 1518, as a translation). For other Promethean references see: Boccaccio, *La geneologia de gli dei de gentili* (Venice, 1569), foll. [71v]-[73v]; Ficino, "Five Questions concerning the Mind," tr. Josephine L. Burroughs, in *Renaissance Philosophy of Man*, ed. Cassirer et al., pp. 191, 208; Henry Peacham, *Minerva Britanna* (1612), p. 189; Charles W. Lemmi, *The Classic Deities in Bacon: A Study in Mythological Symbolism* (Baltimore, 1933), pp. 128-140; D. T. Starnes and E. W. Talbert, *Classical Myth and Legend in Renaissance Dictionaries* (Chapel Hill, N.C., 1955), pp. 120-123; Ernst Cassirer, *Individuum und Kosmos in der Philosophie der Renaissance* (Leipzig, 1927), passim; Erwin Panofsky, *Studies in Iconology: Humanistic Themes in the Art of the Renaissance* (New York, 1939), pp. 50-51; Eugene F. Rice, Jr., "The Wisdom of Prometheus," *The Renaissance Idea of Wisdom* (Cambridge, Mass., 1958), pp. 93-123. On the continuity of the myth, including also Renaissance art, see the article "Prometheus" in *Paulys Real-encyclopädie der classischen Altertumswissenschaft*,

Shakespeare's age Aeschylus' *Prometheus* could have been available, not only in Greek but also in Latin translations and scholia: for example, Greek text with Latin scholia, *Aeschyli tragoediae VII . . . Petri Victorii cura . . . Henrici Stephani observationes* ([Geneva], 1557); Latin translations of *Prometheus* by Joannes Sanravius in *Aeschyli . . . tragœdiæ sex* (Basel, 1555) and by Matthias Garbitius (Basel, 1559), whose version appears also in *Tragœdiæ selectæ. Æschyli, Sophoclis, Euripidis* ([Geneva], 1567), III, 853-943.[108] In 1577, in the course of an extensive Greek education, Peter Young gave his pupil, James VI of Scotland, a copy of *Aeschyli tragœdiæ gr. cum commentario.*[109] Little more than conventional eulogy was presumably intended in Jonson's comparison of Shakespeare to "thund'ring *Æschilus*."

In order to clarify *Lear*'s affiliations with the conventional Promethean prototype, rather than to urge any more direct relation, it may be relevant to point out other Aeschylean resemblances. Such motifs as resentment of divine betrayal, ingratitude, and injustice, defiance of the heavenly powers, and challenge of the thunder, as they may tend to characterize the seventeenth-century Don Juan convention, also mark both dramas. In addition, the time of *Prometheus Bound*, like that of *Lear*, is in a far distant or primeval past, and the setting, like that of the Shakespearean heath, is a rocky wilderness, "far Earth's limit."[110] Both Prometheus and Lear—a Prometheus

---

XXIII, Pt. I (Stuttgart, 1957), 653-730; and Károly Kerényi, *Prometheus: Archetypal Image of Human Existence* (New York, 1963). See also Raymond Trousson, *Le thème de Prométhée dans la littérature européenne* (Geneva, 1964).

108A French translation of Aeschylus' *Prometheus* was produced by Jean Dorat (Auratus) for his pupil Ronsard; see Claude Binet, *La vie de P. de Ronsard* (1586), ed. Paul Laumonier (Paris, 1910), p. 12. The verse tragedy *Parabata vinctus*, attributed to Jacques Auguste de Thou (Lutetiae, 1595), imitates the *Prometheus vinctus*. Coriolanus Martirus included a Latin translation of *Prometheus Bound* in *Tragoediae VIII, Comoediae II* (Naples, 1556, 1563). (I am indebted to my student Mrs. Evaline S. Berry for suggestions regarding Aeschylus' play.)

109*The Library of James VI. 1573-1583. From a Manuscript in the Hand of Peter Young, His Tutor*, ed. George F. Warner (Edinburgh, 1893), p. xlvii; see also Baldwin, *William Shakespeare's Small Latine & Lesse Greeke*, I, 541. Baldwin (II, 245, 459) cites Erasmus and Sir Thomas Elyot on the use of the Promethean myth in education. Cf. Baldwin's *Shakspere's Five-Act Structure* (Urbana, Ill., 1947), pp. 284-288, quoting Matthias Garbitius' critical comments in his edition (Basel, 1559) of Aeschylus' play.

110*Prometheus Bound*, p. 297. Spatially, *Lear* (despite household elements) thus more closely resembles *Prometheus Bound* in contrast to the settings within corrupted court and palace of *Hamlet* and *Macbeth*.

mal enchaîné—are at once victims and rebels, both in their defiance are regarded as mad, and their apparently arbitrary tormenter is alike the highest cosmic power. Both set self-conscious human awareness and character against a seemingly meaningless or destructive universe.

But, whereas Prometheus is the eponymous "pro-vident one" or "Fore-thinker,"[111] and Lear seems to pursue, by his questions, a type of Promethean knowledge, Shakespeare's hero resembles also Prometheus' legendary brother, Epimetheus,[112] the improvident "After-thinker." For a chief difference is that the Greek play opens with the hero already captive, while the English work gradually discloses to him the dimensions of his prison. In the Promethean light, therefore, *King Lear* is a tragedy which celebrates not only the divine mystery but also its correlative, the human condition.

The theme of divine betrayal and cosmic treachery, implicit in both *Prometheus Bound* and *Lear*, is counterpointed in Aeschylus by Io's complaint against Zeus and orchestrated in Shakespeare by betrayal on every level. Whereas the mortal Io, in beast form, passively laments her wrong at the hands of divine power and suicidally tries to cast herself from a high precipice to cut short her suffering, the divine Prometheus stands up defiantly against the god.[113] Shakespeare's play also juxtaposes, through its protagonists, two alternative reactions against seemingly arbitrary cosmic power, the spiritlessly and the dignifiedly human.

Connected with the religious level, betrayal in *Lear* reverberates through every situation, political, familial, and personal. The experiences of both Gloucester's "planetary influence" and Edmund's "whoremaster man" show these to be deceptive reliances. Indeed, divine betrayal reaches through the chain of Edmund's goddess Natura, instinct and desire betraying Edmund, as Edmund betrays

[111]See *Prometheus Bound*, p. 300.

[112]See Hesiod, *Theogony*, tr. Hugh G. Evelyn-White, Loeb Classical Lib. (1929), p. 117; *Works and Days*, ibid., p. 9.

[113]Related to the Promethean thunder challenger is the Theban king, Capaneus (cf. Dante, *Inferno* xiv.49-75); disdaining divine punishment, he defies the god's joyful vengeance and meets his death as he remains standing under Jove's thunderbolt; see Statius, *Thebaid*, Bk. X. Like Lear, Calderón's Sigismondo in *La vida es sueño* rebels against his powerful tormenter and, like him, proclaims the inferior state of mankind to that of beasts. Chained, like Aeschylus' Prometheus, Sigismondo in Act I demands: "¿y teniendo yo más alma, / tengo menos libertad?" (Pedro Calderón de la Barca, *Dramas*, ed. Angel Valbuena Briones, *Obras completas*, I [Madrid, 1959], 367).

Gloucester and the sisters betray each other. Moreover, appearances betray the betrayers, as Edmund is fatally betrayed by Edgar's "outside" which "looks so fair" (V.iii.142). In the denouement's cataclysm of betrayal Lear confuses the identity of his truest friend, Kent, who had earlier warned, "See better, Lear" (I.i.158), and shouts out his indictment of betrayal by the world: "A plague upon you, murderers, traitors all!" (V.iii.269). Gloucester's prediction is thus ironically fulfilled: "machinations . . . treachery . . . follow us disquietly to our graves" (I.ii.118-120). Further, if Edgar's charge against Edmund, "False to thy gods" (V.iii.134), contains truth, the betrayal theme might also reverse the syntax. For, as in the case of Prometheus, the gods, Lear feels, have been "false" to him; thus Lear's "traitors" may be also the gods. Like Aeschylus, Shakespeare probes both the limits of betrayal and the limits of human endurance.

Disillusion at cosmic unrequital characterizes both protagonists: Prometheus, who had been instrumental in Zeus's accession, and Lear, who for eighty years had, presumably, faithfully served and propitiated his gods. Their only reward is to be placed on "the rack of this tough world" (V.iii.314), like Prometheus, "bowed with chastisement, / Painful to bear and piteous to be seen" (p. 306).

> Such benefit that tyrant of the gods
> Rewards with this unequal recompense. (p. 305)

Further, their deity is alike a god of arbitrary and cruel injustice:

> Seems not this lord of gods to all alike
> Impartial in his ruthless violence? (p. 324)

> . . . Zeus with uncouth decrees
> Old ordinance hath altered at his ease,
> And hoary might he hath cruelly defied, (p. 302)

while petitions alter not his hard power, "for Zeus is deaf to intercession, / And . . . ever harsh in will" (p. 298).

When Prometheus asserts, "I hate the race of Heaven, / That meet my benefits with acts of wrong," the "pious" Hermes, Zeus's "servile minister," rejoins, "What madness past belief thy words disclose!" (p. 333). With Lear's "Reason in madness" Prometheus implies irreverence to be a suitable reply to injustice: "If hatred of a cruel foe be madness, / Let me be mad" (p. 333). Apparently corrupt as well as cruel, Zeus, who has attempted rape upon Io, may, as Hermes and Oceanus intimate, also be bribed by favors. Similarly, cosmic depravity may suggest a broader and higher application of Lear's indictment of justice, indeed, his judgment of the lust-and-greed-driven Goneril: "Corruption in the place!" (III.vi.55).

Like the royal British demigod, the Greek hero exclaims,

> look on me and see
> How I, a god, am wronged by gods....
> Ye see me prisoned here, a god ill-starred,
> Of Zeus the enemy, hated of all (pp. 300-301)

somewhat as Lear complains,

> You see me here, you Gods, a poor old man,
> As full of grief as age; wretched in both! (II.iv.274-275)

and later, "here I stand, your slave, / A poor, infirm, weak, and despis'd old man" (III.ii.19-20). Yet neither Prometheus nor Lear will play the woman and despairingly weep. "Never imagine it," says the first,

> that I, in fear
> Of His resolve, will play the woman's part,
> With meek uplifting of my suppliant hands...
> ...Far from me
> Such base humility! (p. 334)

while the second at this stage still invokes the gods against such an occasion:

> And let not women's weapons, water-drops,
> Stain my man's cheeks!...
> No, I'll not weep. (II.iv.279-285)

Though not weak themselves, they pity the weak. Prometheus stole heaven's fire for human warmth, and it is Lear's Promethean pity for mankind, "defenceless" against the "seasons," which expresses itself in his "Poor naked wretches" speech (III.iv.28-32). Lear "gave... all" (II.iv.252) and won no sympathy, like Prometheus, who, "Compassionating mortals in my heart," was "Myself refused compassion" (p. 306). Such unrequited sympathy the heroes lavish on "frail mortals" (pp. 297, 317), the ephemeral "flies" and "birds" of *Lear*, and Prometheus' "brief-dated" men, "creatures creeping for an hour" (pp. 300, 317).[114]

[114] With "frail mortals" cf. *Lear*, IV.i.36; V.iii.9, 13; and Ch. vii above.

From one point of view the arbitrary thunder may be the cosmic equivalent of lawless nature, inexorably ruled at the top only by might: "Say, if I do, the laws are mine, not thine," boasts Goneril. "Who can arraign me for't" (V.iii.158-159). Elsewhere, as if in reply to Lear's pitiful entreaty of the gods, the storm is heard at a distance (II.iv.286). Indeed, the thunder-challenge *topos* appears prototypically Aeschylean, as does the description of the cosmic storm. Like Lear in Act III, Prometheus depicts the storm as the assault of the god upon him:

> . . . The earth heaves and rolls like a storm-
> troubled sea,
> And the roar of her waves is deep thunder that
> momently bursts at my side,
> And the lightning's fierce spirals gleam vividly
> forth, while in horrible glee
> Many whirlwinds are wildly careering with
> columns of dust far and wide.
> All the winds leap to loveless contention,
> each blast by his brother defied.
> The sky and broad main in one chaos of turbid
> commotion are blent;
> And on me this assault from high Zeus,
> making awe where it moves, hath been sent. (p. 337)

Yet, in terms similar to Lear's, Prometheus defies it:

> Then let his darted lightning singe the world;
> With rumbling earthquake and white fluttering snow
> Let him confound and choke all things that are! . . .
> Then be darted upon me in fury the pine-piercing
> flame!
> Let the calm Empyrean be fretted with thunder,
> fierce agony shoot
> Far through Ether with racking of tempest, and
> Earth from her nethermost root
> Rock with wind till she quake to her centre;—
> wave heaped upon wave with harsh roar
> Disorder the stars in their courses,
> confounding the sea with the shore. (pp. 334-336)

Similarly, "Singe my white head!" challenges Lear, "let fall / Your horrible pleasure . . ." (III.ii.6, 18-19), and the Promethean struggle is echoed in the Gentleman's description of Lear, who,

Contending with the fretful elements;
Bids the wind blow the earth into the sea,[115]
Or swell the curled waters 'bove the main,
That things might change or cease.... (III.i.4-7)[116]

Anatomy of Hard Hearts

When I had ripp'd me, 'and search'd where hearts did lye....
—Donne, "The Legacie"

I have observed the progressive disintegration of Lear's religious confidence; his "failure of nerve," to use the term Gilbert Murray applied to the Hellenistic period,[117] is the unnerving discovery of presumably eighty years' commitment to an unreliable presiding

[115]Folio directions: "Storme still." Lear's cosmically destructive imprecations recall not only the scriptural apocalypse but also the end of the world in a deluge as described by Seneca (*Quaestiones naturales*, tr. Clarke, pp. 143-147) and Leonardo.

Appropriately, since Act III contains the great dissolving movement of the play, it is one conveying images of liquidation: cf. the destructive storm itself, with its wind and rain, and Lear's contention with it, bidding "That things might change or cease" (III. i.7); the apocalyptic deluge imagery (III.i.5-6, III.vii.58-61) and the "roaring sea" (III.iv.10). Metamorphosis is sensed also, for example, in the fluid imagery of Poor Tom. "'Tis a naughty night to swim in" (III.iv.113-114), according to the Fool; and the mad beggar's diet of things that swim includes small amphibious animals, "the swimming frog, the toad, the todpole ... and the water" (III.iv.132-133). Amidst the third act's Empedoclean turbulences, a centuries-old cosmological structure seems wrenched from its fixed place. In consequence, the start of the last scene suggests a world in Heraclitean dissolution, where "packs and sects of great ones / ... ebb and flow by th' moon" (V.iii.18-19).

[116]Subsequently, the thunder's moral ambiguity, as has been noted of the Power in Shelley's "Mont Blanc," might relatedly be conceived as secularized neutral force: "... the Power is inaccessible to man, its character is discoverable in its consequences. ... The Power is neither benevolent nor hostile; it is self-contained and indifferent to everything but its own need to act.... the Power, unlike the Christian God, has no human concerns.... man [is taught] to doubt—that is, in the sceptical sense, to recognize that the Power is neither good nor evil, neither benevolent nor vicious, but only amoral ... indifferent ..." (Earl Wasserman, *The Subtler Language: Critical Readings of Neoclassic and Romantic Poems* [Baltimore, 1959], p. 228).

Still later than Shelley, Melville, writing to Hawthorne (letter, April 16[?], 1851, *The Portable Melville*, ed. Jay Leyda [New York, 1959], pp. 427-428), was to define the heroic human attitude toward that Power, as well as "... the tragicalness of human thought in its own ... profounder workings.... By visible truth, we mean the apprehension of the absolute condition of present things as they strike the eye of the man who fears them not, though they do their worst to him,—the man who ... declares himself a sovereign nature (in himself) amid the powers of heaven, hell, and earth. He may perish; but so long as he exists he insists upon treating with all Powers upon an equal basis. If any of those other Powers choose to withhold certain secrets, let them; that does not impair my sovereignty in myself; that does not make me tributary.... There is the grand truth about Nathaniel Hawthorne. He says NO! in thunder...."

[117]"The 'Failure of Nerve': Mysticism and Superstition," *Stoic, Christian and Humanist* (1940), pp. 64-69.

pantheon. And I have noted that the thunder, traditionally the voice of the providential heavens, is in actuality an ambiguous accompaniment to human suffering. So that as, on the one hand, Lear registers a pained surprise at the macrocosm, the microcosm, which, on the other hand, parallels it, is the subject of his disaffected shock. In the same crucial third act, which registers Lear's intellectual and personal peripeteia, there seems to be a complementary echo of his increasing skepticism, one which would be more perceptible to the Jacobean age of transition than to our own; and this shock of discovery communicates itself not to the thunder but to his own flesh and blood: "Then let them anatomize Regan," the mad king exclaims, "see what breeds about her heart. Is there any cause in nature that make these hard hearts?" (III.vi.77-79).[118]

In this seemingly innocent question, superficially a product of his madness, Lear reveals the distance he has traveled from his reliance on "the power that made me" (I.i.207) of the first scene. From one point of view, as a pagan polytheist and naturalist, he would be expected to refer to a "cause in nature" for the solution to his problems. Seen from another point of view, however, Lear's resort to natural, rather than divine, causation is a measure of his developing skepticism.

Yet, on the other side, the Renaissance could have observed in Lear an analogue with itself, with the growing naturalism of which the ambivalent Bacon is the *buccinator*. This appeal to second causes rather than to first, to nature rather than to God, was a mark of the new materialist doubt. But, to aggravate the problem, Lear turns paradoxically to natural causation for the solution to a question traditionally within the divine realm. "Hard hearts" were caused, as every devout Elizabethan knew, by falling from grace, by reprobation and sin. As innumerable Renaissance texts testify, "hardening of the heart" is an ailment peculiarly theological (cf. Exodus iv.21, vii.3, and vii.13; *Faustus*, II.ii.18), to be remedied, if at all, by repentance and grace and subject to the spiritual, rather than to the anatomical, art ("More needs she the divine," as was said of Lady Macbeth, "than the physician," V.i.82).[119] Still unilluminated by Descartes' revelation concerning the pineal gland, some opinion followed Aristotle on the

[118]Such topics seem to have been current; e.g., Thomas Andrewe, *The Unmasking of a Feminine Machiavell* (1604), sig. C2v; and Warner, *Albions England*, p. 172.

[119]Among Renaissance references to "hard hearts" are: William Tyndale, *Doctrinal Treatises*, Parker Soc. (Cambridge, Eng., 1848), p. 195; Homilies, *Certaine Sermons*,

heart as the center of intelligence, and the Stoics, as cited by Montaigne (II, 253), on the soul as situated "within and about the heart."[120]

From a Renaissance point of view, Lear's question indicates a twofold falling away: first, by the substitution of the natural for the divine and, second, by the imputation of a spiritual malady to physical causation—to the body rather than to the soul. Indeed, Lear's remark recalls a characterization in the epistle to the reader of the *Second Part* of La Primaudaye's *French Academie* (1594), regarding those men who "sticke fast in the very matter and forme of their bodies, so that many of them become meere Naturalists and very Atheists" (sig. b). In contrast, affirming the orthodox view, John Yates in *Gods Arraignement of Hypocrites* (Cambridge, Eng., 1615) cites the popular Perkins as follows: ". . . God is *independent* from all *second causes*; yet all second causes are dependent upon him . . ." (p. 128). Relatedly, in his influential *A Golden Chaine* (1592) Perkins defines "Hardnes of heart or carnall securitye, when a man neither acknowledge Gods judgement nor his owne sinnes, dreameth that he is safe from Gods vengeance, and such perils, as arise from sin. Romans.2.5. . . . Luke.21,34" (sig. F4).

Rejecting the search for natural causation, Mornay argues "Against the false naturalists (that is to say professors of the knowl-

---

sig. [Kk8r-v]; Thomas Wilson, *A Discourse uppon Usurye* (1572); Théodore de Bèze, *An Evident Display of Popish Practices, or Patched Pelagianisme* (1578), p. 246; Pierre Viret, *The Second Part of the Demoniacke Worlde, or World Possessed with Divels* (1583), sigs. [E6], [E8v]; Richard Rogers' entry in his diary regarding his "hardnes of hart" by which he was "sodainly overtaken" in 1588 (M. M. Knappen, ed. *Two Elizabethan Puritan Diaries* [Chicago, 1933], p. 78); Thomas Lodge, *Wits Miserie and the Worlds Madnesse* (1596), sig. [Giv]; Richard Greenham, *Propositions containing Answers . . . with an Epistle against Hardnes of Heart* (Edinburgh, 1597), "Cum Privilegio Regio"; Hooker, *Ecclesiastical Polity*, in *Works*, II, 588-591, and "A Remedy against Sorrow and Fear: Delivered in a Funeral Sermon," *Works*, III, 646; José de Acosta, *The Naturall and Morall Historie of the East and West Indies*, p. 340; George Downame, *Lectures on the XV. Psalme* (1604), p. 299; William Perkins, . . . *A Treatise of Christian Equitie* (Cambridge, Eng., 1604), pp. 88-89; Dekker, *The Seven Deadly Sinnes of London* (1606), in *The Non-Dramatic Works of Thomas Dekker*, ed. Alexander B. Grosart, II (1885), 37; George Herbert's poem, "Grace"; Thomas Wilson, *A Christian Dictionary* (1622), s.v. "Hardening," "Hard-heart."

[120]Cf. Edgar (IV.vi.262), "To know our enemies' minds, we rip their hearts"; Webster's *The White Devil* (IV.ii.23), Brachiano on a letter to Vittoria Corombona: "Ile open't, were't her heart." Yet see Huarte de San Juan, *The Examination of Mens Wits* (1594), p. 24. He defends the brain, rather than the heart, as the "principall seat of the reasonable soule." Contrast Ruth L. Anderson, "As Heart Can Think," *Shakespeare Association Bulletin*, XII (1937), 246-251.

edge of nature and naturall things)" and cites "Anatomists or Decipherers of nature."[121] In like fashion, Thomas Scott's *Philomythie or Philomythologie* (1616) attacks the atheist, who knowing "some Philosophy, no Divinity . . . is so inquisitive after the cause, that he forgets both the end and the causer" (pp. 49-50). In Massinger's *A Very Woman* Paulo finds the necessity of a First Cause, while the Viceroy indicates the prevalence of attempts to ascribe natural events to physical law (II.ii). Above other things, the heart, insists Thomas Adams' *Mystical Bedlam, or the World of Mad-Men* (1615), about the time of William Harvey's innovations, is inscrutable to man and visible only to God: "But how can this evill juyce in our *hearts* be perceived? what beames of the Sunne ever pearced into that abstruse and secret pavilion? The *anatomizing* of the heart remaines for the worke of that last and great day. Rom, 2.16. As no eye can looke into it, so let no reason judge it" (p. 22).[122] Similarly, a divine, rather than natural, causation is evident in the title of Thomas Watson's sermon (1649), *Gods Anatomy upon Mans Heart.*

Thus, at this juncture Lear finds himself at the skeptical pole to Gloucester's superstition. Between Gloucester and Lear stands another old man, the sympathetic Lafeu, who in *All's Well That Ends Well* is a negative barometer of the new Jacobean dispensation: "we have our philosophical [i.e., scientific or skeptical] persons, to make modern [i.e., commonplace] and familiar, things supernatural and causeless" (II.iii.1-3); neither superstitious nor skeptical, Lafeu would preserve the old mysteries. There are some mysteries of things which are in God's hands, William Fulke's *A Most Pleasant Prospect . . . to Behold the Naturall Causes of . . . Meteors* (1602) points out: "Concerning the formall and finall cause, wee have litle to say, because the one is so secret, that it is knowne of no man: the other so evident, that it is plaine to all men" (sig. A4^{v}). Fulke thus runs counter both to Aristotle, who holds that we know things when we know their causes, and to Hobbes, who asserts, "Ignorance of natural causes, disposeth a man to credulity, so as to believe many times impossibilities."[123]

[121] *A Woorke concerning the Trewnesse of the Christian Religion* (1587), sig. ***r-v.

[122] Cf. Samuel Garey, *Two Treatises . . . the Foode of the Faithfull* (1605).

[123] *English Works*, III, 92. See Howard Schultz, *Milton and Forbidden Knowledge* (New York, 1955), on the seventeenth-century continuation of the obscurantist tradition, and the discussions elsewhere in the present study on the *Deus absconditus* and on "the mystery of things."

In his question, then, Lear seems, in effect, to be withdrawing an area from the Department of Theology and requesting a grant for a scientific research project: "Then let them anatomize Regan, see what breeds about her heart. Is there any cause in nature that make these hard hearts?" Implying a connection with the scientific anatomist, Lear's remark recalls, more than the traditional bodily ascriptions of Renaissance psychology, the naïve assumption of pioneers in morbid anatomy who associated abstract human vices and virtues with anatomical changes—a kind of pre-Lombrosan typology. Such an identification of human qualities with the physical body was, as a Renaissance physician observes, made by the Greek materialist Democritus of Abdera, who "that he might finde out the seate of anger and melancholy, cut in peeces the bodies of beasts. . . ." A sidenote by the same physician declares: "Anatomy the most sure guide to the knowledge of our selves."[124] Similarly, that frequent indicator of skepticism, Pliny, in his *Historie of the World* anticipates later naturalists in ascribing character to the *cor villosum,* whose possessor was considered to be strong and valorous. "Such was *Aristomenes* the Messenian," of whom, when captured, the Lacedaemonians caused the "breast to be cut and opened, because they would see what kind of Heart he had: and there they found it all overgrowne with haire."[125] Leonardo's anatomical studies set out to "reveal to men the origin of their second—first or perhaps second—cause of existence,"[126] and Renaissance anatomists deduced character traits from anatomical changes. Anticipating Lear, Antonio Benivieni, for example, "amazed at the fellow's wickedness," had a thief's body opened and his heart examined.[127]

[124]Helkiah Crooke, *Microcosmographia. A Description of the Body of Man* (1615), p. 12.

[125]Pliny, tr. Holland (1601), Bk. XI, Ch. xxxvii, p. 340. Cf. Aristotle, *De partibus animalium,* tr. A. L. Peck, Loeb Classical Lib. (1937), p. 245, 667a, ll. 7-32, and reference in Sebastián de Covarrubias Horozco, *Tesoro de la lengua castellana . . .,* ed. Martín de Riquer (Barcelona, 1943), p. 355, s.v. "coraçón." *The Problemes of Aristotle* (1597), sig. D2v. In *Don Quixote* (Pt. II, Ch. xxiii) Montesinos' "philosophic" words reverse the correlation between heart and courage in Aristotle's *De partibus animalium.*

[126]*The Notebooks of Leonardo da Vinci,* ed. Edward MacCurdy (New York, 1938), I, 101.

[127]*Libellus de abditis nonnullis ac mirandis morborum & sanationum causis* ([Paris], 1528), fol. 17. Based on about twenty autopsies and considered the first treatise of pathological anatomy, the work describes the dissection of the thief's body: "Quare hominis admirati nequitiam, mortui cadaver incidendum curavimus, & inventum est cor eius ob

But stronger evidence still for the interpretation of Lear's seemingly innocent remark is its echo in a work which apparently borrowed from Shakespeare's play, Tourneur's *The Atheist's Tragedie*. As has been pointed out, in its beast and thunder parallels and elsewhere Tourneur's work, through its relatively naïve proportions, helps reveal significances in the more complex tragedy of Shakespeare. In Tourneur's play the avowed atheist D'Amville, not satisfied with urging upon the Doctor closer physiological scrutiny of dead bodies, proposes an anatomy in terms whose equation of moral traits with physiological substance precisely echoes Lear's "let them anatomize Regan. . . . Is there any cause in nature that make these hard hearts?" Seeking to determine, in Lear's phrase, what "cause in nature" makes Charlemont's virtue, the skeptical D'Amville, like Shakespeare's hero, proposes an anatomy:

> I begge a Boone. . . .
> His body when t'is dead for an Anatomie. . . .
> I would finde out by his Anatomie;
> What thing there is in Nature more exact,
> Then in the constitution of my selfe. . . .
> The cause of that, in his Anatomie
> I would finde out. (V.ii.156-169)[128]

eximi an caliditatem undique pilis refertum" (fol. 17). Following Democritus, Pliny, and Benivieni, Scipion Dupleix's *The Resolver; or Curiosities of Nature* (1635), pp. 99-100, identifies hairy hearts with moral characteristics.

Lear's directive suggests Benivieni's motive, as well as a possible reflection on Regan: cf. "An Elegie on the Death of the Lady Rutland" in *Sir Thomas Overbury His Wife* (1616), sig. [A7], complaining that anatomizing physicians forgot "that the State allowes you none / But only Whores and Theeves to practise on." Cf. Nashe, I, 196; II, 304-305; Webster, *The Duchess of Malfi*, V.ii.76-77; John Stow, *A Survey of the Cities of London and Westminster*, ed. John Strype (1720), II, Bk. V, 209.

[128]Cf. Robert Anton, *The Philosophers Satyrs* (1616), sig. A2: "Some Surgeon might have begd a dead body from the fanges of execution, whose Anotomy might have taught the age the constitution of vice. . . ." The materialistic investigation of such physical "causes" recalls the tradition of the atheistical physician; see Paul H. Kocher, *Science and Religion in Elizabethan England* (San Marino, 1953), pp. 239-257. In William Bullein's *A Dialogue . . . against the Fever Pestilence* (1564), sigs. Biii-Biiii^v, [Dvii-Dviii], Medicus observes, "I medle with no Scripture matters, but to serve my tourne . . ." and confesses himself "a Nulla fidian . . . there are many of our secte." Eschewing the Bible for Aristotle, he attributes pestilence to natural causes. Cf. Jonson's *The Magnetic Lady* (1632), I.ii.38-40:

> *Rut* is a young Physician to the family:
> That, letting God alone, ascribes to nature
> More then her share . . .

and Massinger's *A Very Woman*, II.ii. (*Dramatic Works*, p. 372), on physicians'

"Poor Naked Wretches"

Justice and injustice, are the most generall of all other morall or politicall habits. There is no vertue or vice, which they do not comprehend.

—Francesco Guicciardini, *Aphorismes Civill and Militarie* (1613; citing Aristotle, *Ethics*)

An aspect of the play's general treatment of justice, the protagonists' plea for distribution to the poor has been misconstrued into a manifesto primarily of social reform. Yet their perception of economic injustice is more a measure of progress in feeling, a preparation for Lear's indictment of justice, as in the "trial" scene of III.vi, and a recognition of the profounder breakdown of justice on the divine as well as secular levels. For the poor become, in the protagonists' eyes, a test case of providence. As Burton's *Anatomy* (Oxford, 1628) asserts, "It cannot stand with Gods goodnesse, protection and providence. . . . when as a wicked Catiffe abounds in superfluitie of wealth . . ." (p. 616).

Traditionally the virtue *quae suum cuique distribuit*, justice includes not only the remedial, or suitable retribution of punishment, but also the distributive, specifically, the proper apportionment of goods. In his *Governour* (1531) Sir Thomas Elyot observes: "Justice . . . is . . . described in two kyndes. . . . The one is named justyce distributive . . . the other is called commutative or by exchaunge, and of Aristotell it is named . . . *Diorthotice*, whiche is in englysshe corrective."[129] Bacon's *Advancement of Learning* (1605) inquires: ". . . is there not a true coincidence between commutative and distributive justice, and arithmetical and geometrical proportion?" alluding to the Aristotelian distinction between the commutative, based on identity, the concern of the judge, and the distributive, based on proportionality, the concern of the legislator.[130] Quixote remarks of knight-errantry, "Whoever professes it, ought to be learned in the laws, and understand distributive and commutative Justice, in

---

Attributing so much to natural causes,
That they have little faith in that they cannot
Deliver reason for. . . .

See also Thomas Fuller's *A Pisgah-Sight of Palestine* (1650), p. 95.

[129] *The Boke Named the Governour,* ed. H. H. S. Croft (1883), II, 187.

[130] *Works,* III, 348.

order to right all Mankind."[131] Moreover, human justice in all aspects is reflected in cosmic justice, whose failure is suggested in W. S.'s dedicatory poem to *Sir Thomas Overbury His Wife* (1616), a popular work which went through numerous impressions. Entitled "Upon the Untimely Death of . . . Sir Tho: Overbury Knight Poysoned in the Towre," the poem demands of heaven the reason that, rather than providence, chance seems unjustly to operate in the distribution of the world,

> and *Her blinde Hand*
> Thy *Benefits* erroneously disburse,
> Which so let fall, ne're fall but to the *worse*?
> Whence *so, great crimes* commit the *Greater* sort. (sig. [¶ 6v])

In the opening scene Lear's maldistribution violates the justice of persons and of property, as well as that "Justice" which may limit even the sacred prerogatives of kings.[132] Ironically, Lear most deeply realizes his own injustice ("O! I have ta'en / Too little care of this"), at the same time as he discovers the larger cosmic injustice (e.g., III. iv.32-33, 36). Similarly, Gloucester discovers human injustice (e.g., IV.i.67-69) as he senses, after his blinding, the larger cruelties (IV.i. 36-37). Hence, also, gratitude and ingratitude, as Seneca[133] and Cervantes, for example, insist, are aspects of justice. Indeed, Don Quixote asserts, "Of all the Sins that Men commit . . . none . . . is so great as Ingratitude . . . if I am not able to repay the Benefits I receive in their Kind, at least I am not wanting in real Intentions of making suitable Returns."[134] As it points forward to the "trial" scene and its aftermath, the hope that "distribution should undo excess" (IV.i.70) serves also as ironical reminder that it is Lear's "distribution" which has itself created "excess," releasing excesses of other kinds which are beyond "undoing."

Further, since "ordinance" is inseparably the divine will of providence in worldly government, "the superfluous and lust-dieted man, /

[131] Pt. II, Ch. xviii, p. 556.

[132] On the two types of justice, see Robert Recorde, *The Whetstone of Witte* (1557), sig. Biv; La Primaudaye, *The French Academie* (1586), p. 393; Cudworth, *True Intellectual System* (1678), Preface. Cf. Rabelais, *Oeuvres* (Paris, 1835), p. 129.

[133] *Ad Lucilium epistolae morales*, tr. Richard M. Gummere, II (1920), 223. See E. Catherine Dunn, *The Concept of Ingratitude in Renaissance English Moral Philosophy* (Washington, D.C., 1946).

[134] Pt. II, Ch. lviii, p. 835.

That slaves your ordinance" (IV.i.67-68), in effect, subverts and denies the heavens' power. ". . . Tu vois clerement," explains Pierre Viret's *Familiere instruction en la doctrine chrestienne* ([Geneva?], 1559), "que ceus qui mettent une providence de Dieu sans l'ordonnance, par laquelle il ait ordonné de toutes choses, ce qui en doit estre, ils abolissent aussi la prevoiance de Dieu, & consequemment toute sa providence" (p. 352). Thus, Gloucester's urgent plea to the heavens to let such a subverter of divine ordinance "feel your power quickly" (IV.i.69) functions not only as a measure of desperation but also as negative suggestion of the absence of that power in the government of his world. In addition, "slaves" implies "contempt of . . . [divine] Ordinance"[135] and contributes to the recurrent theme of "world upside down" by implying that the highest possible law or ordinance has been inverted and made slave to the lowest. Hence, the breakdown of natural law, announced earlier (I.ii) by Edmund, is now echoed in his father's pitying plea against the defiance of cosmic law.

For Shakespeare's age such divine "ordinance" was identified in, for example, the Homilies: ". . . his lawe and ordinaunce (wherein hee commanded them that they should open their hand unto their brethren that were pore. . . ." "And you, who have great plentie of meats and drinkes, great store of moth-eaten apparel," the Homilies continue, will not "part with any peece of your superfluities, to helpe and succor the poore, hungry, & naked. . . ."[136] Anticipating IV.i.67-71, Henry Bedel's *A Sermon Exhorting to Pitie the Poore* (1573) argues Gloucester's point in similar language: "Let the Glutton serve nature to suffise, and leave hys surfet, then shall the poore bee fed with that . . ." (sigs. [Ciii^v]-[Civ]). "For if," Bedel notes earlier, "the ritch would once become liberall, there is superfluous enough to helpe the poore and needy, for nature is soone pleased" (sig. [Ciii^v]), foreshadowing Lear's observation, "our basest beggars / Are in the

[135]Bilson, *Sermon* (1603), sig. [B5].

[136]*Certaine Sermons*, sigs. [U7], [X7]; cf. sigs. O3v-O4. On the "superfluity" tradition see Hermenegildus Lio, "Determinatio superflui in doctrina Alexandri Halensis eiusque scholae . . .," *Antonianum*, XXVII (1952), 429-498; reference supplied by Morton W. Bloomfield. See also Bloomfield's *Piers Plowman as a Fourteenth-century Apocalypse* (New Brunswick, N.J., 1961), pp. 141-143 and passim. Helen C. White, *Social Criticism in Popular Religious Literature of the Sixteenth Century* (New York, 1944). The superfluity motif is carried through to Lear's final interlude with Cordelia; see the present writer, "Lear's 'Good Years,'" *MLR*, LIX (1964), 177-178.

poorest thing superfluous" (II.iv.266-267). "But would they thinke," Spenser's *Faerie Queene* remarks,

> with how small allowaunce
> Untroubled Nature doth her selfe suffise,
> Such superfluities they would despise. (II.vii.15)[137]

In the opposition between "superfluity" and "necessity," Shakespeare recalls not only the "nothing" motif and "Necessity's sharp pinch" (II.iv.213) into which her father has cast Cordelia and himself has been cast. He emphasizes also the marked disproportion in the workings of human justice and foreshadows the arraignment of divine justice to follow. Such a judgment of justice mounts in the last acts to the final "distribution" by Albany (V.iii.296-304), which is sharply and ironically detonated by Lear's denunciation of justice and by his death (ll. 305-311).

[137]Cf. Tyndale, "The Parable of the Wicked Mammon," *Doctrinal Treatises*, p. 99. Richard Eaton, *A Sermon Preached at the Funeralls . . . of Thomas Dutton* (1616), p. 22. See resemblances to the protagonists' pleas in Arthur Warren's *The Poore Mans Passions. And Poverties Patience* (Stationers' Register, Jan. 14, 1605); *The Pilgrimage of Man* (1606), sig. [C4v]; Nashe, III, 389. Cf. also *Timon of Athens*, III.ii.79-94, IV. iii.227-231; Palingenius, *Zodiake*, p. 22. As represented by the influential William Perkins, many Puritans tended to consider the expropriated and homeless poor as outcastes, beyond both church and law; see Christopher Hill, *Puritanism and Revolution: Studies in Interpretation of the English Revolution of the 17th Century* (1958), p. 231.

In addition, a Puritan notion may also be implicit in Lear's polemical use of the *topos* "natura paucis contenta" (cf. Ch. vi, n. 22, above). Against the Puritan hypocritical insistence on necessity and utility rather than luxury, Lear's cry to his deceitful daughters may be also directed:

> Allow not nature more than nature needs, . . .
> If only to go warm were gorgeous,
> Why, nature needs not what thou gorgeous wear'st,
> Which scarcely keeps thee warm. (II.iv.268-272)

(With this may be compared Alexander Niccholes, *A Discourse, of Marriage and Wiving* [1615], sig. G.) Puritan hypocrisy may have been sensed in the claim to the right of excess in apparel, against the wishes of Shakespeare's patron, by the king's first Parliament in 1604. Not long before the probable date of *Lear*'s composition, in a sudden, dramatic opposition to the bill of March 24, 1604, enabling James to regulate dress by proclamation as Elizabeth had done, Commons made void centuries of sumptuary legislation controlling excess in apparel. As Elizabeth's reign had marked a high point in such legislative restraint, this unprecedented abolition would have attracted public notice. See Wilfrid Hooper, "The Tudor Sumptuary Laws," *English Historical Review*, XXX (1915), 448-449; Frances E. Baldwin, *Sumptuary Legislation and Personal Regulation in England*, Johns Hopkins Studies in Historical and Political Science, XLIV (Baltimore, 1926), 248-250; John Davies of Hereford, *Wittes Pilgrimage* [1605?], sig. T1r-v.

Deus Absconditus: LEAR

THE TRIAL OF JUSTICE

Per alta vada spatia sublimi aethere;
testare nullos esse, qua veheris, deos.
—Seneca, *Medea*

After Lear passes the turning point in the bitter disenchantment of Act III, his denunciation of human justice becomes in Act IV more savage. And as it does, it implies a more-than-secular attack on authority, on the powers that be, which he has so long worshiped and represented; the king's "fourscore and upward" makes the disillusion both more unbearable and more dramatic. Lear, the guardian of justice himself and the vicar of the gods on earth, turns against law and piety in an implicit self-denunciation that at once transforms his earth and his cosmos; order is seen as nonorder, justice, viewed from below, is seen as specious, and the gods are viewed as dubiously attainable. So we note in Act IV, in one condensed passage (vi.151-175), Lear's denunciation of the principle of authority, which he has so long represented and venerated. The great chain of being, whose bond, disintegrating, sounds metallically like sweet bells jangled, out of tune and harsh: disorder in the heavens, disorder in the state, disorder in justice, disorder in the family, disorder in the brain produce the contrapuntal cacophonies of the middle acts of *King Lear*.

As chief justice of the land, Lear in his trial and sentence of Cordelia and in his banishment of Kent preserves some outward forms of office, at the same time as he grows increasingly injudicious. Confounding "our sentence and our power" (I.i.170), his faulty regal example opens the way to Edmund's elevation of nature over law (I.ii.1-2), to Cornwall's recognition that, while legal trappings must be regarded, his power puts his cruelty beyond the law (III.vii.24-27), and to Goneril's claim to be above the law, indeed, to possess it (V.iii.158-159). In a universe where "law" has passed into the hands of the lawless and where the room at the top seems occupied by powers who are irrationally and insatiably cruel, cosmic disillusion comes, inevitably, to include the gods.

"NO GOOD DIVINITY"

The earth is given into the hand of the wicked:
he covereth the faces of the judges thereof....
—Job ix.24

"When the thunder would not peace at my bidding, there I found 'em, there I smelt 'em out," the mad Lear recalls (IV.vi.103-105); disillusionment in his gods during the storm scene accompanies disillusionment in his daughters. "To say 'ay' and 'no' to every thing that I said! 'Ay' and 'no' too was no good divinity" (IV.vi.100-102), he observes, lapsing, as does the play from time to time, into scriptural paraphrase (II Corinthians i.18; James v.12).[138] Such syncretistic mixture is present, also, in his church-fatherly excoriation of female depravity (IV.vi.128-130), mingling St. Augustine with centaurs (l. 126), the gods with the pagan-Christian vision of hell.[139]

But Lear's disillusionment, once begun, sweeps all before it, toppling the analogical edifices of God and man, divine and human justice. In addition, this radical questioning of human justice, as the introduction to the sixteenth-century *Dialogues of Guy de Brués* suggests, was characteristic of Renaissance skeptics. The connection between religious skepticism and attacks on worldly justice, made manifest in *Lear*, is illustrated by the skeptical voices in the *Dialogues*, which, recalling the tenth trope of Sextus Empiricus, assert that laws are mere opinion (p. 56). Like Edmund, Lear comes to see law as lacking higher sanction. In various places Montaigne insists that "whatsoever is profitable is also [considered] just and honest . . . That customes and lawes frame justice" (III, 329); "As in times past we were sicke of offences, so now are we of lawes" (III, 323); "Lawes are now maintained in credit, not because they are essentially just, but because they are lawes. It is the mysticall foundation of their authority; they have none other . . . They are often made by fooles;

[138]The scriptural use of "ay" and "no" appears in Thomas Rogers' *The Catholic Doctrine of the Church of England, an Exposition of the Thirty-nine Articles*, Parker Soc. (Cambridge, Eng., 1854), p. 356. Enjoining against swearing, he cites James v.12 and urges, "But let your communication be Yea, yea; Nay, nay." In addition, Renaissance usage provides a context signifying flattery. For instance, Thomas Heywood's second part of *If You Know Not Me* (1606), sig. C2v, connects the "yea and nay" with "smooth-tongu'd" knavery. Those flatterers, declares John Carpenter's *A Preparative to Contentation* (1597), p. 202, "sooth them cunningly with yea Sir, no Sir, whose favour they seeke to obtaine." Montague Summers, ed. *Shakespeare Adaptations: The Tempest, the Mock Tempest, and King Lear* (Boston, 1922), pp. 130, 268-269, relates the phrase to anti-Puritan satire. See also Francis Lenton, *The Young Gallants Whirligigg* (1629), p. 9. Cf. *Don Quixote*, Pt. II, Ch. xix, p. 565; Tilley W660, M1258.

[139]Lear's "To have a thousand with red burning spits / Come hizzing in upon 'em" (III.vi.15-16) resembles, more closely than Harsnet (cited by Muir), a description of Persian punishment for ingratitude. La Mothe Le Vayer's essay "De l'ingratitude" (*Oeuvres* [Paris, 1662], II, 272) recalls: "Et les Perses, dit Themistius dans une de ses Oraisons, avoient establi quelque peine contre eux, que j'ay leû ailleurs avoir esté la marque d'un fer chaud." Themistius (*Orationes XXXIII* [Paris, 1684], p. 268) observes: "Propterea Persicis legibus ingrati animi constituta poena est, quod ubicumque sit, maxime odium atque inimicitiam ingeneret."

more often by men, who in hatred of equality, have want of equity. . . . There is nothing so grossely and largely offending, nor so ordinarily wronging as the Lawes" (III, 331); "There is nothing wherein the world differeth so much, as in customes and lawes" (II, 298).

Voices in Brués' *Dialogues* argue further that laws favor a certain class, as Lear asserts; laws create economic inequalities. Lear makes a point of poverty as against superfluous wealth, just as the skeptic in Brués speaks of the rich gorging themselves with more than they need, while the poor are miserable (pp. 57, 60).[140] Regarding venality in the lawyer,[141] Montaigne asserts: ". . . you perceive it is indifferent unto him to defend either this or that side . . . Have you paid him well, have you given him a good baite or fee, to make him earnestly apprehend it, beginnes he to be enteressed in the matter . . . and so perswades himselfe" (II, 281). Lear's world has reached the "extreame kinde of injustice," which, Montaigne says, is "(according to *Plato*) . . . that that which is unjust should be held for just. The common people suffered therein greatly then . . ." (III, 298).[142]

Finally, the attack on magistrates in Brués parallels that by Lear—laws "are administered by magistrates who act like wolves instead of functioning like watch-dogs [Lear: "A dog's obey'd in office," IV.vi. 161], and who, abusing their authority [Lear: IV.vi.159-160], become ambitious and tyrannical, and dispose of our goods to their own advantage" (p. 62).[143] Like Lear, Montaigne himself had dispensed justice. Yet the magistrate's partiality, declares the essayist, prejudices his judgment, "his inclination unto freindship, unto kindred, unto

[140]See, e.g., Robert Pricket, *Times Anotomie* (1606), sig. C2, condemning the legal partiality accorded the rich. Cf. Alemán, *Guzman de Alfarache*, I, 54; III, 220.

[141]Such conventionally ascribed venality may be suggested, in anticipation, by the Fool (I.iv.135-136).

[142]Justice has fled this earth, declares Christopher Middleton's *Historie of Heaven* (1596), sig. D2r-v. Justice as banished from earth is a *topos*, e.g., in Hesiod, *Works and Days*, tr. Evelyn-White, p. 17, ll. 197-200; Webster, *A Cure for a Cuckold*, I.ii.24; cf. Astraea, in John Carpenter, *A Preparative to Contentation* (1597), pp. 225-226; Spenser, *Faerie Queene*, V.i.11. See *Titus Andronicus*, IV.iii.39-40; *The Eumenides*, in *Aeschylus: The Seven Plays*, tr. Lewis Campbell (1890), pp. 268-270. Cf. Frances A. Yates, "Queen Elizabeth as Astraea," *JWCI*, X (1947), 27-82.

[143]Regarding judicial bias and corruption, references are of course innumerable: Arthur Golding, *A Discourse upon the Earthquake* . . . (1580), sig. C1; Palingenius, *Zodiake*, pp. 95-96, 167; Nashe, II, 155, referring to magistrates who "will have theyr eyes put out with gyfts, and will not see it, but wincke" at justice; *Hamlet*, III.iii.57-60; Samuel Garey, *Two Treatises . . . Deaths Welcome* (1605), pp. 55-56; *The Pilgrimage of Man* (1606), Ch. vi; Samuel Rowlands, *More Knaves Yet?* (1612?), sig. E1v, re-

beauty, and unto revenge, and not onely matters of so weighty consequence, but this innated and casuall instinct, which makes us to favour one thing more then another . . ." (II, 279). "Consider," he observes, "the forme of this Law . . . a lively testimony of humane imbecility; so much contradiction, and so many errours are therin contained. . . . this Office of humanity had brought them to much trouble. How many innocent and guiltlesse men have we seene punished?" (III, 328-329). In short, as the skeptic in Brués' *Dialogues* suggests, "Laws are ineffective. They punish only the small transgressors, but not the powerful criminals" (p. 62), precisely the point that Lear emphasizes:

> Thorough tatter'd clothes small vices do appear;
> Robes and furr'd gowns hide all. Plate sin with gold,
> And the strong lance of justice hurtless breaks;
> Arm it in rags, a pigmy's straw does pierce it.
> (IV.vi.166-169)[144]

In Act III Lear had used legal language in connection with the thunder and lightning, "dreadful summoners" (III.ii.59),[145] persons who warn offenders to appear in court. Arraigning the arraigners,[146] in an anticipation of the reversals of the "promis'd end" (V.iii.263), Lear's assault on justice is also an arraignment of the "servile ministers" (III.ii.21), thunder and lightning, as well as of the justice of the gods. In addition, the bitterness of Lear's "Judicious punishment! 'twas this flesh begot / Those pelican daughters" (III.iv.74-75) suggests not justice but ironical aptness, analogous to that in Edgar's possibly ambiguous comment to Edmund on their father's blinding (V.iii.170). One who had been chief justice of his realm and chief

garding "A Wicked Majestrate" who is like fowlers who close one eye to aim; Francis Meres, *Palladis Tamia* (1598), sig. [Gg7]; Tilley F604; Exodus xxiii.8. Recalling Lear's reference to "glass eyes" which "seem / To see the things thou dost not" (IV.vi.172-174), S. S.'s *The Honest Lawyer* remarks of suspicion which, "Like to a winking Justicer shall see me, / And yet not see me" (1616, sig. C3v).

144Cf. Tilley L116.

145Their relation to ecclesiastical courts suggests that the gods may be behind their "dreadful" errands.

146Of eight occasions on which Shakespeare employs a form of "arraign," most are in connection with treason; e.g., *Hamlet*, IV.v.93; *Winter's Tale*, II.iii.202; and Lear's arraignment of Goneril, III.vi.47, as well as Goneril's assertion that the laws are hers, V.iii.158-159.

priest, Lear discovers the mocking vanity of those offices and those "justicer[s]" (III.vi.21, 56).[147] Still more rebellious in Act IV, he appears to reflect the tradition of those who, like the sixteenth-century Brués and Montaigne and the seventeenth-century libertines Théophile de Viau ("Contre un juge")[148] and Rochester ("A Satyr against Mankind"), match skepticism with antijudicial sentiment.

In his mad repudiation of justice and the folly of judgment, Lear recalls the drawings of Bruegel[149] as well as Daumier. "Thou rascal beadle, hold thy bloody hand!" Lear continues:

> Why dost thou lash that whore? Strip thine own back;
> Thou hotly lusts to use her in that kind
> For which thou whipp'st her. The usurer hangs the cozener,
> (IV.vi.163-165)

where vices and sin may suggest at once the secular and the nonsecular. Corruption afflicts human judges[150] as it does, according to Aeschylus' Prometheus, divine ones. With the officer of the law, suspected of lechery (IV.vi.162-165), may be compared Montaigne's

[147]The sense of weighty power appears, for instance, in Luther as translated by Richard Argentine, on "Justicers, ryche and wise before the world," *A Ryght Notable Sermon* (1548), sig. [bvii]; cf. George Wilkins, *Three Miseries of Barbary* (1606?), "Divine Justicer" (sig. D3); John Day's *Law-Trickes* (1604-07), "fathers to the wrong'd, heaven's Justicers" (1608, sig. B1v). Yet another Shakespearean use is, like *Lear*'s, not unqualified (*Cymbeline*, V.v.213-214). With *Lear*, IV.vi.158-169, cf. William Parkes's *The Curtaine-Drawer of the World* (1612), pp. 16-17.

[148]*Une seconde révision des œuvres du poète Théophile de Viau*, Le libertinage au XVIIe siècle, ed. Frédéric Lachèvre (Paris, 1911), p. 122. See also Théophile de Viau, *Oeuvres complètes*, ed. Charles Alleaume (Paris, 1856), I, 6, 216. Cf. the author of "poésies libertines," Madame Deshoulières, in "Réflexions diverses" (1686), *Les derniers libertins*, ed. Lachèvre (Paris, 1924), p. 86, addressing man as: "Misérable jouët de l'aveugle Fortune, / Victime des maux et des loix."

[149]Cf. the engraving in the series, attributed to Bruegel, of virtues, 1558-59, following the vices; plate in René van Bastelaer, *Les estampes de Peter Bruegel l'ancien* (Brussels, 1908), Pl. 135, and in Max J. Friedländer, *Pieter Bruegel* (Berlin, 1921), Pl. 37. In "Justicia," the artist omits the cushion, symbol of mercy, while another attribute, the bed, becomes the rack; a crucifix neighbors the gallows; the world, resembling, on this occasion, Shakespeare's Globe itself, consists only of spectators, torturers, and tortured.

[150]Cf. Antonio de Guevara, *The Diall of Princes*, tr. Thomas North (1557), Bk. III, Ch. ix, sig. [Hviv], and *The Duchess of Malfi*, IV.ii.329-330. "Magistrats," notes Burton's *Anatomy* (Oxford, 1621), "Democritus to the Reader," "make laws against theeves, and are the veriest theeves themselves" (p. 25). On the small-vs.-large-thief paradox, see also Sir David Lindsay, *Ane Satyre of the Thrie Estaits* (Edinburgh, 1602), sig. [M4]. Cf. Ch. x, n. 56, below.

portrait of a judge who wrote "even now the condemnation against an adulterer" and will write on it a love letter "to his fellow-judges wife" (III, 237). It is thus appropriate that Lear's bitter and not illogical conclusion should be, "None does offend, none, I say, none" (IV.vi.170),[151] applying, in its anti-Pauline overtones, to mankind in both human and divine realms at once. It therefore becomes clear, once again, that Lear's negation is total and includes, as well, the religious sphere.

Before blind Gloucester, Lear shows justice to be all but blind:

> A man may see how this world goes with no eyes. Look with thine ears: see how yond justice rails upon yond simple thief. Hark, in thine ear: change places, and, handy-dandy, which is the justice, which is the thief? Thou hast seen a farmer's dog bark at a beggar? . . .
>
> And the creature run from the cur? There thou migh'st behold
> The great image of Authority:
> A dog's obey'd in office. (IV.vi.151-161)

Presumably, this canine office of authority is similar to that in the bearbaiting allusion of Gloucester, "I am tied to th' stake, and I must stand the course" (III.vii.53), where, in keeping with the old earl's view of the gods, man is a creature torn for sport. When we recall the proximity of bear pits to the Globe and the fact that sometimes the very theaters themselves were dismantled for bearbaiting,[152] we recapture part of the powerful analogy in the spectators' minds. "A dog's obey'd in office" suggests that "They that have power to hurt" *will* do some, recklessly disinheriting themselves of heaven's graces; but, as may be deduced elsewhere, if "They that have power to hurt" are themselves also the heavens, then their graces are inconsiderable. It is important to recognize, as against those critics, for example, who intone, "after being bound upon his fiery wheel in this life, attaining humility and patience," Lear is "fit for heaven,"[153] that the king has

[151]Cf. Homilies, in *Certaine Sermons*, sig. [B7], "all have offended & have need of the glory of God." Hobbes draws a conclusion more analogous to Lear's: where there is "war of every man, against every man . . . nothing can be unjust. The notions of right and wrong, justice and injustice have there no place. Where there is no common power, there is no law: where no law, no injustice" (*English Works*, III, 115).

[152]John Briley, "Of Stake and Stage," *Shakespeare Survey 8*, ed. Allardyce Nicoll (Cambridge, Eng., 1955), pp. 106-108.

[153]S. L. Bethell, "Shakespeare's Imagery: The Diabolic Images in *Othello*," *Shakespeare Survey 5* (1952), p. 78.

here touched the abyss of disbelief in a nihilism that discounts the heavens themselves.

In addition to the other evidences of Lear's increasing skepticism, we may take his attacks on worldly justice as an indication of his developing point of view. Thus Lear's condemnation of human equity operates parallel to, and coordinate with, his shattered vision of divine justice. So we have, in two great scenes, the theological (IV.vi. 180-185) and the secular (III.vi.36-56), Lear as stage manager of bitter sermon and parodied trial. In III.vi.36-56 he has his daughters tried by the unstable Fool, the mad Tom, and the rustic Kent, the last two disguised and all addressed with judicial esteem by the insane king. As world-upside-down reversal, this scene of "reason in madness"—the insane, yet all-too-sane, probing of sane, yet all-too-mad, human justice—leads into Lear's naturalistically skeptical speech (III.vi.77-79).

It is appropriate that Lear should at once slip into the religious mode of discourse; whereas before (III.vi.36-56), the former chief justice stage-managed a trial scene denying human justice, now the former chief priest undertakes the role of a preacher, denying human felicity (IV.vi.180-185).[154] Again, like Cordelia, Edgar, the Fool ("Fortune, that arrant whore," II.iv.52), and Kent, Lear makes the conventional reference to fortune: "I am even / The natural fool of Fortune" (IV.vi.192-193), but the significant point is the progression in his awareness of himself as victim, from the turning point of Act III (ii.59-60), "I am a man / More sinn'd against than sinning." Approaching the nadir of Gloucester, though consistently and with more heroic courage and more articulate power, Lear has attained the Tantalus vision, the insufficiency of all aids, human and divine.

The lower depths, the point of no apparent return, have been reached; but, as elsewhere in Shakespeare, the depths may be areas of conversion, Hamlet's sea and grave seeming to function as transforming devices. Lazarus-like, Lear, in short, has reached the brink foreseen by Kent (II.ii.165-166): "Nothing almost sees miracles, / But misery." If from one point of view miracles are a manifestation of the intervening power of God's providence, in a world where the

[154]Connected with Plinian skepticism and Renaissance pessimism, Lear's "When we are born, we cry that we are come" (IV.vi.184) is a very frequent *topos* from Wisdom vii.3 which suggests, like the seventh book of Pliny's *Natural History*, that man is from the moment of his entrance an unfavored outcast upon earth.

providence of the gods has been shown to be at best a baffling thing, miracles have no place; that may account, in part, for the "almost" of Kent's remark and for the fact that no other unqualified reference appears in the tragedy. Two other qualified allusions are: first, France's incredulous reply (I.i.221-223) to Lear's accusation of Cordelia,

> which to believe of her,
> Must be a faith that reason without miracle
> Should never plant in me,

or, the possibility is so unlikely that only the unlikely possibility of a miracle would persuade me. Second is Edgar's comment to Gloucester, after the attempted suicide, "Thy life's a miracle" (IV.vi.55). In the context of deception—it is obvious to the audience that no miracle, but Edgar's benevolent trickery, was operative—and in light of the continual superstitious language in which the old man is addressed by his sons, the allusion seems suspect. In an unprovidential universe, it is suggested, miracles are absent and prayers are generally ineffective. Such mention of miracles dramatically recalls to the spectator their absence—a sharply contrasting beam of tenuous light in a grimly dark and Godforsaken world.

"The Promised End"

> *The heavenly bodies are a wheel of fire. . . .*
> —Anaximander[155]

> *proud Ixions paine,*
> *Or great Prometheus. . . .*
> —Spenser, *Faerie Queene*, VII.vi.29

The king, in the imagery of Kent's great line, climbs up the Jacob's Ladder of misery to the "almost" miracle (cf. II.ii.165-166) of Cordelia's forgiveness:

> You do me wrong to take me out o' th' grave;
> Thou art a soul in bliss; but I am bound
> Upon a wheel of fire, that mine own tears
> Do scald like molten lead, (IV.vii.45-48)

once again a syncretic image, which the New Arden editor annotates merely as Christian in its reference to hell and purgatory. On

[155]As reported by Hippolytos, in John Burnet, *Early Greek Philosophy* (New York, 1957), p. 66. But see also Charles H. Kahn, *Anaximander and the Origins of Greek Cosmology* (New York, 1960), pp. 85-93.

the other hand, the authors of *Classical Myth and Legend in Renaissance Dictionaries* explain it merely in terms of pagan mythology perhaps derived from Thomas Cooper's *Thesaurus linguæ romanæ & britannicæ* (1578), suggesting that the legend of Ixion and his offspring was in Shakespeare's mind throughout much of Act IV.[156] Cooper's account is of "*Ixion*, A king of Thessalye. . . . Jupiter . . . made a cloude lyke unto Juno, and delyvered hir to him, on whome hee begat the people called *Centauri*. But when hee had avaunted, that he had companyed with Juno, hee was driven downe into hell, and there bounde to a wheele alwayes turning and full of Serpentes, as poets feigne" (sig. 7Lii). Ixion, like Prometheus, was a rebel against the gods and, indeed, has been considered the Greek Cain.[157] In addition, Harsnet in his *Declaration* (1603) refers to "*Ixion* with his wheele" (p. 73), and Mornay observes of "the Tragediewryter, that ere hee leave the Stage, he will tye the wicked Ixion to the Wheele."[158] Instead of in hell, Ixion's "wheel of fire" was sometimes placed in the heavens; the connection is made in Christopher Middleton's *Historie of Heaven* (1596), describing "the Wheele that wrought *Ixions* paine . . ." and the gods that placed "his rack within the firmament" (sig. E1^{v}).[159] The traditional association between the wheel and the sun recalled, for example, by Verstegen's figure of ancient English worship, cited earlier, as well as by the Delphic cult of Apollo and by Rhodes's worship of an Apollo Ixios, may ironically connect Lear's trust in "the sacred radiance of the sun" (I.i.109) and in his centaur daughters with his "wheel of fire." Finally, the authors of the study of Renaissance dictionaries mentioned above conclude that "The excerpts from the play and the *Thesaurus* show that Lear was father of the lustful daughters as Ixion was of the lecherous Centaurs; that Lear, like Ixion, was bound to a wheel (of fire)" (p. 116). But both the New Arden annotator and the authors of this treatise ignore the point that the wheel-of-fire allusion, like others in *Lear*, is syncretic, a product of the play's peculiarly multiple syncretic vision.[160]

156Starnes and Talbert, pp. 115-116.

157Cf. *The Odes of Pindar*, tr. John Sandys, Loeb Classical Lib. (1915), pp. 173, 175.

158*A Woorke concerning the Trewnesse of the Christian Religion*, p. 197.

159See also Henry Hutton, *Follie's Anatomie . . . with a Compendious History of Ixion's Wheele* (1619).

160Iconographically, the burning wheels of the sun were familiar in the Renaissance; cf. a panel by Piero di Cosimo (ca. 1510) at Strasbourg, which shows Prometheus

After the death of an illusion, in a life that converges in madness to a living death, Lear (like Gloucester by Edgar) is taken back to "life" by Cordelia's forgiving grace. To say, with some commentators, that Lear repents and attains humility and patience, thus becoming fit for heaven, in a kind of revivified morality pattern, is to underestimate the complexity both of the play and of Lear's character. Such yearners for poetic justice are well, if only partially, answered in the memorable words of Lamb: "A happy ending!—as if the living martyrdom that Lear had gone through,—the flaying of his feelings alive, did not make a fair dismissal from the stage of life the only decorous thing for him. . . . As if the childish pleasure of getting his gilt robes and sceptre again could tempt him to act over again his misused station. . . ."[161]

Lear, we conclude, returns "purged," but with a difference; the drama is not reversible, and nothing is as it was; the "living martyrdom" has been intellectual as well as physical, religious as well as secular, and has gone much too far. When the convalescent old man murmurs, "You are a spirit, I know; where did you die?" (IV.vii.49), and when he attempts to kneel before Cordelia as she asks benediction of him, we reach the forgiveness scene which some critics, conveniently forgetting that the tragedy has an act yet to run, take, in effect, to represent the conclusion. Brought back from the living dead, Lear can only murmur, "Pray you now, forget and forgive:

lighting his torch at the sun's wheels (Piero borrowed some details from Boccaccio's work, translated as *La geneologia de gli dei de gentili*). Cf. Verstegen's illustration of the sun as a wheel of fire, *A Restitution of Decayed Intelligence*, p. 69. On the wheel as image of the sun, later becoming Fortune's wheel, see Henri Gaidoz, *Études de mythologie gauloise* (Paris, 1886), pp. 8-9, 47-49, 56-60. Cf. the commentary on Jacob Boehme (Hans L. Martensen, *Jacob Boehme: His Life and Teaching* [New York, 1949], p. 57): ". . . when the greedy egoism is minded . . . to rise out of its abyss, and to ascend so as to outstretch its dark huge wings. . . . the *Wheel of Birth* is set on fire. . . . The *Wheel of Birth* now becomes, in the most literal sense, a *Wheel of Anguish*." Cf. *The Shepardes Kalender* (1570?), sig. [Evv], showing sufferers in hell bound on wheels, with fiery dragons at them. Lear's "wheel of fire" suggests also Fortune's wheel, as well as the wheel (cf. V.iii.314) upon which prisoners were punished. Lear is, ultimately, the fool of Fortune (IV.vi.192-193), racked upon its wheel (V.iii.314-315); cf. the *rota nativitas* (Vulgate reading of James iii.6; *Biblia Sacra* [Roma, 1592]). See John E. Hankins, *Shakespeare's Derived Imagery* (Lawrence, Kan., 1953), p. 18, on the figure of a man stretched upon the wheel, bearing the inscription: "Sic ornati nascuntur in hac mortali vita. Est velut aqua labuntur deficiens ita." Hence, Edmund's wheel of Fortune and Lear's wheel of fire may finally be related.

[161]In New Variorum *Lear*, p. 421.

I am old and foolish" (IV.vii.84); in his momentary decline to passivity he falls from the Lear we know to something else, not Lear but more like his partner in sorrow, the Earl of Gloucester. "This is not Lear," as he himself earlier (I.iv.234-235) exclaims; "Does Lear walk thus? speak thus?" With the exception of this brief interlude after a lengthy madness, which commentators mistakenly take as the be-all and the end-all of the play, the defiant Prometheus and Lear-Agonistes of the previous passages comes back to us in the final scene.

Nevertheless, it is true that still, for a time, Lear's reconciliation with Cordelia may seem to involve a kind of return to "piety," but it is a "piety" that hangs by the single thread of reunion and is expressed solely in terms of his daughter. The prison to which, captive, they are led is, microcosmically, the world which surrounds good; yet evil has no power over the Stoic and the Christian martyr. Boethian in their *contemptus mundi* view and syncretic, Cordelia and Lear make a clearing in the universe of evil through their love. Evil and the failure of justice in this world are accepted: "We are not the first," she explains, suffering not for herself but through her love for her father (V.iii.3-6). When she asks, "Shall we not see these daughters and these sisters?" Lear replies, apparently purged of the rancorous threats we found earlier,

> No, no, no, no! Come, let's away to prison;
> We two alone will sing like birds i' th' cage:
> When thou dost ask me blessing, I'll kneel down,
> And ask of thee forgiveness: so we'll live,
> And pray, and sing, and tell old tales, and laugh
> At gilded butterflies, and hear poor rogues
> Talk of court news; and we'll talk with them too,
> Who loses and who wins; who's in, who's out;
> And take upon 's the mystery of things,
> As if we were Gods' spies. . . . (V.iii.8-17)

By a transcendent stroke Shakespeare has replaced the gods, who are now almost inert in Lear's pantheon, with a pair of doomed prisoners, who in their earthly suffering become in turn the observers of mortals. To this cyclical irony does the vision of the gods lead.

If Gloucester's

> As flies to wanton boys, are we to th' Gods;
> They kill us for their sport (IV.i.36-37)

has been more than appreciated for its comment on the human condition, Lear's "We two alone will sing like birds i' th' cage" appears in its implicit sense of passive affliction to have escaped critical emphasis. Indeed, it seems from one standpoint to carry Gloucester's observation further: while there may be a purpose, play or sport, in the gods' cruelty, and man can at least have the flies' illusion of escape, Lear's later vision is of a cage—a prisoned microcosm worse than the prison of Richard II—stationary and enclosed, perhaps at times covered, or borne about for unacknowledged purposes by those greater mysterious powers which imprison man. "Wee thinke cag'd birds sing," aptly observes Flamineo in Webster's *The White Devil*, "when indeed they crie" (V.iv.117).[162]

"Flies" (IV.i.36), "birds" (V.iii.9), "butterflies" (V.iii.13)—fragile creatures of an at most trifling *raison d'être* and, on their various levels, passive, hunted, and ephemeral. Humanity is the passive victim of—what? for—what? Human suffering, Gloucester and Lear seem to imply, is meaningless, at best trivial, anticipating Hobbes's vision of primitive human life as nasty, brutish, and short.

Like Chaucer's Troilus rising at the end to the "eighthe spere" whence he "fully gan despise / This wrecched world, and held al vanite" (Bk. V, ll. 1809, 1816-17), like Lycidas, "sunk low, but mounted high," Cordelia and Lear seem momentarily cleared of earthly despair. Indeed, Lear affirms, developing the irony expressed above, that "Upon such sacrifices . . . / The Gods themselves throw incense" (V.iii.20-21).[163] As in Donne's "The Canonization," the paradoxical reversal of orthodoxy has the function of illuminating an altered perspective. Just as, a few lines earlier, Lear and Cordelia

[162]Cf. *Arcadia*, I, 139:

The house is made a very lothsome cage,
Wherein the birde doth never sing but cry;

and William Alexander, *The Alexandraean Tragedy* (1605-07), ll. 2389-90:

As birds (whose cage of gold the sight deceives)
Do seeme to sing, whil'st they but waile their state.

(*The Poetical Works of Sir William Alexander*, ed. L. E. Kastner and H. B. Charlton, I [Manchester, 1921], 308).

[163]Regarding pagan use of incense, see Edward G. C. F. Atchley, *A History of the Use of Incense in Divine Worship*, Alcuin Club Collections, No. 13 (1909), p. 76: ". . . though all could offer it, it could only be presented to a deity or deified man, and to offer it was to acknowledge the divinity of the person to whom it was offered," supporting the "apotheosis" interpretation above. See Stephen Harrison, *The Arch's of Triumph* (1604), sig. I, contrasting Christian worship with incense and sacrifice as elements of pagan superstition and "Ethnick rite."

are to assume the mantle of divinity by virtue of their sufferings, at least to the extent of becoming "Gods' spies," overlooking transient folly and mutability, so here the father-king protracts the reversal: the gods themselves are to do homage to unique mortals, and a platonized version of Donne's poem is suggested, paradoxical canonization or ironical apotheosis through suffering.[164]

"AND TELL OLD TALES"

If Coleridge's opinion is just that "Old age . . . is itself a character,"[165] it is also true that in *Lear* old age stands for a code of values. For while the identity of some participants nominalistically dissolves, that of others, for example, the Thunder, the Fool, even old age itself, appears to take on a symbolic and realistic value status. In opposition to *Hamlet*, for example, where old men have "a plentiful lack of wit, together with most weak hams" (II.ii.202-203) and to *Troilus and Cressida*, where Nestor's senility is mocked, "old," with its connotations of primogeniture, legitimacy, and hierarchy, has in *Lear*, as in *Macbeth*, a eulogistic sense. On the other hand, as Edmund's hungry generation treads its elders down, old age is dyslogistic among the wicked.

According to *The Booke of Common Prayer* (1590), reciting Psalm 90, "Our tyme is threescore yeares and ten." And "if one see fourscore . . . we count him wondrous old." Yet "of this tyme the strength . . . is nothyng els but paynefull griefe, and we as blastes are gone" (p. 124). Whether Lear's "fourscore and upward" necessarily implied mental decrepitude was, in fact, a disputed point. "Virilitas," as defined by John Withals' school text *A Short Dictionarie for*

[164]Lear's "birds i' th' cage" speech may be related, like Edgar's Dover description (IV.vi.11-24), to Panofsky's (and others') notion of perspective as symbolic form. See also Harry Levin, "The Heights and the Depths: A Scene from 'King Lear,'" in *More Talking of Shakespeare*, ed. John Garrett (1959), pp. 87-103. Both Lear's and Edgar's speeches suggest illusory perspectives, Lear's from the heights of "permanence" upon mutability, a temporal (and spatial) distancing that recalls Donne's "Of the Progresse of the Soule.... The Second Anniversary," ll. 49-50:

> Forget this rotten world; And unto thee
> Let thine owne times as an old storie bee.

Further, both Lear's and Edgar's descriptions involve a *consolatio* of a beloved one: while Lear's is deludedly temporal, and he is shortly to be pulled back into "reality," Edgar's is pseudospatial; and both together underline the pathos and illusory character of the human dimensions.

[165]*Coleridge's Shakespearean Criticism*, ed. Thomas M. Raysor (1930), I, 62.

Yonge Beginners (1556), sig. Wiii, continued from twenty-one until forty, "senectus" from forty to fifty or sixty, and "senium," the age of the protagonists, was the last scene of all. Thomas Wright, however, in *A Succinct Philosophicall Declaration of the Nature of Clymactericall Yeeres, Occasioned by the Death of Queene Elizabeth* (1604), finds the divisions to be products of seven. Man is *in statu virili*, therefore, from twenty-eight to forty-nine (p. 9).[166] In ambivalent fashion, Lear's shadow, Kent, can function with his master; but at forty-eight, "Not so young . . . to love a woman for singing, nor so old to dote on her for anything" (I.iv.40-41), Kent can also stand virile proxy against the villainous young. Although he is at the endpoint of "virilitas," or within "senectus," his "grey beard" (II.ii.63), comparable to Lear's white head (III.ii.24), does not prevent Kent's dominating Oswald, one of the "new" men, who calls him an "ancient ruffian" (II.ii.62).

Although Lear's "infirmity of . . . age" and the "unruly waywardness that infirm and choleric years bring with them" (I.i.293, 298-299) are insisted upon by the wicked sisters, who refer to his state as "dotage" (I.iv.302, 336; II.iv.199), Sir John Davies' *Nosce teipsum* (1599), for example, would dispute their premise, holding that the mind itself need not decay. Replying to such questions as,

> How comes it then, that aged men do doate?
> And that their braines grow sottish, dull, and cold,

Davies explains that, if there is "dotage," it

> is no weakenesse of the mind,
> But of the *Sense*: for if the mind did wast,
> In all old men we should this wasting find,
> When they some certaine terme of yeares had past.
>
> But most of them even to their dying howre,
> Retaine a mind more lively, quick, and strong,
> And better use their understanding power,
> Then when their braines were warme, & limmes were
> yong.[167]

166Precise divisions of man's age varied somewhat; cf. *Batman uppon Bartholome* (1582), fol. 70v; Levinus Lemnius, *The Touchstone of Complexions* (1581), foll. 29v-31; *The Most Excellent . . . Booke, of . . . Arcandam* (1592), sig. M2v; Andreas Laurentius, *A Discourse of the Preservation of the Sight*, tr. Richard Surphlet (1599), pp. 173-174; Henry Cuffe, *The Differences of the Ages of Mans Life* (1607), pp. 117-121.

167*The Poems of Sir John Davies*, ed. Clare Howard (New York, 1941), pp. 180, 184.

Indeed, the evil daughters' hopeful estimate of their father's senility —"Old fools," observes Goneril, "are babes again" (I.iii.20)—anticipates a modern critical evaluation of Lear's "puerile intellect."[168] In contrast, at his undiminished force and intensified reaction the villainesses might, like the astonished Lady Macbeth, have exclaimed: "Yet who would have thought the old man to have had so much blood in him?" (V.i.44-45).

If, in *Lear* and the relatively close *Macbeth*, Shakespeare was more disposed to favor the old, it was not because much time had elapsed since *Hamlet* and *Troilus and Cressida*, composed, in fact, only a few years earlier. Rather, it may have been related to the expedient affirmation of the antiquity and right of the foreign intruder, who in 1603 had succeeded hard upon the nearly half-century reign of the beloved English queen. Following the fabricators of the "Tudor myth," supporting Elizabeth, the King's Men's chief dramatist, about the time of the Gunpowder Plot, sketched in sequence the new ruler's ancestral predecessors on the English and the Scottish thrones.

For the Stuart innovator was repeatedly hailed as the second founder of the British realm, "our second Brute and King,"[169] and himself spoke of "the heritage of the succession and Monarchie, which hath bene a kingdome, to which I am in descent, 300. yeeres before Christ."[170] Contemporary evidence suggests the widely felt necessity of publicizing such ancient claims.[171] In 1604 George Owen Harry, for example, outdid himself in *The Genealogy of the High and Mighty Monarch, James . . . with His Lineall Descent from Noah, by Divers Direct Lynes to Brutus, First Inhabiter of This Ile of Brittayne.*[172] In the same year Lodowick Lloyd's *The Practice of Policy* was dedicated to James, who, he says, "in one day enriched England

[168] G. Wilson Knight, *The Wheel of Fire: Interpretations of Shakespearian Tragedy* (1960), p. 162, among other disparaging commentators.

[169] See John Nichols, *The Progresses . . . of King James the First* (1828), I, 572.

[170] *His Majesties Speech to . . . Parliament . . . the Last Day of March 1607* ([1607]), sig. F2.

[171] See Charles B. Millican, *Spenser and the Table Round: A Study in the Contemporaneous Background for Spenser's Use of the Arthurian Legend* (Cambridge, Mass., 1932); A. E. Parsons, "The Trojan Legend in England: Some Instances of Its Application to the Politics of the Times," *MLR*, XXIV (1929), 253-264, 394-408.

[172] "Lhyr" figures in this "lineall descent" on pp. 8-9.

& Ireland with a king, and the whole Empire of Brytayne with a Prince, to whome it was reserved and continued from *Brutus* the first King, to your Majesty the second King, not as to a stranger, but to a just & a lawfull king of the stocke and linage of *Brutus*, to succeed and sit on *Brutus* seat 2800. yeeres after *Brutus*" (sig. A2). Significantly, Edward Coke found it advisable to insist in the Court of Star Chamber on May 18, 1603, that James's "lawfull, juste & lineall title to the Crowne of Englaunde, comes not by succession onelye, or by election, but from god onelye, (so that there is no *interregnum*, as the ignoraunte dothe suppose, untill the ceremonie of coronation), by reason of his lineall discente."[173] Such pagan English progenitors, indeed, were supposed by some contemporaries really to have existed, Richard Harvey's *Philadelphus* (1593) arguing that Brutus "is no *fabulous Prince* . . . no counterfeit man, but a corporall possessor of this Iland; let them saye what they can" (p. 13). Because of the stage, few men by James's time, adds Heywood's *An Apology for Actors* (1612), could not "discourse of any notable thing . . . from the landing of *Brute*, untill this day . . ." (sig. F3).

On August 27, 1605, at Oxford, with Shakespeare possibly present, Dr. Matthew Gwinn recited some Latin verses to James: "There is a story, O renowned King, that once in the olden time the fateful sisters foretold to thy descendants an endless empire. . . . Bring back great Canute . . . Greater than thy ancestors. . . ." Striking a popular note, Gwinn exclaimed, "Hail thou whom Britain, now united though formerly divided, cherishes."[174] Returning to such "olden time," Shakespeare delineated the pagan pathos of a predecessor who, in obvious contrast to James's wisdom in uniting Scotland and England—compare the title of Anthony Munday's *The Triumphes of Re-united Britania* (1605)— had foolishly divided those realms.[175]

[173]*Les reportes del cases in Camera Stellata 1593-1609*, ed. William P. Baildon (1894), pp. 163-164.

[174]Cited in Henry N. Paul, *The Royal Play of Macbeth* (New York, 1950), pp. 163-164; Gwinn's *Vertumnus* (1607), sig. H3.

[175]On James's determined stand against division, expressed notably in 1604, see David H. Willson, "King James I and Anglo-Scottish Unity," in *Conflict in Stuart England: Essays in Honour of Wallace Notestein*, ed. William A. Aiken and Basil D. Henning (New York, 1960), pp. 41-55. James hoped even that the names of England and Scotland should vanish in the name of Britain. In Munday's work Thamesis calls James "my second Brute" (sig. [Biv^{v}]); cf. sig. Ciii. Numerous pamphlets appeared ca. 1604

Further, that Lear, following his own unilluminated paganism, offered little threat of identification with the king or of infection to his subjects, is made clear, for example, from James's own remarks at the Hampton Court conference of 1604: "... neither did wee now border upon Heathenish nations, neither are any of them conversant with us, or commorant [dwelling] among us, who, thereby, might take occasion to bee strengthened, or confirmed in *Paganisme*."[176] The distance between Christianity and heathendom is still further emphasized, for instance, in *The Judgement, or Exposition of Dreames* of Artemidorus Daldianus (1606): "... seeing that in the worke it selfe there are many superstitions of the Pagans, which wold have bin ridiculous at this present" (sig. A2^v).

Hence, *Lear*, like *Macbeth*, appealed not only to a paramount interest of James, styled by Laud "The most learned prince that this kingdom hath ever known for matters of religion,"[177] a king "so fond of theology," complained Casaubon, "that he cares very little to attend to any literary subject."[178] Nor did these plays merely appease his antisuperstitious bias, through *Lear*'s protagonists of superstitious and skeptical leanings and *Macbeth*'s villain-hero, a victim of deceptive supernatural soliciting who later became a victim of what James in another connection termed a "cauterized conscience"—the last, the royal theologian declared, was the "mother of Atheisme."[179] Gratifying his patron's genealogical concerns, these tragedies of Shakespeare, by their pageantry and *tableaux vivants*, also vividly reminded the Stuart king's new English court and public of the venerable seniority of his line. Not without reason did Ben Jonson, an expert in such matters, pronounce Shakespeare to have pleased both "Eliza, and our James."

---

favoring unity of Scotland and England. Interestingly, in the light of our play, the rejected daughter figures as Scotland and the father as England in John Thornborough's *A Discourse... Proving the... Necessitie of the... Union of... England and Scotland* (1604), pp. 24-25: "And albeit some fathers can be content to disinherite their owne daughters.... I account such parents unkind and unnaturall, where selfe love of their name, maketh them forget themselves, and forsake their owne flesh."

[176]William Barlow, *The Summe and Substance of the Conference* (1604), p. 74.

[177]*The Works of... William Laud*, VI (Oxford, 1857), 6.

[178]Mark Pattison, *Isaac Casaubon, 1559-1614* (1875), p. 321.

[179]*Basilicon Doron*, p. 15.

"THIS GREAT DECAY"

But keepes the earth her round proportion still?
—Donne, "An Anatomie of the World. . . .
The First Anniversary"

As Lear's "O Heavens . . . if you yourselves are old" (II.iv.191-193) suggests the *senectus mundi* and decay-of-nature theme, it may further recall Renaissance disclosures that corruption afflicted not only the sublunar world but also the heavens themselves. For such discoveries as new stars in the firmament ran counter to the pious notion of "the firmnesse of the heavens," as described in Henry Church's *Miscellanea philo-theologica* (1637). Citing Psalms xix.1, cxix.90, 91, and Hebrews xii.28, Church explains, "They are called Firmament for stability. . . . Our bodies are generated and soone corrupted, but the Heavens continue to this day" (p. 177). Hence, Lear's suggestion of the heavens' old age may anticipate his final hyperbolic onslaught (V.iii.257-259) upon their permanence.[180]

Similarly, if Lear insinuates heavenly mutability, he seems elsewhere in conflict with the Renaissance ideal of earthly perfection. Asserting the incorruptible perfection of the heavens, José de Acosta's *The Naturall and Morall Historie of the East and West Indies* (1604) assails the vain philosophers of his age who question this position. "Without doubt," piously explains Acosta, while "the Heaven is of a round and perfect figure . . . the earth likewise . . . joyning with the water, makes one globe or round bowle framed of these two elements. . . . to the most perfect body . . . we must give the most perfect figure, which . . . is round . . ." (pp. 5-6). Alexander Ross in his *The New Planet No Planet* (1646) agrees with Jerome, who holds "that the opinion of the earths roundnesse is the most common opinion . . ." (p. 45).[181] As Lear finally exhorts his listeners to "crack"

[180]See the traditional notion in Oedipus' speech to Theseus (Sophocles, *Oedipus at Colonus,* tr. F. Storr, Loeb Classical Lib. [1912], p. 207, ll. 607-609):

to the gods alone
Is given immunity from eld and death;
But nothing else escapes all-ruinous time.

Cf. the remark on the heavens' susceptibility to old age in Montaigne, III, 278, and Lucian's *Timon, or the Misanthrope*, tr. Harmon, Loeb Classical Lib. (1915), II, 329.

[181]See also Marjorie Hope Nicolson, *The Breaking of the Circle: Studies in the Effect of the "New Science" upon Seventeenth Century Poetry* (Evanston, Ill., 1950). This title suggests another assault upon special providence implicit in the probings of sixteenth- and seventeenth-century astronomers. Mentioning Copernicus and Kepler, e.g., Burton in his *Anatomy* (Oxford, 1621), p. 328, asks regarding possible inhabitants of a plurality of worlds, ". . . are we or they Lords of the World, and how are all things made for man?"

"heaven's vault" (V.iii.259),[182] at a midpoint he bids the thunder "Strike flat the thick rotundity o' th' world" (III.ii.7), recalling perhaps also the "round-womb'd" fertility that Gloucester glances at in the opening lines (I.i.14). It is, indeed, that natural "rotundity" and "perfection," containing Cordelia's "bless'd secrets" and "unpublish'd virtues of the earth" (IV.iv.15-16), which Lear in his final scene finds unprofitable, stale, and flat: Cordelia, he mourns, is "dead as earth" (V.iii.261).[183]

Related to the "ripeness" motif, Renaissance "decay" thus afflicted both heaven and earth. "The opinion of the Worlds decay," observes George Hakewill in 1627 (*An Apologie of the . . . Providence of God* [Oxford], p. 1), "is so generally received, not onely among the Vulgar, but of the Learned both Divines and others, that the very commonnes of it, makes it currant with many, without any further examination." That the world was deteriorating and that men also appeared progressively smaller and shorter-lived were views which, indeed, on the macrocosmic and microcosmic level, seemed widely accepted. In antiquity Horace (*Odes*, Bk. III, Ode vi) had spoken of an increasing vileness and degeneracy from parent to offspring; and, similarly, Seneca, Petrarch, and Luther, among others, had offered testimony to the *topos* of the degradation of the world. The Homilies (*Certaine Sermons*, II, sig. H2) say that "good things do by litle and little ever decay." Spenser reflects the idea of decay since the Golden Age,[184] while Donne is eloquent on the subject: "And freely men confesse that this world's spent."[185] Andreas Laurentius' *A Discourse of the Preservation of the Sight* (1599) observes "the lamentable times and miserable daies, that are come upon us in this last and weakest age of the world . . ." (sig. A3). Human senility

[182]In similar terms, Lear's shadow, Kent, anticipates his master's subsequent outburst; Kent "bellow'd out," says Edgar, "As he'd burst heaven" (V.iii.212-213).

[183]"The earth grosest and basest of all the elements," notes Barnabe Googe in the margin, p. 112, of his translation of Palingenius' *Zodiake* (1576). Cf. "base earth," *Two Gentlemen of Verona*, II.iv.159; *Richard II*, II.iv.20, III.iii.191; "vilest earth," *1 Henry IV*, V.iv.91. More important, dull earth, the heavy center of the world, itself lacks motion. Cf. Palingenius, pp. 111, 218, and 112: ". . . the senslesse Corse, doth stirre as doth a stone." Lear's lament over Cordelia's motionless body, "She's dead as earth" (V.iii.261), emphasizing the distinction between the quick and the dead, prepares for the absoluteness of "Thou'lt come no more" (V.iii.307).

[184]"Two Cantos of Mutabilitie," *Faerie Queene*, VII.vi, vii.

[185]"An Anatomie of the World. . . . The First Anniversary," l. 209.

is employed by John Downame in *Foure Treatises* (1613) to describe "the world now waxing old, and as it were horeheaded . . ." (p. 97). "The *Sunne, Moone, Stars* . . . ," Thomas Draxe's *The Earnest of Our Inheritance* (1613) laments, "are much altered & mightily decayed . . ." (p. 17).[186]

Man's life, complains Robert Anton in *The Philosophers Satyrs* (1616), is shorter than before. Mourning the "totall *wrack* of *earth* and *heaven* above" (sig. C3ᵛ) in this last age, Anton records the shrinking of height and life-span of

> *man* that *noble creature*,
> Scanted of *time*, and stinted by weake *nature*,
> That in foretimes saw *Jubiles* of *yeares*.

In our day, unfortunately,

> man to *wormes meate* turnes in fewer *dayes*:
> *Pigmies* for *Gyants*, that with *Babell power*
> Were wont to scale the high *Olympiade Tower*,
> And wrastle with the *Gods*: now *dwarfes* are borne,
> Ne're made to fight, but made to *natures* scorne:
> The *Arcadian Kings* two hundred yeares did live,
> But now the thriftie *heavens* doe scarcely give
> Halfe of that *pension* to the noblest *man*,
> His *grave* but *sixe foot long, his life a span.* (sig. [C4])

Such contemporary views of the Arcadian and relatively early period of the world in which *Lear* is set may reveal the dramatic use which Shakespeare has made of the Renaissance idea of decay. Indeed, Lear may himself be a microcosm of what Downame above termed "the world now waxing . . . horeheaded." "Infirmities of this last age of the world, like to the infirmitie of olde age," summarizes John Carpenter's *A Preparative to Contentation* (1597, sig. [Ee2ᵛ]). "O ruin'd piece of Nature!" cries Gloucester at sight of his king; "This great world / Shall so wear out to naught" (IV.vi.136-137). Later, Albany describes him as "this great decay" (V.iii.297). Kent refers to his "difference and decay" (V.iii.288). After ripeness, rot; after rottenness, decay; comparable are Gloucester's "a man may rot even here" (V.ii.8) and Lear's remark on Kent, "He's dead and rotten" (V.iii.285). Underlining the prevailing irony of unripeness,

[186]See also Victor Harris, *All Coherence Gone* (Chicago, 1949).

Gloucester and Lear are overripe, the latter having "but usurp'd his life" (V.iii.317); and Cordelia is hardly ripe. Ripeness, at least here, does not seem to be "all."

Finally, Lear and Gloucester, part of a world and a world of values that are passing away, are held to have exceeded both in suffering and longevity those who will follow. Although Bradley, reading them apart from their Renaissance context, judged the last two lines "a poor conclusion to such a play" (p. 377), the final couplet brings the wheel full circle, remirrors the protagonists, and appropriately prophesies the decline:

> The oldest hath borne most: we that are young
> Shall never see so much, nor live so long.

"TAKE UPON 'S THE MYSTERY OF THINGS"

> *Oh fonde is he, who thinkes to understand*
> *The mysteries of Jove his secrete mynde.*
> —Gascoigne, *Jocasta*, III.ii.87-88

When Lear promises Cordelia they two alone will "take upon 's the mystery of things, / As if we were Gods' spies" (V.iii.16-17), a Renaissance sense of "take upon" seems to have eluded commentators. That the phrase, in its customary context of divine mystery and forbidden knowledge, indicated a presumption beyond permitted human limits may be deduced from such passages as the following: Florio's Montaigne, "These people who . . . know nothing themselves, and yet will *take upon them* to governe the world and know all" (II, 247);[187] Nashe, *Pierce Penilesse* (1592), ". . . therefore doo we *take upon us* to prophecy, that we may . . . bringe men in admiration . . . and so be counted for Gods" (*Works*, I, 237); Thomas Tymme's *A Plaine Discoverie of Ten English Lepers* (1592), "let no man *take upon him* to scan and sift Gods workes. . . . But wicked men take unto themselves . . . to murmur against God" (sig. [L4]); John Dove's *Confutation* (1605), ". . . *taking upon them* to be the great Polititians of the worlde . . . their zeale is Atheisme" (p. 4); *Cymbeline* (ca. 1609), ". . . you must either be directed by some that *take upon them* to know, or to *take upon yourself* that which I am sure you do not know . . ." (V.iv.185-188), rebuking human presumption in claiming knowledge of the "undiscover'd country" after death;

[187]Here, and in following citations, I have italicized the phrase in question.

Thomas Draxe's *The Worldes Resurrection* (1609), "So that *Paul* doth not *take upon him* the office of an interpreter, but applieth it to his time. . . . *I would not have you ignorant of this mistery*. Mistery here importeth a thing unknowne unto men or not sufficiently understood of them. . . . *God hideth the knowledge of his secrets* . . ." (pp. 91-92); *Looke Up and See Wonders* (1628), ". . . it is not fit that any man, should *take uppon him*, to write too broad and busie Comments on . . . these [celestial bodies, etc.]. Let us not be so daring as to pry into the closet of Gods determinations" (p. 17); and John Selden's *Table-Talk* (1689), "We cannot tell what is a Judgment of God, 'tis presumption to *take upon us* to know" (p. 26).

John Wilkins' *A Discourse concerning the Beauty of Providence* (1649) declares, "If there be a Commonwealth amongst Ants and Bees . . . 'twould make a man smile to think, that they should *take upon them* the censure of State-matters amongst us men . . ." (p. 78). He argues in "reproof of those, that murmur and repine at the works of providence, that *take upon them* the magisteriall judgement of events . . . we should not *take upon us* the peremptorie censure of . . . things which we cannot understand . . . 'tis extreame folly for men to *take upon them* the censure of Times and Providences, as if they were competent Judges of such matters" (pp. 77, 83).[188]

Like Lear's "take upon 's," his "mystery of things" thus may be seen to contain presumptuous or blasphemous overtones. In *Coriolanus*, for example, Volumnia alludes to "those mysteries which heaven / Will not have earth to know" (IV.ii.35-36). Although Lear starts by rendering unto the gods that which is theirs and swears by "The mysteries of Hecate and the night" (I.i.110), he ends by presuming to violate the gods' prerogatived arcana, as Draxe above defines "mistery," the mysteries of things. The "mysteria caelestis operis," as Ficino translated Plato,[189] was an obsession of Shakespeare's world, poised between traditional beliefs and the empirical new age. Innumerable treatises chastise the presumption of such innovators and of all overcurious souls. For example, Luther condemns "all those . . . fools who, like Aristotle, seek the knowledge of things

188Cf. also Huarte de San Juan, *The Examination of Mens Wits* (1594), pp. 217-218: ". . . men that *take upon them* to governe the whole world . . . ," paralleling Montaigne above; John Carpenter, *A Preparative to Contentation* (1597), pp. 237-238.

189Cited in Raymond Klibansky, "Plato's Parmenides in the Middle Ages and the Renaissance," *Medieval and Renaissance Studies*, I (1941-43), 314.

through their causes, for they are incomprehensible."[190] Similarly, Calvin is vehement against those who trespass on the mysteries of God's "secret counsels"; the reasons governing His will are concealed from us.[191] In addition, Montaigne denounces such presumption on the part of astrological prognosticators and of "interpreters and controulers of Gods secret desseignes, presuming to finde out the causes of every accident, and to prie into the secrets of Gods divine will, the incomprehensible motives of his works" (I, 230). "The ill successe of our age," laments La Primaudaye's *The French Academie* (1586), "affoordeth us too manie miserable testimonies, wherin at this day we see nothing but contrarieties of opinions and uncertainties . . .", the result, he observes, of the "bold curiosities" of those "who have sought to plucke . . . out of heaven the secrets hid from the angels . . . filling our times with trouble and confusion under that false pretence" (p. 161). In a letter to Spenser, Gabriel Harvey, regarding the 1580 earthquake, decries the new science's prying into the mystery of things: "I cannot see . . . howe a man on Earth, should be of . . . so familiar acquaintance with God in Heaven, (. . . without any . . . warrant) to reveale hys incomprehensible mysteries . . . to give sentence of his Majesties secret and inscrutable purposes. As if they had a key for all the lockes in Heaven."[192]

"I see many over-bold with God Almighty," declared Queen Elizabeth in 1585, "making too many subtle scannings of His blessed will. . . ."[193] And James, in a proclamation of 1610, rebukes men's probings into the "highest Mysterys in the Godhead," complaining that they would sit with God "in his most private Closet and become privy of his most inscrutable Counsels."[194] Concerning the "deeper misteries" and those who search "more curiouslie into the secrets of nature," Nashe demands, "Who made them so privie to the secrets of the Almightie . . . ?" (I, 23; cf. I, 133).

Hooker alludes several times to the "heavenly mysteries," the "Cœli mysterium," the "mystery whereof is higher than the reach of

[190] *Werke*, LVI (Weimar, 1938), 116.

[191] *Institutes*, I.xvii.2. In answer to the question of what God did before he created the world, Calvin, echoing Augustine, cites the reply that "he buylded Hell for curious fooles" (I.xiv.1).

[192] *Works*, ed. Grosart, I, 56-57.

[193] G. W. Prothero, ed. *Select Statutes and Other Constitutional Documents . . . Elizabeth and James I* (Oxford, 1913), p. 221.

[194] John Cowell, *A Law Dictionary: Or the Interpreter* (1708), Preface, sig. b1v.

the thoughts of men."[195] Barnabe Rich's *Faultes* (1606) declares, "I will not presume to wade any further into the secret judgements of God . . ." (fol. 35). "Man, dreame no more of curious mysteries . . .", advises Greville's *Cælica*, "*For Gods works are like him, all infinite*."[196] Despite such warnings, George Carleton's *An Examination* (1626) points out, "it hath beene the unbridled humour of some, to be still prying into Gods secrets, and to runne rashly and irreverently into these Mysteries" (sig. B1^{v}). "We are ignorant of the back-parts or lower side of his Divinity," admits Sir Thomas Browne's *Religio medici*. "Therefore to prie into the maze of his Counsels is not only folly in man, but presumption even in Angels."[197]

If the sense of "take upon" and "mystery of things" involves a presumption in Renaissance religious terms, "Gods' spies" may suggest, in addition, a syncretic or pagan reference.[198] Familiar to Shakespeare were "daemons," known also as spirits, geniuses, or angels, who are, says Plutarch, in place of God, who is not present "to intermeddle or employ himselfe in person," "ministers of the gods . . . as if they were deputies, officers, and secretaries . . . those be the Dæmons which are their espies and escouts, going too and fro throughout all parts, some to oversee and direct the sacrifices, and sacred rites and ceremonies performed to the gods: others to chastice and punish the enormious and outragious offences and wrongs committed by men."[199] Mornay in *A Woorke concerning the Trewnesse*

[195]*Ecclesiastical Polity,* in *Works,* II, 541; I, 258, 262.

[196]Sonnet LXXXVIII, *Poems and Dramas,* ed. Bullough, I, 136, 279.

[197]*Works,* I, 18. See also Jewel, *Works . . . Third Portion* (1848), 327. The natural man's heart, declares Carpenter's *A Preparative to Contentation,* p. 280, "is blinded with his owne malice, which understandeth not the mysteries of the spirit of God. . . ." John Wilkins' *A Discourse concerning the Beauty of Providence* (pp. 71, 72) advises that we should "be content to be ignorant in the *finall* cause of things. . . . We do in this world (for the most part) see onely the *dark side* of Providence."

[198]Both Quarto and Folio have "Gods." Whether Muir, following Wilfrid Perrett (*The Story of King Lear from Geoffrey of Monmouth to Shakespeare,* Palaestra, XXXV [Berlin, 1904], 250-251), is correct in reading "Gods'," or most other modern editors in reading "God's," the audience could have heard the perhaps deliberately ambiguous word in the same way.

[199]*Morals,* tr. Holland, p. 1329. See Michael Lloyd, "Plutarch's Daemons in Shakespeare," *N&Q,* N.S. VII (Sept. 1960), 324-327. Cf. Pettazzoni, *The All-Knowing God,* pp. 150-151, on the Neoplatonist Porphyry's association of divine providence with the good *daimones,* whose observation nothing can elude; and on Epictetus' *Discourses,* treating the universal vision of deity and the assignment to each man of a watchful *daimon;* see also Pettazzoni, p. 158, regarding daemons in Chrysippus and other writers.

of the Christian Religion recalls Socrates' remark that "when the good man departeth this world . . . he becommeth a Demon" (p. 346). Heinrich Cornelius Agrippa, *Of the Vanitie and Uncertaintie of Artes and Sciences* (1569), defines "*Dæmon,* that is, a Spirite, as if it were *Sapiens,* that is, Wise" (fol. 2). And Nashe refers to daemons as "spies & tale carriers" (I, 232).[200] Those "visible spirits" sent down by the heavens, in Albany's exclamation, "to tame these vilde offences" (IV.ii.46-47), hence may be related to Plutarch's daemons. As divine secretaries, they are privy to providence and the "mystery of things." Such beliefs regarding divine assistants are present not only in Plutarch but also generally in Stoicism. The high irony in Lear's desperate presumption is thus achieved by the brutal sequence, demonstrating father and daughter to be not only *not* "Gods' spies" but, from Lear's point of view, to be lower than the lowest in creation.[201]

"THOU'LT COME NO MORE"

> *For the condition of the children of men, and the condition of beasts are even as one . . . As the one dyeth, so dyeth the other: for they have al one breath, and there is no excellencie of man above the beast: for all is vanitie.*
>
> –Ecclesiastes iii.19

> *She, shee is dead; she's dead: when thou knowest this,*
> *Thou knowest how poore a trifling thing man is.*
>
> –Donne, "An Anatomie of the World. . . .
> The First Anniversary"

No human power, Lear asserts, is ever again to sever them:

> Have I caught thee?
> He that parts us shall bring a brand from heaven,
> And fire us hence like foxes.
>
> (V.iii.21-23)

The old king's defiance, at the moment of their remanding by Edmund ("Take them away," V.iii.19), is hardly the humility and pa-

[200]See also E. Vernon Arnold, *Roman Stoicism* (Cambridge, Eng., 1911), pp. 232-233; Pierre de Ronsard, *Hymne des Daimons,* ed. Albert-Marie Schmidt (Paris, 1938); E. C. Knowlton, "The Genii of Spenser," *SP,* XXV (1928), 439-456; George Puttenham, *The Arte of English Poesie* (1589), ed. Gladys D. Willcock and Alice Walker (Cambridge, Eng., 1936), Bk. I, Ch. iii, p. 7; *Winter's Tale,* V.i.203.

[201]See the spy-intelligencer motif which may prepare for the last-scene reference: I.v.2-4; II.iv.249; III.i.22-25, 30-34; III.v.11; III.vii.12.

tience that are, according to critics mentioned earlier, to make him fit for heaven. Instead, we are given warning of the return of an intensified old Lear whom we have known for most of the play; and this warning occurs in his last speech before his final and most choleric outburst. We next see him some two hundred lines later, cued by the pious Albany's "The Gods defend her!" (V.iii.255); pat upon this cue enters Lear with Cordelia dead in his arms, an irony noted by Bradley, as well as by Wyndham Lewis, who saw in it evidence of Shakespeare's nihilism.[202] If such critical antipodes as Bradley and Wyndham Lewis can discern similarly, it may not be implausible to suggest that this juxtaposition provides irony which annihilates claims to heavenly reconciliation. The ritual aspect of Lear's dead march, his entrance carrying Cordelia in his arms, is matched by the verbal accompaniment of his blasphemous defiance of the gods:

> Howl, howl, howl! O! you are men of stones:
> Had I your tongues and eyes, I'd use them so
> That heaven's vault should crack. She's gone for ever.
> I know when one is dead, and when one lives;
> She's dead as earth. (V.iii.257-261)
>
> I might have sav'd her; now she's gone for ever!
> Cordelia, Cordelia! stay a little. (V.iii.270-271)

In the light of the earlier discussion it is evident that Lear is a "pagan"; and, if superstition is a heathen manifestation, so, as Fitzherbert suggests, "Atheisme" is one "of the children of Paganisme."[203] Whatever Christian meanings may be present in *King Lear*, I have attempted to demonstrate that, for the most part, the play is at least ostensibly pagan in its premises—Shakespeare seems deliberately striving for fidelity to heathen life and experience as the Renaissance could have understood them. As a further blow to the simple Christian-salvation hypothesis, it may be added that Lear's attitude

[202]Lewis, *The Lion and the Fox: The Rôle of the Hero in the Plays of Shakespeare* (1927), pp. 179-180. While Bradley (p. 260) recognizes the irony at V.iii.255-257, Lewis feels that he draws back from the nihilistic implications of that recognition: "He implies that in this irony there is no ultimate despair, but rather that it is to be referred to a christian optimism. That does not seem likely. . . . But the punctual arrival of Cordelia, brought in like a Christmas present, so *narquois* and so pat, cannot be anything but what it forces us at once to see it as: an expression of the poet's mockery at the vanity of human supplications, and notions of benevolent powers, of which we are the cherished children" (p. 180).

[203]*Second Part of a Treatise,* p. 74.

toward Cordelia's death, his sense that death ends all, as opposed to the Christian view of eternity, is essentially the heathen attitude as the Renaissance knew it. The sixteenth-century Bishop Jewel, for instance, observed: "We are not therefore forbidden to mourn over the dead; but to mourn in such sort as the heathen did we are forbidden."

What, then, was different about the heathen, as opposed to the Christian, mode of mourning? Jewel explains of the pagans that "They, as they did neither believe in God nor in Christ, so had they no hope of the life to come. When a father saw his son dead, *he thought he had been dead for ever*," almost the words of Lear over Cordelia, "now she's gone for ever!" (V.iii.270), and his five-times-shouted "Never!" (l. 308). Recalling Lear, Jewel's pagan, at the death of his child,

> became heavy, changed his garment, delighted in no company, forsook his meat, famished himself, rent his body, cursed his fortune, cried out of his gods. O my dear son (saith he), how beautiful, how . . . virtuous wast thou! *Why shouldest thou die so untimely? why have I offered sacrifice, and done service to my gods? they have made me a good recompence. I will trust them no more, I will no more call upon them. Thus they fell into despair, and spake blasphemies.*[204]

"Hopefull Christians, and hopelesse Heathens" is the conventional antithesis expressed, for instance, in William Sclater's *An Exposition . . . upon the First Epistle to the Thessalonians* (1619, p. 319). "Neither neede we as the Pagans of consolations against death," observes Mornay's *A Discourse of Life and Death* (1592), "but that death serve us, as a consolation. . . . For unto us it is . . . not the end of life, but the end of death, & the beginning of life" (sig. D3ᵛ). "They who mourne excessively," remarks Henry Hoddesdon in *A Treatise, concerning the Death and Resurrection of Our Bodies* (1606), follow the "custome of the gentils, who had no hope" (sig. [C6ᵛ]). Traditional prototypes of sorrow, for example, are condemned for heathen immoderateness:

[204] "The First Epistle of St. Paul to the Thessalonians" (1611; also published in 1584 and 1594), in *Works . . . Second Portion* (1847), p. 865 (italics mine). Jewel was an early patron of Hooker, and his *Apologia ecclesiæ anglicanæ* (1562), later translated by Lady Ann Bacon, Francis Bacon's mother, was both in Latin and English regarded as an official statement of the position of the Church of England; like Foxe's *Book of Martyrs*, Jewel's works were often put in churches.

mourning as Niobe did, in continuall silence and heavines: or raging for sorow as Hecuba did, tearing the cheekes, renting the breasts, beating the heade . . . These . . . were the manners of the Heathen thus to mourne, thus to lament without measure, without end, for the deathe of their friends: but christians doo not so. . . . (sig. [I7^{v}])

Old Testament instances of grief, such as II Samuel xii.23, David on his son's death, "he shall not returne to me," and Job vii.9-10, "he that goeth downe to the grave, shall come up no more. He shal returne no more . . ."; which seem to anticipate Lear's "Thou'lt come no more," could be explained, like his, in the light of their pre-Christian "paganism." Hence, Hoddesdon points out that the Jews "wept, & no marvel, for christ was not yet come. Who by the example of his resurrection . . . sholde comforte us, in death and give us cause to forbeare from any great & immoderat sorrow or weeping." "Let them mourn for their dead," he concludes, "who have no hope of a resurrection, or ever to see them more" (sigs. [C7], [I8]). Similarly, Thomas Draxe's *The Earnest of Our Inheritance* (1613) points out that the heathens, "not knowing the *waies* and word of God, utterly denie that the *bodie* being once dead, can arise againe the same. . . ." But, "if wee beleeve the doctrine of the resurrection, wee must not immoderately weepe, or mourne for our friends departed. . . . For they die not . . ." (pp. 57, 58).[205]

Resurrection in the Christian sense was thus foreign to varying Renaissance interpretations of pagan belief. Although heathens may have "believed the immortality of the soul," explains Samuel Clarke's *An Antidote against Immoderate Mourning for the Dead* (1659), "yet they were never able to comprehend or believe the resurrection of the bodies, and re-uniting them with the souls . . . *Acts* 17.32. and 26.23, &c." Therefore, "The Heathen use to be immoderate in their mourning for the dead; because they want a hope of the present blessednesse of their souls, and the future resurrection of their bodies" (pp. 3, 5-6).[206] "The body rotteth in the ground," remarks

[205]Similarly, David Person's *Varieties* (1635), sigs. [L6v], [L5], M2, asserts "That Christians ought not to feare death, as the *Ethnicks* did." The latter "wanted the true consolation which a beleeving and faithfull Christian hath." Augustine in *De cura pro mortuis habenda*, he declares, aimed at the excessive mourning of pagan Greeks.

[206]". . . That the soule of man is an immortall substance . . . was . . . well known also to the heathen, by the light of nature," remarks Robert Pricke's *A Verie Godlie . . . Sermon . . . of Mans Mortalitie* (1608), sig. D3^{v}. The Epicureans, who make the soul die with the body, were placed by Dante in his *Inferno* x.13-16.

Bishop Jewel, "yet God preserveth it" (p. 866); but Kent, according to Lear, is merely "dead and rotten" (V.iii.285), as Cordelia is "dead as earth" (V.iii.261).[207]

Although, reminds Nilsson, pagans had some belief in immortality, including an underworld, the immortality of the body and the resurrection of the flesh were rejected by them.[208] Significantly, Agrippa's *Three Books of Occult Philosophy* (1651, p. 475) cites Ovid on the four constituents of man, which at death disperse to their appropriate states: corruptible flesh goes to earth; the ghost hovers over the grave; the soul descends to the abode of the dead; and the spirit rises to the stars.

The pagan in Jewel's description above who laments over his child, "Why shouldest thou die so untimely?" is echoed by the pagan in Shakespeare's play. When, once again, the pious Albany proffers the poetic-justice recipe which it seems one of the tragedy's concerns to examine, the indomitably blasphemous Lear makes it a cue for denunciatory passion. "All friends," Albany predicts,

> shall taste
> The wages of their virtue, and all foes
> The cup of their deservings. O! see, see!

into which neatly optimistic calculus Lear visibly and violently intrudes:

> And my poor fool is hang'd! No, no, no life!
> Why should a dog, a horse, a rat, have life,
> And thou no breath at all? Thou'lt come no more,
> Never, never, never, never, never! (V.iii.302-308)[209]

[207]In Lear's dispensation the finality of death and the distance of nature from any possibility of grace bring to mind R. H. Tawney's remark contrasting the Reformation and the Middle Ages (*Religion and the Rise of Capitalism* [1929], p. 98): "Grace no longer completed nature: it was the antithesis of it."

[208]Martin P. Nilsson, *Greek Piety* (Oxford, 1948), pp. 154-155.

[209]Lear's reference to a horse and a dog (see discussion above on the beast in man for other references) is repeated in Coverdale's attack on heathen heresies: "In this book my handling is of natural death, which before our eyes seemeth to be an utter destruction, and that there is no remedy with the dead, even as when a dog or horse dieth; and that God hath no more respect unto them. Yea, the world swimmeth full of such ungodly people . . ." (*Remains of Myles Coverdale*, Parker Soc. [Cambridge, Eng., 1846], p. 48). Samuel Rowlands, *Looke to It: For, Ile Stabbe Ye* (1604), sig. [C4], assails "God-lesse Athists" who hold "that the dead in earth shall make abode, / and never rise from out their graves againe."

In view of pagan attitudes to the afterlife and the absence of textual evidence of Christian immortality, none of *Lear*'s references to ghost, soul, or spirit necessarily requires an exclusively Christian interpretation. Lear's shadow, Kent, at the last exclaims, "Vex not his ghost: O! let him pass" (V.iii.313), "ghost" perhaps suggesting also, as in Ovid, the pagan ghost, or *umbra*. The finality of Lear's "Thou'lt come no more, / Never, never, never, never, never!" is echoed, in a line succeeding Kent's, by Lear's other surviving follower, Edgar: "He is gone, indeed" (V.iii.315).

Moreover, Lear's earlier outcry to Cordelia, "Thou art a soul in bliss" (IV.vii.46), may indicate as well the happy state of the virtuous soul. Like Lear's other "soul" allusions, mainly figurative, the play's "spirit" references are either figurative or, in this case, irrelevant (II.i.53; IV.ii.12, 23, 46; IV.vi.219; V.iii.139). The exception, if any, may be argued to be Lear's "You are a spirit, I know" (IV.vii. 49). Here, pagan, as much as Christian, doctrine may suggest the happy ascent of Cordelia's *spiritus* ("Thou art a soul in bliss"), as his own *manes* descends to the torment of his "wheel of fire" (IV. vii.47). For, as Agrippa's syncretic application of the ancients declares in *Three Books of Occult Philosophy*, if the soul has been virtuous in its earthly life, it "rejoyceth together with the spirit," rising to a perpetual felicity, while the guilty soul, "being left to the power of a furious phantasy, is ever subjected by the torment of corporeall qualities . . ." (pp. 475-476).[210]

Yet Lear's end involves more than an *in-consolatio*. For as in life he has transgressed against the *ars vivendi*, so at his death he violates the *ars moriendi*.[211] The art of dying well, in the Renaissance as well as the Middle Ages, sought to instruct *Moriens* in his last encounter. "For as every man sleepeth with his own cause," declare the Homilies, "so every man shall rise againe with his owne cause. And looke in what state hee dyeth, in the same state hee shalbe also judged, whether it bee to salvation or damnation" (*Certaine Sermons*, sig. [Q6^v]). The *ars moriendi* included the method of handling the five

[210]See also Chapman, *Bussy D'Ambois*, V.iv.147-148; Robert Hunter West, *The Invisible World: A Study of Pneumatology in Elizabethan Drama* (Athens, Ga., 1939).

Lear's "Do you see this? Look on her, look, her lips, / Look there, look there!" (V.iii.310-311) may suggest not only breath, but also, as in the traditional notion, the passage through her mouth of Cordelia's soul.

[211]See Sister Mary Catharine O'Connor, *The Art of Dying Well: The Development of the Ars Moriendi* (New York, 1942), p. 7.

temptations: unbelief, despair, impatience, vainglory, and worldly attachment, as to relatives. Yet in his concluding scene, the old king, long past the usual age of reconciliation, seems prey to all of these, including defiance of the heavens, commission of a confirmed murder (V.iii.274-275), and a final heroic vaunt (V.iii.275-278).

Presumably, Samuel Rowlands, a theatergoer acquainted with Shakespearean drama, could have related cases (cf. Lear's "Fourscore and upward," IV.vii.61)[212] in mind when he asks in *Democritus, or Doctor Merry-Man* (1607):

> Have you liv'd now, some fourescore yeares and odde,
> And all this time are unprepar'd for God?
> What greater foole can any meete withall? (sig. E3)[213]

For Lear violates a ritual of preparation demanded even by Montaigne, who condemned the lack of a rehearsal for death as a "nonchalance bestiale."[214]

That the desire for a happy ending mindlessly transcends the mere facts of the play and common sense itself is demonstrated by Nahum Tate's sugar-coated travesty which "improved" Shakespeare for over a century and a half; by the preference of Tolstoy for the unconsciously comic and pietistic old *Leir*; by the misreading of respectable contemporary scholars motivated less by the text than by anti-Burckhardtian a priori commitments; and by the inveterate pull and conditioning of the twentieth-century Hollywoodized mind in a climate of revived theologizing dedicated to the more consoling aspects of the paradox of the fortunate fall. The conclusion follows from the heathen premises as they are prepared throughout the play; neither as pious polytheist nor as blaspheming skeptic was the pagan (with the possible exception of the *prisca theologia* type, which Lear is not) in any position to expound Christian immortality. In every

[212]Cf. the conventional use of "fourscore," as in Sir David Lindsay, *Ane Satyre of the Thrie Estaits* (Edinburgh, 1602), where Folie (sig. V2) would sell his hood to one "that is baith auld & cald," and who is "Reddie till pas to hell or heavin," being "of age fourscoir of ȝeir."

[213]In the preface to *Martin Mark-All, Beadle of Bridewell* (1610), S. R. [Samuel Rowlands] seems to echo Lear's "this great stage of fools," IV.vi.185:

> I shall bring upon this great Stage of fooles
> (for *omne sub Sole vanitas*) a peece of folly.

[214]See Montaigne, I, 79. See also M. Dréano, "Montaigne et la préparation à la mort," *BHR*, XXII (1960), 151-171.

respect Lear fulfills the criteria for pagan behavior in life and, according to Jewel's description, for pagan behavior regarding death; indeed, he even follows Jewel's heathen into total blasphemy at the moment of his irredeemable loss.

In sum, Lear as a pre-Christian pagan could only with difficulty have believed in a type of Christian corporeal life after death in eternity. After death, instead of Christian *lux aeterna*, occurred pagan *nox aeterna*. To the pagan, as Nilsson points out, "it was self-evident that the body decays in death"—"thou'lt come no more."[215] "The Gentils, and their Poets," Donne notes, "describe the sad state of Death so, *Nox una obeunda*, That it is one everlasting Night; To them, a Night; But to a Christian, it is *Dies Mortis*, and *Dies Resurrectionis*, The day of Death, and The day of Resurrection. . . ."[216] In addition to ordinary expectations of sorrow, this distinction accounts for the violence and vehemence of the father's grief and for the dramatic impact of his expression. After all his previous pagan manifestations, to have turned Lear at the last moment into a sentimental Christian believer in immortality would have made Shakespeare's tragedy ridiculous, reducing pathos to bathos.[217]

To sum up Lear's development is to rehearse the development of the play, its gigantic inversions and its complexities. From an opening scene of maximal religious confidence of a heathen sort, we move toward a testing of that confidence—Lear's love test of the opening scene begins to involve an extrafamilial, political, and cosmic love test, one which encompasses the heavens themselves (whom also he had "Made" his "guardians," as he accuses his daughters, II.iv.253; cf. III.ii.21-24). Human love betrayed reaches into divine love betrayed; thus the question of providence obtrudes, analogically, into the question of a daughter's affection.

Lear's polytheism impinges on an animism whose deities are exten-

[215]*Greek Piety*, p. 155; he notes that "The resurrection of the body was unintelligible to the pagan."

[216]Funeral sermon for Alderman Sir William Cokayne (1626), *The Sermons of John Donne*, ed. Simpson and Potter, VII (Berkeley, 1954), 272.

[217]Cf. Herbert Weisinger, *Tragedy and the Paradox of the Fortunate Fall* (East Lansing, Mich., 1953), p. 246: "Poetic justice . . . stems from the distrust of the audience and is intended to bring about mass deception on a mass scale. But tragedy can exist only when the issue is left in doubt, when the conflict of forces is left free to play itself out, when the audience can be trusted to understand what is at stake. . . ."

sions of nature, as, for example, the sun-god, Apollo; hence, the king's devout polytheism, adoring the nature goddess, could yet embrace what would seem, to a Renaissance Christian, symptoms of naturalism and therefore skepticism. Living before the Christian revelation, as well as outside it, Lear could not know or accept the basic paradox of Creation, that God created the world out of nothing. Thus Shakespeare's ascription to him, expositionally twice-mentioned, that nothing could come of nothing, could signify, ambiguously, that Lear was a pagan, although a skeptic from a Christian standpoint; and that, although a good pagan, his expression of his belief in such terms might serve as a foreshadowing of disbelief to come.

In Acts II and III Lear's pagan devotion begins to undergo its trial, commencing that tension between belief and fear not to believe that surcharges his already strained mind. Again, the failure in humanity parallels the failure in the heavens; the storm occurs on all levels at once, cosmic, familial, and personal. And Lear's questioning of man's state above the animals is a corollary of his questioning of divine providence and justice above man. Once more, from the Christian view of Shakespeare's audience such denial of man's unique place was characteristic of skepticism; and from a pagan view Lear's doubtful defiance of the heavens is also a manifestation of a growing skepticism. The latter becomes even clearer when at one point the king dares, in his madness, to question the divine source of thunder, which to Christians, and to many pagans, was ever the dread voice of the heavens. When Lear exclaims at the midpoint of the play, "I am a man / More sinn'd against than sinning" (III.ii.59-60), we know we have proceeded to a point where a previous confidence in divine and poetic justice has become, in his own person, a bewildered sense of injustice. Ambivalence has overtaken faith.

The storm is the test of the gods. Divine justice above, Lear hopes, will be shown by human justice and charity below (III.iv.34-36); their mutual dependence is the reason for the paramount significance of the religious meaning of this play. In Act IV the maddened Lear has given up his confidence in the sense of the thunder: "when the thunder would not peace at my bidding," and this cosmic debacle involves a human one, as he continues, "there I found 'em, there I smelt 'em out" (IV.vi.103-105). As Lear hints at natural causation for the traditional voice of the gods, thunder, so he hints at natural causation for a traditional divine malady in humans, "hard hearts" (III.vi.77-79); Lear implies skepticism on the macrocosmic and microcosmic levels, operating here, as elsewhere, analogically, in thrusts which could have been evident to Shakespeare's audience but which may be lost on our own. Indeed, the measure of religious change between Shakespeare's time and the present is perhaps a measure of the incomprehensibility to modern spectators of his most cosmic tragedy.

By the end of Act IV Lear's madness has run its course, as have also the tension and breakdown caused by the failure of belief on all levels; and he is ready for "belief" of some kind, though not, of course, for anything resembling his previous tenets. Like Gloucester's, this belief has here a syncretic Christian-Stoic coloring, though there is no reason that we should not reverse the usual order and say it is Stoic-Christian, for the pagan has as great a claim to the syncretism as the Christian element. Lear's new belief is negative and exclusive, one of abnegation, *contemptus mundi*, and forfeit; it is not simply one of "salvation," which recent commentators have sought to fasten on him. It is, ironically, one whose fixity will, Lear vainly hopes, oppose all mutability, although it is immediately to be undermined. Lear's newfound "faith" is pathetically and suddenly withdrawn from him by the murder of Cordelia.

His laments against divine providence, his insistent "why?", his sense of man's reduced place in the scheme of things beneath the lowly animals, his offering of violence to "heaven's vault," are in large part motivated by an inconsolable view that death, excluding resurrection, ends all. This view, which is the premise of the play, implicit in its beginnings and never contradicted, is by definition a pagan, not a Christian, attitude to immortality. It thus explains the funereal chorus at the end of the play, which, syncretically, also invokes the Last Judgment (V.iii.263-264), while at the same time it heathenishly denies that any immortality is possible; here syncretism intensifies despair, implying the disparity between pagan hopelessness and Christian possibility. The pagan attitude also disposes of modern critical contentions that Lear is "saved" or that salvation operates in the denouement. For we have, among others, the evidence of a Renaissance English bishop that Lear's attitude was explicitly and even verbally the pagan attitude toward death, with the grief consequent upon an awareness that death ends all.

Lear's last speeches thus touch on the following ideas: immortality

(V.iii.270, 307); providence, general or particular (V.iii.306-307); and man's special status above the beasts. In earlier analyses I have indicated similar attitudes, questionable from the point of view of Christian orthodoxy. These deviations may, indeed, suggest that Shakespeare might have conceived Lear's views partially in relation to Renaissance outward skepticism, toward which his disabused polytheism could credibly have led him. Un-Joblike, certainly un-Christlike, the king, "Unhousel'd, disappointed, unaneled," goes to a reward the premises for whose existence he has just vehemently questioned; in his case, rather than an angelic chant *in Paradisum* or a Faustian exit with devils, the rest is a perplexing silence.

Finally, among other aims, this discussion has tried to show that the obstacles to an orthodox theological reading of *King Lear*, in which the protagonist moves from sin and suffering to redemption, are more formidable than has generally been realized. The so-called stumbling block, to the Shakespearean neo-Christianizers, of Lear's last appearance is, it may now be evident, scarcely a *hapax legomenon* but a carefully anticipated culmination of Lear's previously expressed tendencies.

Part III

CHAPTER IX

Double Plot

According to Bradley, the double plot chiefly contributes to Lear's "structural weakness," "the secondary plot fills out a story which would by itself have been somewhat thin," and "the sub-plot simply repeats the theme of the main story."[1] Although the double action is thus held to be fatally defective and to be filling which is "simply" repetitive, some critics have excused it on the grounds that it universalizes ingratitude and intensifies the tragic effect. Since Shakespeare succeeded, however, in the neighboring tragedies of *Othello* and *Macbeth*, in achieving intensity and universality without recourse to such devices, a further attempt to account for its unique and apparently uneconomic occurrence may be appropriate.

Among other explanations for the double plot is that which identifies in Lear and Gloucester traditional aspects of the sensitive soul: the irascible and the concupiscible matching the protagonists' anger and lechery. This traditional dualism could, because of its medieval and Renaissance conventionality, tend to dramatic recognition.

Following Plato's conventional division,[2] Erasmus' Folly believes Jupiter has set up against our diminutive reason "two . . . masterless tyrants." These are "anger, that possesses the region of the heart, and consequently the very fountain of life, the heart itself; and lust, that stretches its empire everywhere."[3] King James's teacher, George Buchanan, in *De jure regni apud Scotos* points out that

> two most loathsome monsters, anger and lust, are clearly apparent in mankind. And what else do laws strive for or accomplish than that these

[1]Pages 205, 210, 211. Cf. Harley Granville-Barker, *Prefaces to Shakespeare* (1958), I, 270, who charges that *Lear* "suffers somewhat under the burden" of the double plot.

[2]*The Dialogues of Plato,* tr. Benjamin Jowett (Oxford, 1953), e.g., I, 451 (*Phaedo,* 94d); II, 293-294 (*Republic*, 439e); III, 143-144 (*Phaedrus*, 237d-238b). Cf. ". . . Account of the Allegory of the Poem," in Torquato Tasso, *Jerusalem Delivered*, tr. Edward Fairfax, ed. Henry Morley (1890), pp. 441-442.

[3]Erasmus, *Praise of Folly,* p. 26.

monsters be made obedient to reason? . . . He, therefore, who releases a king, or anyone else, from these bonds does not merely release a man, but sets up two exceedingly cruel monsters in opposition to reason. . . .[4]

In addition, the second book of the *Faerie Queene* presents the familiar opposition of wrath and lust, the irascible in Cantos i-vi, the concupiscible in Cantos vii-xii. Guillaume Du Vair's *The Moral Philosophie of the Stoicks*, translated by Thomas James (1598), speaks of the senses as disturbing "that part of the soule where concupiscence and anger dooth lodge" and raising a "tumult . . . in the mind, that reason during this furie can not bee heard."[5] Huarte de San Juan's *The Examination of Mens Wits* (1594) notes, regarding their ability to repress inferior powers, that "our first parents . . . lost this qualitie, and the irascible and concupiscible remained . . ." (p. 250). Montaigne's influential disciple, Pierre Charron, in *De la sagesse* (1601) distinguishes between "*Concupiscible*, and *Irascible* Faculties."[6] Lodowick Bryskett's *A Discourse of Civill Life* (1606) identifies "the two principall appetites, the irascible and the concupiscible" (p. 48).[7]

Because in Renaissance drama differences in rank may imply other personal distinctions, the royal Lear represents the higher portion of the human creature, his reason being closer to the divine; while the more lowly Earl of Gloucester represents its nether portion. Rank also has its afflictions. Tommaso Buoni's *Problemes of Beautie and All Humane Affections*, whose translation appeared in 1606, attempts to explain an accepted fact: "Why are great Princes commonly afflicted with the griefes of the mind, and men of baser con-

[4]*The Powers of the Crown in Scotland*, tr. Charles F. Arrowood (Austin, Tex., 1949), p. 128.

[5]Ed. Rudolf Kirk (New Brunswick, N.J., 1951), p. 64.

[6]*Of Wisdom*, tr. George Stanhope (1697), I, 174.

[7]See also Nicolas Coeffeteau, *A Table of Humane Passions* (1621), pp. 5-6, 61-63. See "La Luxure et la Colère. Chapiteau roman à Vézelay," in Raimond van Marle, *Iconographie de l'art profane* (La Haye, 1931-32), II, 73, fig. 85. William Blandie's *The Castle . . .* (1581), fol. 13, finds the amatory and the choleric implanted in us. On the connection of the irascible passions with the heart and the concupiscible with the liver, see Sir Thomas Browne, *Pseudodoxia epidemica* (1646), p. 110.

Such writers as Du Vair and Charron lead to Descartes; and since Descartes believed he was the first to demonstrate the untenability of the traditional irascible-concupiscible distinction, it may be supposed that, with few exceptions, the difference was recognized through the Renaissance. See Descartes, *Les passions de l'âme*, ed. Pierre Mesnard (Paris, 1937), pp. 45-46, 111-119.

dition with those of the body" (p. 235).[8] Since passions, as Du Vair's *The Moral Philosophie of the Stoicks* remarks, "darken and obscure the eye of reason" (p. 62), anger and madness assail the king, who suffers most in the mind, putting out his reason's light; while the "dark place" of physical lust and "nether crimes," as well as the physical darkness of blinding, attend his fellow *persona patiens*. Mankind's upper half, closer to the angels, and the nether half, bestial, are symbolized, for example, in Lear's centaur speech (IV.vi.126-134).[9]

Before the end of the fourth act the protagonists, in this last of meeting places, grope together, minds dim and eye sockets empty, like creatures out of Bruegel's "Parable of the Blind."[10] Lacking even the compensatory vision of the mad Cassandra or the blind Tiresias, they enact a parable of the limitations of human knowledge. Yet, if Lear and Gloucester cannot, in a sense, "know" or "see," they can feel; but the irony is that their hard-earned gift of feeling only makes them suffer more. The limit of their knowledge, like Edgar's, is the suffering it brings. As do Montaigne[11] and Sidney's *Arcadia* (I, 227),

[8]See Buoni's work for other mind-body parallels; e.g., cf. Lear's "Nature, being oppress'd," which "commands the mind / To suffer with the body" (II.iv.108-109); cf. also III.iv.11-12 with Buoni's "Why are griefes of the body communicated unto the minde, and those of the minde unto the body?" (p. 227). Yet Buoni suggests that the "griefes of the minde" are "farre greater then those of the Body" (pp. 232-235). On the mind-body relationship, see also Chapman's *Sir Giles Goosecap* (1601-03), V.ii.1-50.

[9]Cf. Lear's description (IV.vi.126-129) and Anthony Copley's *A Fig for Fortune* (1596), sig. B. Cf. Tilley W520. See Montaigne's citation from Jerome, "Diaboli virtus in lumbis est," III, 86. The distinction is, of course, Platonic. See also Horace, *De arte poetica*, l. 4 (tr. H. Rushton Fairclough, Loeb Classical Lib. [1926], p. 450). From the name of Sidney's Arcadian villainess, Cecropia, Shakespeare could have recalled the notion of bodily division, for Cecrops, mythical first king of Athens, had a serpent's form below the waist. On the "woman-serpent" convention see John M. Steadman, "Tradition and Innovation in Milton's 'Sin': The Problem of Literary Indebtedness," *Philological Quarterly*, XXXIX (1960), 93-103. Analogously, Richard Linche's *The Fountaine of Ancient Fiction* (1599), sig. Kii, presents an image of Jupiter, the upper parts naked, suggesting divine light, the lower parts clothed, suggesting darkness and the "illecebrous blandishments" of the world's delights. Benjamin Rudyerd's *Le prince d' amour* (1660), p. 33, observes, regarding woman, "The Equinoctial maketh even the day and the night at the girdle; the upper Hemisphere hath day, and the lower night." To Chapman, centaurs are a symbol of what man has become. Cf. Jonson's Lady Centaure in *Epicoene*; Dekker, *The Seven Deadly Sinnes of London* (1606), in *The Non-Dramatic Works of Thomas Dekker*, ed. Alexander B. Grosart, II (1885), 79.

[10]If Coleridge correctly compares the heath scene of III.iv to Michelangelo, the protagonists' Bruegelesque decline one act later may suggest a significant commentary.

[11]Pierre Villey-Desmeserets, "Montaigne et les poètes dramatiques anglais du temps de Shakespeare," *Revue d'histoire littéraire de la France*, XXIV (1917), 380-381. Cf.

Webster's *The Duchess of Malfi* (III.v.81-84), for example, expresses the Sophoclean position:

> Thou art happy, that thou hast not understanding
> To know thy misery: For all our wit
> And reading, brings us to a truer sence
> Of sorrow....

According to the traditional irascible-concupiscible distinction, Lear's intellectual error of anger receives the conventional punishment of madness (*ira furor brevis*), and Gloucester's physical sin of lechery the conventional retribution of blindness. Yet it is evident that Gloucester, in addition to such irascible passions as fear and despair, also participates in Lear's angry propensities; the earl's rash and premature fury at Edgar parallels Lear's outburst at Cordelia. "I am almost mad myself" (III.iv.170), Gloucester confesses to Kent. On the other hand, Lear, at least figuratively, shares Gloucester's blindness. Blind from the start, dim of sight at the end ("Mine eyes are not o' th' best," V.iii.279), he anticipates both Gloucester and the darkening of his own mind's eye: "Old fond eyes, / Beweep this cause again, I'll pluck ye out" (I.iv.310-311).

A further iterated parallel is that between joy and sorrow, both of which were usually ascribed to the concupiscent faculty. Renaissance psychology recognized the perverse and convulsive effects of such extremes. For example, Nashe speaks of "many whom extreame joy & extreame griefe hath forced to runne mad" (II, 114-115), and

---

Ecclesiastes, passim; Tilley S141 ("Much Science much sorrow") and K188. Cf. *The Defence of Contraries*, tr. Anthony Munday (1593), pp. 23-32: "That ignorance is better than knowledge." See *The Tragedie of Crœsus* (1604), *The Poetical Works of Sir William Alexander*, ed. L. E. Kastner and H. B. Charlton, I (Manchester, 1921), p. 82, ll. 2083-84. See also Webster's *The White Devil*, V.vi.259-260, on the unhappiness of confounding "knowledges."

In addition, compare Lear's name and the current sense of "lere" as learning (cited in *Oxford English Dictionary* s.v."lear," from Spenser, *The Shepheardes Calender* [1579], May, l. 262; John Ferne, *The Blazon of Gentrie* [1586], p. 22; Lyly, *Mother Bombie* [1594], II.v). Lear, who "hath ever but slenderly known himself" (I.i.293-294), invokes "marks of . . . knowledge" (I.iv.240-241), as he presses further, "Who is it that can tell me who I am?" (I.iv.238). Cf. Curtius' "Etymology as a Category of Thought" (pp. 495-500), the tradition of *nomen atque omen*, and the literary practice of symbolic naming in virtually all ages. The heroic eponym, like "Oedipus" (suggesting both knowledge and pride), functions here as ironical leitmotiv, emphasizing not only self-identity and the means of the work's unfolding but also the irony of the dramatic quest.

Timothy Bright in *A Treatise of Melancholie* (1586), which Shakespeare probably knew, remarks, "What marvell . . . if contraries in passions bring forth like effects; as to weepe & laugh, both for joy & sorow? For as it is oft seene that a man weepeth for joy, so is [it] not straunge to see one laugh for griefe" (pp. 148-149).[12]

In this regard, the similarity between the deaths of Gloucester and Lear accentuates their difference: Gloucester perishes between extremes of grief and of joy at the knowledge that his son was "miraculously" preserved (V.iii.196-199); Lear dies between extremes of a kind of joy in his desperate illusion of her lips' movement and of grief in his emphatic knowledge that his daughter was needlessly butchered. While such emotional extremities were divisive, immoderateness of joy alone could cause death. "Sudden Joy," says the Renaissance proverb (Tilley J86), "kills sooner than excessive grief." "For it is not possible," declares Mabbe's 1623 translation of Alemán's *Guzman de Alfarache*, "that any mans heart should dissemble a sudden joy. Though it sometimes so hapneth, that excesse of joy, doth suffocate the naturall heat, and deprive it of it's life."[13] Especially in an old or enfeebled man, the extremes themselves could wrenchingly cause violence. Apropos, the *Celestina* in Mabbe's translation (1631) remarks:

> on the one side he is oppressed with sadness and melancholy . . . on the other side transported with that gladsome delight and singular great pleasure. . . . And thou knowest that, where two such strong and contrary passions meet, in whomsoever they shall house themselves, with what forcible violence they will work upon a weak and feeble subject.[14]

[12]Cf. Pedro Mexía's opposition between grief and joy, *The Treasurie of Auncient and Moderne Times*, tr. Thomas Milles (1613), p. 716; and the table in Nannus Mirabellius, *Polyanthea* (Venice, 1592), p. 76. See also Nashe, "A . . . Prognostication," *Works*, III, 390; *Venus and Adonis*, ll. 413-414.

[13]III, 167. Death through joy is also mentioned in *The Problemes of Aristotle* (1597), sig. [F7v]; Marston, *Antonios Revenge*, I.v (*Plays*, I, 81); Buoni, *Problemes*, pp. 242-244; Scipion Dupleix, *The Resolver; or Curiosities of Nature* (1635), pp. 250-252. James Hart in . . . *The Diet of the Diseased* (1633), p. 400, cites Galen in support of the view that "some might die of too great joy."

[14]Ed. H. Warner Allen (New York, [1923]), p. 210.

See John Davies of Hereford's *Microcosmos* (1603), pp. 45, 75, on the destructive or fatal effect of extremes of joy and grief. The emotions were familiar subjects in the grammar-school study of Cicero's *Tusculanae disputationes*. Gregory of Nyssa's *De hominis opificio* explains joy, grief, and tears as connected with the expansion or contraction of the blood vessels; and Melanchthon considers joy and sorrow to be the explosion and contraction ultimately related to the heart and blood.

Analogous to the above, as well as to the microcosmic weather analogy of Lear (cf. III.i, ii), is Cordelia's own joy and grief as described by the Gentleman (IV.iii.18-20):

> You have seen
> Sunshine and rain at once; her smile and tears
> Were like, a better way. . . .[15]

Proverbially reflected in the *Arcadia* and in other parallels, the contrast is echoed also in S. S.'s *The Honest Lawyer*: "So I have seene (me thinkes) Sun-shine in raine" (1616, sig. B).[16] Finally, as in Bright, cited earlier, it is anticipated in the perversity of the Fool:

> *Then they for sudden joy did weep,*
> *And I for sorrow sung.* (I.iv.182-183)[17]

Progressively skeptical and Epicurean with regard to the gods, Lear is set up against the superstitious and eventually "Stoic" Gloucester, their differences, like their similarities, being great. In crediting the ominousness of eclipses, Gloucester, although Epicurean on a sensual level, assumes an un-Epicurean position, for followers of Epicurus rejected such prognostication. On the other hand, Gloucester's belief in omens could, like his later tenuous acceptance of "ripeness," associate him with a Stoic view, which also vigorously defended both intuitive and inductive divination.[18]

Further, in an earlier tragedy Shakespeare had already employed the classical distinction as a measure of a character's shifting viewpoint; the scornful and Epicurean Cassius, at a moment of defeat, partially repudiates his previous rejection of omens:

15Cf. Webster, *The Devil's Law-Case,* I.ii.130-131; Joseph Hall, *Epistles,* I (1608), p. 143.

16Tilley L92a. On the *Arcadia* see Muir (at IV.iii.18-25) and Wotton cited by Steevens (New Variorum *Lear*, p. 252). Cf. above, Ch. iii. Samuel C. Chew, *The Pilgrimage of Life* (New Haven, 1962), pp. 120-121, relates smiling and grief together to a Renaissance depiction of patience.

17Robert Armin, who probably played Lear's Fool, speaks in *A Nest of Ninnies* (1608) of one whose manner was "ever to weepe in kindnesse, and laugh in extreames" (*Fools and Jesters: With a Reprint of Robert Armin's Nest of Ninnies*, Shakespeare Soc. [1842], p. 38). The Fool's song echoes a popular one; see Peter J. Seng, "An Early Tune for the Fool's Song in *King Lear*," *SQ*, IX (1958), 583-585; and Hyder E. Rollins, "'King Lear' and the Ballad of 'John Careless,'" *MLR*, XV (1920), 87-89.

18Cicero's *De divinatione* distinguishes the two. See Bk. I, Ch. xi; Bk. II, Ch. xxvi.

You know that I held Epicurus strong
And his opinion: now I change my mind,
And partly credit things that do presage. (V.i.77-79)[19]

As it does with regard to attitudes toward thunder and the stars, *Julius Caesar*'s opposition of the Epicurean Cassius and the Stoic Brutus foreshadows a similar antithesis in *King Lear*. Still earlier, the *Taming of the Shrew* (I.i.27-40) had philosophically posed Epicurean delights against Stoic repressions. In Jacobean, Caroline, and Restoration comedy, moreover, the opposition between Stoic and Epicurean continues, and that duality, as a recent study of Etherege reminds us,[20] underlies works of such dramatists as Chapman, Jonson, Thomas Nabbes, and Fletcher.

As superstitious "over-believer" and skeptical "under-believer," Gloucester and Lear tend to two of the best-known pagan philosophical attitudes in the Renaissance. In 1604 Andrew Willet's *Thesaurus ecclesiæ* juxtaposes those points of view:

First, both the Stoickes and Epicures (which were two of the most famous sects of Philosophers amongst the Gentiles, as we may reade Act. 17.18.) are confuted: The first whereof did bring in a fatall necessitie, making all things to depend, not upon the will and providence of God, but upon a certain connexion of causes, to the which the divine power it selfe should be subject: like as vaine Astrologers and star-gazers do attribute all to their constellations and aspects of starres. But the Scripture teacheth us, *that the Lord doth in heaven and earth whatsoever it pleaseth him, Psal.* 135-6: he is not forced by, or tyed to any such fatall conjunction of causes.

Having piously derogated the fatalistic, astrological, and Stoic pattern, Willet turns next to its equally contemned Epicurean counterpart, which removes God's providence from earthly cares:

[19]Cf. Cassius' earlier view (I.iii.46-52). Shakespeare's recollection could have been strengthened by Plutarch's references to Cassius' Epicureanism: before Caesar's murder, again at Sardis, where Cassius reasons with Brutus against the fanciful vision of spirits, and finally before Philippi (*Lives* of Caesar and Brutus). As Cassius later retreats from Epicureanism, so Brutus later seems to debate some notions of Stoicism (V.i.101-119). In addition, Macbeth's self-proclaimed endurance (e.g., V.iii.9-10) may suggest an analogous dualism in his obdurate scorn of "English epicures" (l. 8).

[20]Dale Underwood, *Etherege and the Seventeenth-Century Comedy of Manners* (New Haven, 1957). Stoic virtue and Epicurean pleasure form antithetical choices in the famous temptation of Hercules; see Erwin Panofsky, *Hercules am Scheidewege* (Leipzig, 1930), and Hallett Smith, *Elizabethan Poetry: A Study in Conventions, Meaning, and Expression* (Cambridge, Mass., 1952), pp. 290-303.

The Epicures . . . [like] many carnall men . . . cannot look into Gods providence, as the Preacher speaketh in the person of such, Eccle. 9.10 *Time and chance cometh to all.* Ambrose hereof writeth well. . . . *The Epicures thinke, that God taketh no care of us: and Aristotle, that Gods providence descendeth no lower then the Moone: but what workeman doth cast off the care of his worke?*[21]

Of the four ancient schools most esteemed by the humanists—Platonism, Aristotelianism, Stoicism, and Epicureanism—the last is espoused by More's Utopians, who regard the Stoics as their particular adversaries.[22] ". . . I wil no Stoickes of my Jury," pronounces Sir John Harington in *An Apologie* (1596, sig. Cc1v); "of the twoo extreames, I would rather have Epicures." Yet in a chapter on "the opposite opinions of the Stoicks and Epicures" Thomas Jackson's *A Treatise of the Divine Essence and Attributes*, Part II (1629), notes that "The Stoicks did well in contradicting the Epicures, which held *fortune* and *Chance* to rule all things . . ." (p. 179).

Moreover, cosmic Epicureanism and Stoicism had personal corollaries, which are attacked, for instance, in Miles Mosse's *Scotlands Welcome* (1603), assailing contemporary atheists: ". . . *Epicures* they are, for they hunt after pleasure as after their chiefest good. . . . *Stoikes* they are: for though they love to dispute of Action and Practise, yet themselves covet to sit in ease and quietnesse" (p. 76). In addition, William Fulbeck's *A Booke of Christian Ethicks or Moral Philosophie* (1587) describes the alternatives facing his contemporaries, who may seem, according to their actions, "fooles to the Stoikes, blockes to the Epicures" (sig. E). It is such want of feeling that evokes Marullus' outcry in *Julius Caesar*, "You blocks, you stones, you worse than senseless things!" (I.i.40), as well as Mon-

[21]Cambridge, Eng., pp. 24-25. In his *De natura deorum*, Cicero singled out the two schools; see introduction, A. S. Pease, ed. *De natura deorum. Liber primus* (Cambridge, Mass., 1955), pp. 13-14. Cf. Cicero's refutation of Epicurean ethics in *De finibus*, Bk. II; reply in Seneca, *Moral Essays*, tr. John W. Basore, II (Cambridge, Mass., 1935), 121, 123, and Lucian's Epicurean attack on Stoicism. See Ficino on Stoicism and Epicureanism in "De quatuor sectis philosophorum," *Supplementum Ficinianum*, ed. Paul O. Kristeller (Florence, 1937), II, 7-11; Montaigne repeatedly juxtaposes the two sects; e.g., II, 108-109; II, 203.

[22]More's Utopians share the Epicurean opposition to superstitious fear and dread of death, while they reject Epicurean ethics. The Stoic-Epicurean antithesis is expressed, e.g., in the section headed "Antonius pro Epicureis & pro natura contra stoicos" in Lorenzo Valla's *De voluptate*, tr. Vincenzo Grillo as *Il piacere* (Naples, 1948), p. 33; and in Erasmus' "The Epicurean," *The Colloquies*, tr. N. Bailey (1878), II, 326-345, where the serious Spudæus debates with the Epicurean Hedonius.

taigne's repeated attacks upon "Stoicall impassibility"; compare the commonplace jest in *Taming of the Shrew* on "stoics" and "stocks" (I.i.31). Speaking of a philosopher, Montaigne says, "Hee would not make himselfe a stone or a blocke, but a living, discoursing and reasoning man . . . ;" and the essayist admits himself not "begotten of a blocke or stone."[23] Sidney's *Arcadia*, too, following the tale of the "Paphlagonian" king, observes,

> Griefe is the stone which finest judgement proves:
> For who grieves not hath but a blockish braine. (I, 227)[24]

As Edgar has been shown above to provide indications contrary to Stoicism, so Lear, whom he parallels, repudiates such unfeeling impassiveness. "Howl, howl, howl! O! you are men of stones . . ." (V.iii.257).

Indeed, anger marks both Lear's opening scene, when he rages at Cordelia, and his closing scene, when at her death he storms at the heavens. Although anger was associated with the irascibility of old age, the emotion was not always discredited. On the one hand, ". . . in age," notes *The Pilgrimage of Man* (1606), "man is wonderfully changed, he is prompt to wrath . . ." (sig. D2), as the evil daughters agree, "You see how full of changes his age is . . . the unruly waywardness that infirm and choleric years bring with them" (I.i.287, 298-299). Yet, on the other hand, in Kent's reply to Cornwall, "but anger hath a privilege" (II.ii.71; cf. *King John*, IV.iii.32), and in Lear's prayer for "noble anger" (II.iv.278) may be heard an attitude antithetical to the Stoic injunction. As King James himself confesses, "I love not one that will never bee Angry: For as hee that is without *Sorrow*, is without *Gladnesse*: so hee that is without *Anger*, is without *Love*,"[25] while Bacon points out, "To seek to extinguish Anger utterly is but a bravery of the Stoics."[26] Similarly, William Sclater's *An Exposition . . . upon the First Epistle to the Thessalonians* (1619) argues against Stoic repression of such emotions and, like Lear, indicts "men of stones":

> The opinion of Stoickes, not allowing to their Wise man any use of Affections, not to sigh or change countenance at any crosse accident,

[23] III, 272; II, 207; III, 309; cf. III, 189.

[24] Cf. Tilley M172.

[25] J. L. S., ed. *Flores Regii . . . Spoken by . . . James* (1627), No. 2.

[26] *Works*, VI, 510.

sorts neither with Religion nor Reason. . . . Another sort of men wee have, in practice more then Stoicall; whom no crosse from God or men can affect to sorrow . . . their patience is it, or rather their blockish senselesnesse? (p. 317)

Indeed, a Renaissance point of view, like Lear's, exalted a virtuous anger. Ficino and the Florentine humanists, for example, helped effect a change with regard to the traditional sin of *ira*, transforming it partly to a "noble rage,"[27] as in Lear's desired "noble anger," which, instead of bursting forth, comes deliberately called.

Similar in their deaths, the protagonists provide a basis for comparison also in their lives. Although both are, as Lamb said, on the "verge of life," for Gloucester the verge is symbolized by a physical cliff, while for Lear it is the more terrible Dover of the mind, as in Gerard Manley Hopkins'

> O the mind, mind has mountains; cliffs of fall
> Frightful, sheer, no-man-fathomed.

Yet the common language of their renunciation-resolves, Lear's "To shake all cares and business from our age" (I.i.39) and Gloucester's presuicidal

> This world I do renounce, and in your sights
> Shake patiently my great affliction off, (IV.vi.35-36)

in light of the consequence of such attempts, may suggest that human suffering is unshakable; the attempt to escape leads only to further suffering. Whereas the abject Gloucester falls undignifiedly, Lear stands erect as he challenges the elements to "Singe my white head!" (III.ii.6). The latter's attitude to life as well as to death seems summed up in several lines of *Choice, Chance, and Change* (1606), regarding one who, being "moulded of a noble mind," has "steele unto the backe" and "Cries not with feare, to heare a thunder cracke." Such a person

[27]See Edgar Wind, *Pagan Mysteries in the Renaissance* (New Haven, 1958), p. 69 and *n.* Cf. John Serranus, *A Godlie and Learned Commentarie upon . . . Ecclesiastes*, tr. John Stockwood (1585), p. 321. Eugene M. Waith, *The Herculean Hero in Marlowe, Chapman, Shakespeare, and Dryden* (1962), pp. 44-45, cites other views favoring righteous anger, including St. Thomas Aquinas' *ira per zelum*. Luther's defense of just anger is well known; see Ewald M. Plass, *What Luther Says, an Anthology* (St. Louis, Mo., 1959), I, 28-29; II, 847, 985. See also Frances A. Yates, *The French Academies of the Sixteenth Century* (1947), pp. 116-120, 143.

Stoupes not to death untill the heart do crack:
Lives like himselfe, and at his latest breath,
Dies like himselfe.... (sig. [K3])

If *Hamlet* shows the mature Shakespeare deliberately exploiting parallel ideas for dramatic effect—for example, the various attitudes toward the ghost of the sentinels, Hamlet, and Horatio in Act I—the more complex *Lear* reveals him employing such ideas to provide the very structure of the play itself. Moreover, Renaissance conventions may adequately account for Shakespeare's unprecedented duplication; and I suggest that there may be no real loss of economy, since Lear and Gloucester stand for recognizably antithetical religious positions in this tragedy of man's relation to the heavens.

Conventionally paired, superstition and skepticism (or atheism) assumed a relation of polarity as well as, inevitably, of similarity: extremes to the mean of faith, they were both irreligious. Suggested by Plutarch in "Of Superstition,"[28] the concept of true faith as the *via media* between superstition and skepticism was restated, in terms favorable to itself, by Renaissance Calvinism, which conveniently consigned Catholicism to a superstitious or atheistic limbo. Marking the distinction, Hooker, after castigating atheists, turns his ire on practicers of superstition: "Wherefore to let go this execrable crew [of atheists and Machiavellians], and to come to extremities on the contrary hand."[29] James's *Basilicon Doron* (Edinburgh, 1603), advises his son, regarding his conscience, "especially . . . to keepe it free from two diseases, wherewith it useth oft to be infected; to wit, Leaprosie, & superstition: the former is the mother of Atheisme, the other of Heresies" (p. 15). Elsewhere James utters the aphorism, "The Devill alwaies avoydes the meane, and waites upon extremities; So hath he sought to devide the world betwixt *Athisme*, and *Superstition*."[30] That superstition was the counterpart of atheism, that both were irreligious, is, typically, the conviction of Joseph Hall, who, in his *Characters of Vertues and Vices* (1608),

[28]See also Clement of Alexandria, *The Exhortation to the Greeks*, tr. G. W. Butterworth, Loeb Classical Lib. (1919), p. 51, condemning both atheism and "daemon-worship" as extremes to be guarded against; and Aquinas, *The Summa Theologica*, Pt. II, Qu. XCII, Art. 1, on religion as a moral virtue containing a mean opposed both to excess (superstition) and deficiency.

[29]*Ecclesiastical Polity*, in *Works*, II, 23.

[30]*Flores Regii*, No. 20.

observes: "The Superstitious hath too manie Gods, the Prophane man hath none at all . . ." (p. 93).

Between reason, the soul's left hand, and faith, her right, true religion walked; any deviation to the left led to atheism, any excess to the right led to superstition. Among numerous texts illustrative of the dichotomy, Burton may be cited: "For methods sake I will reduce them [the fallacious doctrines] to a twofold division, according to those two extreames of *Excesse* and *Defect*, impiety and Superstition, idolatry and Athisme."[31] A mock prognostication of 1608, *The Penniles Parliament of Threed-bare Poets* (sig. B3), announces, "Athistes, by the Law, shall be as Odious, as they are Carles: and those that depend on Destiny, and not on God, may chaunce looke through a narrow Lattice at Foote-mans Inne," meaning prison. As Bacon observes in his essay "Of Superstition," the one, atheism, "is unbelief," while "the other," superstition, "is contumely: and certainly superstition is the reproach of the Deity." Just as atheism, he supposes, is related to wariness, so superstition is totally unreasonable and therefore the greater threat to political stability; it "bringeth in a new *primum mobile*, that ravisheth all the spheres of government."[32] By virtue of their superstition, especially, pagans were led to atheism, polytheism tending to break down men's faith. Fitzherbert's *Second Part of a Treatise*, cited above, alludes to the pagan inclination to both atheism and superstition. In like fashion, what has been termed the first sixteenth-century English pantheon of the heathens' gods, Stephen Batman's *The Golden Booke of the Leaden Goddes* (1577) in its dedication claims to show "into what . . . Atheisme, . . . Idolatrye, and Heresie, they have . . . affiaunced their beleeves."

Finally, while the superstitious-concupiscible character might be seen as passively accepting, the skeptical-irascible might be regarded

[31] *The Anatomy of Melancholy* (Oxford, 1628), p. 579. See also Howard Schultz, *Milton and Forbidden Knowledge* (New York, 1955), p. 265, for numerous other references. See John Weemes, *A Treatise of the Foure Degenerate Sonnes* (1636), p. 36; Weemes's religion-between-two-thieves analogy recurs, e.g., in Alexander Ross's *Gods House, or the House of Prayer* (1642), p. 9. Cf. Sidney's allusion to "the *Philosophers*, who shaking off superstition, brought in *Atheisme*" (*The Defence of Poesie*, in *Complete Works*, III, 34). Richard Bernard's *Contemplative Pictures* (1610), sig. E3r-v, lists "carnall Atheistes" along with the "foolishly superstitious." See further Hobbes, *English Works*, II, 277; IV, 293; Tilley D234 ("The Devil divides the world between atheism and superstition").

[32] *Works*, VI, 415-416.

as a dynamically rejecting type. Contemporary ideas of belief and unbelief, of the passive and the active, could also in this manner be assimilated to antithetical structural elements. Ironically, while at the start Lear is caught by belief in his evil daughters and disbelief in his good daughter, he is throughout the middle portion of the play torn between his previous belief and disbelief in his daughters as well as in his gods. For Lear, belief is sanity, and its loss becomes insanity. Having "caught" Cordelia (V.iii.21) and having again lost her, Lear in his last words composes a tension of nihilistic unbelief and the tenuously supported illusion that Cordelia still breathes.

Whether the double plot is, in fact, uneconomic is, of course, relative to interpretative criteria and dimensions, as well as to the type of play it is judged to embody. It is conceivable, for instance, that Bradley's recognition of the work's moral symmetry, its almost equal division into powers of good and evil, might legitimately be extended to structure as to sense. In this drama of duplicity and betrayal the doubleness of man's nature and the irresolution of his mysterious sojourn on earth are mirrored in the two protagonists. Since Shakespearean openings customarily provide clues to the action, it is significant that the initial lines (I.i.1-7) deal in dualities: the Albany-Cornwall antithesis, the division of the kingdom, and the observation that "equalities are so weigh'd that curiosity in neither can make choice of either's moiety." Similarly, the legitimate Edgar is, to Gloucester, "no dearer in my account" than the illegitimate Edmund (I.i.20-21). Further, while near the beginning the state, the family, as well as the protagonists' hearts are split (Gloucester's "old heart is crack'd, it's crack'd," II.i.90), at the end, with the family severed and the state still "gor'd" (V.iii.320), Lear's voice would "crack" the heavens, and both old men die, their hearts cleft in twain. The duality of Hamlet,[33] as reflected, for instance, in his dictional iterations, develops in *Lear* into a structural principle.

In addition, while facilitating an expanding multiplicity, the double plot helps sustain unity and maintain interest by its alternation of diverse characters and events reflecting the focal problems. Hence, in one sense Edgar's succession of quick-change roles may be allied to the general dramatic stategy. Further, through his proxy relation-

[33]See Harry Levin, *The Question of Hamlet* (New York, 1959).

ship, as during Lear's madness, Gloucester also assumes a larger expository and choral burden, thereby freeing the main character for more central utterances. From one point of view, therefore, the Gloucester plot may be said to frame the main plot, producing an effect analogous to that obtained by the contrast between prose and verse usual in Shakespeare. Finally, the Gloucester contrast might, in part, "purge" Lear of some possible theatrical disadvantage of old age and heighten the audience empathy frequently reserved for the *virtù* of a younger hero. For Gloucester's "We have seen the best of our time" (I.ii.117-118) may be, in one sense, an admission somewhat less applicable to Lear.

Indeed, it may be possible to regard the double plot as a developing metaphor, opening up the principal action into two parts that mirror each other. Such a device would be appropriate to a play in which the protagonist expresses a dissociation between his name and his identity (e.g., "This is not Lear: / Does Lear walk thus?" [I.iv. 234-235]), so that his person dissolves into a dual personage, a character in search of himself. Paralleled by Edgar's quest for identity, Lear demands his own identity of his daughters, his retainers, his Fool, and himself (I.i, iv; II.iv), his sane and insane pursuit of his "name" being, in effect, an image of the dramatic action. In the dissolution of identity which marks the opening, Lear and Edgar lose theirs, Cordelia disappears, and Kent and Edgar assume disguises. While the villains hypocritically ply their new roles, and Albany is "ignorant" (I.iv.282) and confused, Edmund provides the nominalistic rationale which dissolves names, as he displaces their possessors.

From one point of view, indeed, Lear may be said sequentially to dissociate into his children, Goneril and Regan (selfish willfulness) and Cordelia (courageous adamancy), as Gloucester may be seen successively to dissolve into his components, Edmund (lust) and Edgar (pathos). Here, fatherhood, as in Dostoievsky's Karamazov family, involves not only the problem of identity but also that of identity in multiplicity. Thus, through self-alienation and division, characters generate proxies for themselves, as well as analogues of each other. As the play moves, therefore, Lear's problem is seen revolving from different angles, above and below, through the continual presence onstage of proxy characters, as well as of the gods who are in their "heavens" while all is not right with the world.

Further, if *Hamlet*'s play-within-the-play holds "the mirror up to nature," Lear's double plot holds the mirror up to the heavens themselves. Just as Cordelia reflects the aspect of steadfast love, Edgar that of unchanging pity, and Kent of virile loyalty, Gloucester generally mirrors, centaur-fashion, Lear's all-too-human side, as the heavens mirror Lear's royal demigod or Promethean side. In addition, while *Hamlet*'s play-within-the-play centripetally reflects its hero in relation to his corrupt courtly audience, *Lear*'s play-within-the-cosmos, with the gods as spectators, more centrifugally throws the image of mankind against the questionable heavens. After a certain point in *Lear*, for example, human actions are invoked to "show the Heavens more just" (III.iv.36).

Lending the central situation sharper reality, Gloucester's physical suffering intensifies Lear's mental anguish, the passion of the blinding (III.vii) preceding the height of Lear's mad frenzy (IV.vi). In addition to its perspective on pain, Gloucester's role fills out the dimensions of Lear's; the latter's function is identified not only through his own words and actions but also through those of the figures who stand proxy for him. When, for example, Gloucester warns against the "purpos'd low correction" (II.ii.142) in putting Kent in the stocks, both earls act partly as anticipatory Lear symbols. Called "shame" by Lear (II.iv.6) and by Kent (II.iv.45), the villains' offense against Kent, the latter observes, is "Against the grace and person of my master" (II.ii.132). Again, as Cornwall and Regan punish both these royal followers, the king's vacated place on the throne descends to Kent's seat in the stocks (II.ii, iv) and to Gloucester's chair during the old earl's blinding (III.vii).

Enriching and underscoring the play's significances, the double plot facilitates its elaborate contrapuntal movements. In I.i the king is actively involved in his own duping; while in I.ii, II.i, and III.iii Gloucester is the more passive victim of a protracted deception. In contrast to Lear's dynamic behavior, the proxy role of the slower-witted Gloucester reveals in less rapid detail how an analogous deception might come about. Similarly, the implicit first-act debate between Gloucester and Edmund (I.ii) is contrapuntal to the Gloucester-Lear antithesis; Edmund's attitude toward Gloucester's credulity in part foreshadows Lear's mounting skepticism of his own previous belief. While the old earl continues to be gulled, Lear in I.iv and v is educated in his folly by the Fool.

In the proxy scene of II.ii the king is shown abused. In II.iv the two protagonists are brought together onstage for comparison, as they are again during the heath scene of III.iv and in IV.vi. While Gloucester continues, in III.iii, to be deceived by Edmund, Lear, in III.ii, has already challenged the supernal deceivers, or at least their elemental messengers. Thus Lear is able, earlier than Gloucester (III.iv versus IV.i), to invoke, through ironically reversed prayers, human examples for heavenly justification. Gloucester's customarily delayed counterpoint reaches his passion of the body (III.vii) after Lear has already begun his passion of the mind (III.ii.67: "My wits begin to turn," and III.iv, vi). While Lear's eyes have been opened, Gloucester's "vile jellies" are being extinguished. Indeed, Lear's mad "trial" of the villains (III.vi) ironically introduces the villains' "trial" (III.vii) of Gloucester; madness and "justice" are juxtaposed. Whereas mental suffering serves to animate Lear, Gloucester's blinding produces a deeper passivity and an implicit presuicidal renunciation of the world of action (IV.i.20-21).[34] Gloucester's attempt at self-destruction (IV.vi) contrasts, in its futile indignity, with Lear's heroic challenge to the elements (III.ii.6), as the latter's fearless jeopardy of life is suggested by Cordelia at IV.vii.31-36. In IV.vi, by a masterly irony, madman and blind man are brought together and confronted.

Although Gloucester for most of the play lags behind and echoes Lear, the last scenes reverse the order, as the antihero foreshadows the hero's concluding lines. Gloucester's "suicide" and "restoration" (IV.vi) prepare for Lear's moving "rebirth" scene (IV.vii). The earl's quiescent acceptance of "ripeness" (V.ii.11) sets the stage for his king's frenzied rejection of Cordelia's most "unripe" extinction (V.iii). And Gloucester's death offstage (described by Edgar, V.iii. 196-199) anticipates, without distracting from, the intensified pathos of Lear's last earthly moment (V.iii.310-311).

While Bradley ascribes confusion to the double plot, it is evident that confusion might only have been compounded by compressing *Lear*'s conceptual elaboration within narrower limits. Indeed, the device may rather be an agent of clarity, assimilating to drama's limited economy the intellectual freight of this cosmic tragedy. For in one respect the double action is related to the fashion in which the play may be said to "think," the work being, in its own terms, a de-

[34]See Ch. v, n. 16, on the problem of works and action.

veloped and dialectical argument. Examining the total conspectus of human existence under the heavens and delving also into "hell," the drama is structurally consonant with Shakespeare's most epic or total play.

Ironically, the structural mode employed depends partly upon the traditional device of analogy in a drama which suggests, through its dissolution of natural law and hierarchy, the incipient breakdown of analogy. In a final sense, however, as the religious poles become assimilated to the dramatic ones, *King Lear* is not "about" ideas at all but acts out rather its essential tragedy of human experience. Ultimately, then, the double plot is an instrument of complexity, the assurance of a multifaceted ambivalence which, contrary to the salvation hypothesis, probes and tests, without finally resolving, its argument of mysterious human suffering.

CHAPTER X

Minor Characters: Kent, Cornwall, Albany, the Fool

Having suggested that in the major characters of *King Lear* four main religious positions may be delineated, I turn next to those characters who, regardless of the number of their lines, are yet in a subordinate role to the more prominent figures. What is implied by this statement is that, disregarding quantitative measurements, Cordelia, Edgar, Goneril, Regan, Edmund, Gloucester, and Lear conduct the business of the two plots and are the substance of the two interrelated families. Behind them stand their servants, their followers, and those who, like Albany, are so unfortunate as to be married into them.

In other words, I am to consider the retinue of Lear, such as Kent and the Fool, and the sons-in-law, Albany and Cornwall, in which characters, appropriately, the main attitudes are echoed but more diffused, chorally or symphonically. It is conceivable, moreover, that the minor characters analogously reflect the fourfold division of the major figures: Kent, a *prisca* type, tied to the Cordelia-Edgar group; Cornwall, at one with the atheistic Goneril, Regan, and Edmund; Albany, in his cosmic optimism, the counterpart of Gloucester in his cosmic pessimism and anxiety; and the Fool, in his disordered perversity, mingled with Lear's growing sense of cosmic irrationality. Yet we cannot invariably expect the relatively clear-cut manifestations of the Cordelia-Edgar group, of the Goneril-Regan-Edmund group, or of Gloucester or of Lear; we sense these subordinate characters also as refractions of those they serve and of the dramatic circumstances in which they appear.

Kent

Tunc autem totius rei publicae salus incolumis praeclaraque erit, si superiora membra se impendant inferioribus et inferiora superioribus pari jure respondeant, ut singula sint quasi aliorum ad invicem membra.

—John of Salisbury, *Polycraticus*, Bk. VI, Ch. x

In contrast to the pragmatic Oswald and Edmund and their sensual "service," Kent is the disinterested feudal liegeman in a self-seeking Jacobean world. Not one who, in the Fool's words, "serves and seeks for gain, / And follows but for form" (II.iv.78-79), Kent sustains the orderly nexus whose post-Renaissance denial Gabriel Marcel has described in his "Dégradation de l'idée de service et dépersonnalisation des rapports humains."[1] In an increasingly dehumanized society, progressively estranged both from God and from man, Kent's personal loyalty contrasts older assurances with contemporary deteriorations. In the absence of other certainties Kent clings loyally to the authority of "the grace and person of my master" (II.ii.132), as Lear, in turn, is to cling ultimately to Cordelia's love. Indeed, Kent worships Lear, to an extent, as Lear had worshiped the gods; and, in a marksmanship metaphor appropriately recalling a sense of the Aristotelian *hamartia*, Kent begs him to "let me still remain / The true blank of thine eye" (I.i.158-159), as the king had thought himself the cynosure of divine attention. Yet while Lear's "service" to his gods changes to disaffection and disillusion, the constant Earl of Kent continues to the end to do "him service / Improper for a slave" (V.iii.220-221).

Since service is the orderly and reciprocal personal bond sustaining hierarchy, deterioration in the former leads to disintegration in the latter. As Shakespeare emphasizes James's political wisdom in uniting instead of dividing, so his defense of service underlines his patron's political concern, divine right and authority: ". . . you have that," acknowledges Kent, "in your countenance which I would fain call master. . . . Authority" (I.iv.29-30, 32).[2] Although, simultaneously with the puritanical leveling of old and valued human relationships, James's own son was eventually to perish, about the time of *Lear*'s composition James could yet implement his principles, his bishops at royal desire ejecting a large number of the Puritan clergy. Defending hierarchy, James argued proverbially: no bishop, no king. Exposing the consequences of the breakdown of hierarchy, Shakespeare's tragedy traces the effect of disintegration in traditional service and loyalties.

[1]*Les hommes contre l'humain* (Paris, 1951), pp. 144-157.

[2]Kent's petition to serve Lear, as well as his intended master's reply in I.iv, appears to follow a set form; cf. *Club Law* (1599-1600), ed. G. C. Moore Smith (Cambridge, Eng., 1907), ll. 2824-29; John Day, *Humour Out of Breath* (1607-08), II.i, ii (in *Nero & Other Plays*, ed. Herbert P. Horne et al. [1904], pp. 286, 291).

In contrast to true service, Edmund, in his second-scene soliloquy, parodies devotion. Juxtaposed with Kent in the opening lines, Edmund extends "My services to your Lordship" (I.i.29). Subsequently, Edmund offers his "services" to almost everyone else, as well as his self-reflexive services to "Nature." He serves his father and his brother (I.ii.185), both against their interests; he serves his proxy father, Cornwall, in his own interest; and, in another sense as well, he serves the lusts of Goneril and Regan. Goneril exclaims that to Edmund "a woman's services are due " (IV.ii.27), as Edgar's serving-man confesses that he "serv'd the lust of my mistress' heart" (III.iv. 86-87).

A lesser Edmund, Oswald is described as

> a serviceable villain;
> As duteous to the vices of thy mistress
> As badness would desire, (IV.vi.254-256)

while Kent portrays him as "one that wouldst be a bawd in way of good service" (II.ii.18-19). Prototypically, the Fool's "sir which serves and seeks for gain" (II.iv.78), Oswald is addressed by Regan in the same quantitative terms she bestowed upon her father: "I'll love thee much," she promises; "Let me unseal the letter" (IV.v.21-22). Hence, Oswald can perversely allude to Gloucester's "treachery, / And . . . the loyal service of his son" (IV.ii.6-7). Against Oswald's practice (e.g., II.ii.13-23), as against Edgar's serving-man confession (III.iv.85-102), is set Kent's prologue to the good servant (I.iv.4-7, 14-38). Borrowing for its connotative effect an analogical *entendre*, Kent defines the selfless limits of the latter (I.iv.5-7): "If thou canst serve. . . ." In contrast, Goneril instructs Oswald, regarding Lear, "If you come slack of former services, / You shall do well" (I.iii.10-11), while the king denounces Goneril in terms recalling the reciprocal principle of service: "the dear father / Would with his daughter speak, commands, tends service" (II.iv.101-102). Ultimately, the breach of reciprocity is enlarged through the "servile ministers" (III.ii.21) to its cosmic dimensions, with the recognition of an all-pervasive alienation and disservice in an inhospitable universe.

Since in Kent and Edmund true and false service are sharply contrasted, the lines of one tend to follow hard upon those of the other. For example, after the manifestation of Kent's solicitude for his master in III.ii, Edmund in III.iii is shown betraying his father to Cornwall. Closing with Edmund's soliloquy on filial treachery, this scene is succeeded by one which opens with Kent's concern for the old king, followed by Kent's repeated further persuasions toward shelter. Scene v reveals Edmund's consummation of his father's ruin, with the usurpation of the old man's title in the exchange between Cornwall and Edmund. Leading from that, Scene vi, in prologue to the blinding, commences with a confrontation of Kent and Edmund's father. The conclusion of Act IV and the start of Act V are similarly linked by Kent and Edmund, and the dying Edmund's speech at V.iii.228-229 is followed by the entrance announcement, "Here comes Kent."

In the *Faerie Queene* (III.x.6.9) Spenser anticipates Shakespeare's depiction "Of vile ungentlenesse, or hospitages[3] breach." Against the evil sister's dispossession of Lear's retainers, whose manner, Goneril complains, "Shows like a riotous inn" (I.iv.252), the protagonists assert the traditional bond of hospitality. Affirming and reaffirming their own status, on the other hand, the villains would sever such profitless relationships. Goneril, for example, in self-justification, objects on grounds both of morality and efficiency (I.iv.249-260, II.iv.262-265) to housing Lear and his useless knights.

The breakdown of Renaissance "hospitality"[4] coincided with a financial crisis in noblemen's estates, and this in turn affected men of letters and others who depended upon patronage. Echoes of their complaints are heard, for instance, in Spenser and in the *Parnassus* plays (1598-1603). As the aristocracy and gentry settled in London to seek advancement, saving themselves the heavy expense of hospitality, some allied themselves with the court, while others joined with the Puritan financial interests. In part it was ultimately the new power of the Puritan economic drive[5] that tended to demolish the older traditions of "great house" hospitality. "I may say to you,"

[3]"Hospitage": that which is due from a guest.

[4]Hospitality's decay was widely lamented; see William Stafford, *A Compendious . . . Examination . . . of Complaints* (1581), sig. Bv.

[5]The Puritan attitude is condemned in Nashe's "A . . . Prognostication," *Works*, III, 389: ". . . diverse poore men shall die at riche mennes doores: pittie shall bee exiled, good woorkes truste over the sea with Jacke a lent, and Hospitalitie banisht as a signe of popish religion." Elsewhere, Nashe assails the hypocritical "puritie" which holds "hospitalitie for an eschewed heresie" (I, 22).

complains Christmas in Nashe's *Summers Last Will and Testament,* "there is many an old god that is now growne out of fashion. So is the god of hospitality."[6]

Although the aged Lear, having tasted his daughters' hospitality, at the second act's close flings himself out into the storm, the old-fashioned Gloucester requires another act to appreciate the breakdown of human reciprocity. In contrast to the daughters' order, "their injunction be to bar my doors, / And let this tyrannous night take hold upon you" (III.iv.154-155), "Th' inviolable rites of hospitality"[7] are, in the old earl's traditional view, humanly enjoined. The supreme test of hospitality comes with the night on the heath. Cordelia would in such a night have let enter her "enemy's dog, / Though he had bit me" (IV.vii.36-37). "In such a night / To shut me out?" (III.iv.17-18), exclaims Lear. Though the Fool warns against trusting the "tameness of a wolf" (III.vi.18), at "that dearn time" Gloucester reminds Lear's daughter and son-in-law,

> If wolves had at thy gate howl'd . . .
> Thou should'st have said "Good porter, turn the key."
> All cruels else subscribe. . . . (III.vii.62-64)

When Gloucester warmly extends to Cornwall and Regan the social relationship of host to guests, "I serve you, Madam. / Your Graces are right welcome" (II.i.128-129), such "hospitage" is, conversely to *Macbeth,* brutally violated by those guests, whose acceptance of the relationship makes the crime still greater sacrilege. Hence, at the scene of his blinding Gloucester astonishedly exclaims,

> What means your Graces? Good my friends, consider
> You are my guests . . .
> . . . I am your host:
> With robbers' hands my hospitable favours
> You should not ruffle thus. . . . (III.vii.30-31, 39-41)

Cf. Jonson, *The New Inn* (1629), I.iii.56-59, and Massinger, *A New Way to Pay Old Debts* (1621-25), I.i, on Wellborn's father who "kept a great house, / Relieved the poor, and so forth" (*Dramatic Works,* p. 291). See also, e.g., Dekker, A *Strange Horse-Race* (1613), in *The Non-Dramatic Works of Thomas Dekker,* ed. Alexander B. Grosart, III (1885), 337.

[6] *Works,* III, 284.

[7] Fletcher, *The Tragedy of Thierry and Theodoret,* IV.i (*The Works of Francis Beaumont and John Fletcher,* ed. A. R. Waller, X [Cambridge, Eng., 1912], 56).

In the Renaissance context of hospitality, such treatment would have been regarded as "foul play" (III.vii.31) indeed. In the macrocosm, analogously, Kent's wishful remark to Cordelia, "The Gods to their dear shelter take thee, maid" (I.i.182), points forward with dramatic irony to the new Renaissance awareness of cosmic inhospitality.

Confronting Lear's angry old man, Kent displays an analogous lack of *mesure*; and, where Cordelia answers rage with silence, Kent replies with his own honest anger (I.i.160-166). In the Renaissance proverb, "He that cannot be angry is no Man."[8] Yet Kent would be the "physician" to Lear's fury (I.i.163-164), as, eventually, Lear, with ironic self-reflexivity, advises, "Take physic, Pomp" (III.iv.33), and Cordelia addresses the Doctor to Lear's madness (IV.vii). As the counterweight of Kent's strength is felt, moreover, the audience can estimate the force of Lear's rashness which overrides it.

If *King Lear* is divided between vacillators (for a time, Gloucester and Albany) and true men, it is Kent who defines the company of the latter. His loyal strength matches the *virtù* of the treacherous Edmund. He is the truly noble Earl of Kent, in contrast to the falsely ennobled Edmund, Earl of Gloucester; and his Cynic forthrightness[9] is, like Timon's, the obverse to libertine hypocrisy. As his diction indicates, Kent is the plain, blunt man of the country, complementing, in truth-speaking, the relatively oblique and court-bred Fool. His encounter with the symbol of false service, Oswald (II.ii), is consummated by the rustic-guised Edgar's dispatch of the villain (IV.vi.232-256). Anticipating Gloucester's proxy role (cf. II.ii.132, 140-147) for the king's hardships, Kent, claiming to carry "years on my back" (I.iv.41-42), is sturdier than his master, who, at the start,

[8]Tilley M172. Lear's angry charge at Kent, "miscreant!" (I.i.161; cf. "recreant," I.i.166) may also suggest disbelief, reinforcing the sense of Kent as dubious of Lear's divine reliances. Cf. discussion of anger in Ch. ix.

[9]Lucian satirically identifies the Cynical manner: "you should be impudent and bold, and should abuse all and each, both kings and commoners, for thus they will admire you and think you manly. Let your language be barbarous . . ." (*Philosophies for Sale*, tr. A. M. Harmon, Loeb Classical Lib. [1915], II, 469).

Cf. Kent's threat in Cornwall's presence to chastise Oswald, "If I had you upon Sarum plain" (II.ii.84), and the fact that Salisbury Plain, noted for its pagan relic, Stonehenge, lies between Kent and Cornwall.

In the same scene Kent's desire to "tread" Oswald "into mortar" (ll. 65-66) echoes Proverbs; cf. Charles Richardson, *A Sermon concerning the Punishing of Malefactors* (1616), p. 20, citing Proverbs xvii.10 and xxvii.22, "For though a man should bray a foole in a morter . . . ," and Tilley F447.

would "Unburthen'd crawl toward death" (I.i.41). Yet Kent's initial inability to vanquish Oswald foreshadows Lear's frustration against his adversaries, as Edgar's slaying of Oswald later prefigures their downfall.

As Gloucester reflects the pathos of Lear's age, Kent—to whose "strong arms" Edgar alludes (V.iii.211)—mirrors the virility of his manhood. For, although "Fourscore and upward," the king is tenacious of the latter: "I am asham'd / That thou hast power to shake my manhood thus" (I.iv.305-306). Hence, Kent is neither so young as to defeat the comparison nor so old as to destroy its effectiveness; he is, as noted above, at the final verge of, or past, "virilitas" but not yet within the protagonists' "senium" (cf. I.iv.40-42). But if Kent admits to Cornwall, "Sir, I am too old to learn" (II.ii.128), it is in the sense that he is too old to learn the new ways of disservice.

Further, as Kent can "deliver a plain message bluntly" (I.iv.35-36), he is also Lear's symbolic evidence of strength. If such a man as Kent can eventually follow him even unto death, it is implied, Kent's values may be reflected in his master. While the banished Kent reintroduces himself, significantly, as not "so old to dote on" a woman "for anything," he also boasts that he is "Not so young . . . to love a woman for singing" (I.iv.40-41). Yet he is unlike the "old lecher" Gloucester (cf. III.iv.115). For, in contrast to Lear, who has just submitted his "all" to his evil daughters, Kent identifies himself as above womanly weakness: though he condemns Oswald as "an eater of broken meats" (II.ii.13), he himself professes "to eat no fish" (I.iv.18).[10]

While Kent's

> It is the stars,
> The stars above us, govern our conditions;
> Else one self mate and make could not beget
> Such different issues. . . . (IV.iii.33-36)

seems, like the Servants' and Albany's exclamations, choral hyperbole shaken loose by the cumulative horrors, it also reflects a Stoic

[10]Cf. Barnabe Rich's *The Irish Hubbub* (1617), p. 25, "the whoremaster . . . *Senex Fornicator*, an old Fishmonger," and the old "fishmonger" Polonius (*Hamlet*, II.ii.174). See also Robert Greene, *The Black Book's Messenger* (1592), reprinted in *The Elizabethan Underworld*, ed. A. V. Judges (1930), p. 252. Cf. Falstaff on "fish-meals" (*2 Henry IV*, IV.iii.99). See also *double entendres* in Benjamin Rudyerd, *Le prince d'amour* (1660), p. 33. Helge Kökeritz, "Punning Names in Shakespeare," *MLN*, LXV (1950), 240-241, compares "Caius" (V.iii.283) to euphemisms in *Romeo and Juliet*, II.iv.97, and *2 Henry IV*, II.i.17. Yet "Caius" is also used by Renaissance writers in the sense of John Doe; e.g., in John Ferne, *The Blazon of Gentrie* (1586), pp. 301-302.

fatalism.[11] In addition, Kent's observation that Albany and Cornwall have spies "—as who have not, that their great stars / Thron'd and set high?" (III.i.22-23), in its implication that rank is destined, suggests a rationale for his "service."

Although, with his master, Kent betrays un-Stoic anger, he shows Stoic fortitude in the stocks (II.ii.155-157) and alludes, like Cordelia, to fortune: "Fortune, good night; smile once more; turn thy wheel!" (II.ii.173). "Fortune" recurs in the last scene, where, chorally, Kent rehearses the tragic direction; there he defines, like Edgar (IV.i.5), the pitiable decline (V.iii.280-281). Further, Kent (IV.vii. 96-97), like the stoical Brutus and Macbeth, fatalistically[12] stakes his destiny on "th' event." Finally, Kent's "Is this the promis'd end?" (V.iii.263) may carry overtones not only of the Last Judgment but perhaps also of the well-known Stoic notion concerning the antici-

[11]See, illuminating Kent's exclamation, Palingenius, *The Zodiake of Life*, tr. Barnabe Googe (1576). Kent, by his contrasting view, recalls to mind Edmund's opening-soliloquy suggestion (I.ii) of heredity as determined in the womb at the moment of generation. The latter has priority for the Bastard over the moment of birth, especially as he is legally excluded from the advantages of birth. On the one hand, Palingenius seems to tend toward Edmund's notion:

> yet ought we for to pray
> To God, within the mothers wombe that he may give good seede:
> For so we shewe our selves in lyfe, as wee therein doe breede.
> Whosoever doth come nought from thence wil seldom vertuous prove, . . .
> Well maist thou nature rule sometime, but never her expell. (pp. 77-78)

At the end Edmund consistently acknowledges his own "nature" as innately disposed to evil at his "dark and vicious" (V.iii.172) birthplace. Yet, on the other hand, stellar and naturalistic tendencies seem alternately reflected under Palingenius' more general rubric of Nature:

> As oft as under naughty starres the byrth she doth procure:
> While as the childe doth inwarde take the motions of the skie,
> Or else begot of naughty seede: the cause doth often lye
> Amyd the parentes of the childe, when they perfourme the acte. (p. 79)

Kent's declaration thus takes on added significance regarded from one dramatic viewpoint: the implicit debate between Gloucester's faith in the position of the planets at nativity and Edmund's faith in the conceptual moment and its vital heat. Further, Kent's perplexity over identical parentage and different moral issue is resolved in related terms by Palingenius:

> But thou wilt say, what kinde of seede is sowne, such fruit it brings, . . .
> Not so, for oft a Squall is borne of Goodly men, wee see.
> And faire and eke welfavourd men yll favourd knaves have got, . . . nor in the fathers sure
> It lyes, to give the children minde. This, nature doth procure.
> What fruite can noble seede up bring if skyes doe not agree? (p. 92)

[12]Cf. the Gentleman's "The arbitrement is like to be bloody" (IV.vii.94) and Webster's "bloudy audit" in *The White Devil*, IV.i.21.

pated periodical consumption (*ecpyrosis*) of the entire world.[13]

A pagan without hope of immortality, Kent ultimately comes "To bid my King and master aye good night" (V.iii.235). As he loses that relationship which had helped provide his identity, Kent's occupation's gone. Hence, he announces his departure to follow Lear (V.iii.321-322). Emphatically among the king's "no"-sayers, Kent memorably contradicts Lear in the opening scene. Yet his protracted "ay" and "no" exchange in II.iv.15-22, succeeded by Lear's recognition, "To say 'ay' and 'no' to every thing that I said! 'Ay' and 'no' too was no good divinity" (IV.vi.100-102), seems ironically recalled in Kent's resigned last line, "My master calls me, I must not say no" (V.iii.322).[14]

Like Cordelia, Kent is Stoic on his own behalf but pitying for the king, a distinction which she defines (V.iii.5-6). Both from the first perceive the deceitfulness of the world; both foresee the outcome (e.g., Cordelia, I.i.280-281; Kent, I.i.160-161); and both share a commitment to works without hope of reward (cf. I.i.184-185, IV.vii.1-6). Speaking, like Edgar, in the language of one to whom he is bound, Kent in his devotion to Cordelia manifests a *prisca* expression concerning "The Gods" (I.i.182). Lear's "unkindness," Kent notes, "stripp'd her from his benediction" (IV.iii.43-44). Kent's and Cordelia's loyalty to the bond also prompts Kent's indictment of the false servant, Oswald (II.ii.74-76).

Nevertheless, insofar as Kent's disguise soliloquy carries an analogical overtone of the Good Servant and the parable of the talents,

> If thou canst serve where thou dost stand condemn'd,
> So may it come, thy master, whom thou lov'st,
> Shall find thee full of labours, (I.iv.5-7)

it is significant to note that the "master" here is Lear, the pagan king dominating Kent's religious perspective. Like Cordelia's "O dear father! / It is thy business that I go about" (IV.iv.23-24), the scriptural echo is adapted to the heathen monarch's service. It is, indeed, the mortal Lear alone whom Kent has uniquely

[13]See Seneca, *Quaestiones naturales*, tr. John Clarke (1910), pp. 143-156, adding the deluge to the conflagration (p. 150): "Both will take place when God has seen fit to end the old order. . . ." Regarding the final conflagration, cf. Donne's "A Feaver" and Renaissance commentaries discussed in Don Cameron Allen, "Three Notes on Donne's Poetry . . . ," *MLN*, LXV (1950), 104-106.

[14]Cf. Clermont's presuicide speech in Chapman's *The Revenge of Bussy D'Ambois* (ca. 1601-12), V.v.179, 183.

ever honour'd as my King,
Lov'd as my father, as my master follow'd,
As my great patron thought on in my prayers.
(I.i.140-142)

CORNWALL

... for they are of the fierce wrathful property, and know nothing of the light. Fierceness is their strength and might, and enmity their will and life. The more evil and hostile a creature is in the dark world, the greater is its might. As the powerful tyrants of this world often exhibit their power in malignity, so that men must fear them, or as tame animals are afraid of ferocious ones; so has this likewise a property in the dark world.

—Jacob Boehme, *Sex puncta theosophica*

In the reiterated dissension between the dukes of Albany and Cornwall, the political and geographical, as well as the moral, polarities of the play are suggested. Albany, representing the northern part of the British isle, was one of James's titles and a title of his second son; Cornwall, on the other hand, representing its southwestern extreme, was a title of his elder son. At the death of Elizabeth in 1603, Prince Henry became Duke of Cornwall; the dedication of Barnabe Rich's *Faultes* (1606), for example, is addressed to "the most vertuous . . . Prince, Henrie . . . Prince of Wales, Duke of Cornwall. . . ." Such titles, without necessarily being identified with their current holder, could serve also as symbolic abstractions, reminding audiences of the dangers of division as well as of James's role against division. Further, the distant pagan setting could have reduced risk of identification. Yet internal schisms remained an issue which James's politicians sought to resolve, Thomas Egerton's *The Speech of the Lord Chancellor* (1609) pointing out, nevertheless, that to demand an end to "dis-union" through "such an absolute and perfect reconciling or uniting of Lawes as is fancied" is unrealistic. "Is it yet so," he inquires, "betweene *England* and *Wales*? or betweene *Kent* and *Cornewall*?" (p. 115).

Where Albany is inaction, Cornwall is the fury of the deed itself, a rough beast whose unswerving cruelty, too destructive to survive, comes to deadly use. Where Lear's "frame of nature," moreover, was too easily "wrench'd . . . / From the fix'd place" (I.iv.277-278), Cornwall is "unremovable and fix'd . . . / In his own course" (II.iv.

93-94). Self-consumingly, "the fiery Duke" (II.iv.92, 104) is without issue.

Yet for a time he finds a son in Edmund, as Edmund plots against his own father. "I will lay trust upon thee," promises Cornwall, in a near-ritual parody, "and thou shalt find a dearer father in my love" (III.v.24-25). That filial relationship is shortly to be dissolved, when, in the exchange of the blinding scene (III.vii), Edmund loses his father substitute near the instant that his own father is deprived of his eyes. The tragic irony of this bartering of darkness for darkness near the middle of the play foreshadows a similar exchange at the end, when Lear enters with his daughter's corpse while the fatally wounded Edmund himself is borne off.

Further, at the "trial" of Edmund's father, Cornwall is "judge," as in the previous scene Lear is "judge" at the "trial" of Cornwall's sister-in-law and wife. Like that of these sisters, Cornwall's "justice" is above the law; mere anarchy being loosed upon the world, his willful fury is, as he recognizes, beyond human restraint:

> Though well we may not pass upon his life
> Without the form of justice, yet our power
> Shall do a court'sy to our wrath, which men
> May blame but not control. (III.vii.24-27)

Leading directly to his death at the end of this scene, Cornwall's *hubris* is comparable to that, in Marlowe's *Edward II*, of young Mortimer, who utters a similar boast shortly before he is to lose his head:

> All tremble at my name, and I fear none;
> Let's see who dare impeach me for his death. (V.vi.13-14)[15]

Complementary to each other, Cornwall in his outward villainy contrasts with Edmund in his inward Machiavellian guile, as, in effect, the lion with the fox. Indeed, in contrast at least to the initial behavior of the other villains, Cornwall is relatively uncourtier-like and bluntly to the point. Although in this he parallels Kent, Cornwall ironically indicts him as hypocritical (II.ii.102-105).

REVOLT OF THE FIRST SERVANT

Prefiguring the final rebellion of Lear, first servant of the state, against the arbitrary cruelty of the cosmos is the revolt of the First

[15]Ed. H. B. Charlton and R. D. Waller (1933).

Servant against the state torture by his lord, the Duke of Cornwall. Microcosmic to the play, it occurs at the end of the third, the great rebellion, act and sums it up.

Of all the personages, Cornwall, suggesting a combination of the medieval Homicidium and the Miltonic Moloch, seems the most ruthless and unimaginative. With ironic appropriateness, therefore, it is Cornwall's own First Servant, so low as to be nearly anonymous ("A servant that he bred," IV.ii.73), who rises against arbitrary cruelty and fatally stabs his lord. In this deed by that unknown soldier of human dignity, motivations may include a fear that the limits defining mankind have been breached and a need to assert an essential human identity. Despite a familiarity with his master's character, having his whole life unquestioningly obeyed him, the First Servant, like the king himself, reaches a point beyond which silent indifference is impossible:

> I have serv'd you ever since I was a child,
> But better service have I never done you
> Than now to bid you hold. (III.vii.72-74)

Subversive to Cornwall's "new order," the servant's self-sacrificing *non serviam* is nevertheless itself an assertion of order. Although the dying Cornwall commands, "throw this slave / Upon the dunghill" (III.vii.95-96), the First Servant, like the king whom he reflects, is essentially *l'homme révolté*. "The slave who opposes his master," observes Camus, "is not concerned . . . with repudiating his master as a human being. He repudiates him as a master. . . ." For,

> If men cannot refer to a common value, recognized by all as existing in each one, then man is incomprehensible to man. The rebel demands that this value should be clearly recognized in himself because he knows or suspects that, without this principle, crime and disorder would reign throughout the world. An act of rebellion on his part seems like a demand for clarity and unity. The most elementary form of rebellion, paradoxically, expresses an aspiration to order.[16]

Indeed, the slain rebel's companions chorally explicate, within Cornwall and Regan's lawless universe, the motivations of his act:

[16]Albert Camus, *The Rebel: An Essay on Man in Revolt,* tr. Anthony Bower (New York, 1958), p. 23.

Second Serv. I'll never care what wickedness I do
If this man come to good.
Third Serv. If she live long,
And in the end meet the old course of death,
Women will all turn monsters. (III.vii.98-101)

TORTURE AT THE GLOBE

Il faut toujours en revenir à de Sade, c'est-a-dire à l'homme naturel, pour expliquer le mal.

—Charles Baudelaire, *Journaux intimes*

In the deliberate and extreme sadism of the blinding scene may be observed the inevitable acting out of the ideology of the villains, as expressed, for instance, in Edmund's nature soliloquy (I.ii.1-22). "For him, nature is sex; his logic leads him to a lawless universe where the only master is the inordinate energy of desire." Relevant precisely to the libertine creed of the villains, this summary of the next century's Sade significantly points the corollary: that instinct "is the ultimate expression of nature, and . . . the blind force that demands the total subjection of human beings, even at the price of their destruction."[17] Like Shakespeare, Bossuet, before Sade, connected the pleasure principle and sadism: "C'est le génie de la volupté . . . opprimer le juste . . . voilà cette volupté si commode, si aisée et si indulgente, devenue cruelle et insupportable."[18] In his mad perception, indeed, Lear assails the "rascal beadle" who lashes the whore he "hotly lusts to use" (IV.vi.161-164). "If only nature is real," concludes Camus, "and, if, in nature, only desire and destruction are legitimate," then, since "all humanity does not suffice to assuage the thirst for blood, the path of destruction must lead to universal annihilation" (p. 44).

Committed to the pleasure of destruction, the villains identify cruelty and murder with natural law. Such inferences follow inevitably from the dissolution of traditional natural law's restraints. "Qui doute . . . ," demands Sade, "que le meurtre ne soit une des lois les plus précieuses de la nature? . . . Si la destruction est une de ses lois,

[17]Camus, *The Rebel*, p. 38.

[18]J. B. Bossuet, "Sermon du mauvais riche" (1662; known also as "Sermon sur l'impénitence finale"), *Oeuvres oratoires*, ed. Joseph Lebarq (Paris, [1923]), IV, 208. Cf. Fénelon, who spoke of "the tiger that is in every libertine" (cited in Arthur A. Tilley, *Molière* [Cambridge, Eng., 1921], p. 146).

celui qui détruit lui obéit donc!" Since vicious cruelty conforms to the law of nature, and God tortures and repudiates mankind, there is nothing to stop one from torturing and repudiating one's fellow men. Such ultimate nihilism is, in practice, deduced by the sadistic villains. Yet it is sensed also by the protagonists themselves amidst the seeming cosmic sadism which kills men, like flies, for sport and which later gratuitously slaughters the innocent. If the gods are as they are, then "None does offend" (IV.vi.170). For Lear might partly, in his own terms, ultimately concur with Sade: "Dieu est très vindicatif, méchant, injuste. . . . L'auteur de l'univers est le plus méchant, le plus féroce, le plus épouvantable de tous les êtres."[19]

The logic of Promethean rebellion thus forces Lear, assailing first man, then the cosmos, to bid the thunder "Strike flat the thick rotundity o' th' world!" (III.ii.7) and to wish "Nature's moulds" (III.ii.8) and "heaven's vault should crack" (V.iii.259), in some degree as it impels Sade to desire to destroy the cosmos, "arrêter le cours des astres, bouleverser les globes qui flottent dans l'espace. . . ."[20] Significantly, perhaps, Sade's use of thunder and lightning is analogous to *Lear*'s, the elemental perversity an argument against the benevolence of divine power. After the criminal Noirceuil of Sade's novel promises, "Mes amis, un orage terrible se forme; livrons cette créature à la foudre; je me convertis si elle la respecte," the virtuous Justine is struck by lightning.[21] Connecting the seventeenth and eighteenth centuries, Camus terms this "a freethinker wager that is the answer to the Pascalian wager."[22]

Albany

In addition to the Servants' exclamations, other utterances in the play are, rather than merely personal expressions, definitions of the

[19]Cited in Mario Praz, *The Romantic Agony* (1951), pp. 102-103.

[20]Ibid., p. 105. On "Nature's moulds" in Shakespeare see the present writer, "Timothy Bright and Shakespeare's Seeds of Nature," *MLN*, LXV (1950), 196-197.

[21]In Praz, *The Romantic Agony*, p. 106. Cf. Voltaire's analogous use of the Lisbon earthquake.

[22]*The Rebel*, p. 37. Recalling the alteration from *Leir* to *Lear*, Sade's original version regarded thunder providentially and exclaimed at the injustice of the lightning stroke: "Ceci est trop fort et trop singulier, il n'est pas naturel que la providence punisse aussi cruellement et avec aussi peu de justice un être qui ne servit jamais que la vertu; ça ne m'en impose pas, c'est indirectement que la colère du ciel me frappe, et c'est à moi que tous ces coups s'adressent, à moi seule qui les ai mérités" (in Praz, *The Romantic Agony*, p. 167).

limits which tragedy tends to explore, those *Grenz-Situationen* beyond which man "is" not. Such speeches in a work which also probes the limits of the gods, beyond which the gods "are" not, are delivered by the protagonists, as well as by such secondary characters as the Servants, Kent, and Albany. They provide, like the tragedy itself, an "as if" case: what would become of man if . . . ? For a crucial question of an age torn between traditional and Machiavellian-Hobbesian views of human dignity—all coherence gone through the threatened disintegration, on all levels, of identifying bonds—was: at what point does man cease to be man?

During the storm, for example, Kent repeatedly emphasizes the unprecedented infliction of the heavens upon unaccommodated man (e.g., III.ii.45-48) and the bounds of his endurance:

> man's nature cannot carry
> Th' affliction nor the fear. (III.ii.48-49)
>
> The tyranny of the open night's too rough
> For nature to endure. (III.iv.2-3)

The "wrathful skies" which "Gallow the very wanderers of the dark" (III.ii.43-44), pouring down upon man's "Oppressed nature" (III.vi.100) their "tyranny," also throw into confusion the traditional identities and roles of human victim as well as divine tormenter.

Like Kent, a measuring figure of decency, Albany, in the fourth act, defines the human condition. As the First Servant demarcates human limits by acting them out, the conjunction of sentiments between the lowest servant and the highest noble suggests also a circumscription of the social order. Indeed, Albany's fourth-act detonation echoes that of the First Servant in the third. Taking up the Third Servant's conditional prediction (III.vii.99-101), Albany conditionally envisions the naturalistic apocalypse, the metamorphosis of man without the heavens' justice:

> If that the heavens do not their visible spirits
> Send quickly down to tame these vilde offences,
> It will come,
> Humanity must perforce prey on itself,
> Like monsters of the deep. (IV.ii.46-50)

In contrast to Gloucester's nightmare perception of purposeless existence, conceived in his own "sport-insect" metaphor, Albany imagines the destruction of the last restraining hierarchical and legal principle, reducing man to a beast which preys upon its kind. Recalling one of the traditional signs before doomsday,[23] Albany's apocalyptic vision, in terms reminiscent of Coleridge's prediction above (Chapter vi, note 64), projects *à outrance* Edmund's naturalistic doctrine of the first act and its third-act application by Cornwall.

As supporter of hierarchy, Albany is committed to the bond of humanity on its various levels, organically sustaining each other. Analogous to the Renaissance *exemplum* of the body and its members, moreover, the symbolic tree recurs in both *Leir* (ll. 1242-43) and *Lear*:

> She that herself will sliver and disbranch
> From her material sap, perforce must wither
> And come to deadly use. (IV.ii.34-36)

Albany's "nature" is therefore not Edmund's ruthless chaos of animal vitality, restlessly creating its own "hierarchy" by tooth and claw. It is rather one of rootedly traditional order and restraint:

> That nature, which contemns it[s] origin,
> Cannot be border'd certain in itself. (IV.ii.32-33)[24]

As Albany "fears" Goneril's "disposition" (IV.ii.31), his vision of mankind preying on itself is fulfilled in the murder of Regan by Goneril and in Goneril's suicide.

[23]Formerly attributed to Bede, one version of the fifteen doomsday signs predicts, on the fourth day toward the "promised end," monsters of the deep. See William W. Heist, *The Fifteen Signs before Doomsday* (East Lansing, Mich., 1952), pp. 24-25; see also pp. 26, 28. Cf. *Troilus and Cressida*, I.iii.108-124. See, in this chapter below, the discussion of "world upside down."

[24]Cf. *Queen Elizabeth's Englishings of Boethius, De Consolatione Philosophiae, A.D. 1593* (ed. Caroline Pemberton, E.E.T.S., Orig. Ser. 113 [1899], p. 79): "For they that forsake the common end of all thinges that be, they leave themselves to be. . . . For ther is that, that keps & retaynes Natures order: Ther is that fayles from that, & leaves that in their Nature is grafted." Still closer is Marcus Aurelius Antoninus' *The Communings with Himself*, tr. C. R. Haines, Loeb Classical Lib. (1916), p. 299: "A branch cut off from its neighbour branch cannot but be cut off from the whole plant. In the very same way a man severed from one man has fallen away from the fellowship of all men. Now a branch is cut off by others, but a man separates himself from his neighbour by his own agency in hating him or turning his back upon him; and is unaware that he has thereby sundered himself from the whole civic community." See Epistle to the Romans xi.19-20; Aurelius, *Communings*, p. 85, describing as "a

Although Albany, like the protagonists and Edgar, is deceived by a close relative, he is slowest to be undeceived. Like Edgar, he apparently starts from a kind of worldly *tabula rasa*. Yet, in contrast to Edgar's *éducation sentimentale* or sympathetic involvement in feeling, Albany's is primarily a timed explosion, a retarded awakening to human evil and a transformation from confused disinterest to engaged commitment. His three stages include the "mild husband" who "trust[s] too far" (I.iv.338) and who, in regard to his abused and royal father-in-law, is "guiltless, as I am ignorant" (I.iv.282): "Now, Gods that we adore, whereof comes this?" (I.iv.299), he sums up both his piety and his confusion. After Lear's madness and Gloucester's blinding, however, he is "never man so chang'd" (IV.ii.3); yet, perceiving the moral reversal in his world ("he . . . told me," complains Oswald, "I had turn'd the wrong side out," IV.ii.8-9), he smiles bitterly and does nothing. His last stage emphasizes Albany's almost invariable lateness. Having been last to recognize his own wife's character, he might, with her father, have exclaimed regarding Goneril, "Woe, that too late repents" (I.iv.266). He is too late to prevent the French invaders' landing (IV.ii.4). When, at long last, he is stirred to action, he discovers himself, too late, in the ironical position of one who is wedded to a loathed enemy with whom he must patriotically ally to combat a desired friend. When he grandly resigns the kingdom to Lear, "During the life of this old Majesty" (V.iii.299), it is again too late, for some ten lines later Lear is dead. And, most notably, as he exclaims, "Great thing of us forgot! / . . . Run, run! O, run!" (V.iii.236, 247), his "absolute power" (l. 300) is too late to prevent the murder of Cordelia.

Civil order victorious in the ashes of the state is poised against the ambiguity of the cosmos. Preventing the work from declining into further horror, the survival of Albany and Edgar helps confirm the continuity, within the given universe, of human goodness. Affirming ethical absolutes and natural law, Albany platonically condemns self-involved and "self-cover'd" moral relativism:

> Wisdom and goodness to the vile seem vile;
> Filths savour but themselves; (IV.ii.38-39)

---

limb cut off from the community" one "who cuts off his own soul from the soul of all rational things. . . ." Cf. John xv.5-6; Clement of Alexandria, *The Rich Man's Salvation*, tr. G. W. Butterworth, Loeb Classical Lib. (1919), p. 349.

and, as a norm of public order, he maintains the traditions of chivalry (IV.ii.63-67) and good form (V.iii.233-234). Taking up Kent's earlier role against the villains, Albany, especially after Gloucester's blinding, symbolizes moral indignation; and, as Edgar manipulates the spectators' pity, so Albany's new commitment in the closing acts dramatically channels the audience's outrage. Similarly marked is his newly developed tone of dry and ironic command, as at V.iii.41-46, 71, and 80, culminating in the restrained yet bitter irony of lines 85-90: his wife, Albany explains, is already "sub-contracted" to Edmund, so there can, legally, be no banns between Edmund and Regan. Simultaneously admitting impediments to the marriage of untrue minds, the duke seems implicitly to admit cuckolding by his hierarchical opposite, the excluded and uninheriting Bastard.

Receiver of the kingdom as highest-ranking survivor, Albany, like other figures of the final sequence, thus attains his identity. In his earlier failure to assume his noble prerogative, however, and in his *de facto* submission to the inferior powers of evil, the duke mirrors the king's relinquishment of his hierarchical trust: the self-deposed Lear having "ever but slenderly known himself" (I.i.293-294), he forfeits the "marks of sovereignty, knowledge, and reason" (I.iv. 240-241). Since identity in *Lear* involves both self-knowledge and responsibility to one's place, the realization of his own identity awaits Albany's full expression of his power and rank. In ironic contrast to the restoration, however, and to the denouement's distribution of "deservings" (V.iii.304), crown, titles, and "names," the motif of deprivation pervades the closing lines. For on the difference between Albany and Lear, and their estimate of gains and losses, hangs the tragic balance: the irredeemable loss of Cordelia and with her, amidst the empty vastnesses, the loss of man's cosmic identity.

In the marriage of Albany and Goneril hierarchical justice and degree are wedded to unfathomable evil and chaos, their conjunction suggesting the Hobbesian beast coupled with civilized order. Standing for human decency, against the blood-dimmed tide, Albany for a time seems to lack conviction, while the worst are full of passionate intensity. Firm in the last act, however, the duke demands distributive justice, even on the battlefield (V.iii.44-46), and later promises their due to Kent and Edgar (V.iii.300-302). It is the "judgment of the heavens," moreover, which Albany repeatedly invokes, as at IV.ii.46-47 and 78-80, as well as at V.iii.231-232. In contrast to the pitiful Edgar, solacing and forgiving the father and the brother who had sought his life, Albany's discovery involves only "justice." Inclining here to the terror, rather than the pity, of the Aristotelian tragic effect, the duke exclaims at the death of his wife and his sister-in-law:

> This judgment of the heavens, that makes us tremble,
> Touches us not with pity. (V.iii.231-232)

Yet, while occupying antithetical moral positions, Albany with his poetic justice (e.g., IV.ii.78-80; the gods "So speedily can venge") and the villains with their *lex talionis* seem analogous, insofar as both, from different directions, assume the imminence of appropriate earthly retribution. While Regan holds, like the Fool, that men's follies must be their schoolmasters, Goneril's vindictive insistence that, since "'Tis his own blame," Lear "must needs taste his folly" (II.iv. 292-293) perhaps ironically anticipates the language of Albany's poetic-justice formula:

> All friends shall taste
> The wages of their virtue, and all foes
> The cup of their deservings. (V.iii.302-304)[25]

Appropriately, Albany's term "deservings" is used elsewhere in the play only by a villain, in Edmund's promise to Kent to "study deserving" (I.i.31) and in his anticipation, profiting from his father's indiscretion, of his own rise: "This seems a fair deserving" (III.iii. 25).[26] Joining the term with a kind of poetic justice, Cornwall, too, says of the stocked Kent, "his own disorders / Deserv'd much less advancement" (II.iv.201-202).[27] Whereas Lear initially claims to rely upon the concept of desert and merit, apportioning shares "Where nature doth with merit challenge" (I.i.53), Cornwall employs "merit" in connection with his own retributory poetic "justice"; Gloucester, Cornwall assures Edmund, *deserved* the plot

[25]Cf. the text (Leviticus xxiv.19-20) insisted upon by the Puritans, e.g., John Dod and Robert Cleaver, *A Plaine and Familiar Exposition of the Ten Commandements* (1604), p. 262: ". . . God hath appointed to bee punished by the Magistrate, by inflicting the same hurt upon him, that hee . . . hath done to another: *An eye for eye, hand for hand, foote for foote, & c.* And that most justly too, that hee should drinke of his owne cuppe."

[26]As elsewhere in Shakespeare, an early comment strikes a keynote—the play itself may be viewed as a "study" in "deserving."

[27]The worldly pragmatic Fool anticipates this use at II.iv.64-65: "And thou hadst been set i' th' stocks for that question, thou'dst well deserv'd it."

against his life: "I now perceive it was not altogether your brother's evil disposition made him seek his death; but a provoking merit, set a-work by a reproveable badness in himself" (III.v.5-8). Once again, the only other reference to "merit" is Albany's, in a speech requiring Edmund to use the prisoners according to the equal determination of "their merits and our safety" (V.iii.45). Further, of the three uses of "justicer" in the play, two are employed with sardonic effect by the mad Lear in his trial scene (III.vi.21, 56); these seem to prepare for the third occurrence in Albany's prompt presumption of the heavens' retributive "justicers" (IV.ii.79).

If Albany has been blind at the start in marrying Goneril and in long remaining unaware of her true identity, at the end he appears to transcend a private confusion perhaps only to achieve a cosmic one. For, as at the opening, Albany was said to "trust too far" (I.iv.338) in human relationships, so, of the survivors at the close, he alone retains a cosmic trust. A kind of ducal *deus ex machina*, he can neither control, till too late, the evils of his domestic environment nor fully, perhaps, estimate the darker potentials of his supernatural one. He envisions, for example, an imminent human debacle (IV.ii. 46-50), only to seize hastily upon "evidences" of heavenly providence that prevent it (ll. 78-80). Dramatically questioning such confidence, however, a series of ironies suggests Albany's imperception of the forces that other characters, in the destructive element immersed, more feelingly perceive. It is, appropriately, this personage whom Shakespeare chooses to uphold distributive and cosmic justice at the end (V.iii.300-304)—in effect, to "explicate," like Job's comforter, the mystery of suffering ("Remember, I pray thee: who ever perished being an innocent? or where were the upright destroyed?" [iv.7])—and to be undercut by Lear's unsatisfied outcry (V.iii.305-308).

The Fool

The most artful Part in a Play is the Fool's. . . .
—Cervantes, *Don Quixote*, Pt. II, Ch. iii

RENAISSANCE FOLLY

Les folz, le numbre desquelz est infiny, comme atteste Salomon. . . .
—Rabelais, *Gargantua and Pantagruel*

The Renaissance secularization of folly increasingly transformed it from a context of sinfulness to one of imprudence. Analogous to the newly reemphasized divine "irrationality" and the *Deus ab-*

sconditus, human reason's reiterated darkness implied an all-pervasive earthly irrationality. Universal folly as sinfulness (Brant, Geiler von Kaisersberg, Murner, Bosch) thus gave way to universal folly as immutably inherent in human life (Erasmus, Rabelais, Franck, Bruegel).[28] As earth was transmuted from an ultramundane mirror to a world stage, it presented the struggle, less of good and bad angels or of abstract virtues and vices than, within a universe of folly, of fools and knaves: *psychomachia* yielded to *moriomachia*.

With flawed reason long after the Fall, reflecting Renaissance Pyrrhonist limitations, man occupied a confused realm of folly, mirroring clearly neither heaven nor hell. His altered condition, under the no-longer-immutable heavens, is figured in the juxtaposition of Lear, the heavens' thunder, and the hell-ridden Edgar upon the heath —accompanied by the Fool. Amidst this sound and fury, where all were merely players, folly and imprudence, not sin alone, drove men from cradle to the grave. "All thy other titles thou hast given away; that [of Fool] thou wast born with" (I.iv.155-156), his jester informs Lear. "When we are born," the king echoes, "we cry that we are come / To this great stage of fools" (IV.vi.184-185), as finally he exclaims, "And my poor fool is hang'd!" (V.iii.305).

Indeed, syllogizes Erasmus, "if he is a fool that is not wise, and every good man according to the Stoics is a wise man, it is no wonder if all mankind be concluded under folly."[29] In the absence of wisdom and goodness, the Fool and the Knave, the deceived and the deceiver, become interchangeable *Doppelgänger*, whose dealings inspire this mortal coil: in a world of folly knaves are merely a special kind of fool. Appropriately, Lear's first mention of him, alluding also to the sense of "boy," is "Where's my knave? my Fool?" (I.iv.45-46). Folly's counterpart, reason, becomes practicality and, as in the Renaissance picaresque romance, develops into a cunning principle of knavish advancement through the world. Apropos, Pascal, like La Rochefoucauld, held that men could hardly endure each other's society if they were not the dupes of one another.[30] Similarly, Ma-

[28] I am indebted in this sentence, as well as elsewhere in this section, to Charles de Tolnay's introduction to his edition of *The Drawings of Pieter Bruegel the Elder* (New York, [1953?]).

[29] *Praise of Folly*, p. 127.

[30] *Pensées*, ed. H. F. Stewart (1950), pp. 76, 78: "Ainsi la vie humaine n'est qu'une illusion perpétuelle. . . . L'union qui est entre les hommes n'est fondée que sur cette mutuelle tromperie. . . ."

dame du Deffand divided the world into "les trompeurs, les trompés, et les trompettes,"[31] and La Rochefoucauld's disciple, Swift, spoke of "the sublime and refined Point of Felicity, called, *the Possession of being well deceived*; The Serene Peaceful State of being a Fool among Knaves."[32]

In Shakespeare's world, as in Erasmus' and Bruegel's, Everyman seems less eligible for justification than for a cap and bells. Folly, for Erasmus, includes unreason, the opposite of Stoic wisdom, which is untenable in Folly's realm: "And the Stoics too, that conceive themselves next to the gods, yet show me one of them . . . if he do not . . . for some time commit an act of folly and dotage" (p. 16). For that Stoic wisdom, which Erasmus defines as "nothing else than to be governed by reason," must yield to folly, "to be given up to the will of our passions" (p. 26). In the discrepancy between man's self-vaunted reason and his undignified reality—"Most ignorant of what he's most assured" (*Measure for Measure*, II.ii.119; cf. ll. 117-123)—Shakespeare, like Erasmus, Rabelais, and Montaigne, finds wry food for laughter.

FOLLY AND CONTRADICTION

Il est plus fol, qui a fol sens demande.
—Bacon, *Promus* (ca. 1594)

The protean Fool is, *in posse*, everything subsumed in the world governed by folly. Mediating between practical necessity and idealistic impulse, he is himself not totally free to choose but is driven by his own principle. Since folly as unreason is inherently contradictory, as well as, to a certain degree, compulsively determined, the Fool's actions belie his words, as his words belie his feelings. Contradictorily framing his incessant apothegms of practical self-regard, the Fool's sympathy emerges initially, as it does for him finally, when he selflessly accompanies Lear into the storm. Divided between pragmatism and love, between the villains' quantitative chaos and his master's

[31]*Horace Walpole's Correspondence with Madame du Deffand*, ed. W. S. Lewis and Warren H. Smith, VI (New Haven, 1939), 66.

[32]*A Tale of a Tub*, ed. A. C. Guthkelch and D. Nichol Smith (Oxford, 1920), p. 174. If, as Reformers especially insisted, human nature through Adam was corrupted, it could follow that, where all do offend, in Lear's terms "None does offend" (IV.vi.170).

more traditional cosmos, the Fool is, in part, a reflection of Renaissance transition.

Hence, his inconsistencies juxtapose the frailty of private beliefs with the substance of public realities. In a world composed almost solely of fools and knaves, mistrust becomes a universal principle. Faithful commitments, such as Cordelia's, give way to hypocritical vows, such as her sisters'. Conversely, imprudence or trust is reputed madness: "He's mad," notes the Fool, "that trusts in the tameness of a wolf, a horse's health, a boy's love, or a whore's oath" (III.vi.18-19). As Queen Elizabeth, with the bitter perception of old age, confided to Lambarde in 1601: ". . . now the wit of the fox is everywhere on foot, so as hardly a faithful or virtuous man may be found."[33] His Machiavellian realism defeated by his own foolish sympathy,[34] the Fool is a measure of inevitable human discrepancies, reflected, for instance, in Machiavelli's admonition: ". . . there is such a difference between the way men live and the way they ought to live, that anybody who abandons what is for what ought to be will learn something that will ruin rather than preserve him. . . ."[35]

While ostensibly disappearing in mid-play, the Fool in principle accompanies Lear on his circular journey to human love. The demand for love which devised Lear's torment is his intolerable shirt of flame: deludedly having cast out love through self-love, he pursues love even to the final illusion of his beloved's breathing lips. In this cyclical movement the Fool's "pining away" at Cordelia's banishment in the first act is rounded out by Lear's inconsolable grief in the last: "And my poor fool is hang'd!" In the dark journey from illusion to illusion, on the unlighted path where knowledge is folly but ignorance is not bliss, the king and his Fool ride side by side.

[33] J. E. Neale, *Queen Elizabeth* (New York, 1934), p. 382.

[34] Cf. *The Christmas Prince*, ed. Frederick S. Boas and W. W. Greg, Malone Soc. Repr. (1922); as the editors indicate, in *Ira seu tumulus fortunæ* only Stultus stays faithful to the Prince, while in *Periander* the loyal page Neotinus pursues his master through a night of fearful storm. See also Alfred Harbage, "The Authorship of *The Christmas Prince*," *MLN*, L (1935), 501-505. Cf. the loyal Fool in George Cavendish's *The Life and Death of Cardinal Wolsey*, ed. R. S. Sylvester, E.E.T.S. (Oxford, 1959), p. 104. In Richard Brome's *Queen and Concubine* (1635-39), Andrea, the faithful fool, follows the banished queen Eulalia into exile.

[35] *The Prince and Other Works*, tr. Allan H. Gilbert (Chicago, 1941), p. 141. Cf. Bacon, *Works*, V, 17: ". . . we are much beholden to Machiavelli and other writers of that class, who openly and unfeignedly declare . . . what men do, and not what they ought to do." See "De improvidentia futuri" in Sebastian Brant's *Stultifera navis*, tr. Alexander Barclay (1570), foll. 137-139.

FOLLY AND PRUDENCE

> *I am a Fool that's certain, for if I'd been wise, I had left my Master many a fair Day since; but . . . . I must follow him through Thick and Thin. . . . I love him well, and . . . nothing but Death can part us.*
>
> —Cervantes, *Don Quixote*, Pt. II, Ch. xxxiii

While the Fool, like Polonius, preaches the new bourgeois ethic, he lives the traditional one. Against his own businesslike advice to

> Have more than thou showest . . .
> Lend less than thou owest . . .
> Learn more than thou trowest,
> Set less than thou throwest;
> Leave thy drink and thy whore,
> And keep in-a-door,
> (I.iv.124-131)

prudent folk counsel of caution against displaying, lending, wasting, trusting ("Distrust and caution," noted Franklin, "are the parents of security"),[36] the Fool throws in his lot with the old king, repudiates the ethic of accumulation, and does not "keep in-a-door." Discarding both warmth and prudence, Lear rushes headlong into the storm. Ignoring the Fool's "Set less than thou throwest," he utters to the heavens, as to his daughters, the gambler's cry, "take all" (III.i.15),[37] and he is accompanied by

> None but the Fool, who labours to out-jest
> His heart-strook injuries. (III.i.16-17)

If Lear heeds the rhymed counsels above, he will, the Fool guarantees, "have more / Than two tens to a score" (I.iv.132-133), an arithmetical absurdity, or the warranty of "interest" on his moral principle, in keeping with the inappropriateness of his advice. Recalling Coleridge's "*cui bono? . . . quid mihi?*" or "ant-hill" principle of vir-

[36]Franklin, 1773, in Tilley F135. Cf. I.iv.338, on trusting; Tilley A202. Cf. the Fool's other prudent admonitions, e.g., III.ii.25-34, apparently echoed in Richard West, *The Court of Conscience* (1607), sig. E1, and anticipatory of Tilley W874.

[37]As reported by the Gentleman, and recalling Lear's "I gave you all" (II.iv.252).

tue,[38] he also mocks Lear's concern with the rise and fall in price (I.i.197). As in his prognostication, the Fool at the end subverts any apparent sense with a sudden *reductio*. Predicting, as *homme chiffre*, the king's quantitative nadir ("now thou art an O without a figure," I.iv.200-201),[39] his promise of "more" foreshadows Lear's reduction to less (cf. II.iv.261-265) and finally to "nothing."

THE WARM FOOL

If he have wit enough to keep himself warm.
—*Much Ado about Nothing*, I.i.68[40]

Since, in contrast to the rustic Kent, the shivering domestic Fool yearns visibly for house and hearth, he is a measure of Lear's "foolish" exposure and alienation upon the heath. When he was at home, to quote Touchstone, he "was in a better place." Where the Fool is weak and cowardly, moreover, Kent is courageous; yet both the indoor domestic Fool and the outdoor rustic clown, with whom Kent shares some traits, undertake the folly of loyalty. Shelterless, the Fool and Lear, like the naked beggar, "acting out" some negative implications of special providence, provoke the question of covering and protection. Hence, reiteratively, upon the heath and elsewhere, house references occur in the Fool's speeches (e.g., I.v.27-32; III.ii.10-11, 25-26, 27). After Regan's excuse, "This house is little" (II.iv.290), Kent offers the king "a hovel" lending "friendship," in contrast to the castle, "this hard house . . ." (III.ii.63-64). And Lear, too, comes to address himself to "houseless heads" and "houseless poverty" (III.iv.30, 26). The Fool is domestic, moreover, even in his imagery of eggs (I.iv.162-171) and breeches (I.iv.180-181), of cooking and feeding (II.iv.122-127). His ambition is centered on the

[38]*The Political Thought of Samuel Taylor Coleridge*, ed. R. J. White (1938), pp. 94-95.

[39]Cf. Tilley C391 ("He is a Cipher among numbers"). Gerta Calmann, "The Picture of Nobody: An Iconographical Study," *JWCI*, XXIII (1960), 70-71, cites a fifteenth-century Italian representation of the fool as card O of the Tarot pack; she notes the analogy between the fool and the sign O during initiations at German universities, conducted to the chant, "O beane . . . o asine . . . o cifra, o figura nihili, o tu omnino nihil." Cf. Alemán's *Guzman de Alfarache*, II, 194. Cf. *As You Like It*, III.ii. 307-308. A character in *Club Law* is named Mr. Cipher. C. T.'s *Laugh and Lie Downe* (1605), sig. Biii, describes a "Ladie" who "asked me who I was? I aunswered, a Cipher among figures."

[40]Cf. Tilley K10.

hearth: Truth "must be whipp'd out," he mutters bitterly, "when the Lady Brach may stand by th' fire and stink" (I.iv.117-119). Although Henry VIII's fool, Will Somers, is described as lying down to sleep among the dogs,[41] these latter might often have been the Fool's rivals for the preferred fireside place. If "Truth" is also Cordelia, "the Lady Brach" may suggest her flattering sisters, who are eventually to hasten the Fool's exit into the cold.

But even flattery is preferable, as the Fool's speech (III.ii.10-11) implies, to the cold. Describing *The Honestie of This Age* (1614), Barnabe Rich says that upon wisdom, "some *Court holy water wordes* . . . wee will bestowe, but for our owne advantage, & when our turne is served, our kindnes is estranged" (p. 37). As the Fool's expressions seem the antithesis of the sentimental and the religious, so for him holy water becomes "court holy-water" (III.ii.10),[42] his remark being flippantly antithetical to the "holy water" from Cordelia's "heavenly eyes" (IV.iii.31). Representing the indoors-loving courtier ("This is a brave night," he puns, "to cool a courtezan," III. ii.79), the Fool, unable to "smile as the wind sits," catches "cold shortly" (I.iv.105-106). For, as Lear's comparison with him shows (III.ii.68-69), neither the Fool nor his master is "ague-proof" (IV. vi.107-108). As the warmth-sensitive Fool had predicted, "Winter" was indeed "not gone" (II.iv.46; cf. II.iv.68). Amidst the naked beggar's shouts of "Tom's a-cold" (III.iv.58), Lear's "warm fool"[43] emphasizes the king's new-found place among the "poor naked wretches."

Household plays including a memorable domestic fool, *Twelfth Night* and *Lear*, both influenced by Sidney's *Arcadia*,[44] also enact the topical issue between *arriviste* hypocrisy and traditional hospitality. As Malvolio longs to dispossess the reveling Sir Toby and his Knight, Goneril and Regan carry out the ejection of Lear's "debosh'd" (I.iv.250) knights. Paralleling Malvolio in his distaste for

[41]Robert Armin recalls that "Such, like Will Sommers, sleepe amongst dogs" (*Fools and Jesters: With a Reprint of Robert Armin's Nest of Ninnies* [1608], Shakespeare Soc. [1842], p. 48).

[42]See Tilley H532. Cf. Ch.v, n.18.

[43]On another sense of "warm fool," see Leslie Hotson's *Shakespeare's Motley* (New York, 1952), p. 66.

[44]See Fitzroy Pyle, "'Twelfth Night,' 'King Lear' and 'Arcadia,'" *MLR*, XLIII (1948), 449-455.

"cakes and ale," Goneril, for example, expresses her opposition to "epicurism" and "tavern[s]" (I.iv.252-253). Also intimating the crisis of traditional nobility, Lear's "knights and squires" (I.iv.249) reemerge in the Fool's prognosticatory hope concerning "No squire in debt, nor no poor knight" (III.ii.86). Appropriately, the domestic fools of both plays sing versions of the same song, emphasizing warmth and shelter. Yet Feste's song, containing the line "'Gainst knaves and thieves men shut their gate," is acted out in bitter earnest by Lear's knave, the king, and the pathetic remains of his retinue, shivering outside the gates which men have shut against them. According to the Fool's song (with its possible thrust at the groundlings who, unsheltered, stood fronting his stage),

> He that has and a little tiny wit,
> With hey, ho, the wind and the rain,
> Must make content with his fortunes fit,
> Though the rain it raineth every day. (III.ii.74-77)

For the Fool, in the Renaissance proverb, has wit enough to wish to come in out of the rain;[45] the king, with "a little tiny wit," has not.

WORLD UPSIDE DOWN: "ADYNATA" AND "IMPOSSIBILIA"

> *Loe, nature chaunged upside downe, and out of order tornde. . . .*
>
> —*Agamemnon* in *Seneca His Tenne Tragedies* (1581)

> *All goes topsie-turvy; all Kim, Kam; all, is tricks and devices; all Riddles and unknowne Mysteries; you shall not finde man, with man; we all live in ambush, lying in wait one for another, as the Cat, for the Mouse, or the Spider for the Fly. . . .*
>
> —Alemán, *Guzman de Alfarache*, II, 19-20

A constant and topical refrain, heard in the translation of Louis Leroy in 1594, "Every where the publike estates have bin afflicted, changed, or destroied; and every where the Religion troubled with

[45]Tilley F537. C.T., *Laugh and Lie Downe,* seems to echo both *Twelfth Night* and the Fool's lines sung in the "purgatory" of *King Lear*: "These passages who hath paste, and is come unto the ende of his pilgrimage [cf. *Lear,* V.iii.196], let him sing with me in this purgatorie: Oh the winde, the weather, and the raine," sig. [Biv^{v}]. (C. T.'s work alludes also to "a Foole in a pied coat," sig. F2^{v}.)

In his earlier rhyme mentioning rain, the Fool promises: "But I will tarry; the Fool will stay, / And let the wise man fly" (II.iv.82-83). Employing (as in III.ii.40) the conventional fool-wise-man conjunction, the Fool may here also utilize a proverbial ex-

heresies . . . . there was never in the world more wickednes, more impietie, or more disloialtie; Devocion is quenched . . . there remayneth but a shadow of Justice. All is *turned upside downe* . . . ,"[46] is echoed in Montaigne: "I live in an age, wherein we abound with incredible examples of this vice [cruelty] . . . And read all ancient stories, be they never so tragicall, you shall find none to equall those, we daily see practised. . . . I could hardly be perswaded, before I had seene it, that the world could have afforded so marble-hearted and savage-minded men . . ." (II, 121).[47] The late Elizabethan and the Jacobean sense of the inversion of values,[48] reflected in Gloucester's and the Fool's entirely conventional prognostications and in the play's *adynata*, is revealed also in Philopatris' *An Humble Petition Offered to the . . . Estates of This Present Parliament Assembled at Westminster Pallace* (1606), ". . . thus is the worlde there turned topsie turvie: The good and faythfull are taken away, and the wicked and ungratious are hoysted up in their roomes" (pp. 9-10). It is summarized again in Chapman's Byron:

> The world is quite inverted, Virtue thrown
> At Vice's feet, and sensual Peace confounds
> Valour and cowardice, fame and infamy.[49]

As *raisonneur* of chaos, the Fool is the incessant chorus of value inversion. In this he is reminiscent of the *topos* Curtius traces in the Virgilian *adynata* known in the Middle Ages, suggesting the reversal of the entire natural order. The collocation of *adynata* or *impossibilia*

---

pression; see *A New Enterlude of Godly Queene Hester* (1525-29), ed. W. W. Greg, in *Materialien zur Kunde des älteren englischen Dramas*, V (Louvain, 1904), l. 673: "And fooles be fayne to fyght when wise men runne away." Cf. also the speaker's name, Hardydardy, and the Fool's "handy-dandy" vision as asserted by Lear, IV.vi.155.

[46] *Of the Interchangeable Course* . . . , tr. Robert Ashley (1594), fol. 112ᵛ (italics mine).

[47] See Pierre Villey-Desmeserets, *Les sources & l'évolution des essais de Montaigne* (Paris, 1933), II, 489, who speaks of the ". . . chaos intellectuel où le XVIe siècle s'était débattu."

[48] Asserting that gratuities were basic to Elizabethan court life, J. E. Neale's *The Elizabethan Political Scene* (Oxford, 1948) notes the sharp decline in public morality during the queen's last decade; the new accumulative ethic in the Tudor and Stuart era has frequently (e.g., by R. H. Tawney, L. C. Knights, Christopher Hill) been documented.

[49] *The Tragedy of Charles Duke of Byron* (1608), I.ii.14-16. Cf. Spenser, *Faerie Queene*, Bk. V, Proem, st. 4.

led to the world-upside-down *topos*. By the twelfth century the former, supplemented by Ovid and the Roman satirists, recur as the church and social conditions become subjects of world-upside-down censure; similarly, in the medieval *Carmina Burana*, in Nigel de Longchamps' *Speculum stultorum*, as well as, following Lucian, in Rabelais and others, the *topos* survives.[50] This theme of inversion proceeds in its literary career to a point beyond Curtius' purview in Swift's *Gulliver's Travels*, whose method Dr. Johnson similarly perceived and whose substance has more than one analogy with Shakespeare's drama.

Structurally as well as conceptually, the world-upside-down motif, which embraces the play, manifests also the Fool's principles. The anonymous early lyric, for instance, "This werlde es tournede up-so downe,"[51] anticipates the Fool's characteristic expression. Among sixteenth-century examples, the fifth book of Rabelais' *Gargantua and Pantagruel* shows the Queen of Whims's officers engaged in such perversities as ploughing the sandy shore with yoked foxes, extracting water out of stones, shearing asses, gathering figs from thistles, milking he-goats, and catching the wind in nets. "Others," declare Rabelais' seventeenth-century translators, "set carts before the horses,"[52] recalling the ox behind the cart in the *Carmina Burana* and the Fool's "May not an ass know when a cart draws the horse?" (I.iv.232-233). Anticipating the Fool's "impossible" instructions

[50]In addition to such impossibilities rehearsed, e.g., in *Romeo and Juliet*, I.i.182-187, see the numerous *adynata* in Petrarch and in Salutati; cf. Klaus Heitmann, *Fortuna und Virtus: Eine Studie zu Petrarcas Lebensweisheit* (Cologne, 1958), p. 237 (Heitmann provides a useful register of some revelant Renaissance *topoi*). See Curtius, pp. 94-98; Ernest Dutoit, *Le thème de l'adynaton dans la poésie antique* (Paris, 1936); Robert M. Grant, *Miracle and Natural Law in Graeco-Roman and Early Christian Thought* (Amsterdam, 1952), pp. 57-58; H. V. Canter, "The Figure *Adynaton* in Greek and Latin Poetry," *American Journal of Philology*, LI (1930), 32-41.

[51]See *The Index of Middle English Verse*, ed. Carleton Brown and Rossell Hope Robbins (New York, 1943), No. 3778; cf. Karl Brunner, "Hs. Brit. Mus. Additional 31042," *Archiv für das Studium der neueren Sprachen und Literaturen*, CXXXII (1914), 318. See also Carleton Brown, "The 'Pride of Life' and the 'Twelve Abuses,'" *Archiv*, CXXVIII (1912), 72-78, connecting the "world upside down" and social satire; and *Religious Lyrics of the XVth Century*, ed. Brown (Oxford, 1939), p. 238: "lo! how þis werld is turnyd up & downe." See also *Poets of the English Language*, ed. W. H. Auden and Norman H. Pearson, Viking Portable Lib. (New York, 1950), I, 426-427. Cf. Klaus Lazarowicz, *Verkehrte Welt: Vorstudien zu einer Geschichte der deutschen Satire* (Tübingen, 1963).

[52]*The Urquhart–Le Motteux Translation of the Works of Francis Rabelais*, ed. Albert J. Nock and Catherine R. Wilson (New York, 1931), II, 817. Cf. the rhetorical

(I.iv.132-133),[53] ironically echoed also in his exchanges with Lear over "nothing," still others at Rabelais' Paradise of Fools "out of nothing made great things, and made great things return to nothing."

Iconographically, the perversity of Rabelais' Queen of Whims's court appears, for instance, in Bruegel's painting of Flemish proverbs (1559). At the sign of the world turned upside down, the inn and its environs witness such performances as shearing a pig, filling up a fountain after the calf has been drowned, and carrying light in a basket into the bright day. As Nashe reminds us, the world upside down was a familiar alehouse sign: ". . . it is no marvaile if every Alehouse vaunt the table of the world turned upside downe, since the child beateth his father . . ." (III, 315).[54] In the Fool's perception of Lear's topsy-turvy world[55] the daughters instruct their parent ("Which they will make an obedient father," I.iv.243) and indeed, recalling the alehouse sign, chastise him like a child: ". . . thou mad'st

---

form—"the Greeks call it *Histeron proteron,* we name it the Preposterous" (George Puttenham, *The Arte of English Poesie* [1585], ed. Gladys D. Willcock and Alice Walker [Cambridge, Eng., 1936], Bk. III, Ch. xiii, p. 170); cf. Tilley C103, P434.

[53]As do other characters, the Fool chorally points the downward direction of the tragedy. Paralleling his father's astrological pessimism, Edgar's philosophical remarks (IV.i.5; IV.i.27) are matched by the Fool's more specific folk pessimism: e.g., "Winter's not gone yet, if the wild-geese fly that way" (II.iv.46-47). Similarly, Kent's proverbial "out of heaven's benediction / . . . To the warm sun!" (II.ii.161-162), addressed to the king, underscores the progressive deterioration of the royal party. Such alteration of condition to a worse one seems insinuated in the Fool's reply to the query of his still not fully disabused master: "Be my horses ready?" "Thy asses are gone about 'em" (I.v.34-35). Although the Fool's jest in the sequence seems to have escaped notice, "From horses to asses," in Erasmus' *Adagia* ([Frankfurt am Main], 1629), p. 161, "ab equis ad asinos" is a Renaissance proverb analogous to that of Kent above and implies a similar deterioration in one's estate; see Tilley H713, omitting *Lear* as well as George Ruggle, *Ignoramus,* 1st Prologue: "Imo transcendes ab Equo ad Asinum" (1630, p. 3).

[54]On the child beating the father, cf. the Fool, I.iv.180-181, and McKerrow (Nashe, *Works,* IV, 448), who declares the inversion is probably based on Aristophanes and cites Thomas Wilson's *Rule of Reason* (1551); nevertheless, it was not uncommon in ancient and later comedy. Nashe's sign recurs in Edward Guilpin's *Skialetheia* (1598), sig. [D8]:

> The ale-house *Ethicks,* the worlds upside downe
> Is verefied: the prince now serves the clowne.

[55]In addition to references in Tilley (A328, K35, T165, W903, and, analogously, R40), the theme of the world upside down is expressed, *inter alia,* in Anthony Copley's *A Fig for Fortune* (1596), sig. [H2], "Fortunes topsie-turvie to confound"; Thomas Dekker and George Wilkins' *Jests to Make You Merie* (1607), p. 10, where an old man compares the present age with the past: "now the world was cleane found upside downe"; Wilkins' *The Miseries of Inforst Mariage* (1605-06; pr. 1607), sig. [I4v]: "Turnes the world upside downe, that men orebeare theyr Maisters"; John Bulwer, *Anthropometamorphosis* (1653), sig. ***1v, "The World is Topsie Turvy

thy daughters thy mothers . . . when thou gav'st them the rod and putt'st down thine own breeches . . ." (I.iv.179-181). In effect, he tells his master, "thou bor'st thine ass on thy back o'er the dirt" (I.iv.168-169). Eventually, as its cruel inversion is implied also in Albany's image of the self-devouring monsters of the deep (IV.ii.46-50),[56] the Fool's technique is absorbed into Lear's: for example, "which is the justice, which is the thief?" and "The usurer hangs the cozener" (IV.vi.155-156, 165).[57]

Since the world upside down is thus not only a physical but also a moral revolution, subversion becomes inversion, and all values "change places" (IV.vi.154). If, after the best have yielded up rule to the worst, might is right and justice and injustice are indistinguishable, then, as Lear, with "Reason in madness" (IV.vi.177), concludes, "None does offend" (IV.vi.170). More ominously, Hamlet's fear that "reason pandars will" (III.iv.88), suggesting a revolt in the order of nature, so that the basest becomes the norm of the natural, is consummated in Lear's horror of nature and of his own flesh (e.g., II.iv.223-227), which "smells of mortality" (IV.vi.135). In *Lear*, further, the cosmos seems enlisted in that reversal, against order and on the side of anarchy. Having acquired from the Fool less practical judgment than the "handy-dandy" vision which subverts it, the king becomes, like the antic Hamlet, his own vice. In sum, while the Fool reflects the comically grotesque aspect of the world upside down,

---

turn'd." See the series of Renaissance illustrations of "Mundus Perversus," "De verkeerde Wereld," in L. Lebeer, "De Blauwe Huyck," *Gentsche Bijdragen tot de Kunstgeschiedenis*, VI (1939-40), 161-229, e.g., figs. pp. 213, 215, 217. "Le monde renversé" is discussed in Jean Rousset, *La littérature de l'âge baroque en France: Circé et le paon* (Paris, 1960). Related to the world upside down is Fortune's wheel, whose turning motivates the work's continual inversion. Both motifs are illustrated in Bruegel's "Children's Play," containing numerous whirls and circles; while his "Christ in Limbo," in addition to displaying the self-seeking monster of the deep and Lewdness, shows the turning wheel of hell, casting its impaled old men from limbo into hellfire.

[56]See the present writer, "Addendum: Lest Men, Like Fishes," *Traditio*, XVIII (1962), 421-422. See also Henri Estienne, *A World of Wonders . . . Preparative Treatise to the Apologie for Herodotus*, tr. R. Carew (1607), p. 81: "It is a thing very . . . proper to this age (. . . it is more practised) that greeat theeves rob the lesse, as great fishes devoure the yong frie." Charles Richardson in *A Sermon against Oppression and Fraudulent Dealing* (1615), p. 8, cites Diogenes Laertius on great thieves hanging little thieves.

[57]Cf. Tilley T119. Citing the punishment of hanging merely for theft, including a first offense, while worse offenders go free, Erasmus (*Christiani matrimonii institutio*) sees the laws as an example of the world upside down.

Lear mirrors its grotesquely tragic side. For him, indeed, the hierarchy of the sacred has been overturned.[58] As Curtius, citing the early seventeenth-century libertine Théophile de Viau, points out, "In the twilight of a distracted mind the 'world upsidedown' can express horror" (p. 97).

Having severed the bond of communication and, by his disposal of the kingdom, the bond of social duty as well, the king has, in effect, isolated himself. Since, in Aristotelian as well as proverbial terms (Tilley M380), unsocial or solitary man is either a god or a beast, the king descends to a level where his companion must be the Fool. No longer able to sustain the orderly intercourse of dialogue, Lear for the most part finds his interlocutors outside the human order, as the thunder and the elements, and outside the social order, as beggars, madmen, and fools. His remaining confidant, of all the glittering court, is its solitary, whipped, and whimpering plaything. Amid the general failure of communication, the Fool, in rhymes, songs, parables, and riddles, replaces the futile directness of Lear's friends by his own disordered obliquity. Accompanying the king's unreasoned state, his staccato maieutic is thus an implicit invitation to madness: "O Fool! I shall go mad" (II.iv.288).

Further, the ambiguity of terms, as well as the shifting nature of concepts, provides the richness of irony of both Erasmian *declamatio* and Shakespearean drama. That the rashly mad Lear should be taught by a Fool is ironical, since, as Erasmus' *Praise of Folly* insists, "folly is the next degree, if not the very thing. For what else is madness," Folly asks, Polonius-fashion, "than for a man to be out of his wits?" (p. 61). Although "folly doctor-like" may prescribe prudence, what is prudence, asks Erasmus, but another kind of folly? "If prudence depends upon experience," the wise man's self-distrust constrains him to his books, where he learns only the "subtleties of words"; while the Erasmian fool picks up from practical experience what a blind man may have seen. In addition to experience, Erasmus' Folly claims even judgment and prudence for her own, since human appearances are deceptive and double-faced, like Alcibiades' Sileni: "common sense, that is to say, folly" (pp. 42-43, 53). Hence, self-defeating from the beginning, the Fool's instruction of the king cannot teach

[58]In chronological sequence Shakespearean tragedy appears to develop this recognition; where, it may be suggested, Hamlet questions, and Lear challenges, Macbeth assassinates, the divine order.

him prudence but only helps turn him into another kind of fool, that is to say, a madman.[59]

Combining the recurrent motifs of world upside down and antigeneration, the Fool and his master in Act II encounter the crisis of Lear's last filial rejection. His final hope threatened, Lear is seized with a paroxysm foreshadowing his end: "O me! my heart, my rising heart! but, down!" to which the Fool replies, "Cry to it, Nuncle, as the cockney did to the eels when she put 'em i' th' paste alive; she knapp'd 'em o' th' coxcombs with a stick, and cried 'Down, wantons, down!'" (II.iv.121-125). The eel, as in Rabelais[60] and *Pericles* (IV.ii.154-156), is, in the work's *dissuasio nubendi* context, a generative symbol. The Fool, in effect, seems to imply that Lear could have avoided heartache, putting down both the *hysterica passio* which "swells up toward" his heart (II.iv.56-57) and the "rising heart" itself, had he also put down his wanton impulse to reproduction. Joining the antigenerative theme with that of ingratitude, the Fool continues his topsy-turvy parables: "'Twas her brother that, in pure kindness to his horse, buttered his hay" (II.iv.125-127). Although in Robert Wilson's *The Three Ladies of London* (ca. 1581) it is charged, "Thou didst grease the horses' teeth, that they should not eat hay,"[61] and "An Ostler," according to *Sir Thomas Overbury His Wife* (1616), "hath certaine charmes for a horse mouth that he should not eat his hay" (sig. E2^{r-v}),[62] the cockney's foolish brother presumably acted merely out of the goodness of his heart. In an upside-down world, which binds generation to "filial ingratitude"

[59]Cf. *Praise of Folly*, p. 94, and Shakespeare's Sonnet 66. Cicero's *Paradoxa* defends the Stoic paradoxes (derived from the Cynics and indirectly from Socrates), including the position that all foolish men are mad. See also Lollio's remark in Middleton and Rowley's *The Changeling*, I.ii.46-49, "We have but two sorts of people in the [mad]-house, and both under the whip, that's fools and madmen; the one has not wit enough to be knaves, and the other not knavery enough to be fools" (*The Works of Thomas Middleton*, ed. A. H. Bullen [1885]).

[60]*Oeuvres* (Paris, 1835), "Glossaire," p. 580, s.v. "Anguille"; with the cockney's perversity in beating the eels, cf. Rabelais, the Queen of Whims's court, where (p. 316) "Aultres escorchoyent les anguilles par la queue, et ne crioyent lesdictes anguilles avant que destre escorchees, comme font celles de Melun" ("écorcher l'anguille par la queue": to take things by the wrong end foremost). The Fool's cockney is evidently attempting a "pâté d'anguille."

[61]*A Select Collection of Old English Plays*, comp. Robert Dodsley, ed. W. Carew Hazlitt, VI (1874), 255.

[62]Cf. Nashe, "A . . . Prognostication" (*Works*, III, 391), on "wicked Ostlers, that steale haie in the night from gentlemens horses, and rub their teth with tallow, that

(III.iv.14), "pure kindness" becomes perversity where thanklessness is the norm.

With symbolic bauble, which ladies will "be snatching" (I.iv.161), and rooster's coxcomb, the Fool pointedly speaks of "grace and a cod-piece; that's a wise man and a Fool" (III.ii.40-41). In contrast to his traditionally ithyphallic comic role and to the concerns for the flesh shared by Touchstone, Feste, Pompey, and Lavache, *Lear's* "all-licens'd" Fool seems paradoxically repressive and antiprogenitive. "Down, wantons, down!" is his theme, against Edmund's invocation to potency (I.ii.22) and Goneril's bestowal on the Bastard of a kiss which,

> if it durst speak,
> Would stretch thy spirits up into the air.
> Conceive. . . . (IV.ii.22-24)

Conception may have been a blessing, the Fool and his master might suggest, but not as Edmund would conceive. Even the once-sportive Gloucester finds corruption in generation:

> Our flesh and blood . . . is grown so vile,
> That it doth hate what gets it. (III.iv.149-150)

As Lear exclaims, "'twas this flesh begot / Those pelican daughters," Mad Tom interpolates the generative cause: "Pillicock sat on Pillicock hill" (III.iv.74-76).[63] "No, do thy worst, blind Cupid,"[64] concludes the king, "I'll not love" (IV.vi.139).

---

they may eate little. . . ." Cited in connection with Nashe (V, Supplement, 72) is *The Eclogues of Alexander Barclay*, ed. Beatrice White, E.E.T.S. (1928), Eclogue v, ll. 698-699. Marston, *The Dutch Courtezan*, III.i (*Plays*, II, 106). See also Dekker, *Lanthorne and Candle-light*, in *Non-Dramatic Works*, ed. Grosart, III, 299.

[63]Similar suggestions may lie in III.ii.3 and IV.vi.83; see, in contrast, Sonnet 11. Cf. Florio, *Queen Anna's New World of Words* (1611), s.v. "púga," "piuiólo"; see the seventeenth-century *Urquhart–Le Motteux Translation of . . . Rabelais*, ed. Nock and Wilson, I, Bk. I, Ch. xi, 225.

Folly is associated with the act of generation itself, e.g., in Othello's charge against Desdemona, "She turn'd to folly, and she was a whore" (V.ii.132); cf. *Troilus and Cressida*, V.ii.18, etc. In treatment of the subject, *Lear* is here, and in a number of other ways, directly antithetical to *As You Like It*, with its amiable "country copulatives" (V.iv.58): contrast the bitterness of Lear's "Let copulation thrive" (IV.vi.117).

[64]Not merely, as editors assert, a brothel sign but also an allusion to the blind Eros which befuddles man's intellect by exciting Voluptas unguided by reason; cf. John Downame, *Foure Treatises* (1613), p. 152: ". . . *Cupid* was said to be blind, because they who are possessed with this filthie lust, lose the sight of their understanding . . .";

"LUDICRA-SERIA": FOOL AND TRAGIC HERO

As when upon the stage a foole comes dreste up like a King.
—Palingenius, *Zodiake* (1576)

When Coleridge remarks that Shakespeare prepares for the Fool's introduction, unlike that of his other common clowns and fools, by bringing him "into living connection with the pathos of the play, with the sufferings,"[65] the critic's perception touches upon an implicit *topos* of the Fool-Lear relationship, the *ludicra-seria.* In contrast to Sidney's condemnation of the tragic "mingling" of "Kinges and Clownes" and matching of "horne Pipes and Funeralls,"[66] the mingling of jest and earnest, well documented in the literature of antiquity and the Middle Ages, recurs in Shakespeare's most pathetic tragedy.

In Homer, the juxtaposition of the base Thersites and the heroic Achilles; in classical mime and pantomime, the alternation of comic and tragic actor; in Ovid, the opposition of wanton against serious Muse and Thalia against Melpomene; in later antiquity, the rhetorical schema, *ioca seriis miscere*; the clerical mixture of laughter and solemnity and the admission of grotesque humor even to the sufferings of martyrdom, as in Prudentius' hymn of St. Laurence, and the *vita sancti*; Renaissance proverbs,[67] to add to these illustrations of Curtius (pp. 417-428), expressing the antithesis, and Raleigh's observation, "Onely we dye in earnest, that's no Jest";[68] and numerous other instances of the collocation of jest and earnest—testify to an enduring rhetorical and poetic tradition.

Robert Henryson, *Testament of Cresseid* (ca. 1480), Assembly of the Gods, ll. 169-175. Cf. Nashe, III, 195-196; Pleberio's lament over his daughter Melibea's suicide, *Celestina*, tr. James Mabbe (1631), ed. H. Warner Allen (New York, [1923]), p. 262: "They paint thee blind . . . but more blind are they that serve thee." See Erwin Panofsky's chapter on the subject in *Studies in Iconology: Humanistic Themes in the Art of the Renaissance* (New York, 1939) and Edgar Wind, *Pagan Mysteries in the Renaissance* (New Haven, 1958), pp. 56-77. See also A. A. M. Esser, *Das Antlitz der Blindheit in der Antike* (Leiden, 1961). Cf. above, Ch. v, n. 80.

65*Coleridge's Shakespearean Criticism,* ed. Thomas M. Raysor (1930), I, 63.

66*The Defence of Poesie,* in *Complete Works,* III, 39-40. See George Whetstone, dedicatory epistle to *Promos and Cassandra* (1578), "Manye tymes (to make mirthe) they make a Clowne companion with a Kinge"; *Virgidemiarum* (1597), *The Complete Poems of Joseph Hall,* ed. Alexander B. Grosart (Blackburn, Eng., 1879), Bk. I, Satires III, IV; Robert Kittowe's *Loves Load-starre* (1600), sigs. D3r-v.

67E.g., Tilley D532, J42, J46.

68*The Poems of Sir Walter Ralegh,* ed. Agnes M. C. Latham (1929), p. 48.

Although jest and earnest exist side by side in the convention which Curtius explores (pp. 417-435), he omits comment on the reciprocal aesthetic effect of their blending. In the transformed Renaissance moral framework, for example, the jest-earnest polarity at times dissolves ambiguously into fool and knave. The *topos* is indicated, again on both sides, ambivalently, in such collocations as Sancho Panza and Don Quixote, Sganarelle and Dom Juan, the *gracioso* and the hero. The morality Vice having changed from grim devil to jesting clown, the conventional duality is transposedly suggested in the opposition of the "antic" Hamlet and the "vice of kings." In Shakespeare, indeed, this mixture of jest and earnest reaches a culminating point, matched only by the emergent Spanish drama.

In Renaissance drama, moreover, the double plot seems related to the jest-earnest polarity and similarly contributes an ambivalent and ironical relationship. That the duality may also involve implicit social and hierarchical commentary is evident from the discrepancy in rank and diction of the personages and plots opposed. Such juxtapositions, providing some versions of "pastoral," may therefore suggest multiple evaluatory perspectives. In this sense the Fool, Lear's partner in irrationality, functions analogously to Lear's other *Doppelgänger*, his partner in suffering, the double plot's Gloucester. Ultimately, the *ludicra-seria* antithesis, through its sense of *ludere*, to play, is related to the topic of world as stage, upon which the supposedly serious gods trivially fool with mankind. The eventual identity of king and jester lies in the recognition that under the omnipotently sportive deities all men, whether solemn or foolish, are ludicrous.[69] From this standpoint, Coleridge's apprehension of the Fool as brought "into living connection with the pathos of the play" seems still more fully justified.

In addition, a related *topos* may indicate the inversion in the relationship between the Fool, often addressed as "boy," and the octogenarian king. This is the *puer senex* convention, established, as Curtius observes (p. 99), by the beginning of the second century

[69]The relationship between king and jester on a secular level is suggested by Ernst H. Kantorowicz, *The King's Two Bodies: A Study in Mediaeval Political Theology* (Princeton, 1957). As in the ritual *forma degradationis* of *Richard II*, an inverted coronation rite, the king dissolves into his component figures, god, man, and fool. Nominalistically, Richard, too, questions the identity of king as man and name (III.ii.83 ff.).

A.D. and continuing at least to the seventeenth century.[70] Employed by Scaliger, he recalls, to praise the fifteen-year-old Grotius, and by Góngora in praise of the Viceroy of Naples, the *puer senex* topic was memorably sustained by means of a much-used text: Gregory the Great started his life of St. Benedict with "Fuit vir vitae venerabilis . . . ab ipso suae pueritiae tempore cor gerens senile" (Curtius, p. 100). If, as Goneril notes, "Old fools are babes again" (I.iii.20), and, in contrast to Lear's imprudence, the "boyish" Fool is full of practical worldly wisdom, the convention may be reflected in Shakespeare's tragedy.

According to Solomon's saying (Wisdom iv.8-9), "wisdome," not age alone, "is the gray heare" unto men. For, while age is honorable, it is not merely to be measured by years. Paradoxically, Lear's "white head," it is evident from dramatic beginning to end, lacks the judicious attributes of age, while his "boy" Fool seems abundantly supplied with apt perceptions, sage counsel, and prudent forebodings. "How ill white hairs become a fool and jester!" exclaims one of Shakespeare's more practical kings (*2 Henry IV*, V.v.52). "Better," observes Ecclesiastes iv.13, "is a poore and wise child, then an olde & foolish king, which wil no more be admonished."[71]

Moreover, not only Goneril but also Cordelia, later, describes Lear as "this child-changed father" (IV.vii.17). Hence, according to the conventions of youth and age, the Fool may be partly related to the *puer senex*, or wise youth, whereas, conversely, Lear after his madness confirms: "I am a very foolish fond old man" (IV.vii.60). Lear, indeed, in one sense fulfills Wager's titular *The Longer Thou Livest, the More Foole Thou Art* (ca. 1559-1568). Like Cordelia, Goneril, and Lear himself, the Fool sums up Lear's immature old age, which shows his master to be the opposite of the *puer senex*: "Thou should'st not have been old till thou hadst been wise" (I.v. 45-46).

"*And I'll Go to Bed at Noon*"

Like Mercutio, disappearing at midpoint, the Fool seems absorbed into the play's tonal complexity; Mercutio's Elizabethan note of

[70]See the discussion of old men as children in John Carpenter, *A Preparative to Contentation* (1597), pp. 229-230.

[71]The childish king of Ecclesiastes x.16 recurs in the Homilies, *Certaine Sermons* (1587), sig. [Ll7v]; in *1 Henry VI*, IV.i.192; and in *Richard III*, II.iii.11. Cf. Tilley W600, as well as R40 and S1050.

amorous gaiety is succeeded by the Fool's note of antiromantic jest. Although *Romeo and Juliet* is a tragedy of young love and *King Lear* is a tragedy of aged death, both share the wanton ripping from earth by a preventable mistake and underline the prevalent irony of unripeness. Moreover, as the joyousness of the Queen Mab speech appears contrapuntally absorbed into the pathos of the earlier tragedy's denouement, so the Fool's grotesqueries seem mingled with the less endurable pathos of *Lear*'s close. If, then, a character's physical presence onstage need not be the only measure of his dramatic relevance, Cordelia's absence and the Fool's *in medias res* disappearance raise noteworthy considerations regarding modes of theatrical significance.

Although Bradley, for example, complains that we are left in ignorance as to the fate of the Fool, probably owing to Shakespeare's "carelessness or an impatient desire to reduce his overloaded material" (p. 208), the Fool's fate may be visible on the stage in the person of the king. "I have . . . stuck close to my good Master," the departing Fool, like Sancho Panza, might claim, "and kept him Company this many a Month; and now He and I are all one."[72] For there are characters, like Cordelia, whose silences are audible and whose departures are permanent presences. If the Fool disappears, folly itself remains, reverberating like the thunder. Like the latter, too, the Fool is also a principle; and in the merging of human folly with cosmic irrationality his principle transfiguredly persists. In Act IV, for example, the mad Lear plays the Fool to Gloucester's sorrow, the Fool's riddling grotesqueness, however, intensifying into the king's bitter jests. As the Fool's "all-license" becomes Lear's vision of licentiousness everywhere, the king continues in his Fool's interrogations, culminating in that final Fool's question, "Why?" (V.iii.306).

If eventually in the physical sense superfluous, the contradictory clown seems eclipsed only *in propria persona* by the higher irrationalities. For the Fool is not at home in spaces, and he whimpers and cowers before the adversary of the thunder. Yet both the Fool's pragmatic *prudentia* and his master's reckless *imprudentia* appear "but a trifle here" before the vastness of the apparent retribution. Where mankind seems a guilty victim deluged with disproportionate suffering, mystery repudiates causation.

Further, the perverse untimeliness of the Fool's last utterance,

[72] *Don Quixote*, Pt. II, Ch. xxxii, p. 652.

"And I'll go to bed at noon" (III.vi.88), is matched by the perverse and untimely extinction of Lear's other "poor fool," Cordelia. His exit line is couched, appropriately, in the world-upside-down form which he bequeaths to Lear's vision. The insane king's departing "We'll go to supper i' th' morning" (III.vi.86-87) is in ironical contrast to his first act's imperious demand, "Dinner, ho! dinner! Where's my knave? my Fool?" (I.iv.45-46). The eternally departing Fool replies with a corresponding "And I'll go to bed at noon." The conventional polarity between the "prudent" boy Fool and the "foolish" old king having been noted in the *topos* of *puer senex* above, it is evident from Ecclesiastes x.16-17 that in Lear's "We'll go to supper i' th' morning" an antithesis also recurs:

> Woe to thee, O land, when thy King is a childe,
> and thy princes eate in the morning.
> Blessed art thou, O lande, when thy King is the sonne of nobles,
> & thy princes eate in time.

Thus in his own topsy-turvy way the Fool, like Lear's other fool, Kent, bids his "King and master aye good night" (V.iii.235). Saying good night at the "noon" of the play, the day's clearest moment, the Fool contradictorily evokes the confusion between sleeping and waking of Poor Tom's jolly shepherd in the same scene (III.vi.42-45) and of Lear's own earlier "waking?" (I.iv.237). His comment foreshadows also the sleep which descends at Lear's crescendo point of madness and from which Lear later awakens to encounter death. In part, the phrase alludes further to the traditional topsy-turviness of fools; Joseph Hall's *The Discovery of a New World*, for instance, speaking of fools, declares that "Tapers and noone day meete ordinarily at every dinner time amongst them."[73] Yet "And I'll go to bed at noon" foreshadows metaphorically, as Edgar's "Ripeness is all" anticipates ironically, Cordelia's own leave-taking. Such unhappy prematurity occurs, for example, in a love poem of 1577:

> My Lady . . . Doth force my harte with woe to pine
> And biddes my joyes at noone good nighte.[74]

[73]Ed. Huntington Brown (Cambridge, Mass., 1937), p. 79. Cf. Thomas Adams, *The Gallants Burden* (1612), fol. 16v, regarding the Epicures, who "invert the Order God hath disposed to the times preposterously, makeing the night day, and the day night; at midnight they revell, *at noone they sleepe*" (my italics).

[74]Tilley B197, citing also John Heywood, "It semeth ye wolde make me go to bed at noone," . . . *Proverbs* (1546), II.vii, sig. Kiv. John S. Farmer's edition (1906),

Closer to *Lear*'s time, however, is the eulogy of Essex, untimely cut off, in Robert Pricket's *Honors Fame in Triumph Riding* (1604), appending verse by "Ch. Best":

> All his lifes morne he like a *Romaine* led,
> At noone like a Divine went to deaths bed. (sig. E)[75]

"*And My Poor Fool Is Hang'd*"

> *Thou art the Scrutator without knowledg, the magistrate without jurisdiction: and when all is done, the vice of the play.*
>
> —Montaigne, *Essays*, III, 253

In the "ruinous disorders" of his new world Gloucester finds "son against father" and "father against child" (I.ii.115-119). The "bond" being "crack'd 'twixt son and father" (ll. 113-114) and daughters becoming "guardians" of parents (II.iv.253), family identities, like individual ones, dissociate. The Bastard shifts from his natural father to Cornwall, Gloucester's "arch and patron" (II.i.59), who "adopts" Edmund as a son, as the latter usurps his own sire. While Edgar is godson (II.i.91) of the "child-changed" Lear, he is first deprived of his own father and then of his royal godfather. Beginning with references to "Our son of Cornwall" and "our no less loving son of Albany" (I.i.41, 42), Lear himself first disowns Cordelia, then his other daughters. In turn, Kent twice describes Cornwall and Regan to Lear as "Your son and daughter" (II.iv.14, 44). Eventually, the king-father, protecting bond symbol of state and family, senses himself, analogously, deprived of his own paternal divinities. Amidst this shifting familial context, early foreshadowed in Gloucester's prognostication, Lear's daughter, his "lytell yong fole,"[76] could, in the ambiguous boy-actors' convention, more easily be transposed

---

p. 180, *A Dialogue of the Effectual Proverbs in the English Tongue concerning Marriage by John Heywood*, glosses Heywood's phrase, "betimes, unconscionably early." Cf. Tilley D570.

[75]The Essex eulogy quoted recalls the title of "Essex's Last Good Night," a lamentable ballad so popular that eighteen months after Essex's execution a German visitor heard it sung by the people everywhere, even in the court (Neale, *Queen Elizabeth*, p. 381).

[76]*The Interlude of Calisto and Melebea* (ca. 1527-30), Malone Soc. Repr. (1908), l. 490. See also *Oxford English Dictionary* s.v. "fool," on the word's Renaissance sense of "endearment or pity." Cf. *Venus and Adonis*, l. 578.

with the Fool. "My poor fool" thus appears to complete a series of substitute parent-and-children relationships.[77]

That Lear associated the Fool and Cordelia may be deduced from the jester's continual reminder of her absence; indeed, for Lear, Cordelia's absence is a function of the Fool's presence. Working upon the father's emotional recollection, the Fool, in the king's mind, becomes one with Cordelia. The play's initial allusion to the Fool indicates Lear's support of him against the villains (I.iii.1-2). Moreover, "fool" was a term of endearment, sometimes, as above, applied to a child. Erasmus' *Moriae encomium,* for example, carries with its title his affectionate regard for Thomas More, his dear fool. "We must become little Children and Fooles againe," as Sebastian Franck's *The Forbidden Fruit* (tr. 1640) recalls.[78] From this it is but a step to the notion of fool as victim, or fool as hapless instrument of higher powers, as (recalling Romeo, at III.i.141) in Lear's "I am even / The natural fool of Fortune" (IV.vi.192-193).

Both Fool and Cordelia appear such instruments, the Fool by profession and Cordelia by victimization. Both are, at the start, childlike dependents upon Lear, and both follow and are devoted to him unto death. Yet both share an unyielding devotion to truth, Cordelia's initial refusal to temporize suggesting the truth-telling function of the Fool. Since she is the fool who dares tell the truth, she, too, is "whipp'd out" (I.iv.118). As in the Renaissance proverb, children and fools speak the truth.[79]

From the king's first mention of the Fool, moreover, there appears a connection in Lear's mind between him and the daughters: "Where's my . . . Fool? . . . where's my daughter?" (I.iv.45-47). Although this daughter is Goneril, woven into his impending disappointment with her is his second reference, combining the Fool and Cordelia: "Since my young Lady's going into France, Sir," the Knight remarks, "the Fool hath much pined away." Significantly, Lear replies, "No more of that; I have noted it well." And he adds, recurring to the elder daughter, "Go you, and tell my daughter I would speak with her. Go you, call hither my Fool" (I.iv.77-81).

Connecting the Fool here with the daughters, Shakespeare also

[77]Deprived of his last and most precious attachment, Lear in his "my poor fool" significantly echoes the villains' repeated possessives (e.g., II.iv.311, IV.ii.25, V.iii.158).

[78][August Elutherius, pseud.], p. 50. Cf. I Corinthians iii.18, iv.10.

[79]Tilley C328.

appears, in the Fool's seemingly irrelevant jests, to plant ironical foreshadowing of Cordelia's end. In such apparently haphazard jokes as those concerning the "breath" which Lear gave him—like Cordelia —nothing for (I.iv.135-136),[80] and the mirror into which fair ladies make mouths (III.ii.35-36), the mouth-breath-voice-lips pattern of Lear's last lines is anticipated. There Lear alludes to the truth-speaking Cordelia's mouth, "no breath at all," glass-staining breath, and lips, as well as her voice, which was "soft, / Gentle and low" (V.iii. 272-273). Not inappropriate, too, is the Fool's rhyme offering to exchange his identity symbol, the coxcomb, for a hanging, as he joins "daughter"-"slaughter"-"halter." In the same rhyme "A fox, when one has caught her" (I.iv.327) may contrariwise anticipate the reversal of Lear's "Have I caught thee?" in the latter's vision of father and daughter as potentially heaven-hunted foxes (V.iii.21-23).

Echoed in Mad Tom's allusion to the demon possessing "chambermaids and waiting-women," of "mopping and mowing" (IV.i.61-62),[81] grimacing and making mouths, the Fool's "For there was never yet fair woman but she made mouths in a glass" (III.ii.35-36)[82] re-

[80]"*Fool.* Then 'tis like the breath of an unfee'd lawyer; you gave me nothing for 't." The "unfee'd lawyer" is proverbially recurrent; see, e.g., Francis Lenton, *The Innes of Court Anagrammatist* (1634), sig. C, regarding the lawyer's demand for "his due fee," "Or else his tongue will very silent be."

[81]Cf. Tilley M1030; Nashe, III, 259. Mowing was associated with apes: see Lyly, *Pappe with an Hatchet* (1589), *The Complete Works of John Lyly*, ed. R. Warwick Bond (Oxford, 1902), III, 406; *The Works of Gabriel Harvey*, ed. Alexander B. Grosart, II (1884), 223-224; Ruggle, *Ignoramus*, IV.xi, p. 144.

[82]The Fool, looking up at a fair woman making mouths in a glass, is depicted in Brosamer's "Le Fou et la Femme," reproduced in Raimond van Marle, *Iconographie de l'art profane* (La Haye, 1931-32), II, 453, fig. 485, giving further instances. On Notre Dame, central porch of the façade, the lower series includes the Fool (Stultitia) beside the falling rider (Superbia) and a wanton observing herself in a mirror (Luxuria). The description of human vices in the medieval *summa*, sketched by A. E. M. Katzenellenbogen (*Allegories of the Virtues and Vices in Mediaeval Art*, Warburg Inst. Studies, X [1939], 79-80), as it evokes the evil sisters with symbolic mirror and treasure chest, cites "the two most dangerous material desires, lechery and avarice. . . ." Katzenellenbogen also notes Luxuria regarding herself in a mirror, window of the choir apse, Lyons Cathedral (ca. 1220); choir window of Auxerre Cathedral (ca. 1230), Luxuria with a mirror. A fourteenth-century Venus, Luxuria holding a mirror, is instanced in Jean Seznec, *The Survival of the Pagan Gods* (New York, 1953), pp. 107, 197. Cf., *inter alia*, the title of Nigellus Wireker's *Speculum stultorum* (in Nigel de Longchamps' *Speculum stultorum*, ed. John H. Mozley and Robert R. Raymo, Univ. of Calif. English Studies, No. 18 [Berkeley, 1960]). See Gustav F. Hartlaub, *Zauber des Spiegels: Geschichte und Bedeutung des Spiegels in der Kunst* (Munich, 1951). I am indebted for this reference to Jean Rousset. See also a work useful for numerous other relevant topics, Samuel C. Chew, *The Pilgrimage of Life* (New

calls that Lear, who at the opening hung on Cordelia's mouth for a word, at the end hangs on her lips for a breath. The Fool's satirical comment on feminine vanity persists through his insinuations against the knavery of deceitful daughters, as well as against the reproductive process itself; it continues through the dramatic irony of Goneril's scathing rebuke, "O vain fool!" (IV.ii.61); and it comes to a halt with the final revelation of the vanity of human wishes: unhappily, neither at the beginning nor the end can Cordelia "heave / My heart into my mouth" (I.i.91-92). The lifeless visage of Cordelia, who was of all women least vain, is imagined by Lear to make mouths in a glass (V.iii.261-263). From the above may be deduced an evident intention to infuse part of the Fool's symbolism into the pathos of Cordelia's death and of Lear's ultimate anagnorisis.

As the chattering Fool is a human analogue to the meaningless thunder, he is also the quotient between man and the gods, embodying both reason and unreason. At once more than a character and less, he is, like Erasmus' goddess Folly, an omnipresent influence. Hence, incarnating the principle of contradiction, he is both timely and timeless, first slipping betimes away, then reemerging, *sub specie stultitiae*, in Lear and finally as Lear's "poor fool." As "The Epytaphye of Lobe, the Kynges Foole," points out, "For folys be alyve, Lobe, thouȝh thou be gone."[83] Whereas Lear is "bound / Upon a wheel of fire" (IV.vii.46-47), the Fool, from another point of view, seems less bound to Fortune's wheel since, in a sense, with "Fortune, that arrant whore" (II.iv.52), his principle helps turn it; his worldly advice is to "Let go . . . a great wheel" that "runs down a hill" (II.iv.71-72). Immortal like evil, resembling the Iago who is finally wounded, not dead, folly like knavery is always in the world. Since the universe is doomed to its influence, folly, as much as love, could

---

Haven, 1962), p. 97. Superbia, in Bosch's "Seven Deadly Sins" at the Escorial, presents a housewife admiring herself in a mirror held up by a devil (Bruegel has a similar image of Superbia); see Otto Benesch, "Hieronymus Bosch and the Thinking of the Late Middle Ages," *Konsthistorisk Tidskrift,* XXVI (1957), 21-42. Cf. Hartmann Schopper, *De omnibus illiberalibus . . . artibus* (Frankfurt, 1574), sig. [O8], a fool looking in a mirror. Henry Peacham's *Minerva Britanna* (1612), p. 5, castigating self-love, illustrates a woman regarding herself in a glass. See Barnabe Rich, *My Ladies Looking Glasse* (1616). The legend of Goya's work, showing an old hag before her mirror, completes the cycle: "Hasta la Muerte."

[83]From MS. Rawlinson C258, in James Orchard Halliwell-Phillipps, *Nugæ poeticæ* (1844), p. 45.

be said to move the sun and the other stars. In contrast to the Dantean epilogue, Renaissance man, looking up and confusing knowledge with knowledge, might only deduce dark nescience—or the Catullan "sidera . . . cum tacet nox."[84]

ALL FOOLS

. . . the Foole of all Fooles . . .
—Jacke of Dover, His Quest of Inquirie
. . . for the Veriest Foole in England (1604)

Thus, in addition to the "allowed fool," under such aspects as the above, the characters of Shakespeare's *speculum stultorum* invariably share motley, albeit with a difference. Indeed, the probable date of *Lear*'s composition recalls that shortly before, on January 1, 1605, a court presentation occurred of Chapman's *All Fools*.[85] While Kent, it might be concluded, is the fool of loyalty and service, Edgar the "fool to sorrow," and Cordelia the "poor fool" of piety, of truth, and ultimately of cosmic irrationality, Albany, a fool by marriage (cf. IV.ii.28, 58), is also the fool of cosmic optimism. Duped by his son and a victim of his own anxieties, Gloucester is a fool of the stars, while Edmund, bastardized by Gloucester, is a fool of nature, worshiping the force that has blindly spawned him. Like Edmund, the other villains are fools of their own desires and compulsive self-interest and are, at the last, fools of one another. Dissemblers, as Guzman de Alfarache observes, are themselves "fooles of the first forme."[86] Fools of time, they are, despite their expectations of "thriving," astonished to be ripped untimely from its womb (cf. Cornwall at III.vii.97; Oswald at IV.vi.252-253). As fools of their own worldly prosperity, the villains are also its victims. For the victors belong to the spoils, and, as Luther, before Touchstone, proverbially observed, "Fortuna quos fovet, stultos facit."[87]

[84] *The Poems of . . . Catullus*, tr. F. W. Cornish, Loeb Classical Lib. (1912), p. 10.

[85] Chapman's title recalls a large and here unrecountable Renaissance fool literature; e.g., Tommaso Garzoni, *The Hospitall of Incurable Fooles* (1600). The "all fools" *topos* receives intensified treatment in the sixteenth century: agreeing with Ecclesiastes (Vulgate) i.15, Rabelais, e.g. (Bk. III, Ch. xxxviii of *Gargantua and Pantagruel*, *Oeuvres* [Paris, 1835], pp. 180-181), catalogs and enumerates at some length the variety of fools.

[86] Alemán, *Guzman de Alfarache*, III, 334.

[87] *As You Like It*, II.vii.19; Luther, *Werke*, XLIII (Weimar, 1912), 52.

Chief actor in the play, Lear himself is the fool of fools. For, if other characters are proxy to Lear, the king is shown to be proxy to the universal principle of folly. In this drama, which involves a quest for identity, human and divine, the king is shown on a fool's pilgrimage, an errand which brings back at the close the "Fool," as well as the concept of human and cosmic meaninglessness. Having passed through the paradigm of "fool," Lear thus fulfills his jester's prediction, "thou would'st make a good Fool" (I.v.39), as well as Kent's warning against the time "When majesty falls to folly" (I.i.149). In this *Narrendämmerung* the king, in Montaignian terms, discovers himself: "Tu es le scrutateur sans connoissance, le magistrat sans jurisdiction, et après tout le badin de la farce."[88] The tragic hero as clown, Lear accomplishes the traditional or mythic identification of king and jester. Hence, in addition to linking Cordelia to the Fool, his "my poor fool" may also be self-reflexive: in Hopkins' phrase, "poor Jackself," it is Lear also he mourns for.[89] Further, amidst the mysteries of folly the "puissances trompeuses" appear to share, by analogy, a similar identity. If Lear is a fool of the gods, they themselves seem moved by the highest irrationality. In the twilight of Prometheus, reverberating "fool" to the end, Shakespeare's tragedy questioningly investigates the credentials which certify Olympus.

[88]Cf. Rochester's skeptical libertine ["A Satyr against Mankind"], *Poems*, ed. Vivian de Sola Pinto (1953), p. 119. The "reas'ning *Engine* . . . / Who was so proud, so witty, and so wise," at last perceives that not reason, but folly, drove him on:

> Then Old Age, and experience, hand in hand,
> Lead him to death, and make him understand,
> After a search so painful, and so long,
> That all his Life he has been in the wrong.

[89]"My own heart let me have more pity on," *Poems of Gerard Manley Hopkins*, ed. Robert Bridges (1918), p. 67.

CHAPTER XI

Irony as Structure

IN *Lear* structural irony is a principle of action which, with the safety of indirection, probes the ways of the gods to man. From Senecan tragic irony, as from effects similar to those of Calvinism and Montaigne, Renaissance drama drew some of its climate for tragedy; the vengefulness of the Senecan deities and the obscurity of providence fostered a sense of divine inscrutability and human victimization. As in Marlowe, Kyd, Greville, and Webster, for example, such tragic irony of cosmic disproportion emerges in Shakespeare. Ironically suggesting, perhaps, that one level might as effectively be appealed to as the other, *Macbeth* demonstrates the treachery of dependence upon hell, while the relatively close *Lear* may indicate the fallibility of pagan heavenly reliance.

Such indications in *King Lear* are expressed notably through sequential irony, the tacit commentary which the dramatist, operating *ab extra*, may legitimately introduce. The histrionic sensibility operates through a dynamism of action in which certain sequent juxtapositions, as in the *liaison des scènes*, themselves may take on meaning. In the *Henry IV* plays, for example, the fact that a scene at the tavern is followed by one at the court may itself involve a meaning dimension, the sequence in its contrariety suggesting a significant assertion in formal terms on the part of the composer; and the sharp contrast, in sequence, between the dark, cold, supernatural opening scene of the Ghost in *Hamlet* and the subsequent superficial and glittering scenes in a court presided over by Claudius offers, by simple collocation, a type of commentary. In regard to the dramatic dialogue itself, we find, for example, in *Julius Caesar* an instance of ironical juxtaposition as meaning; in the crucial exposition of Caesar's character Shakespeare has broadly sketched the *hubris* and vanity, the susceptibility to flattery, of the consul, who reveals himself ripe for the kill. And two successive lines brilliantly uncover him to the audience, when he has just vaunted himself above such common human failings as fear:

I rather tell thee what is to be fear'd
Than what I fear; for always I am Caesar. (I.ii.211-213)

The very next line undoes him: "Come on my right hand," he tells Antony, "for this ear is deaf."[1] Eventually, the irony arrives full circle through Prince Hamlet:

Imperious Caesar, dead and turn'd to clay,
Might stop a hole to keep the wind away. (V.i.236-237)

Sequential ironies, which reflect a tendency of the play, are exposed like a series of trapdoors in *Lear*. When, for example, the aged sire petitions the heavens for the first time,

O Heavens,
If you do love old men, if your sweet sway
Allow obedience . . .
Make it your cause; send down and take my part!
(II.iv.191-194)

as if in reply, the evil daughters join forces both by gesture and by word. "O Regan! will you take her by the hand?" (II.iv.196), Lear exclaims, and both attack him with their reprobate complaints (ll. 197-265). Either the heavens are deaf, the sequence may suggest, or they seem to delight in malicious mischief. Once again, Lear appeals pitifully to the heavens (II.iv.273-275); his appeal is answered by a devastating storm that threatens the earth. Perhaps, the sequence appears to imply, the gods are indifferent to weakness and oppression; perhaps, even further, such appeals serve only to exasperate them and summon their cruelty. At the end of this speech Lear shouts,

I will do such things,
What they are, yet I know not, but they shall be
The terrors of the earth,[2] (II.iv.282-284)

when the sound of the storm is heard; mankind seems, ironically, an impotent and pathetically miserable creature, futilely absurd in his

[1] The dramatic irony in Caesar's remark does not exclude a proverbial sense involving skepticism (Tilley E11, "He cannot hear on that Ear [side]").

[2] Although Muir, after Ritson, cites only Golding, this is a Senecan *topos*; cf. *Thyestes,* tr. Jasper Heywood (1560), in *Seneca, His Tenne Tragedies,* ed. Thomas Newton (1581), Tudor Trans. (1927), I, 64. See also Ovid, *Metamorphoses,* tr. Arthur Golding (1567), Bk. VI, fol. 78; *The Misfortunes of Arthur* (1588), I.ii.39-44 (*Early English Classical Tragedies,* ed. John W. Cunliffe [Oxford, 1912]).

powerless rage, in contrast to the irrational menacings of the skies.

In the next act when Edmund has concluded, within Gloucester's castle, his cold calculation against his father (III.iii.25-27), we are thrown, in the following line, into the cold and inhuman atmosphere of the storm on the open heath. The sequence is here meaningful, but not so much in the way of ordinary irony as of the coincidence between human and natural evil; and this, in itself, may be irony, insofar as humankind and kinship might be expected to provide love and warmth, while the more distant heavens may not.

Once again, when Lear concludes his "prayer" before sleep, beginning "Poor naked wretches, whereso'er you are," and pleading, through charity, to "show the Heavens more just" (III.iv.28-36), the next lines reveal a "poor, naked wretch" in the person of Edgar as Poor Tom, and the Fool terrified, running out of the hovel (ll. 37-40). Later, at the point when the mad king seeks restorative sleep, "Make no noise, make no noise; draw the curtains: so, so. We'll go to supper i' th' morning" (III.vi.85-87), Gloucester enters, revealing, "I have o'erheard a plot of death upon him" (l. 92). The gods whom Lear adored seem very busy.

Even when, Job-like, man feels himself at the worst of his misfortunes, the gods can directly afterward with a few swift strokes make him yearn for the good old days. Thus Edgar, banished, deprived of love and property, homeless, may describe himself at the bottom of his misfortunes (IV.i.1-9). Having rationalized his depression into a reasonably bearable state, he at once sees enter his newly blinded father led by an old man:

> My father, poorly led? World, world, O world!
> But that thy strange mutations make us hate thee,
> Life would not yield to age. (IV.i.10-12)

The irony of the gods has delivered its message; Edgar now understands:

> O Gods! Who is't can say "I am at the worst"?
> I am worse than e'er I was. (ll. 25-26)

Human misery, in other words, is bottomless. And divine cruelty apparently has no limits.

Like Edgar, Kent furnishes some undertones of Lear's despair. For example, with regard to the gods' special providence and Cordelia's eventual fate, the ironical implications of Kent's "The Gods to their dear shelter take thee, maid" (I.i.182), like those of some comments of the Fool, are evident. Indeed, the Quarto text also underlines the providential commentary, reading "protection" for the Folio's "deere shelter." In addition, Kent's parallel speech at III.vi.5 in the Quarto, "the Gods deserve [Folio: reward] your kindnes," to Gloucester embraces a similarly pointed and subversive irony. In fewer than two hundred lines (III.vii.67) Gloucester's kindness to Lear is "rewarded" by his savage blinding; such kindness, in a jussive subjunctive phrase suggesting multiple ironies, "the Gods deserve."

As the most optimistic believer in poetic justice, Albany, when the killing of Cornwall by a servant is described to him, excitedly acclaims it as proof of heaven's justice. Yet in the same breath, with a kind of unaware irony, he hastily recalls himself, "But, O poor Gloucester! / Lost he his other eye?" (IV.ii.80-81). At another point Gloucester has been converted to existence rather than suicide (IV.vi.218-220); the old man, in other words, looks forward to a gradual deliquescence. Reconciled both to life and to the heavens, he thanks his benefactor, Edgar:

> Hearty thanks:
> The bounty and the benison of Heaven
> To boot, and boot! (IV.vi.225-227)

At this point of Gloucester's achievement of a *modus vivendi* and acceptance of continued life, the villainous Oswald enters with drawn sword as a potential instrument of fate (IV.vi.227-231). Gloucester, it seems, cannot die; but at the very moment of persuasion that life is preferable, it seems he cannot live. Little wonder that he earlier compared men to flies whom the gods kill for their sport; not only does Gloucester express that sentiment, but the gods appear to make it good.

The concluding act delivers a consistent series of ironic blows. Edgar, having brought his blind father into "the shadow of this tree / For your good host," bids him pray "that the right may thrive" and assures him,

> If ever I return to you again
> I'll bring you comfort,

to which Gloucester replies, "Grace go with you, sir!" (V.ii.1-4). Instantly, Edgar runs back upon an alarum and a retreat:

> Away, old man! give me thy hand: away!
> King Lear hath lost, he and his daughter ta'en.
> Give me thy hand; come on. (ll. 5-7)

So much for human comfort. Like Gloucester and his son, Lear, even at the end, has a momentary blind faith in a permanence and immutability (V.iii.11-19) that is brusquely shattered by Edmund's harsh "Take them away" and Cordelia's hanging. So much for human comfort, even that which is resigned to oppression and hopes merely for endurance. Pathetically pointing ahead to the close, Lear's consolation of Cordelia at the opening of the last scene is rich in irony: the "mystery of things" which they are to take on themselves as "Gods' spies" is shortly to enfold them both.

With poetic justice, the demolition of poetic justice is left to the Duke of Albany; aptly, his hierarchical status analogically allies him with the heavens. When, having heard about the plot against Cordelia, he exclaims, "The Gods defend her!" (V.iii.255), his answer arrives immediately in the person of Lear carrying Cordelia dead in his arms. Replies come rapidly at the denouement; irony builds to a crescendo. In an echo of the old Leir's happy restoration, Albany offers to relinquish the throne ("our absolute power") to its rightful owner "During the life of this old Majesty" (V.iii.298-300); a dozen lines later Lear is dead. Justly, he promises Edgar and Kent,

> you, to your rights,
> With boot and such addition as your honours
> Have more than merited. (ll. 300-302)

And finally he announces, after overwhelming demonstration of irrationality and injustice, a program of rewards for virtues and punishments for vices (V.iii.302-304), a promise which is interrupted by Lear's last speech, and his final annihilation of human trust in divine justice (V.iii.305-308).

Beyond the lines themselves of this concluding scene, however, there is an irony in the lack of inevitability, which Bradley points out, in the catastrophe; at various moments, for example, in the unnecessary delay of Edmund's confession, the tragedy could have been avoided. "It is not even satisfactorily motived. In fact it seems expressly designed to fall suddenly like a bolt from a sky cleared by the vanished storm" (p. 204). This is true, and its *Tragik des Zuspät* is a transcendent illustration of sequential irony. Evidently, therefore, an element of gratuitousness is integral to the tragedy. Hence, Lear's arbitrary opening, held to be unsatisfactorily motivated, and in *Shakespeare und Kein Ende* called absurd by Goethe, seems an analogically appropriate overture to such a work. A pattern of gratuitousness, indeed, appears to pervade not only the beginning and end but also two of the play's crucial events, Gloucester's blinding and Cordelia's hanging. Accompanied by the irrational menacings of the thunder, the willful operations of an upside-down providence in an apparently deranged universe would suggest an implicit metaphysical "absurdity." In this respect Shakespeare's drama evokes, to an extent, the "absurdity" of Quixote's quest (Part I of *Don Quixote* was published in 1605) and adumbrates, in a work which owes much to *Lear*, the "absurdity" of Ahab's frenzied pursuit of the White Whale.

In conclusion, I have indicated, through an inspection less of the lines themselves than of what is expressed in the relation of the lines and in the sequence of dialogue and event, confirmation of an implicit direction of the tragedy: annihilation of faith in poetic justice and, within the confines of a grim, pagan universe, annihilation of faith in divine justice. In this dark world, the last choruses tell us, we find the promised end, or the image of that horror, in which man's chief joy is to be removed from the rack of this tough world and in which man's pathetic solace is—ultimate irony!—the *illusion* that that which he has most loved still breathes: "Look on her, look, her lips, / Look there, look there!" (V.iii.310-311). No redemption stirs at this world's end; only suffering, tears, pity, and loss—*and* illusion.

CHAPTER XII

Conclusion

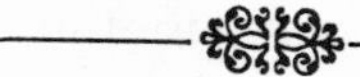

In order to answer the question with which this study started, "What is the validity of the optimistic Christian interpretation of *King Lear*?" I have had to consider the play in relation to its Renaissance religious background. A brief recapitulation may serve to bring to mind the relevance of the parts to the aim of the whole study.

The first chapter indicated that a majority of recent interpretations tended to the theory of Christian optimism in one or both of its aspects: (1) that, by analogy with the morality tradition or with Dante, the protagonist was somehow redeemed; and (2) that presiding over the human action was a benevolent or personal providence.

The second chapter offered evidence that in Renaissance Italy, France, and England the concept of a special providence came increasingly into question; this questioning coincided with a period of renascent skepticism. In addition to the skeptical disintegration of providential belief, another factor was the breakdown of the medieval analogical relation, and the progressive distancing of God from man. Thus the Deity became, in effect, a *Deus absconditus*, whose seemingly arbitrary and capricious workings were, according to such influential figures as Calvin and Montaigne, beyond the power of feeble human reason to grasp or to evaluate.

Moreover, while expressing the leitmotiv of inescapable human affliction, a major source, Sidney's *Arcadia* in its rendering of a heathen landscape also suggests three other attitudes to providence: (1) the *prisca theologia* or virtuous heathen; (2) the atheistic; (3) the superstitious. Such attitudes to providence, as well as (4), the shiftingly indeterminate reaction to an inhospitable cosmos, comprise the religious alternatives ascribed in the Renaissance to heathens; and they foreshadow, without necessarily being the source of, the providential attitudes of the chief characters in *Lear*.

Next, it was shown that Shakespeare's probable source play, the old *King Leir*, is permeated with Christian emphases that, from comparison of the two works, Shakespeare evidently wished to avoid; the change from the orthodox to the ambiguous use of thunder is especially noticeable in the later work. From such comparisons it was suggested that Shakespeare intended a more complex perspective than that afforded by the Christian optimism of the old *Leir*, as well as that of many recent interpretations. Moreover, although it would seem to be self-evident or, at least, to follow by definition, citations were adduced to show that Renaissance expectation, except for the *prisca theologia* exemption, was to view heathens as atheistic or superstitious, or both.

Succeeding chapters indicated that in the major characters of *King Lear*, comprising the Gloucester and Lear families, the four attitudes, the main religious alternatives ascribed to pagans in the Renaissance and those in the *Arcadia*, clearly emerge: (1) The first category, or *prisca theologia*, includes Cordelia and Edgar; (2) Goneril, Regan, and Edmund possess an atheistical outlook; (3) Gloucester's excesses mark him as at least kin to the superstitious pagan; and (4) Lear is shown to develop from pagan belief to disbelief.

In addition to relating the minor characters of *Lear* to the thematic preoccupations of the play, a final section, by an examination of sequential ironies, considered implicit as well as explicit directions regarding providence. Evidently these move far from the Christian optimism asserted by modern critics. Furthermore, if the explanations advanced thus far are correct, they may partly aid in accounting for the anomaly that *Lear* alone, among all of Shakespeare's tragedies, has a fully developed and apparently repetitive double plot. Insofar as Lear and Gloucester have contrasting and complementary functions, evidence has been suggested to indicate that *King Lear* comprises not a wasteful duplication of primary and iterative secondary plot but, *inter alia*, a juxtaposition of four attitudes toward providence, which helps sustain the structure of the play itself.

From the indications presented above, it may be concluded that the optimistic Christian interpretation of *King Lear* is probably invalid as: (1) no evidence exists to show that Lear arrives finally at "salvation," "regeneration," or "redemption," and (2) the purported benevolent, just, or special providence cannot be shown to be operative. While reasons which may have misled modern criticism into such assumptions have been touched upon earlier, a full account is beyond the scope of this study. Yet it may at least be observed that those interpretations which see the tragedy as a traditional morality and those which see it as following the sin-suffering-redemption pattern are a result of unhistorical, a priori misreading of the work's significance. To a certain extent, those critics seem to be correct; the play seems to start with such premises and appears to progress to such a conclusion, but only through the fourth act; for the devastating fifth act shatters, more violently than an earlier apostasy might have done, the foundations of faith itself.

What, therefore, are we left with, and how shall we answer the question regarding the tragedy's religious significances? Several points of view suggest themselves, and their result indicates no simple solution. For one thing, the play ends with the death of the good at the hands of the evil; and among the sacrificed good is a virtuous heathen believer, while among the evil are atheists. Thus, it may seem to be a play which leans to the side of faith overcome in this world by the forces of evil and so, from a Christian point of view, an indictment of atheistic wickedness. But we find that among these forces of evil the chief villain at the end becomes converted to a virtuous view, exchanges forgiveness, and repents. And, further, among the sympathetic who are destroyed is a heroic king who appears to blaspheme against the heavens. Hence, we are left with a *Hamlet*-like confusion of values in terms of a chiasma of ethical and religious ideas and consequences.

To add to the confusion, moreover, we have the problem that the play is in its premises ostensibly pagan. Thus, from one point of view whatever happened to its characters might be irrelevant to the Christian universe of Shakespeare's spectators. It might be said, for example, that in a pagan world of unbelievers religious values are both confused and erroneous, and thus the consequence of such values would not concern the Renaissance viewer's own religious problems. Hence, the play in its temporal irrelevance might have failed to interest the more egocentric spectator.

But, on the other hand, if we assume that the Shakespearean spectator analogically transformed the characters and situations in *Lear* into Christian terms, we are left with the spectacle of a Christian tragic hero who ends as a skeptic blaspheming his Deity, a unique occurrence in the dramatist's work and one fraught with danger, both politically and artistically. At a time when *The Atheist's Tragedie,* in all its naïve scourging of the disbelieving villain, trod the boards, are we to expect the limited sophistication of a Jacobean audience to have applauded a Shakespeare turned Shavian?

We must, therefore, in view of the antinomies of dramatic evidence and contemporary circumstance, conclude: (1) that Shakespeare's creation was intended as an ostensibly "realistic" depiction of pagan life; (2) that, nevertheless, an unhistorical, Christian-conditioned Renaissance author and audience could only with difficulty have objectively and detachedly viewed a presentation of religious problems without converting them to some extent into Christian terms; that, therefore, while the play's paganism weighs more heavily and is intended as prima-facie datum, the work contains certain inevitable Christian allusions, which would, to its religiously conditioned audience, have made the depiction more dramatically palatable; and, further (3) the audience would have the more sympathetically regarded the heathen's difficulties with *his* gods insofar as the Jacobean age was experiencing an analogous crisis in religion and the idea of providence; moreover, an attack on heathenism could have been taken as a blow for Christianity.

The conclusion, in brief, of this study is that Shakespeare's *Lear*, despite its Christian allusions, is intentionally more directly a syncretically pagan tragedy; on the other hand, although its "realistic" depiction of heathen religious attitudes, far from simple camouflage, is not intended to provide allegorical one-to-one correspondences with the world of Jacobean Christianity—and could not, without serious consequences to the author—its contemporary analogical significance would not have been lost on some members of a sympathetic audience, circa 1605, undergoing in related terms its own theological crisis. By depicting a superstitious pagan progressing toward doubt of *his* gods, Shakespeare secured for the play the approbation of the less speculative devout, who saw in its direction the victory of the True Faith ("Païen unt tort, e chrestien unt dreit," as the *Chanson de Roland* has it). Moreover, he obtained for it the interest of those more troubled and sophisticated auditors who were not to be stilled by pious assurances in the unsteady new world of the later Renaissance. For the latter, *King Lear* carried its own *tua res agitur* significance: it made more vivid the image of that horror, the all-dissolving chaos, for those who could not turn aside and stop their beating minds.

King Lear Studies
1967-1987

FOR THIS new issue of *"King Lear" and the Gods*, I have been asked to supply a brief, selective sketch of *Lear* research in the score of years since the book's publication (1966).[1] In that period, Shakespearean studies have included emphasis on theatrical performance and related interests. Such concerns contrast with the critical fashions of previous decades, which comprised application of Renaissance psychology, image-pattern approaches, and orthodox political-religious contextualizing. Relatively little is now heard of "wrath in old age" as a key to Lear, of patterns of sight-imagery, or of Tillyardian conformity to order and degree.

In *Lear* studies, which have proliferated since the displacement (c. 1960) of *Hamlet* as central tragedy in the canon,[2] fashionable emphases have included performance and text. These two have combined to produce the recent revelation of *Lear* as not one, but two theatrically separate and individual Shakespearean plays: the Quarto (1608) and the Folio (1623). Overnight (post-1978), enthusiasm for Shakespearean mitosis appears to have imbued many in the field: as with *Lear*, quarto and folio versions of *Hamlet*, *Troilus*, and *Othello*, for

For critical reading of this essay, I am indebted to S.F. Johnson and to David Bevington, Peter Blayney, G.B. Evans, and Richard Knowles. The essay is not included in the index.

[1] See for general surveys: G.R. Hibbard, "*King Lear*: A Retrospect, 1939-79," *Shakespeare Survey* 33 (1980): 1-12; Peter Wenzel, *Die "Lear" Kritik im 20 Jahrhundert: Ein Beitrag zu einer Analyse der Entwicklung der Shakespeare-literatur* (Amsterdam: B.R. Grüner, 1979). For bibliography: Larry S. Champion, comp., *"King Lear": An Annotated Bibliography*. 2 vols. (New York: Garland, 1980). For collected essays: Janet Adelman, ed., *Twentieth-Century Interpretations of "King Lear"* (Englewood Cliffs, N.J.: Prentice-Hall, 1978); Kenneth Muir and Stanley Wells, eds., *Aspects of "King Lear": Articles Reprinted from "Shakespeare Survey"* (Cambridge University Press, 1982); Kenneth Muir, ed., *"King Lear": Critical Essays* (New York: Garland, 1984).

[2] R.A. Foakes, "*King Lear* and the Displacement of *Hamlet*," *Huntington Library Quarterly* 50 (1987): 271-76.

example, now are announced as distinguishably separate plays and stages in Shakespearean revision.

CRITICISM

More closely related to concerns of this book are the conflicts that remain between proponents of a redemptive and of a skeptical *Lear*. In *Lear* criticism, as a bibliographer notes, emotion tends to preempt description,[3] and Lear's last scenes continue to generate more heat than light. A recent textual scholar decries "the thirty-six literary critics who are all writing the same essay on Shakespeare's last scenes, an activity known as original research."[4] Those who feel a kinship to salvation and the educational value of suffering persist in perceiving optimism; others find a less benevolent closure. Still others try to work out, between such polarities, a more subtle ending, not always clearly related to the lines.

Religious preoccupations also include recognition of *Lear*'s morality play heritage (Emrys Jones; Edgar Schell). Robert H. West finds the play's suffering and end bespeak divine mystery; there is mystery of redemption in *Lear* (p. 145). Similarly, Robert G. Hunter, evoking Reformation theology, considers that the mystery of God's judgment is here at its most profound. Herbert R. Coursen, Jr., believes that Lear's journey is toward the "Christian" insight represented by Cordelia (p. 238). While John Reibetanz finds that the play embraces a dark Jacobean world, he associates Cordelia with Christ (p. 120), and sees the work as a validation of Christian humanism. For Derek Peat, the play generates the tension of uncertainty. Leo Salingar examines Harsnett's *Declaration of Egregious Popish Impostures* (1603) as providing the tragedy's access to a world of demonic evil. Inspecting exorcism and *Lear*, John L. Murphy also studies implications of the play's use of Harsnett, as well as the polemical divinity of *Leir*. He finds in Edmund's end a "drama of redemption" (p. 214). Finally,

[3] Edward Quinn, introduction to "King Lear" in Quinn, James Ruoff, and Joseph Grennen, comps., *The Major Shakespearean Tragedies: A Critical Bibliography* (New York: Free Press, 1973), p. 152.

[4] Ernest A.J. Honigmann, "Shakespeare as a Reviser," in Jerome J. McGann, ed., *Textual Criticism and Literary Interpretation* (Chicago: University of Chicago Press, 1985), p. 10.

Joseph Wittreich reads *Lear* in relation to St. John's Revelation and the apocalyptic tradition.[5]

Another critical concern continues to be language. Two concordances are here of use: Spevack's, based on G.B. Evans's Riverside text, provides a concordance to *Lear*. Howard-Hill supplies a concordance to *Lear*'s First Folio text. Application of linguistic analysis to the tragedy is exemplified in Madeleine Doran's essay.[6]

Returning to theatrical interests, we may note Marvin Rosenberg's study of the history of *Lear* performance, traced by act and scene. Theatrical emblems in the play are examined by Reibetanz. Urkowitz's essay inspects *Lear*'s interrupted exits. Stephen Booth considers a tragic audience's multidimensional theatrical experience, its awareness and knowledge.[7]

[5] Emrys Jones, *Scenic Form in Shakespeare* (New York: Oxford University Press, 1971), pp. 152-94. Edgar Schell, *Strangers and Pilgrims: from "The Castle of Perseverance" to "King Lear."* (University of Chicago Press, 1983). Robert H. West, *Shakespeare and the Outer Mystery* (Lexington: University Press of Kentucky, 1968), pp. 127-66. Robert G. Hunter, *Shakespeare and the Mystery of God's Judgments* (Athens: University of Georgia Press, 1976), pp. 183-96. Herbert R. Coursen, Jr., *Christian Ritual and the World of Shakespeare's Tragedies* (Lewisburg, Pa.: Bucknell University Press, 1976), pp. 237-313. John Reibetanz, *The King Lear World* (University of Toronto Press, 1977). Derek Peat, " 'And That's True Too': *King Lear* and the Tension of Uncertainty," *Shakespeare Survey* 33 (1980): 43-53. Leo Salingar, "*King Lear*, Montaigne and Harsnett," *Aligarh Journal of English Studies* 8 (1983), 124-66. John L. Murphy, *Darkness and Devils: Exorcism and "King Lear"* (Athens: Ohio University Press, 1984). (See also Murphy, rev. of *Division of the Kingdoms*, ed. Gary Taylor and Michael Warren, *Papers of the Bibliographical Society of America* 81 [1987]: 53-63, relating the play to Catholicism and censorship.) Joseph Wittreich, *"Image of That Horror": History, Prophecy, and Apocalypse in "King Lear"* (San Marino, Calif.: Huntington Library Press, 1984).

[6] "A Concordance to *King Lear*," in Marvin Spevack, ed., *A Complete and Systematic Concordance to the Works of Shakespeare* (Hildesheim: Georg Olms, 1968), 3: 892-1017. T.H. Howard-Hill, ed., *"King Lear": A Concordance to the Text of the First Folio* (Oxford, 1971). Madeleine Doran, " 'Give me the map there!': Command, Questions, and Assertion in *King Lear*," in *Shakespeare's Art: Seven Essays*, ed. Milton Crane (University of Chicago Press for George Washington University, 1973), pp. 33-67; revised in Doran, *Shakespeare's Dramatic Language* (Madison: University of Wisconsin Press, 1976), pp. 92-120.

[7] Marvin Rosenberg, *The Masks of King Lear* (Berkeley: University of California Press, 1972). John Reibetanz, "Theatrical Emblems in *King Lear*," in *Some Facets of "King Lear": Essays in Prismatic Criticism*, ed. Rosalie L. Colie and F.T. Flahiff (University of Toronto Press, 1974). Steven Urkowitz, "Interrupted Exits in *King Lear*," *Educational Theatre Journal* 30 (1978): 203-10. Stephen Booth, *King Lear, Macbeth, Indefinition, and Tragedy* (New Haven: Yale University Press, 1983).

TEXT

Readers of this book may be interested in a controversial innovation in *Lear* studies: the assumption not only that there are two *Lear* plays, but also that the later (Folio) text is an authorial revision of the earlier (Quarto). (F has been estimated to contain about 133 lines or part-lines not in Q. In contrast, Q has about 288 lines or part-lines not in F.) Regarding this controversy over Shakespeare self-improved, one proponent, lauding the dramatist's revisionary mastery, notes his "preternatural brilliance . . . his capacity . . . to strike us dumb with amazement."[8]

In this revisionary dualism, the pendulum has swung against E.K. Chambers's opposition to the disintegration of Shakespeare (*The Disintegration of Shakespeare*, 1924; repr. 1944). Once again, the canon is a target for disintegrators. Within a fractionating or deconstructive climate of textual indeterminacy, innovators have tended to disjunction and consequent multiplication. Indeed, in the new Oxford edition of the *Complete Works* (1986), what the editors consider two *Lear* plays (both Q and F) are printed.

Following is a selective chronological summary of recent textual positions regarding *Lear*.

• Michael J. Warren, "Quarto and Folio *King Lear* and the Interpretation of Albany and Edgar," in *Shakespeare: Pattern of Excelling Nature*, ed. David Bevington and J.L. Halio (Newark: University of Delaware Press, 1978), pp. 95-107. Based on 1976 paper. Argues that as there can be no single "ideal" *Lear* text, conflation is invalid; Q is an authoritative text of *Lear*; F may be a revised version by Shakespeare; there are two *Lear* plays.

• Steven Urkowitz, *Shakespeare's Revision of "King Lear"* (Princeton University Press, 1980). Conflation of the two texts distorts the good qualities of each; both Q and F are suited for theater; F, as containing Shakespeare's second thoughts, is more exciting than Q, and is Shakespeare's final version.

8 Steven Urkowitz, *Shakespeare's Revision of "King Lear."* (Princeton University Press, 1980), p. 149.

• Gary Taylor, "The War in *King Lear*," *Shakespeare Survey* 33 (1980): 27-34. On Folio changes, in preparation for and as aftermath of battle in V.ii; these are definitely Shakespeare's.

• P.W.K. Stone, *The Textual History of "King Lear"* (London: Scolar Press, 1980). Argues that Q1 is a theatrical report obtained by repeated visits and copied in longhand; F is unreliable—a revision not Shakespearean, possibly by Massinger; using a new promptbook (the old destroyed in Globe fire, 1613), F is based on a revised version of Q2 (Pavier, 1619).

• Peter W.M. Blayney, *The Texts of "King Lear" and their Origins*. Vol. 1, *Nicholas Okes and the First Quarto* (Cambridge University Press, 1982). Analyzes printing of Q1 in Nicholas Okes's printshop, by analogy with Charlton Hinman's study (1963) of the printing of F1. On the basis of an examination of type recurrences, the study concludes that Q1 was printed *seriatim*.

• T.-H. Howard-Hill, "The Problem of Manuscript Copy for Folio *King Lear*," *The Library*, ser. 6, 4 (1982): 1-24. Opposed to view that F was printed from Q1. Suggests Q2 influence on F was intermediated through a manuscript.

• Gary Taylor, "The Folio Copy for *Hamlet*, *King Lear*, and *Othello*," *Shakespeare Quarterly* 34 (1983): 44-61. Rejects Howard-Hill's 1982 suggestion that Q2's influence on F was intermediated through a manuscript. Argues Folio Compositor E set directly from Q2.

• Gary Taylor and Michael Warren, eds., *The Division of the Kingdoms* (Oxford, 1983). Twelve essays by eleven contributors, opposed to conflation and favoring Shakespearean revision and the two *Lears*. Taylor attempts to prove that F derives from a Shakespearean revision of 1609-10.

• T.-H. Howard-Hill, "Q1 and the Copy for Folio *Lear*," *Papers of the Bibliographical Society of America* 80 (1986): 419-35. F derives from a playhouse manuscript, or promptbook, and Q2. Removes Q1 as direct influence on F.

Whatever the scholarly merits of their case, dual-*Lear* and Shakespearean-revision proponents evince easy slippage from hypothesis into fact. Questionable logic tends, moreover, to accompany a rhetoric of compulsion. What the proponents assert, *must* be true; what opponents' doubts are raised, *must* be false. To illustrate, a few instances will suffice.

Although Warren's pioneer essay (1978) starts by announcing his intention to prove that "Q and F *King Lear* . . . should be treated as two versions of a single play" (p. 97), his conclusion (p. 105) slides into "we have two plays of *King Lear*." Urkowitz's title, *Shakespeare's Revision of "King Lear,"* assumes what it proposes to prove—that there is revision, and that such revision is by Shakespeare. In that book, too, slippage can be observed from the early "working presumption" to the final absolute fact. Early (p. 11), "the Quarto is at least an approximation of Shakespeare's draft of the play before it was adapted for the stage," and "the Folio is a generally accurate reproduction of a promptbook" (p. 13). Later, the author asserts that "except for only a very few variants that are obviously the result of errors in copying or printing, the vast majority of the changes found in the Folio must be accepted as Shakespeare's final decisions," and that "the Quarto is genuinely Shakespeare's and not a corruption." Further, "I contend that all the objections used against the theory of revision must be discounted . . ." (pp. 129-30). Limited hypotheses thus become absolute facts, which *must* be accepted. All objections, on the other hand, *must* be discounted.

In addition to simplification of tangled evidence, proponents regularly assert Shakespeare's Folio revision as fact. While Taylor recognizes that "a circle . . . is not the best logical proof," he claims an absolute certainty, which itself raises questions: "That the play was revised, and that Shakespeare was responsible for the revision, seem to me incontestable." For this incontestability, he offers curiously inverted logic, shifting the normal *onus probandi*: "I thus regard the doubts for the redaction as unproven and unprovable."[9]

Although it has excited enthusiasm and elicited favorable reviews (along with some reviews more critical),[10] the case for two *Lear* plays

[9] Gary Taylor, "Folio Compositors and Folio Copy: *King Lear* and Its Context," *Papers of the Bibliographical Society of America* 79 (1985): 74; Taylor and Warren, *Division of the Kingdoms*, pp. 428-29.

[10] See, chronologically, among the latter: Richard Knowles, review of Urkowitz, *Shakespeare's Revision*, *Modern Philology* 79 (1981-82): 197-200. Philip Edwards, review of Urkowitz and P.W.K. Stone, *Textual History*, *Modern Language Review* 77 (1982): 694-98. Kenneth Muir,

and Shakespearean revision can be considered "not proven." To return to an initial proponent of the hypothesis: Michael J. Warren has announced his edition of materials for the study of the problem. Four parts will include photographic facsimiles of Q1, Q2, and F1 and a parallel-text version of Q1 and F1. Perhaps, upon their publication, scholars will be better equipped to evaluate, cautiously and judiciously, relations among these versions of *King Lear*.

"The Texts of *King Lear*: An Interim Assessment of the Controversy," *Aligarh Journal of English Studies* 8 (1983): 99-113; reprinted with "Postscript" in Muir, *Shakespeare: Contrasts and Controversies* (Brighton: Harvester Press, 1985), pp. 51-66. (Against the notion that Shakespearean "responsibility for the [Folio] changes is proved by their brilliance," Muir contends [p. 100], that, rather than improving the text, "some of the alterations are dramatically disastrous.") Sidney Thomas, "Shakespeare's Supposed Revision of "*King Lear*," *Shakespeare Quarterly* 35 (1984): 506-11. Richard Knowles, "The Case for Two *Lears*," review of *Division*, ed. Taylor and Warren, *Shakespeare Quarterly* 36 (1985): 115-20. T.-H. Howard-Hill, "The Challenge of *King Lear*," review-article on *Division*, ed. Taylor and Warren, *The Library*, ser. 6, 7 (1985): 161-79. See also Frank Kermode, "How Do You Spell Shakespeare?" review of *Complete Works* (Oxford, 1986-87), 2 vols. (modernized and original-spelling editions), ed. Stanley Wells and Gary Taylor, *London Review of Books*, 21 May 1987, pp. 3-5; David Bevington, "Determining the Indeterminate: The Oxford Shakespeare," review of *Complete Works*, ed. Wells and Taylor, and *William Shakespeare: A Textual Companion* (Oxford, 1987), by Wells and Taylor, *Shakespeare Quarterly* 38 (1987): 501-19.

Index

PASSAGES REFERRED TO OR QUOTED

(Page numbers are in parentheses.)

INDEX

SUBJECTS AND NAMES

INDEX